D1187699

SCOTTISH HISTORY SOCIETY

FOURTH SERIES

VOLUME 17

———

Stirling Presbytery Records

STIRLING
Presbytery Records
1581–1587

edited by James Kirk, PH.D.

★

★

EDINBURGH
printed for the Scottish History Society *by*
CLARK CONSTABLE LTD
1981

ISBN 0 906245 01 x
Printed in Great Britain

PREFACE

Grateful acknowledgment is made to the Presbytery of Stirling for permission to publish its earliest records in a volume which, coincidentally, commemorates the quater-centenary of the creation of presbyteries in 1581. When I first gained access to the records in 1968, the volumes were preserved in the Church of the Holy Rude, Stirling; and I would express my thanks to the Rev. Thomas Kinloch, then Clerk to the Presbytery. The records were subsequently transmitted to the Scottish Record Office in January 1973, but they are due shortly to return to the burgh from which they came, for deposit in the Central Regional Archives at Stirling.

I would also record my thanks to Dr Ian Rae for seeing my manuscript through the press.

JAMES KIRK

University of Glasgow
June, 1981

Generous contributions from the
Carnegie Trust for the Universities of Scotland
and the Hope Trust
towards the cost of producing this volume
are gratefully acknowledged by the
Council of the Society

CONTENTS

INTRODUCTION

STIRLING presbytery records merit particular attention not only as the earliest surviving presbytery records in Scotland but also as the only presbytery records for the late sixteenth century whose minutes commence with the presbytery's formal constitution and erection in 1581. As an ecclesiastical court, the presbytery came into being two decades after the institution of kirk sessions, provincial synods and general assemblies, but its appearance, as the history of its antecedents suggests, was less innovatory and less disruptive than is sometimes imagined.

Antecedents to the presbytery's erection: From its inception, the reformed church had developed a system of conciliar government which subordinated individual overseers to the supervision of a concentric series of church courts. The wide-ranging responsibilities attributed to superintendents and commissioners of provinces in the 1560s were never permitted to obscure the accountability of overseers, as regional administrators, to the ministers and elders within their jurisdiction and to the graded courts where authority collectively resided. During visitations, the superintendent was encouraged to act with the advice of assessors and with the assistance of the minister and elders of the congregation. Elsewhere, his activities were associated with the work of the synod and of the kirk session of the chief town of the province which became his court when he was resident. The existence of an appellate jurisdiction from kirk session and synod to general assembly (presided over by an elected moderator), to whose judgment the superintendents and commissioners were obliged to submit themselves for trial at every meeting, suggests a system essentially at variance with what are usually understood to be the principles of episcopacy.[1] 'Episkopē', it has been observed, 'originates with the bishop . . . and descends through

---

[1] J. K. Cameron, *The First Book of Discipline* (Edinburgh, 1972), 126–7; *The Works of John Knox*, ed. D. Laing (Wodrow Society, 1846–8), ii, 147, 150; *The Booke of the*

permanent moderators from the highest to the lowest in the Church.'[1] Yet, it was indeed with some success that the Scots from 1560 had sought to repudiate the traditional apparatus of episcopal government and to replace it by a system where discipline was exercised primarily through the eldership.[2]

That this is a correct reading of events is supported by the church's reaction to the attempts of King James' government to ignore the assembly's repeated claims to dissolve the bishoprics of the unreformed church and to argue instead for their retention and (after further dispute) for their integration within the machinery of the reformed church. Such an arrangement reached in the financial and political compromise worked out at Leith in 1572 presaged the introduction of bishops, so recognised, within the church. But in 1572, the assembly, after protesting at aspects of the compromise, declined to accept the agreement as lasting, while criticism of the new 'counterfett bischopis' led the assembly in 1575 to question whether 'the bischops, as they are now in the Kirk of Scotland, hes thair function of the Word of God or not', and to resolve to dispense with its unsuccessful experiment in episcopal administration by returning in 1576 to a system of visitation whereby ministers received commissions from the assembly to act as visitors. Within four years of its introduction, the Leith episcopacy had been effectively eclipsed in so far as bishops had been eliminated from playing any distinctive part in ecclesiastical government.[3]

Universall Kirk of Scotland (*BUK*), (Edinburgh, 1839–45), i, 266 (accountability); Knox, *Works*, vi, 450; *BUK*, i, 17, 113, 161, cf. 19; *Register of the Minister, Elders and Deacons of the Christian Congregation of St Andrews* (*RStAKS*), ed. D. H. Fleming (Scottish History Society, 1889–90), i, 257 (assessors); *BUK*, i, 195; *The Buik of the Kirk of the Canagait*, ed. A. B. Calderwood (Scottish Record Society, 1961), 24, 36, (ministers and elders); *BUK*, i, 29, 75, 162, 191, 193, 237, 241; St Andrews University Archives, MS. 30451, fo. 5v.; *RStAKS*, i, 110, 140, 143, 145, 151, 168–9, 183–4, 188, 190, 221, 229, 231, 233, 277–8, 308, 315, 318–9, 331, 343, 362 (synod and session); *BUK*, i, 33; *Acts of the Parliaments of Scotland* (*APS*), edd. T. Thomson and C. Innes (Edinburgh, 1814–75), iii, 23, c. 7 (appeals); *BUK*, i, 25–6, 31, 39–40, 52–3, 65, 77, 112, 123, 157, 175, 184 (trial)

[1] P. Collinson, *The Elizabethan Puritan Movement* (London, 1967), 179
[2] J. Kirk, '"The Polities of the Best Reformed Kirks": Scottish achievements and English aspirations in church government after the Reformation', *Scottish Historical Review*, lix (1980), 22–53
[3] J. Kirk, *The Second Book of Discipline* (Edinburgh, 1980), 13–42

Concern for effective and efficient oversight, which the Leith bishops so frequently had failed to provide, led the assembly to place further reliance on the collective responsibility of decisions taken in the ecclesiastical courts and on the work of ministers acting as temporary overseers commissioned by these courts rather than on a system which, regardless of any intended safeguards, looked as if it might permanently raise individual bishops to a position of superiority over their brethren (especially so, when one archbishop declined to acknowledge his subordination to the assembly) and which was designed to secure a measure of 'conformity with England', thereby placing at risk the survival of a distinctively reformed church order. In 1576, the assembly reiterated how, in exercising oversight and supervision, 'the power stands not in the visiter but in the kirk'; and in 1578 the Second Book of Discipline reaffirmed the essence of earlier ideals by recognising that 'nather may the name of ane bischop be attributit to the visitour onlie, nather is it necessar to abyd alwyse in ane manis persone', and that 'everie assemblie hes power to send furth frome thair awine nomber ane or ma visitouris to sie how all things be reulit in the boundis of thair jurisdictioun'. This was strictly in accord with the assembly's explanation in 1565 that 'every true preacher of Jesus Christ is a Christian bishop', and with the system of administration exercised by superintendents and commissioners in association with the courts of the church.[1]

In itself, the assembly's resolve to eliminate diocesan episcopacy implied a renewed emphasis on conciliar government rather than entrusting the government of the church at its highest levels to individuals. Such a tendency was apparent in England, too, where adherents of the anti-episcopal movement advocated the supersession of episcopacy and the adoption of the 'presbytery' or congregational eldership, and of the *classis* or district court, subordinate to the provincial synod and national assembly. In Scotland, however, where 'presbyteries' (in the English sense) had operated from 1559, there was no corresponding urgent advocacy in the 1570s for the introduction of any entirely new court modelled on the English or continental *classis*. What did emerge, however, was a recognition

[1] *BUK*, i, 367, 376–7, 385–6 (archbishop); *BUK*, i, 357 (visitor); Knox, *Works*, vi, 434 (minister as bishop); Kirk, *Second Book of Discipline*, 196–7

that not every church need have a separate eldership of its own, which had a particular relevance for areas where kirk sessions had not yet been fully established, and that, in rural areas especially, several contiguous churches might share a common eldership on a basis somewhat akin to the general sessions which had long been a familiar feature in the larger burghs.[1]

This recommendation adopted in the Second Book of Discipline was motivated less by an attachment to doctrinaire principles than by the need to meet the very urgent problems associated with the Regent Morton's policy of uniting, under the supervision of one minister, three or four adjacent churches, otherwise served only by resident readers. All this helps to explain the Second Book of Discipline's decision that not every 'particular paroche kirk cane or may have thair awin particular eldarschip, especiall to landwart, bot we think thrie or four, ma or fewar, particular kirkis may have ane commoun eldarschip'.[2] In 1578, 'presbytery' was used as a synonym for 'eldership', when the general assembly admonished the existing bishops 'to usurp not the power of the presbytries'. But, as yet, the communal elderships commended in the Second Book of Discipline existed on paper and not in practice until, in reply to the synod of Lothian's plea for 'a general order to be taken for erecting of presbyteries in places quher publick exercise is used', the assembly finally determined in 1579 that 'the exercise may be judgit a presbyterie'. The exercise, which met in the burghs and market towns where ministers from the rural hinterland were expected to resort for scriptural exegesis, became the embryonic presbytery; and such an arrangement for linking the exercise with the disciplinary functions of the eldership proved a convenient enough device since the exercise already had assumed the rôle of an executive organ of administration from at least the early 1570s. Nevertheless, as an institution the exercise was by no means in universal operation throughout the country, and even where exercises did exist their history was tenuous and far from being an uninterrupted one. The need for a more systematic approach towards establishing presbyteries already had been indicated in the Second Book of Discipline's call for the assembly, with the king's consent, to appoint a committee 'to unit and devyd the parochis as necessitie and commoditie

[1] Kirk, *Second Book of Discipline*, 102–3   [2] *Ibid.*, 199

requires' and to 'designe places quhair the assembles of particular elderschipps sould convene'. This was achieved by the spring of 1581 when consultations with the privy council led to a revision of the parochial and diocesan structure so that 'presbitereis or elderschippis may be constitute', and thirteen model presbyteries were thereafter set up in central and southern Scotland to serve as 'exemplars to the rest', though no effective attempts were made to merge the work of the existing kirk sessions with the newly established presbyteries.[1]

The presbytery's constitution and composition: In selecting Stirling as one of the thirteen initial centres for establishing presbyteries, the assembly of April 1581 had assigned the task of erecting the presbytery, somewhat surprisingly, to Bishop Andrew Graham of Dunblane and to Robert Montgomery, then minister of Stirling and soon to be provided to the archbishopric of Glasgow, who, along with Graham, made preparations for founding the presbytery or 'elderschip of Striviling', as the minutes reveal, on 8th August, 1581. A foretaste of the presbytery's composition had been revealed in the Second Book of Discipline's definition that 'be eldarschip is meint sic as ar constitut of pastouris, doctouris and sic as now ar callit eldaris'. The presbytery's inaugural meeting was duly attended by the ministers of Stirling, St Ninians, Falkirk, Dunblane, Logie, Alva, Fossoway and Muckhart, accompanied by elders from the churches of Stirling, Dunblane, St Ninians and Logie. Shortly thereafter, further recruits were forthcoming when elders from Alva, Fossoway and Glendevon were elected to serve as presbytery elders for life in response to the presbytery's decision that each kirk session should elect 'twa or thre elderis', approved by their congregation, to serve on the presbytery.[2]

The recognition that a presbytery elder should be elected for life and that he promise 'faythfullie to exerceis his office thairin unto the end of his lyif as God sall minister to him the giftis of his Spirit' was

[1] *Ibid.,* 105–7, 232; *Register of the Privy Council of Scotland* (*RPC*), edd. J. H. Burton and D. Masson, 1st ser. (Edinburgh, 1877–98), iii, 383; D. Calderwood, *The History of the Kirk of Scotland,* ed. T. Thomson (Wodrow Society, 1842–9), iii, 523; *BUK,* ii, 482
[2] *BUK,* ii, 487; Kirk, *Second Book of Discipline,* 202; see below, 1–2, 4–5; for further recruits, see below, 8, 14, 23, 46, 59, 64–65, 68, 113

strictly in accord with the Second Book of Discipline's understanding that an elder 'anis lauchfullie callit to the office and having
giftis of God meit to exercyse the same may not leave it agane', but
he was not of course expected to serve continuously without release
from his duties.[1]

The size of the presbytery, in practice, turned out to be consider-
ably larger than the 'thrie or four, ma or fewar, particular kirkis'
commended in the Second Book of Discipline, but noticeably
fewer than the 25 constituent churches envisaged in the assembly's
scheme of April 1581 which assigned to the presbytery 14 churches
from the diocese of Dunblane, 9 churches from St Andrews diocese
and 2 detached parishes from the diocese of Dunkeld. The assembly's
plans seem to have been based not on any earlier units of administration either secular or ecclesiastical (other than the parish) but on
the need to create a streamlined, compact and localised system of
supervision adapted to meet the changing needs of society. Both
crown and church in 1581 agreed that no 'formal order' could be
achieved until 'the ancient bounds of the Diocies be dissolved, where
the parishes are thick together, and small be united; and where they
are too great and large bounds, be divided, and thereafter Presbyteries or Elderships constituted for a dozen of parishes or thereabout,
some moe, some fewer, as the commodity of the Countrey lyeth,
where the Ministrie and Elders in these bounds conveening may
commodiously exercise Ecclesiastical Discipline, and take order with
affairs of the Kirk'. The large and populous parish of St Ninians near
Stirling was earmarked for division, though this was not so readily
effected. Besides, the presbytery still lacked its complement of
constituent churches.[2]

Although one of the ministers of Dunblane had attended the
presbytery's inaugural meeting and took his place as a member, the
other minister of the city – Bishop Andrew Graham – seems only to
have been present as a commissioner from the assembly for erecting
the presbytery and was accordingly admonished, along with the
ministers of Aberfoyle and Kilbride, at the presbytery's second
meeting in August to give attendance 'becaus thai ar appointit be

[1] See below, 1, 4–5, 8, 23; Kirk, Second Book of Discipline, 192
[2] Kirk, Second Book of Discipline, 199; BUK, ii, 484 (where Stirling is mistakenly
omitted from the list of 24 churches); Calderwood, History, viii, 36; see below, xlii

the generall ordur to be under the jurisdictioun thairof'. Bishop
Graham's disinclination to sit as a member of Stirling presbytery
arose not from any distaste on his part for presbyteries – he had,
after all, submitted to the assembly and accepted its programme –
but from his desire to inaugurate a separate presbytery of Dunblane.
Supported by several dissenting presbytery members from the area
of Dunblane, Graham chose to appeal from the presbytery's judgment (albeit in an unsuccessful bid) to the general assembly where
the dispute was first noted in October 1581. The ground for their
dissent was that when they had taken part at the request of king and
kirk 'with uthir brethrein and gentilmen' in determining how the
'ordour of union and divisioun of the kirkis and erectioun of the
presbyteriis' might take effect, they had not intended their assistance
to imply their assent to becoming members of Stirling presbytery,
especially since, as they contended, 'we haif a presbytery of our
awin erectit of a lang tyme past in Dunblane be the ordur approvit
be the generall kirk affoir our visitour standand undischairgit, our
assembleis and conventionis mentenid, our exerceis haldin and
keipit and the materis of our kirk intreattid'.[1] Such was the affinity
between the duties already undertaken by the exercise and those
assumed by the presbytery in 1581 that the ministers of Dunblane
could readily mistake their exercise for a presbytery. In any event,
once established, presbyteries simply absorbed the functions of the
exercise; and at its inaugural meeting Stirling presbytery made due
provision for holding the exercise for scriptural exegesis as a regular
and integral part of its proceedings. At the same session, a candidate
for presbytery clerk was forthcoming in James Duncanson, reader
at Stirling, and the moderator was then elected by the votes of the
presbytery members to serve for a half-yearly term from the meeting of one provincial synod till the next.[2]

Authority and jurisdiction: Although disposed to concur with the
church in setting up presbyteries, the crown was disinclined to
lend its support to the assembly's condemnation of diocesan episcopacy. The assembly might readily remove the existing bishops
from episcopal administration but it did not so readily succeed in

---

[1] See below, 1–6, 12–18, 59; *BUK*, ii, 524
[2] See below, 2

preventing fresh nominations by the crown to vacant bishoprics, for even where the church declined to operate the machinery for episcopal appointments, set up in 1572, the crown could still promote a titular bishop to possess the revenues of the title and to sit in parliament. The issue directly affected the presbytery, from its inception, when the government, in effect, accepted the assembly's challenge and nominated Robert Montgomery, minister of Stirling and one of the presbytery's founders, to the vacant archbishopric of Glasgow. A licence to elect James Boyd's successor to the vacant see had been issued in August 1581, and by October Montgomery had been granted provision by the crown. When the chapter of ministers declined to elect the crown's nominee, the privy council declared that the bishopric had fallen to the crown for disposal. The courts of the church retorted by threatening to excommunicate the new archbishop and although forbidden by the crown to proceed against him, the assembly in April 1582 finally declared Montgomery deposed and excommunicated. Undeterred, Montgomery raised an action against the presbytery of Glasgow, and the privy council declared his excommunication to be null and void.[1]

The matter first came before the presbytery in September 1581 when Montgomery's absence from his parish and his reputed 'necligence in his offeice bayth in doctrein and disceplein' were promptly censured. Unimpressed by his letter which appeared 'to accuse utheris rather than to excuse him self', the presbytery ordered Montgomery to compear in October before the synod of Lothian (in whose province Stirling then lay with the presbyteries of Linlithgow, Edinburgh and Dalkeith). With the general assembly's intervention in October, the king sought to delay proceedings against the aspiring archbishop but the assembly nonetheless went ahead to investigate, in his absence, sixteen accusations against the archbishop, who, it was said, not only 'denyed that in the New Testament any mentioun was made of the presbyterie or Elderschip', but also 'to prove the corrupt estate of Bischops in our tyme, he broght foorth the examples of Ambrose and Augustine'. After commanding him to remain as minister of Stirling and to decline the

---

[1] D. E. R. Watt, *Fasti Ecclesiae Scoticanae Medii Aevi ad annum 1638* (Scottish Record Society, 1969), 151; *RPC*, iii, 474–7, 496–7; *BUK*, ii, 524–5, 528–9, 533–4, 542, 543–4, 546–7, 558–66, 571–5, 583

archbishopric on pain of excommunication, the assembly granted the presbytery a commission to examine Montgomery further and to submit its report to the synod of Lothian.[1]

Turning from defence to attack, Montgomery complained to the presbytery that he 'was nocht bruthurlie nor cheritablie handillit', and he declined to give 'ane plaine answer' to the town council's inquiry about whether or not he would remain as minister. Only belatedly was he persuaded to give an assurance that he would continue at Stirling, at least until the next assembly met – 'and langer as the kirk wald command him' – but he evasively avoided renouncing his claim to the archbishopric on the ground that 'the mater was wechtie'. His continued failure either to remain at Stirling or to promise to decline the archbishopric led the presbytery to conclude that Montgomery had disobeyed the acts of assembly and so was liable for excommunication. Nor was the presbytery wholly satisfied with Montgomery's disarming profession that 'he meinis nocht nor will, nor sall be ony uthir bischop bot sic ane bischop as Paull teichis in his epistillis to Titus and Timothie, that is, a minister and preichour of the Word of God and promesis nevir to trublle or vex his brethrein with his admissioun to the bischoprik of Glasgw'. As a committee of the presbytery proceeded to investigate his behaviour, Montgomery, in turn, lodged a complaint against the elders of his own kirk session. For his part, however, Montgomery admitted that 'sumtymis thruch laik of memorie and negligence in his studie and awaytting on his buik' he had failed to maintain 'sic furmalitie and sensibilnes in doctrein as become him', but he denied ever to have been 'swa ovircumit with drink that his sencis faillit him'. Although he did not 'preceislie deny' lending money at a high rate of interest, he did at least accept that he should not enjoy the fruits of the archbishopric, if the church so ruled.[2]

Nonetheless, after hearing that Montgomery had secured letters charging the ministers of Glasgow to admit him as archbishop, the presbytery lost no time in suspending Montgomery from the ministry. Not only had the kirk session complained of their minister's 'intollarablle negligence', but the presbytery itself firmly censured Montgomery's pursuit of 'warldlie effairis and ungodlie suittis

[1] See below, 6–10; *BUK*, ii, 528, 533–4, 542, 546–7
[2] See below, 9–10, 13–15, 17–22

B

of unlauchfull honouris, pre-eminence and riches expres againis the Word of God, the actis of the generall assemblie and dewatie of ane trew pastour', and it condemned his actions which, it considered, were designed 'to steir up ane lamentablle schisme and trublle in the kirk of God and this commone wealthe, and to inflame the hairttis of our souverane lord and his cheif nobilitie againis his maist fayhtfull subjectis'. Under threat of imminent excommunication, Montgomery was summoned before the synod of Lothian in April 1582 but after failing to compear before either synod or general assembly, he was deposed from the ministry and, in June, was finally excommunicated.[1] Not only did the presbytery continue to lack its contumacious founding member, but it also faced the task of securing a replacement for Montgomery as minister of Stirling. More importantly, the Montgomery episode had turned out to be a vital trial of strength for the presbytery's newly assumed jurisdiction and competence.

Although recognition of the authority of presbyteries was withheld in statute law until 1592, the crown and privy council had acknowledged from 1581 that presbyteries possessed a jurisdiction in so wide an area as in matters affecting ecclesiastical discipline. The extent of this jurisdiction was not immediately defined – at least in the surviving acts of the general assembly – but an indication of the scope attributed to elderships or presbyteries was forthcoming in the Second Book of Discipline, which the assembly had endorsed and engrossed in its register in April 1581. The examination, ordination, admission (and, indeed, deposition) of ministers, the supervision and visitation of the parishes, the formulation of enactments and the execution of ordinances made in the higher courts, the licensing of marriage contracts, the correction of manners, and the ultimate sanction of excommunication were all understood to be functions appropriate to be discharged by presbyteries.[2] As early as November 1581, Stirling presbytery granted to a candidate for the ministry a testimonial of his suitability 'becaus he hes bein tryit bayth be the brethir of the exerceis of Dumfarmling, as David Fargusonis teste-

---

[1] See below, 26-31, 35-41; *BUK*, ii, 558-62; *Calendar of State Papers relating to Scotland*, vi, ed. W. K. Boyd (Edinburgh, 1910), nos. 124, 130

[2] Calderwood, *History*, viii, 35-6; Kirk, *Second Book of Discipline*, 179-80, 185-6, 194, 196-202, 223-4

moniall gevin thairupon beris, and also be us bayth in exerceis and publict doctrein and fund ablle to proffeit the kirk of God be his doctrein'. Proof of his good character was also attested 'bayth be ane testemoniall of the gentilmen of Clakmannan quhair he dwellis and als be report of our brothur, Thomas Swintoun, send be us thair to that effect'.[1]

The tendency for candidates to undergo examination at the exercise had already emerged before the erection of presbyteries, so that the assumption of this power by presbyteries from 1581 was achieved with little dislocation. In another instance, William Scott, 'allegit to be admittit minister' at Callander was required in 1582 to demonstrate his fitness by preaching before the presbytery in private, on an assigned text of scripture, 'in the minister of Strivilingis chalmir'. Although the assembly, somewhat belatedly in 1582, had instructed presbyteries to examine candidates for the ministry 'and such as they find qualified, to provyde them to kirks', there is no indication in the period before parliament's proscription of presbyteries in 1584 of the rôle which Stirling presbytery played in selecting and admitting suitably qualified ministers to parish churches. Hitherto, from 1576 much of this work had been undertaken by visitors (commissioned by the assembly) in association both with the exercise and the synod, and there are incidental references in the presbytery minutes to the duties earlier performed by the visitor in the diocese of Dunblane, including the terms of an act made by the visitor 'with the advis of the assembly present' at a visitation of Tillicoultry in July 1577.[2]

Once constituted, however, presbyteries were seen as the appropriate body empowered to conduct visitations; and the assembly saw fit not only to recognise in 1582 that each presbytery might select 'two or ma' of its members to act as visitors 'according to the Booke of Policie', but also to restrict the activities of its own commissioners and visitors to those areas not yet possessing presbyteries. Where presbyteries operated, therefore, the powers of commissioners and visitors of provinces were understood to have lapsed; and the assembly's appointment in October 1581 of David Lindsay, minister at Leith, as commissioner for West Lothian and Stirling-

[1] See below, 12
[2] See below, 68, 87; *BUK*, ii, 570; *BUK*, i, 357; see below, 3–5, 119–20

shire was apparently for the specific purpose of negotiating with the modifiers of ministers' stipends.[1]

From its inception, Stirling presbytery had supervised the conduct of its ministers, readers, schoolmasters and congregations, though the first presbyterial visitation of a parish recorded in the minutes did not occur until April 1583 (some twenty months after the presbytery's creation) when the presbytery granted a commission to three of its members to visit the parish of Muthill to 'tak inquisitioun and tryell of sic thingis in that parrochun as concernis the glorie of God and weill of his kirk, and farther to travell with the congregatioun thairof and desyr thame to provyd a sufficient dwelling for Mr Alexander Chisholme, thair minister'. Somewhat earlier, in January 1582/3, the presbytery had introduced the practice whereby ministers of the parishes were obliged to produce before the presbytery for scrutiny, on a regular basis, 'thair buikis and proces of the disciplein usit be thame in thair particular sessionis' so that 'ane uniform and generall ordur of disceplein may be establischit, usit and execute . . . in tymis cuming'.[2]

In a process somewhat akin to the procedure for admitting men to the ministry, presbyteries were encouraged to receive presentations of candidates from patrons and to grant them collation to benefices. Earlier, visitors had been recognised by the assembly in 1576 as the appropriate agents for receiving presentations and giving collation, provided they acted with the advice of the synod and exercise; and by 1580 the assembly had declared further collations by 'any pretending the style of bishops' to be wholly void. The logical sequel was the assembly's claim in 1581 that presentations be directed to presbyteries. Although this was at variance with the crown's preference for directing presentations to benefices in royal patronage to commissioners or bishops, it would be harder to demonstrate that the assembly's plans were contrary to statute law which, after all, had approved collation by superintendents 'or utheris havand commissioun of the kirk'.[3] And from 1581 presbyteries, and their representatives, had received just such a commission from the church.

---

[1] *BUK*, ii, 568; Kirk, *Second Book of Discipline*, 196–7, 223–4; *BUK*, ii, 537, 535–6
[2] See below, 11–12, 25, 31–32, 59; 118; 76–77; see also Index *sub* 'Ministers', 'Readers', 'Schoolmasters'
[3] *BUK*, i, 357; ii, 419, 459, 514, 568, 602; *APS*, iii, 23, c. 7

Within Stirling presbytery's jurisdiction, however, no parochial benefice in the crown's patronage appears to have been disponed between 1581 and the onset of the 'Black Acts' of 1584. The presbytery was not immediately involved, therefore, in granting collation to these benefices. But an indication of the rôle which presbyteries were expected to play is apparent in 1583 when Archibald Livingston, on informing the presbytery of his provision to the parsonage of Culter, 'acknawlegit him self to be bund thairby of his dewatie to serve in the cuir of the ministrie at the kirk thairof and to the effect he may entir in the said cuir with the bettir ordur desyris the brethrein of this presbytery to gif him thair testemoniall of his lyf and conversatioun direct to the presbytery of Lainrig, in the quhilk boundis the said kirk of Cultir is, that thaireftir he may be lauchfullie admittit thairto be the said presbytery of Lainrig'.[1] Provision to a parochial benefice was understood to incur an obligation on the recipient to undertake the cure of souls, and in this process the church, and more specifically the presbytery, was expected to have a say in examining the suitability of the candidates presented. Abuses such as nonresidence and pluralism were therefore roundly condemned by presbytery and general assembly alike.[2]

As a competitor for the kind of jurisdiction which in an episcopal system is usually exercised by a bishop or his delegate, the presbytery was seen by the assembly as competent even to examine the abilities and performance of the Leith bishops appointed since 1572. As early as 1578, the general assembly had admonished the bishops in general terms 'that they impyre not above the particular elderschips but be subject to the same' and 'that they usurp not the power of the presbytries'. More specifically, in October 1582, the assembly assigned to the presbyteries of Perth, Edinburgh, the Mearns, Dundee and Glasgow the examination of the bishops of Moray, Aberdeen, Brechin, Dunkeld and St Andrews respectively; and it committed to Stirling presbytery the trial of the bishops of Dunblane and the Isles.[3] The bishops' performance in Word and sacraments, in discipline and behaviour, as well as in utilising episcopal patrimony and granting collation to benefices in defiance of acts of assembly came under the presbytery's scrutiny.

[1] See below, 177   [2] See below, 9, 117, 222
[3] *BUK*, ii, 425, 593

Even before it received its commission from the assembly to investigate the bishops' activities, the presbytery had ordered Andrew Graham of Dunblane, in April 1582, to account to the general assembly 'for negligence in his offeice' in accordance with an act of synod; and in May, after criticising 'the lang absence of Mr Andro Grahame fra his kirk of Dunblane and negligence of his flock', the presbytery had insisted that the bishop reply to the charge. The accusations were by no means new, for Graham had a history of being less than a satisfactory bishop. His career as bishop effectively dated not so much from 1573 when the crown had first issued to the chapter its licence to elect but from 1575 when the crown confirmed his election and issued a mandate for his consecration. But although a graduate, Graham had no pastoral experience, and in 1575 the assembly, finding itself in a dilemma on discovering that 'it is not yitt decided that all bishops sould be first preachers' had hastily ordered the bishop to demonstrate his aptitude for the office by preaching a sermon on Romans 5 before so many of the ministry as might be present at the Magdalene chapel in Edinburgh.[1] Thereafter, his shortcomings in performing his duties as bishop had been duly observed by the assembly from as early as 1576. Nor was this wholly unexpected, for his promotion to the bishopric had the characteristics of a dynastic appointment secured by his kinsman the Earl of Montrose, who, as Master of Graham, had earlier acquired rights to the temporalities of the bishopric during its vacancy, and who, after gaining the installation of his own candidate, obtained from the bishop a feu of the entire lands of the bishopric. Such a grant posed a potential threat to the security of the sitting 'kindly tenants' of the bishopric who successfully sought the protection of parliament in 1578 on the ground that 'ane thowsand of our soverane lordis commonis and pure people wilbe put to uter heirschip and extreme beggartie . . . quhen as sa grite rowmes quhairupoun sa mony ar sustenit salbe reducit in the handis of ane particular man'.[2]

These were the antecedents to the presbytery's proceedings which

[1] See below, 41, 44; Watt, *Fasti*, 78; Calderwood, *History*, iii, 341–2; *BUK*, i, 316, 317, 321, 325
[2] *BUK*, i, 349; *The Register of the Privy Seal of Scotland*, vi, ed. G. Donaldson (Edinburgh, 1963), nos. 590, 729; *APS*, iii. 111–2

commenced in December 1582 when Graham was assigned the task
of making the exercise on the text of Ephesians 13, 'to the effect the
brethrein may juge on his doctrein', which was considered to be
both 'sound and proffitablle'. But the bishop admitted having
failed to preach and exercise discipline at Dunblane for a year; he
affirmed that he 'nevir gaif ony collatioun of beneficis to na persone
sen his admissioun to the foirsaid bischoprie'; and he sought a
postponement to answering the charge of dilapidating episcopal
patrimony. The presbytery, however, found Graham's inventory of
feus and tacks to be incomplete and unsatisfactory; grants of episcopal property to the Earl of Montrose and Masters of Mar and
Livingston had not been entered; and it admonished Graham 'nocht
to styll him self bischop in tymis cuming nather be word nor wrett'.
At the same time, John Drummond of Pitkellany, on behalf of the
kindly tenants of the bishopric, took the opportunity of complaining
to the presbytery that Graham had 'nocht onelie to the grit hurt
damnage and skayth of his successuris bot alswa to the extreim hurt
of us, possessuris and tennentis of the said kirk lands, sauld, delapidat
and put away the haill leving of the said bischoprie or at the lest ane
gret part thairof in gret menis handis by us, the saidis possessuris and
kyndlie tennentis'. Another tenant with a lease of the teinds of
Kinbuck protested at how the bishop had not only declined to renew
her lease but 'maist ungodlie intendis to set the samin to utheris ovir
hir hed'. These 'bills of complaint' seeking redress for wrongs had
the intended effect of securing promises from the bishop to recognise the tenants' rights. Yet further investigations led the presbytery,
by October 1583, to pronounce Graham guilty of 'negligence in
doctrein and disciplein, waisting of the patrimony of the kirk,
setting of takis againis the actis of the kirk'.[1]

Although he promised the presbytery in January 1583/4 that he
would make no further grants of episcopal property 'without the
advys and consent of the brethrein of the said presbytery', Graham
continued to be less than responsive in fulfilling his duties. He
procrastinated when ordered to admonish the Earl of Montrose for
associating with an excommunicated kinsman; he was fined for
absence from the synod in April; and in May, a few days before

---

[1] See below, 66–74, 76–78, 82, 85–86, 88, 93–95, 97, 102, 105–6, 110–12, 155, 167,
171, 174–6

parliament banned presbyteries from meeting, the bishop was again censured for his habitual failure to preach in Dunblane during the preceding six months.[1]

John Campbell, the other bishop whose activities the presbytery was required to investigate, had been promoted in 1572 to the bishopric of the Isles where clan Campbell had succeeded in extinguishing the rival claims of the Macleans of Duart. The selection of Stirling as the appropriate presbytery for examining the bishop of the Isles, 'sasone as he may be apprehendit' for 'he is nocht presentlie in thir boundis', was possibly made with an awareness of Argyll's own interests in the locality at Castle Campbell near Dollar. After he had preached a trial sermon on Ephesians 2, Campbell's doctrine was considered 'generall, aggreing with the grundis of religioun bot nocht sufficient in opning up of the sense and mening of the said text'. He claimed that he had preached and ministered at Iona until a dispute with Maclean over a feu, in March 1580/1, had forced him to return to the mainland of Argyll where he preached at Ardchattan 'oft tymis quhen he was thair'. But after arriving in the lowlands to seek redress from the king and council, he had 'preichit in na plaice' for half a year. He denied having given collation to any benefices since the assembly's act of 1580 or having dilapidated the patrimony of the bishopric (other than a confirmation of a feu to Argyll) or of the annexed abbacy of Iona (which he had resigned in favour of Alexander, his son). The presbytery nonetheless warned him 'nocht to styll him self bischop, nor lord, in in tymis cuming'. Witnesses duly summoned to give evidence included Argyll, Campbell of Ardkinglass and Maclean of Duart. Even Glasgow presbytery was consulted. Yet nothing 'bot honestie' could be found in the bishop's behaviour, and the presbytery absolved him from all charges 'excep the disjunctioun and separatioun of the abbacie of Ycolumkill fra the bischoprik of the Yllis laitlie procurit be the said Mr Johnne as als ane confirmatioun gevin be him to the Erll of Argyll'.[2]

The disciplining of negligent ministers and readers, as well as bishops, also occupied the presbytery's attention. James Dalmahoy, minister of Cambuskenneth, was duly censured by the presbytery in

---

[1] See below, 185, 194–5, 208–10, 215–18
[2] Watt, *Fasti*: 206; see below, 66–67, 78–80, 82–84, 103–5, 112, 146–9, 164–5

1581 for marrying (despite an objection being voiced) a couple who did not even belong to his parish, 'without testemoniall or lycence of the elderschip'. In another instance, he had conducted the marriage of a woman whose first marriage remained undissolved. Other irregular marriages, including one which he had solemnised at six o'clock in the morning, were brought to the presbytery's attention. His approach to ministering the sacrament of baptism was equally lax. He admitted baptising in a barn 'becaus of the foull wathir', and was said to have received payment for baptisms and marriages. The presbytery had therefore no hesitation in deposing him from the ministry.[1] In 1583, a reader was suspended by the presbytery for officiating at the marriage of a woman who was not his parishioner and whom he knew to have been 'divorcit fra hir first husband for adultrie'. Another reader, whom the presbytery censured for usurping the minister's office, was understood 'to have abusit the sacrament of baptisme and mariage in ministratioun of thame without ony lauchfall admissioun thairto in wret'. After he underwent examination by being assigned 'ane chaptur in the New Testament and commandit to reid the same and eftir reiding of ane portioun thairof thair was gevin to him twa prayeris in the psalme buik to reid', the presbytery soon concluded that the candidate 'can nocht proffeit the kirk of God be his reiding becaus he reidis nocht distinctlie, keipis na point in his reiding nor understandis nocht quhat he reidis', and so deposed him from all office in the ministry. An 'allegit reder' at Lecropt, who baptised a child 'abusitlie in ane prophane hous in the Latein langage', was also deemed by the presbytery to have been 'nocht lauchfullie admitted to ministrat baptisme in the kirk of God' and was accordingly deposed 'fra reding in the kirk of God and all functioun thairof . . . at all tymis'. The presbytery even felt it necessary to report the case to the king for secular punishment, but found it harder to determine whether the child 'salbe haldin as lauchfullie baptezit or nocht'.[2]

A minister of Clackmannan, who 'fengzeit in his speikin sayand now that he hes nocht ane buik of disceplein quhilk befoir he confessit to have hade' and who appeared to have torn out some written evidence 'quhilk appeiris to the brethrein to be varie

suspicius', was convicted by the presbytery of 'selling of the sacramentis and utheris benefeittis of the kirk' and so was suspended from
the ministry in 1583.[1] In another instance, a minister who had
permitted bridals, banquets and the playing of pipes during a period
of general fast was fined by the presbytery and ordered to make
public repentance in his own parish church; and aware of the 'grit
abuse and superstitioun usit be sindrie personis that cumis to parroche
kirkis to be mareit in causing pyperis and fidlayeris play befoir thame
to the kirk and fra the kirk, to the grit dishonour of God', the
presbytery proceeded to prohibit all such ceremonies and to insist
that couples 'cum to the kirk reverentlie as becumis thame without
ony playing'.[2] More mysterious was the presbytery's investigation
into whether Alexander Mure, a minister who had officiated at the
laird of Tulliallan's marriage, was 'musellit or ony wayis disgysit the
tyme he mareit him'. The laird maintained that the 'minister was na
manir of way disgysit on his faice nor utherwayis the tyme of the
said mariage bot was honestlie claid in blak as becumis ane minister'.
Yet the presbytery still sought the depositions of witnesses who
testified that the marriage had taken place on St Lawrence's day 1581
'be ane honest lyk man cled lyk ane minister, with ane taffety hatt,
quhais name thai knew nocht, undisguysit on faice or utherwayis',
with which the presbytery declared itself satisfied.[3]

In an effort to regulate and standardize disciplinary procedures in
the parishes, the presbytery had undertaken to inspect the 'books of
discipline' or registers of disciplinary cases kept by ministers and
kirk sessions; and by 1583 it was 'statute and ordeinit' that these
records should include a list of all marriages, baptisms and alms
collected and distributed to the poor, and that inspections of the
books should take place twice-yearly.[4] In a similar manner, the
exercise for interpreting scripture, which formed an initial part of
presbytery meetings and which might take place in public before an
assembled congregation or in private behind the closed doors of the
session house, had an important rôle to play not only in examining
prospective ministers and in increasing educational standards among
ministers, but also in maintaining a uniformity in doctrine.

At each weekly meeting of the exercise, one minister was ex-

---

[1] See below, 134, 142   [2] See below, 190–2
[3] See below, 196–7, 199   [4] See below, 76–77, 88, 102, 106, 224, 253

pected to preach on an assigned text and another then undertook to make some practical observations on the first speaker's exposition. In December 1581, the presbytery had ordered the schoolmaster and reader at Dunblane to attend the exercise at Stirling and by 1582 'the haill ministeris of the elderschip and brethir of exerceis' agreed to impose fines on absent members to ensure regular attendance. A list of the members discloses the names of 16 ministers, exhorters and readers, the schoolmasters of Stirling and Strageith, and the commissary of Dunblane; but there was noticeably no word of the participation on the exercise of the presbytery elders, whose names appear only on the sederunts of the presbytery meetings.[1] The presence at the exercise of schoolmasters, however, was consistent with the Second Book of Discipline's definition of the doctor's duty 'to oppine up be simple teaching the mystereis of the fayth' and with its recognition that the doctor's, or teacher's, office comprehended 'the ordour of scoles'. Thus, from 1583, Alexander Yule, the Stirling grammar schoolmaster, was generally distinguished in the sederunts as 'ane brothur of exerceis' from the rest of the elders who attended presbytery meetings, though he was nonetheless recognised as an elder; and all this was also in keeping with the Second Book of Discipline's claim that 'the doctour being ane eldar, as said is, sould assist the pasture in the governament of the kirk and concurre with the uther eldaris, his brethrene, in all assembleis'.[2]

Once the exercise had been held, the ministers, teachers and elders retired to a separate part of the church where the presbytery, formally constituted as an ecclesiastical court, assumed responsibility for governing the constituent parishes. From the outset, elders of the presbytery showed a readiness to attend meetings on a regular basis. Their members included such elders from Stirling kirk session as Adam Erskine, the lay commendator of Cambuskenneth abbey, Humphrey Cunningham and James Pont, the commissaries of Stirling and Dunblane respectively, John Laing, possibly the maltman burgess of that name, Robert Alexander, a bailie, and William Norwall, the burgh's treasurer. From St Ninians came two lairds,

---

[1] See below, 18, 21–23 ; see also Index *sub* 'Exercise'
[2] Kirk, *Second Book of Discipline*, 187–8; see below, 77, 79, 85, 88–89, 94–95, 98, 100, 102, 106, 110 ('ane brothur of exerceis'); 66, 69, 72, 74, 90 (elder); Kirk, *Second Book of Discipline*, 189

Alexander Forester of Garden and Duncan Nairn of Torbrex, and Alexander Paterson, a notary in Corspatrick. Adam Spittle of Blairlogie and James Alexander in Mains represented the parish of Logie across the Forth to the north of Stirling. There are few signs, however, of the attendance of the elders from Alva, Fossoway, Glendevon or Muckhart, who had accepted office for life.[1]

Even so, at some of the earlier meetings of the presbytery, the number of elders present exceeded that of the ministers. Yet, by 1582, in replying to 'certaine doubts proponit concerning the presbyteries', the general assembly expressed the view that 'the number of such as are associat to the eldership for discipline and correctioun of maners, that are not pastours nor doctours, quho travell not in the Word, be not in equall number with uthers, but fewar; the proportioun as the necessitie of the eldership craves'. Nor was this all, for the assembly also observed that in future the presence of elders in presbyteries 'salbe no further straitit, but as the weghtines and occasioun, upon intimatioun and advertisement made be the pastours and doctours, sall requyre; at quhilk tyme they sall give thair godlie concurrence; exhorting them alwayes that may commodiouslie resort, to be present at all tymes'.[2] Thereafter, the elders' attendance at presbytery meetings seems somewhat to have dwindled, though a few were usually still present until Archbishop Adamson's criticism – that the presbytery 'appointed of gentlemen lords of the ground, and others associat with the ministers, is no other thing but to induce a great confusion in the kirk, and an occasioun of continuall sedition' – helped to supply Arran's government with the ammunition which it needed to abolish presbyteries by act of parliament in May 1584.[3] With the resumption of the presbytery's meeting in June 1586, well after Arran's downfall, elders ceased to attend in the period covered by this volume, though schoolmasters continued their association with the presbytery.[4]

Although the Second Book of Discipline had attacked 'the mingled jurisdictioun' of the commissary courts 'in sofar as thay

---

[1] See below, 1, 4–5, 8, 23; see also Index *sub* individual names
[2] See below, e.g., 17; *BUK*, ii, 567
[3] Calderwood, *History*, iv, 54; *APS*, iii, 293
[4] See below, e.g., 220–2, 225, 228–36, 253

mell with ecclesiasticall maters', the participation of the commissaries of Stirling and Dunblane as elders of the presbytery is signifi-
cant, for not only were they accustomed in their own courts to hear
cases concerning testaments and teinds and suits arising from deeds
which they had registered, but their forensic skills had also a relevance to the legal proceedings of the presbytery.[1]

Local commissaries, however, were denied a jurisdiction in
matrimonial causes which exclusively pertained to the commissary
court of Edinburgh, which, as the presbytery records disclose, might
still authorise a local commissary to proceed in hearing an action of
divorce.[2] At the same time, the presbytery also claimed a certain
competence in actions relating to marriage contracts, adherence and
separation.

Before marriage could be solemnized (which the presbytery
required should take place in church on a preaching day, witnessed
by the assembled congregation), the parties had first to express their
consent to contract marriage, and their banns, indicating their
intention to marry, had to be proclaimed on three successive
Sundays in the parishes where they resided so that anyone with
knowledge of an impediment to their marriage might voice an
objection.[3] When one couple complained in 1587 that their minister
had declined to marry them, even though they had 'confessit
mutuall promeis of mariage', the presbytery discovered that after
their banns had first been called, the laird of Gargunnock, 'heritur of
the land' where the girl's father had dwelt, had voiced an objection
as her appointed tutor on the ground that her prospective husband
was 'ane mane that hes na gair and als he spendit all that he hade'
whereas the girl had received 'ane rassonabill portione of gair left to
hir be hir father'. The daughter claimed, however, that 'becaus scho
was of perfyt aige, viz., of xx yeir or thairby' she was 'fre to marie'
whom she chose and was 'nocht bund to abyd be ony of hir freindis
consent'. The couple also 'confessit that thay hade carnall copulatione togethir', but appeared to be penitent 'eftir the moderatour
hade thratnit the jugementis of God'. In giving judgment, the
presbytery rejected the laird's objection as 'na thing relivant' and

---

[1] Kirk, *Second Book of Discipline*, 228; see below, 1; see also Index *sub* 'Cunningham,
Humphrey' and 'Pont, James'
[2] See below, 91   [3] See below, 5, 67, 125, 142

ordered marriage to proceed after the couple had made public repentance.[1]

Failure to fulfil the promise to contract marriage also gave rise to disputes which came before the presbytery for resolution. A woman who failed 'to schaw and declair ane ressonablle caus quhy scho will nocht compleit mariage according to ane matrimoniale contract' after she was 'contractit in mariage with consent of hir parentis', was judged by the presbytery in 1583 to be 'inconstant in passing fra the promeis of mariage quhilk scho haid made', and her father was likewise censured for 'approving hir passing thairfra agains his awin formar consent to the said promeis'. In passing sentence, the presbytery ordered the woman to make public repentance, and it fined her father £10 to be devoted to the decoration of their parish church of Clackmannan. In another case, in 1587, when the presbytery inquired 'quhy mariage is nocht desyrit to be solemnizit', the mother of the betrothed girl, replying that she had sought a delay in the proceedings, explained that she 'could nocht gait thingis necisar for hir dochteris mariage nor banquet as yit', but after the presbytery had urged a day to be named for the marriage, the family then 'cancellat and destroyit the matrimoniall contract', which led the presbytery to declare the girl's fiancé 'frie to marie in the Lord', and to discipline both mother and daughter 'for sclandering of the kirk'.[2]

The ability to prove the validity of a marriage had not inconsiderable legal implications. Authentication might readily be obtained by witnesses and perhaps also by a notary or by an entry in the registers of marriages which ministers were exhorted to keep. In 1581, proof of a couple's alleged marriage was sought from Edinburgh kirk session, and the presbytery soon elicited from the parties that there was merely 'promeis of mariage betuix thame and thair bannis lauchfullie proclamit bot was nocht mareit as yit'. The right of legitimate heirs to inherit property was the reason for a petition in 1584 from two sons who wished to establish the legality of their parents' marriage contracted 'of auld in tyme of papistrie' and held 'in ane hous privallie be ane preist in presens of certane witnessis' who had since died. The presbytery acceded to their request that the minister of the parish should receive from the parents a statement of the validity of their marriage before the congregation and, if no

[1] See below, 240–1, 243–4   [2] See below, 123, 125–6; 248–9, 252–5, 261–4

impediment were raised, that the minister should solemnize the 'band of matremony of new betuix thame according to the ordur reformit'.[1]

The detection of clandestine or irregular marriages also fell within the presbytery's competence. Thus, in 1584, the presbytery sought to determine whether a laird who had divorced his wife and then remarried was 'lauchfullie mareit'. The laird, however, was able to prove that the banns had been publicly proclaimed in church and that the marriage had been held in church before 'ane lairge numbir of honest personis of the parrochun, men and wemen'; and although he could not recall 'gif the day of his mariage was on ane Sonday or nocht', he was able to produce the minister's written testimonial of the marriage and also witnesses of the proceedings. The presbytery therefore found the marriage 'deulie varefeit'.[2]

Promise of marriage followed by cohabitation was also regarded by the presbytery as irregular but not as invalid. An illustration that the presbytery was prepared to concede that cohabitation with habit and repute constituted marriage occurred in 1582 when the presbytery took cognisance in a case where it was claimed that thirteen years earlier 'on ane fasternisevin at nycht eftir supper' in presence of a reader and witnesses, a couple had 'promesit mutuallie to compleit mariage on Sonday immediatelie eftir the fest of peace'. They had then cohabited 'dyveris yeiris' and had 'ane bairne'. But when the man, after separating, claimed that he had promised to marry another and wished his banns to be proclaimed, the presbytery ordered him 'to separet him self in societie' from the second woman, accused him of adultery, and, in view of 'the first woman refusand to persew the said mane for his first promeis made to hir', sought the synod's advice 'quhethir gif he may lauchfullie marie the second woman; gif nocht gif he and the first woman salbe compellit to compleit and solemneiz mariage according to thair first promeis'. The synod's short reply was that 'the second mariage stayis and urge for adherence of the first'. Nonetheless, in another case, in 1586 when a man had 'continewit lang in cumpany' with a woman 'to the grit offence of God and sclandir of his kirk', the presbytery required not only his repentance and his promise to complete marriage but also that caution be acted in the commissary

[1] See below, 19–20, 30–31, 34; 227–8   [2] See below, 196–7, 199

court. A marriage duly contracted and lawfully solemnized, but never consummated, was still regarded as valid by the presbytery.[1]

Actions relating to adherence also came within the presbytery's jurisdiction. With the Reformation, the law relating to adherence and divorce had undergone modification, first, with the acceptance of divorce *a vinculo* for adultery, and then, in 1573, with the statutory recognition of divorce for desertion. A pursuer might therefore raise an action of adherence in the commissary courts, then seek from the court of session letters of horning against the offender, and might also apply to the presbytery for appropriate ecclesiastical proceedings in the expectation of raising an action of divorce in the commissary court if the offender continued obdurate. When a litigant complained in 1582 that 'hir husband wald nocht ressave hir in hous with him and interteny hir as becumis him to do to his wyf', the presbytery ordered the husband to 'interteny hir as becumis him of Goddis law to do to his wyf or ellis to schaw ane ressabble caus quhy'. Recognizing that an obstacle to reconciliation existed in the litigant's admission that 'scho was deforcit agains hir will be ane man quhome scho knawis nocht and hade borne ane bairne to him', the presbytery gave the husband the choice of adherence to his spouse 'or ellis to intent actioun of divorcement agains hir befoir the commissaris of Edinburgh'. In another case, the presbytery insisted that a husband receive 'his spous agane in hous with him and interteneis hir as Godis law prescryvis and nocht to put hir fra him agane undir the paine of excommunicatioun'.[2]

The church's objection to the marriage of guilty parties in divorce cases led the presbytery in 1583 to declare invalid a marriage by a reader of the guilty parties in a divorce. Yet, elsewhere, the presbytery was prepared to approve a second marriage by a penitent adulterer in 1583 who had not been divorced but who was recognized 'to be fre' because of 'the departing of his wyf'. The presumption of death after the prolonged absence of a spouse was an issue on which the presbytery was reluctant to act. In one case, where a woman had presumed the death of her husband 'quha departit fra hir to Flandiris to the weris, thre yeir syne or thairby, and as scho is credablie informit allegis him ded thair ane yeir or mair syne', the

[1] See below, 64, 89–90; 108–9; 226–7; 160
[2] See below, 32; 32–33, 35, 41; 55–56, 58

presbytery could find 'na sufficient testimony of the deathe of hir said husband'. Another defendant's claim that 'he is trewlie informit' that his wife had 'departit furth of this lyf in Ingland lang befoir' left the presbytery with the perplexing problem of whether his 'fault be adultrie or fornicatioun'.[1]

Paternity cases were also heard by the presbytery so that the father might be made responsible for the child's welfare. In 1584, the presbytery sought to establish the identity of the father of a child by interrogating the mother and suspected father, and by examining the evidence of the midwife and witnesses 'insafar as thai knaw'. When a parishioner of Lecropt in 1586 declined to have a child baptised 'becaus it was nocht his', the presbytery ordered him 'ather to intent actione of devorcement befoir the juge ordinar againis his said spous for gaitting of the said bairne in adultrie and thairby to pruif hir ane hure, or ellis acknawlege and confes the said bairne to be his awin', though the matter was finally resolved when his wife 'deponit be hir grit aythe' that he was the child's father. The discovery of a 'fundlein bairne', an abandoned 'mane chyld fund on ane gait syd quhilk passis up fra the fut of Marie wynd to the castell of Striviling', who had been fostered but not baptised, led the presbytery to order Stirling kirk session to admonish the foster father 'to teiche the said bairne the sowme of ane Christiane fayth, viz., the xij articillis of the beleif that he mycht gif ane confessioun thairof the tyme he ressavit the sacrament of baptisme'.[2]

The expectation that an offender should 'confesse his sinne' to the church and recognise that 'he hath offended God and what slander he hath raised in the Kirk' gave rise to the exercise of an exceedingly wide ecclesiastical jurisdiction. The presbytery considered itself competent to take cognisance in cases involving homicide or manslaughter, and slander or defamation, as well as the more obviously ecclesiastical issues of recusancy and nonconformity, blasphemy, fornication, adultery and incest, profanation of the Sabbath by dancing or by holding markets, and the 'superstitious abuses' of clerk plays, midsummer bonfires, and pilgrimages to Christ's well, where the sick and afflicted sought cures for their maladies.[3] Regulations for the administration of the two sacraments

---

[1] See below, I, 91, 96; 142; 182; 202   [2] See below, 214; 225–6, 228; 87
[3] Cameron, *First Book of Discipline*, 168; see below, 38; and Index, *sub* subjects

C

of baptism and the Lord's Supper (the latter of which the presbytery insisted ought not to be administered at Easter or during Lent), for the observance of general fasts, as well as subscription to the Negative or King's Confession of Faith of 1581 were also enforced.[1]

In the case of homicide, the presbytery remitted ecclesiastical censure and sentence to the synod when 'a man slayer' in 1583 confessed that he was 'sorie fra his hairt and hes obteinit remissione fra the kingis majestie and hes satisfeit the partie thairfoir'. An action of defamation, or 'bill of slandir', brought before the presbytery in 1587 by one woman against another who had claimed that the pursuer had 'tane away the milk fra hir fatheris cow be wichcraft' resulted in the presbytery's finding the accused guilty of slander 'in calling hir ane wiche, in effect, quhilk scho could nawayis preive to be of varetie'. Slander of a different sort was evident in 1584 when the presbytery heard that 'ane sclandir is rissin in this toun thruch Mr William Moresone, allegeand that he sould have spokin sclanderuslie agaims the trew religioun of Jesus Christ professit in Scotland to the grit hinderance of Godis glorie and disconfort of the faithfull'.[2]

The problem of Roman Catholic recusancy took various forms. At one level, there existed a simple piety, less overtly Catholic, but nonetheless associated with older beliefs and such traditional practices, steeped in folk lore, as the veneration of shrines and pilgrimages to Christ's well whose water was reputed to heal diseases. In 1581, and again in 1583, the presbytery investigated the 'gret abuse usit be the rascall sort of pepill that passis in pilgrimage to Chrystis woll and usis gret idolatrie or superstitioun thairat expres agains Godis law'. A pilgrim seeking a cure described how he 'sat doun on his kneis and prayit, and drank of the woll and cust waltir on his hed and wosche his hed and breist' and then left behind a piece of clothing at the well. A woman with 'the meigroun in hir hed' and another with 'seiknes at hir hairt and ane sairnes that was in hir arme' performed similar ceremonies. One also claimed that she had 'past to Chrystis woll becaus hir foirbearis past thair', and another with a sick boy 'belevit that be the waschein of the bairne with the waltir of the said woll, he sould ather dee or leive'. The cult seems

---

[1] See below, 99, 224; 44, 178, 190–1, 295–6; 5, 203; see also Index *Sub* 'Baptism', 'Communion', 'Fasts' and 'Confession of Faith'

[2] See below, 174; 247, 249–50; 204

to have attracted more women than men, though one man admitted to visiting the well on behalf of his sick mother 'bot allegit that quhowsone he saw the said woll he belevit weill thair was na help to his mothur to be gottin thair'. In pronouncing its verdict, an unsympathetic presbytery concluded 'his mothur to have bein deliberat in mynd to have committit idolatrie and superstitioun at the said woll' and sentenced both to the social sanction of making public repentance in church.[1]

Catholic gentry who might seek to protect co-religionists in their midst and so revive Catholic worship were challenged by the presbytery to yield to its uncompromising claims. In 1584, Alexander Livingston of Terrintirran, his daughter-in-law (a Graham), and some of his servants were ordered on pain of excommunication to account for their failure to receive communion at Kippen parish kirk, and were admonished by the moderator 'that thai be nawayis absent fra the said sacrament quhen it is ministrat in thair awin parroche kirk in tymis cuming'. Unchecked, such backsliding might end in recusancy. More serious, however, was the behaviour of Walter Buchanan, the laird of Arnprior's brother, whom the presbytery heard had 'newlie returnit with ane Flemis woman, allegit to be his wyf, furth of cuntreis quhair papistrie is publictlie professit and authoresit be sword and fyr, speciallie the cuntreis of Spaine and Flanderis'. As he had 'at na tyme repairit to preiching nor prayeris' since arriving in Stirling, Buchanan was required to provide the presbytery in December 1586 with 'ane confessione and declaratione of his fayth and religione'.[2]

The case well illustrates both the strength and weakness of the presbytery's position. Although his brother-in-law, Alexander Seton of Gargunnock, 'ane godlie mane and weill reportit of', persuaded the presbytery to delay its proceedings for a spell, Buchanan had still to confer with the minister of Stirling who failed to secure his conformity, for he claimed as his 'warldlie excuis that he could nocht subscryve to our religione presentlie nor yit publictlie profes the samin, to wit, becaus the samin will be the tinsall of his wyffis heritage and leving, quhilk scho hade in Flanderis, and thairfor quhill he hade tane sum ordur thairanent he could nawayis

---

[1] See below, 4, 115–16, 120, 128, 130, 132–6, 139–40, 144, 147, 149–51, 154–5, 161
[2] See below, 167, 170, 205, 208–9; 234–5

imbraice our religione'. When Robert Buchanan of Leny sought a further adjournment as the culprit 'hade bot varie laitlie sein the said confessione of fayth and thairfor was nocht weill advysit thairwith', the presbytery agreed, 'willing rather to win the said Waltir than to los him'. Further delays ensued, month by month, as the presbytery exhorted him to 'frequent the kirk in tyme of service, speciallie in tyme of preichein' (which he failed so to do, professedly because 'thais pairttis of Kippen quhair he dwellis is undir sic feir of brokin heland men') until in April 1587 the presbytery, its patience almost exhausted, threatened to excommunicate him 'as ane papeist refusar to profes our religione, agreing with the Word of God'. Undeterred, he declined even to have his child baptised 'according to the ordur approvit be the reformit kirk of Scotland'. His empty promise 'to depart schortlie furth of this cuntrie' delayed the final sentence of excommunication till 1588 when the presbytery declared him 'obstinat and indurit in papistrie'. Action was also taken against his brother, the laird of Arnprior, who had 'declairit him self in sindrie partis to be ane papeist and hes rassonit for defence of the heresie thairof'.[1] By then, however, fears of a counter-Reformation had reached new heights as the Armada crisis threatened England.

There is, however, little indication in the presbytery records of the detection of lay recusants in the burgh of Stirling itself. When a tailor was remitted from the kirk session to the presbytery for trial, the minister and grammar schoolmaster of Stirling had discussions with him 'anent the cheiff heddis of religioun' but it was soon discovered that 'he willinglie aggreit with all heddis of the trew religioun of Jesus Christ professit in Scotland and (as appeirit to thame) he was nocht obstinat and that the wordis that he had spokin in menteinance of the mes was mair of ignorance nor uthirwayis'. Nonetheless, the presbytery insisted in 1584 that he subscribe the Negative Confession of Faith and that he 'rys on his feit' before the congregation of Stirling to 'confes that he hes offendit God in geving of his corporall presens to the mes in France and in speiking in this toun in menteinance thairof, and that he publictlie dam the samin and all papistrie in generall'. In 1583, however, Robert Veich, 'sumtym gwarden of the Gray freiris in

---

[1] See below, 235–43, 245–7, 250, 256, 260–1, 265–6, 284–5, 299, 305–7, 310–11 ; 300, 306

Striviling', who had failed to compear before the synod to give 'ane confessioun of his fayth and religioun' and to be disciplined 'for his formar abusis' was ordered to find surety, from a goldsmith who acted as cautioner, that he would appear before the general assembly; but on finding that 'na obedience was offirit be the said freir', the presbytery, after four admonitions, passed sentence of excommunication. Three inhabitants of Dunblane were also excommunicated 'for nonrecantatioun of the papisticall religioun', a sentence which the presbytery thought advisable to reaffirm in 1584 'incaice the commone pepill pretend ignorance thairof'.[1]

A further threat was perceived in the crown's rehabilitation in 1587 (albeit merely for two years) of William Chisholm, Andrew Graham's Roman Catholic predecessor as bishop of Dunblane, to the neglect of Graham's own title to the see. On hearing of his recent return from France, the presbytery immediately censured Chisholm as one 'quha is notourlie knawin to be ane papeist and ennemie to the reformit religione' and threatened him with excommunication for his 'continuance in that corruptit religione of papistrie repugnant to the Word of God'. When the commendator of Inchaffray and Chisholm of Cromlix excused the bishop's failure to face the presbytery on the ground that the 'bischop haid ane disais fallin in his leg quhairthrow he mycht nawayis travell', the presbytery thoughtfully responded by sending a deputation to meet the bishop at Inchaffray, 'gif he can be personallie apprehendit', but the bishop declined to be interviewed, and only on the king's direct intervention, in January 1587/8, was the sentence of excommunication delayed until the next general assembly in February insisted that it be pronounced and intimated in all the churches of the presbyteries of Stirling and Dunblane.[2]

The resort to excommunication, as the final ecclesiastical sanction, is a measure of the church's failures, not its successes. Yet excommunication carried with it penalties which even the proudest contemner could ill afford to disregard; hence the readiness of some 'to satisfie the kirk' and be absolved from the sentence. Deprived of all benefits of the kirk, the excommunicant was deemed a social outcast, and the presbytery was vigilant in disciplining any who

---

[1] See below, 200, 202–3; 176–8, 180, 183, 185, 187–9, 199–200; 206
[2] See below, 294–5, 301–8

attempted to associate with those whom it had cut off from the society of the church. The Countess of Menteith, a notary and several inhabitants of Stirling were censured for socialising with Robert Montgomery, the excommunicated archbishop. Indeed, a special licence had first to be obtained before an excommunicant might be lawfully approached. In 1583, the brother of an excommunicant received a dispensation from the presbytery to confer with him 'for calling of him fra that damnablle idolatrie' and to provide him with 'neciseris to his awin chalmir allanirlie'; but in renewing the licence in 1584 the presbytery insisted that he be accompanied by 'ane minister and ane elder' on future visits. Inter-presbyterial communications also made it hard for excommunicants to escape from their disabilities by moving from one locality to another. On being informed by Edinburgh presbytery in 1584 of David Graham of Fintry's excommunication 'for his feirfull apostacie' by the minister of Dundee, the presbytery took action against the Earl of Montrose and the Chisholms of Cromlix for befriending Fintry after he had been excommunicated.[1]

In theory, if not always in practice, excommunication was understood to have the concurrent secular sanction of outlawry; and the presbytery in 1583, hearing that the king had 'promesit to the kirk to puneis all excommunicat personis civillie according to the lawis', ordered the names of all excommunicants to be reported in accordance with an act of the general assembly. Invocation of the secular arm in support of the ecclesiastical – reaffirmed most recently in the Second Book of Discipline's claim that 'cheiflie and namelie Christiane princes, kingis and uther magistrates' had a paramount duty 'to assist and fortifie the godlie proceding of the kirk' – had an application in the presbytery's work. The authority of both crown and parliament was sought, where necessary, to reinforce the jurisdiction of the ecclesiastical courts. In 1582, the presbytery took action so 'that the kingis majestie mycht be advertesit of thair unreverent handling' by Robert Montgomery; and in 1583 the recent act of parliament against pilgrimages was invoked for punishing pilgrims to Christ's well. In the localities, the powers and prestige of nobles and lairds, as lesser magistrates, were called upon

---

[1] See below, 36; 252, 258; 147, 154, 166; 46, 48, 50–52, 83, 152–4, 158, 161–2; 168–9, 179–80, 219–20; 113; 200, 207, 209–11. See also Index *sub* 'Excommunication'

to ensure that the presbytery's wishes were heeded. Lord Doun, as steward of Menteith, was urged to punish certain offenders; and, to the presbytery's evident satisfaction, 'the laird of Cars, barroun of the barrony of Alvayth made actis in his court that na mane sould hant' the company of an excommunicant. Sometimes the 'godly magistrate' needed reminding of his duties. In 1584, the Earl of Montrose was exhorted not to receive certain 'freindis, tennentis or servandis' whom the church had excommunicated; otherwise, as the presbytery pointedly explained, 'we can nocht of our dewatie bot pres his lordschip with disceplein thairfoir'. The burgh magistrates, a few of whom conveniently sat as presbytery elders, were also expected to lend their weight by enforcing the presbytery's decrees. In 1582, the presbytery reported an offender to 'the civill magistrattis, viz., to the provest and bailleis of Striviling . . . desyring thame to adjone thair auctoritie to the auctoritie of the kirk in punesing'.[1]

The rôles of minister and magistrate, correctly exercised, were seen to be complementary, not contradictory, but the church's early awareness of 'the faults which the civill sword either doth neglect or not punish' had strengthened its claims to assume an autonomous jurisdiction, in which the presbytery had power to 'statute and ordain' enactments and deliver sentences without experiencing the necessity of 'tarrying for the magistrate'. In the presbytery's proceedings, the civil magistrate's intervention was exceptional; and, indeed, the presbytery itself drew attention in 1587 to 'the grit aboundance of schaddein of blude in this countrie without ony puneisment or remady made thairfoir be the civill magistrat'.[2] Frequently, the presbytery resorted to the convenient device of requiring offenders to find surety for their good behaviour and to have this registered by the commissary court. More serious cases, however, were often remitted to the synod for further determination.[3]

The firm links between the localities and the centre which the church courts had forged, and which were scarcely paralleled in

[1] See below, 113; Kirk, *Second Book of Discipline* 213; see below, 39; *APS*, iii, 212, c. 6; see below, 115–16; 119–20; 208, cf. 209–12; 54

[2] Cameron, *First Book of Discipline*, 165; cf. Knox, Works, vi, 451; see below, 296

[3] See below, 138, 193, 195–6, 202, 237, 242; 92, 98, 103, 159–60, 169–70, 173, 182; see also Index *sub* 'Commissary Court' and 'Synod'

secular society, were further strengthened by the judicial and supervisory work of the presbytery as a district court where ministers, lairds and burgesses deliberated together. This connection is strikingly illustrated in the appointment of commissioners to attend the general assembly. Whereas in October 1581 the presbytery had merely intimated that the lairds of Garden and Keir, and the commissary of Dunblane had been appointed by the synod as commissioners to the general assembly, by April 1582 the presbytery itself had undertaken to elect three ministers, as well as two lairds and the two commissaries as the 'barronis and gentill men', to attend the assembly at St Andrews. This form of election was again observed in June 1582 and in April 1583, but there is no word of the election of commissioners from the presbytery to the assemblies which met in October 1582 and in October 1583. Perhaps, as was so in October 1581, the synod assumed responsibility, as a convenient organ accustomed to meet in April and October. Thereafter, no assemblies met between October 1583 and May 1586; and the attempt by some ministers to convene an assembly in April 1584 ended in failure. Yet after its reconvening in June 1586, the presbytery resumed responsibility for sending commissioners (in this instance, purely ministerial commissioners) to the assembly which met at Edinburgh in June 1587.[1]

Through the presbytery, too, the ordinances of the national and regional courts were circulated and made known in the parishes. Appeals were also transmitted from the presbytery to the general assembly.[2] The links established could scarcely have been closer, but they were in danger of being dissolved when the 'Black Acts' of 1584 revived the authority of bishops and proscribed presbyteries from meeting.

The presbytery minutes abruptly end on 19th May 1584; but in the preceding month, possibly in anticipation of the changes to come, the synod had taken the unusual step of announcing the times and places of the next four synods until April 1585.[3] The eventual collapse of Arran's conservative government in December 1585, and the return from England of the presbyterian exiles who had sought

---

[1] See below, 8, 40, 45, 107, 266
[2] See below, 5, 10-11, 66-67, 79, 86, 113, 224, 281; 109-10, 224; 4-6, 10-11, 143
[3] See below, 220; 215

sanctuary there, prepared the way for attempts at reconciling bishops, whom the king wished to retain, with a presbyterial administration. A conference between some councillors and ministers at Holyroodhouse in February 1585/6 reached agreement in a compromise which recognised that 'presbyteries of persons ecclesiasticall' should be set up throughout the realm in places selected by the general assembly with the king's advice, and that bishops, presented by the crown and admitted by the general assembly (to which they remained accountable in life and doctrine), should each accept a congregational charge, and, with other commissioners, conduct visitations with 'the advice of the presbyterie', which was also assigned a positive rôle in admitting candidates to benefices. Admissions and deprivations by a bishop, without the presbytery's approval, were declared to be invalid. Acceptance that a bishop 'by himself sall doe nothing, but that which a particular minister or moderator is astricted to by his office' was evidently designed to satisfy presbyterian beliefs, but it might also imply recognition that the bishop should become constant moderator of the presbytery, an interpretation which was by no means clarified in the accompanying statement that 'the bishops and commissioners sall visie the presbytereis and the moderator of the presbytereis sall visie the particular kirks'.[1]

When it met in May, the assembly gave hesitant approval to the scheme after making many detailed comments. It insisted that the name of bishop was 'commoun to all Pastours and Ministers', but it permitted the king to present to the assembly for admission a minister nominated to a bishopric. Although affirming that 'visitatioun is in the person of Pastours', the assembly accepted that it might 'send a man, accompanied with such as the Presbitrie sall adjoyne to him in visitatioun', or, again, it might appoint a bishop to visit certain defined areas (but not 'the haill bounds callit of auld, Dyocie') so long as he proceeded with the synod's advice and such as the synod joined with him in visitation. In presentation and collation to benefices, the overseer was to act with the presbytery's advice and with assessors nominated by the general assembly. The work of bishops was to be supplemented by commissioners nominated by the crown and admitted by the assembly. In addition, the

[1] Calderwood, *History*, iv, 491-4

assembly wished to subject the bishop in life and doctrine to the presbytery or synod (as well as to the assembly in respect of his commission); but, on the king's objection, the bishop's subjection to the presbytery or synod was waived.[1]

In drawing up its plans for establishing 16 synods and 52 presbyteries, the assembly separated Stirling and Dunblane into two distinct presbyteries (as Bishop Graham had sought in 1581) with 23 and 20 constituent churches respectively. Detached from the province of Lothian, the two presbyteries were to form a new province of Dunblane with its own synod, an arrangement which persisted until 1588 when both presbyteries were incorporated into the province of the synod of Perth. Since the assembly accepted in 1586 that bishops and commissioners should act as moderators of presbyteries, James Anderson, minister of Stirling and the crown's nominee to the assembly for the office of commissioner, automatically became moderator of Stirling presbytery which resumed its activities on 21st June; but the assembly also gave commission to four ministers from the two presbyteries in the province of Dunblane to observe the commissioner's behaviour.[2]

As efforts were made to effect a scheme along the lines of the bishop-in-presbytery, the first matter to come before the presbytery after its resumption, curiously enough, was the case of Bishop David Cunningham of Aberdeen, formerly sub-dean of Glasgow, whose trial for the 'sclandir of adultrie' the assembly had remitted to the presbyteries of Stirling and Glasgow. Thereafter, the presbytery resumed its supervision of the benefices within its jurisdiction by ordering James Cockburn, a non-resident benefice-holder, to produce his presentation, collation 'with all uthir richtis and documentis that he hes' to the benefice of Muckhart.[3] The candidate, identified elsewhere as the brother of John Cockburn of Clerkington,

[1] *BUK*, ii, 650, 652–4

[2] *Ibid.*, ii, 648–9, 664, 667, 676; see below, 237, 245–6, 256–9; Scottish Record Office (SRO), CH2/722/1, Stirling Presbytery Records, 20 August 1588: 'The generall assemblie ordanis the presbyteriis of Perthe and Dunkeld to concur with thir twa presbyteriis, viz., Sterling and Dunblane in ane synodall assemblie, and the placis of thair conventione to be at the appointment of the said synodall assemblie, and thair first conventione to be in Perth. *Sic subscribitur*, J. Richie'. (This authenticated record varies somewhat from the minute in *BUK*, ii, 738, which does not mention Stirling as part of the enlarged synod.) See below, 220; *BUK*, ii, 667

[3] See below, 220–1; 221–2

had been presented by the king to the benefice of Muckhart on
12th January 1585/6, during the presbytery's abeyance; and the
presentation in his favour had been directed to the archbishop of St
Andrews, or to the commissioner or superintendent of the bounds.
The presbytery's action, though not immediately effective, ulti-
mately led to Cockburn's deposition four years later in 1591.[1]

Although he was present in the sederunts of most presbytery
meetings, the commissioner seems to have played no special part in
the routine business of the presbytery (other than his acting as
moderator) and, indeed, his activities escape mention in the records
until October 1586 when the presbytery ordered him to notify a
congregration of the presbytery's approval for the admission of an
assistant minister. The commissioner, however, was accorded the
right of attending the general assembly, but it was the presbytery, as
a whole, which 'electit and nominat' the ministers to accompany
him to Edinburgh in June 1587; and it was the presbytery, again,
which decided when to resort to excommunication, leaving to the
commissioner merely the task of executing its verdict. Although
responsible for conducting visitations (and also for negotiating with
the modifiers of ministers' stipends), the commissioner was nonetheless accountable to the presbytery, which inspected the parochial
books of discipline and which criticised and fined him for his absence
from the synod in April 1588 'berassone he is nocht onlie ane minister of the Word within thir boundis quhairby he is daitbund to haif
bein thair, bot also, seing he is commissionar of thir haill boundis
quhairby sindrie thingis concerning his offeice was neidfull to be
handlit, and becaus thair was sindrie waightie materis traittit'.[2]

In the examination and admission of candidates to the ministry,
the presbytery again played a leading part. In addition to examining
ministers and prospective ministers at the exercise, the presbytery
proceeded, after due trial, to admit Henry Laing, 'ane yung man of
honest report newlie returnit frome the schollis' to the ministry at
St Ninians in 1586; it licensed William Paton as a minister in 1587,
and when no local church 'that hes only rassonablle stipend' could

[1] SRO, CH4/1/2, Register of Presentations to Benefices, fo. 145r.; PS1/66, Register of
the Privy Seal, fo. 119r.; CH2/722/2, Stirling Presbytery Records, 3 November, 1590;
22 June, 10 August, 1591
[2] See below, 289–90; 266; 305–7; 294; 253; SRO, CH2/722/1, Stirling Presbytery
Records, 9 April 1588

be found for him, it permitted him to seek a charge in the Merse. When requested by a spokesman for the parishioners of Bothkennar 'to appoint ane brother to plaice' William Cowper whom the general assembly had admitted as minister, the presbytery 'ordeinit' the commissioner 'to pas to the said kirk ony Sonday he thocht meit, thair to notifie the parrochinnaris' and 'to desyr thame to signifie thair consent'. All too readily the commissioner might become no more than an instrument of the presbytery, which showed itself prepared to defend its jurisdiction. As soon as it heard of an apparent attempt by St Ninians kirk session 'to elect and admit ane minister', the presbytery denounced the action as 'plaine repugnant to Godis Word and gude ordur', since 'the admissione of all ministeris is onlie in the handis of the presbyteriis and utheris assembleis of ministeris'. Once agreement was reached, the presbytery again appointed the commissioner to induct Henry Livingston as the new minister of St Ninians, 'and to plaice him ordinar pastur thairat'; 'and ordanis the commissionar to report his diligence heirin to the brethrein'. The commissioner's accountability to the presbytery was evidently not to be disregarded, and at the next meeting, a full report of his proceedings 'for obedience of the brethreinis ordinance' was disclosed, 'quhilk the brethrein jugit to be formallie done'. Nor was the commissioner's customary presence at inductions even considered to be essential. In December 1587, at Henry Laing's admission as minister of Airth, the presbytery chose to appoint the minister of Bothkennar to induct the new minister to Airth.[1]

A preference for returning to earlier presbyterian practices, thereby undermining the compromise of 1586, soon became apparent by April 1588 when the device of having the commissioner serve as constant moderator was abandoned in favour of twice-yearly elections, as previously. Even earlier, the synod, by April 1587, had adopted the observance of rotating its meeting-place between Dunblane and Stirling. Thereafter, with the presbytery's incorporation in the synod of Perth, by August 1588, presbyterial visitations were resumed; and a representative other than the commissioner was appointed to the platt for adjusting ministers' stipends. The presbytery's self-confidence in recovering the lost ground of 1584 helped to hasten, as well as to reflect, the presbyterian

[1] See below, 229–34; 244–5; 273; 274–5; 275–8, 280–1, 283–4, 286–7, 289–90; 297

ascendancy within the wider church whose statutory recognition was finally forthcoming in 1592.[1] Statutes might still be annulled, or their force might be nullified, but never again in the history of the established church were presbyteries to be entirely swept away as they were by act of parliament in 1584.

The text and method of editing: The text offered below is contained in the first folio volume of Stirling Presbytery Records, which extends from August 1581 to February 1589/90, and which is presently located in the Scottish Record Office, Edinburgh.[2] The following transcription, ending in December 1587 (with the experiment of the commissioner-in-presbytery showing signs of collapse), illustrates the scope and content of the presbytery's work from the presbytery's erection in 1581 till the onset of the 'Black Acts' of 1584, its revival and recovery in 1586 and its reassertion of its powers thereafter.

The tidy, steady hand of the scribe, James Duncanson, reader at Stirling, continues throughout the volume, which remains unfoliated. The minutes seem to have been composed from notes (perhaps entered in a scroll book) which the scribe took at the meetings and subsequently wrote up. This would help to explain occasional slips, such as the misplacing of certain proceedings relating to Bishop Chisholm of Dunblane which the scribe inserted out of sequence in December 1587. Occasionally, in certain sessions, the scribe has recorded the sederunts but has omitted to enter any account of the proceedings.[3] When the volume was later rebound, folios 2 and 3 were transposed, but the correct sequence is preserved in the text below. Nor is it possible to cross-check any cases in the 1580s with Stirling Kirk Session Records, whose surviving minutes only begin in November 1597.[4]

In transcribing and editing the records, the normal editorial conventions have been adopted. The original orthography has been retained, except for the standardisation of 'i' and 'j'; 'u', 'v' and

[1] See below, 245, 256, 310; SRO, CH2/722/1, Stirling Presbytery Records, 16 April 1588; 3 September 1588; 12 November 1588; *APS*, iii, 541–2
[2] SRO, CH2/722/1. The records have been assigned for transference to Central Regional Archives, Stirling
[3] See below, 61, 193, 225, 230, 233–4, 239, 294; 296–7, 300–4
[4] SRO, CH2/1026/1, Stirling Kirk Session Records, 17 November 1597

'w'; and 'y' and 'z' where appropriate. Abbreviations and contractions have been extended; punctuation has been modernized; editorial comment is italicised within square brackets; and the device of three full stops denotes the omission of a phrase owing to a damaged portion of text. Dates remain in original form.

THE ELDERSCHIP of Striviling was erectit upone the viij day of August the yeir of God im vc lxxxi yeiris be Mr Robert Montgumrie and Mr Andro Grahame, commissionaris appointit be the last generall assemblie haldin at Glasquow to that effect.

The namis of the ministeris and elderis presentlie convenit quha accep[tit] upone thame offeice and plaice in the said presbitry be solem promeis [in] the presens of God thair handis beand haldin up promesing faythfullie to exerceis thair officis thairin, conform to the Word of God, unto the end of thair lyvis, as it sall plais God to minister unto thame the giftis of his Holie Spirit:

Ministeris: Mr Robert Montgumrie, minister at Striviling; Patrik Gillaspie, minister at S. Ninianis kirk; Andro Forester, minister at Falkirk; Mr Andro Yung, minister at Dunblane; Alexander Fargy, minister at Logy; Robert Mentayth, minister at Alvayth; Mr Adame Merschell, minister at Fossowy; Thomas Swintoun, minister at Mukert.

Elderis: for the kirk of Striviling, Adame, commendatar of Cambuskynneth; Umphra Cunynghame, commissar of Striviling; Mr James Pont, commissar of Dunblane; Johnne Layng, burges of Striviling. For S. Ninianis kirk, Alexander Forester of Garden, Duncane Narne of Torbrekis, Alexander Patirsone in Corspatrik. For Logy, Adame Spittall of Blair Logy, James Alschundur in Mainis.

The refuse of Mr Andro Grahame and Michaell Lermonthe to accep plaice in the presbitry and the said Mr Androis protestatioun: Mr Andro Grahame, minister at Dunblane, and Michaell Lermonth, minister at Kilbryd, beand desyrit be Mr Robert Montgomrie and the bretherein foirsaid, thai than beand present, to accept offeice and plaice in the elderschip foirsaid and to submit thame selffis to the jurisdictioun thairof refusit to do the same and protestit the said Mr Andro Graham that this his consent to the erecting of the elderschip of Striviling sould nocht be prejudiciall to him in caice thair sould be ane presbitry heireftir appointit in Dunblane.

Electing of the scryb: The same day the bretherein present with commone consent electit James Duncansone, redar in the kirk of Striviling, clark to the said presbitry.

Electing of the moderator: The same day Patrik Gillaspy, minister at S. Ninianis kirk, was chosin be moniest vottis moderator to the said elderschip unto the nixt provinciall assemblie.

Quhat hour the exerceis sall begin: The bretherein ordanis the exerceis to be kepit ilk Tysday at ix houris and the bell to rigne befoir the hour ane rassonablle spaice.

The xv day of August, 1581

Ordur for electing of elderis to the presbitry: Ordanis ilk minister to convein thair awin particular sessioun and to desyr thame to elect furth of thair parruschun twa or thre elderis to concur and accep offeice and plaice in the presbitry, and, being electit be thair awin sessioun, ordanis the minister to publeis thair naimis in the pulpet and to craif the consent of thair kirk thairunto, quhilk being obtenit ordanis the saidis personis to be presentit to the presbitry to the effect forisaid.

Admonitioun to the moderator to warn the ministeris heir wrettin to accep plaice in the presbitry: Ordanis Mr Andro Grahame, minister at Dunblane, Mr William Stirling, minister at Abirfoull, and Michaell Lermonth, minister at Kilbryd, to be warnit be the moderator to the xxij of August instant to accep upone thame offeice and plaice in this presbitry becaus thai ar appointit be the generall ordur to be under the jurisdictioun thairof, and that undir the pane of disobedience.

The xxij day of August, 1581

Comperance of Michaell Lermonthe and productioun of ane wreting: Mris Andro Grahame, William Stirling and Michaell Lermonth being warnit be the moderatoris wreting according to the tennour of the act maid thairanent in our last sessioun, comperit Michaell Lermonth for him self and in name of Maisteris Andro Grahame and William Stirling and producit ane wreting direct to Patrik Gillaspy, minister of Goddis word, quhairof the tennour followis.

The tennour of the wreting for Dunblane: Brethir, pleis we haif ressavit a letter direct from you . . . the wrett in the name of certan of your brethrein, quhairin ye req[uire] and chairge us to repair unto Stirling the xxij of this instant to adjone us unto the number of your presbytery to keip ordinarie pla[ce] in your exerceis and uthir assembleis thairof, and finallie to bring [the] eldaris of our congregatiounis with us to accept plaice in your presbytery, thretning us heirunto with excommunicatioun. For answer we haif heirtofoir in certane of your assembleis convenit with you to satisfie the desyr of the kingis g[racis] letter and wrettein direct from the moderator of the last generall assemblie, quhilk we undirstand extein[dis] only to this point, that convening with uthir brethrein and gentilmen to quhome the saidis letteris wer direct, we micht gif our avy[s and] jugement quhow the ordour of unioun and divisioun of the kirkis [and] erectioun of the presbyteriis proponit in the plat send to you mycht tak effect, and to reforme be gude avys quhairas it was neidfull and to report answer agane that be gude avyis and deliberatioun gude ordour concerning the saidis pointis micht be finallie con[clu]dit and establischit be the kirk and kingis grace, swa that our metin[g] was nocht to approve quhatsumevir forme and ordour was propon[it] in the said platt without contradictioun. Now we undirstand this ordur to haif tane that finall conclusioun and establischment as yit be the kirk and kingis grace. In respect quhairof we marvell that ye sould exceid the boundis of your commissioun safar as [to] threttin us with censuris incace of our refusall to adjone unto your numbir befoir that this ordur be finallie establischit w[ith] uniform consent of the kirk and kingis grace. And samekill that rather becaus we haif alwayis opponit our selffis afoir and disassentit fra adjoning us unto your presbytery, lyk as we be thir presentis disassentis thairfra for mony gude consideratiounis, namely, becaus we haif a presbytery of our awin erectit of a lang tyme past in Dunblane be the ordur approvit be the generall kirk affoir our visitour standand undischairgit, our assembleis and conventionis mentenid, our exerceis haldin and keipit, and the materis of our kirk intreattid, quhilk ordur ainis sa weill plantid, we can nocht dessolve and brek raschelie be adjoning us to your numbir befoir that our lauchfull rassonis may be hard befoir the generall assemblie quhy we can nocht do the same lyk as we haif alreddy

D

menit our selffis be our letter and message exponit be the laird of Keir to the moderatour of the last generall assemblie and kirk of Edinburgh and sa that thai conclude the sam to be neidfull unto the quhilk tyme we can nocht adjone us to keip place and ordour with your presbytery, our awin ordur standand undischargit, bot will glaidlie furdur you with our counsell and presens as salbe neidfull without prejudice of our awin erectioun. This meikill we haif thocht meit to mak answer to your letter in a modest manir thinking the same salbe fund ressonabyll; uthirwayis gif the same may nocht satisfie, bot that nochtwithstanding ye intend (as ye mak mentioun be your letter) to proceid with censuris of your kirk againis us, we be thir presentis will protest for remade befoir the generall assemblie, and appeallis frome you unto thair sentence. Swa committis you to God, from Dunblane the xxij day of August 1581, youris brethir in the Lord. *Sic subscribitur*, Androu, b. Domblane, Maister Williame Striviling, Michaell Lermonthe, minister.

Quhilk wreting being sein and considderit be the bretherein present, ordanis Mr Andro Grahame, Mr William Stirling and Michaell Lermonthe to produce ane warrand of thair presbytery and visitour specefeit in thair said wreting befoir this sessioun the xxix day of August instant with certeficatioun and thai failze, this presbytery will ordane the censuris of the kirk to proceid againis thame.

Elderris: The quhilk day comperit Johnne Sandis, for the kirk of Fossowy, and William Persone, for the kirk of Glendoven, chosin be the kirkis foirsaidis to be elderis within the said presbytery, quha be halding up of thair handis and solem promeis in the presens of God promesit faythfullie to exerceis thair offecis thairin unto the end of thair lyvis as God sall minister to thame the giftis of his Spirit.

Chrystis well: The brethering, undirstanding ane papisticall pilgramage begun at leat at Chrystis well, ordanis everie minister within thair awin boundis to try quhat personis hes resortit thairto and to call thame befoir thair particular sessioun that thai being convict thairof ordur may be provydit thairfoir.

Dansing: Ordanis the kirk of Striviling to tak ordur with sic personis as dansis on the Sabboth day speciallie with thai that dansit within the nycht in Robert Wysis hous on Sonday last.

Confessioun of the fayth: Ordanis ilk minister to requyr thair parrochinaris to subscryve the kingis gracis confessioun of fayth, conforme to the act of the generall assemblie maid thairanent.

The xxix day of August the yeir of God im vc lxxxi yeiris

Contenuatioun of the matter tuiching Dunblane: In the term assignit to Mr Andro Grahame, Mr William Stirling and Michaell Lermonthe to produce ane warrand of thair allegit presbytery and visitur, comperit Michaell Lermonthe and allegit in his awin name and thairis that the saidis Maisteris Andro and William micht nocht compeir that day berassone of weghtie materis thai haid to do, and thairfor desyrit the term to be contenowit to the fyft of September nixt, quhilk being knawin and considderit be the brethir thair excuse was thocht rassonablle and swa contenuit the mater to the fyft of September foirsaid, with certeficatioun and thai failze the censuris of the kirk sould be execut againis thame.

Tuiching mariage: Ordanis the actis of the generall assemblie to be observit within the boundis of this presbytery, bearand in effect that na minister within brugh minister mariage to ony persone aff ane preching day, and to landwart aff ane Sonday, and that in tyme of preching. Item, that na minister mary personis beand bayth of uthir congregatiounis nor his awin, albeit thai have lauchfull testemoniallis excep thai bring with thame ane lycence from the elderschip.

Elder for Alvethe: Comperit Andro Wilsone for the kirk of Alvayth, chosin be the same to be ane elder within the presbytery, quha be halding up of his hand and solem promeis in the presens of God promesit faythfullie to exerceis his offeice thairin unto the end of his lyif, as God sall minister to him the giftis of his Spirit.

The fyft day of September, 1581

Appellatioun for Dunblane: In the term assignit to Mr Andro Grahame, Mr William Stirling and Michaell Lermonthe to produce warrand of thair allegit presbytery and visitur, compeirit the saidis personis personally and allegit that thai could nocht adjone thame selffis to this presbytery befoir the generall assemblie haid concludit thair determinatioun thairanent and haid hard thair ressonis quhairfore thai could nocht do the same, and adherand unto thair appellatioun gevin in of befoir undir thair hand wrett, protestit that thai mycht be hard befoir the generall assemblie befoir ony proces war led againis thame be us, and incaise of refuse of this thair desyr appellis of new to the determinatioun of the generall assemblie quhom thai promeis to obey. Albeit that the saidis personis satisfeit nocht the desyr of thair terme conforme to the last act, yit inrespect of thair appellatioun the brethir contenwis farder proces againis thame to the said generall assemblie, and ordanis thame to compeir befoir the samin the thrid day thairof to heir thair pretendit appellatioun discussit with certificatioun and thai failze the said appellatioun salbe haldin as nocht proponit, to the quhilk the saidis personis willinglie aggreit.

Admoneis Mr Robert Montgumrie: The brethir, considdering the grit absence of Mr Robert Montgumrie, minister at Stirling, fra his chairge and necligence in his offeice bayth in doctrein and disceplein, ordanis the moderator to admoneis him thairof and to desyr him to compeir the nixt sessioun to schaw the causis of his absence.

The xij day of September, 1581

The quhilk day Patrik Gillaspie, moderatour, schew to the brethir that he haid admonesit Mr Robert Montgumrie of his absence and desyrit him to be present conform to the last act.

Productioun of Mr Robert Montgumreis wreting: Comperit James Duncansone and producit ane wreting of the said Mr Robertis direct to the brethir of the exerceis and presbytery of Striviling, quhairof the tennour follwis.

The tennour of the said wreting: Bretherein, eftir my hairtlie commendatioun, war nocht certane necessar bissines I haif haid ado this tyme bygane, and yit hes in hand, I haid nocht bein absent fra you. Thairfor I pray you haif my absence excusit, for I suppone few ministeris hes kepit bettir recidens nor I haif keipit hethirto, nor mair cairfull for the kirk, bayth towarttis the exerceis and presbytery, as I report your awin rememberens, nocht doutting bot ye will tak in gude part my lauchfull excuse as occasioun may offir to your selffis and the Lord blis your exerceis and presbytery throw

Jesus Chryst. So be it. At Stirling, the xj day of September 1581. *Sic subscribitur*, youris brothur in the Lord, Maister Robert Montgomerie.

The answer to the said wreting: The said wreting being considderit albeit it appeiris to accuse utheris, rather than to excuse him self, yit the brethir willing materis to be handillit brothurlie passis thairfra and ordanis the said Mr Robert to declair in the nixt sessioun the speciall causis of his absence becaus the bill in that part is generall.

Admonitioun concerning adultraris: The moderatour warnit the brethir that gif thair was ony adultraris or incesteus personis within thair boundis that thai sould summond thame (sa mony as was convict thairof) to the synodall assemblie to be haldin in Edinburgh the thrid day of October to ressave thair injunctionis thairfoir.

The xix day of September, 1581

The brethrein inrespect of Mr Robert Montgomreis absence contenwis his mater to the xxvj day of September instant.

The xxvj day of September, 1581

Ordanis to summond Mr Robert Montgumrie: The brethir, considering the absence of Mr Robert Montgumrie fra his chairge to be na thing amendit be thair former admonitioun, bot rather mair necligent nor of befoir, ordanis him to be summond to the provinciall assemblie of the elderschippis of Striviling, Linlythquow, Edinbrugh and Dalkayth to be haldin in Edinbrugh the thrid day of October nixtocum within the tolbuth thairof or quhair it salhappin thame to sitt within the said brugh for the tyme to answer to sic thingis as sould be layit unto his chairge undir the paine of disobedience, and ane summonds to be direct heirupone.

Margaret Leiche, adultrix: Compeirit Malcolme Wallace, elder of the kirk of Striviling, and schew that Margaret Leiche haid confessit in thair particular assemblie that scho haid committit adultry with James Galbrayth of Culcruch desyring the elderschip to wrett and declair the samin to the elderschip quhair the said James dwellis.

James Galbrayth allegit adultrar: The brethir ordanis the moderatour to wret unto the elderschip of Glasquow and to desyr thame to try the said James Galbrayth of Culcruch befoir thame tuiching the adultry allegit upon him be the said Margaret Leiche.

The x day of October, 1581

Presentes: Mr Robert Montgumrie, Patrik Gillaspy, Andro Forester, Mr Andro Yung, Alexander Fargy, Robert Mentayth, Thomas Swintoun, Mr Adame Merschell, my lord Cambuskynneth, the laird of Garden, Mr James Pont, Umphra Cunynghame, Adame Spittall, James Alexander, the lairdis of Keir, Dutreyth, Mairchestoun and Glorat, Mr Johnne Stewart, provest of Striviling, Johnne Auchtmwty, Andro Cowane, Malcolme Wallace, bailleis, and William Norwall, maistir of wark.

Commissionaris to the generall assemblie warnit thairto: The moderatour schew to the lairdis of Garden and Keir and Mr James Pont that thai war appointit be the provinciall assemblie to be commissionaris to the generall assemblie to be haldin in Edinbrugh the xvij day of this instant and desyrit thame to keip the samin.

Robert Mentayth requyrit of ane penalty: Robert Mentayth being requyrit of the penultie contenit in the act of the provinciall assemblie for his absence fra the same allegit that he was seik and mycht nocht travell.

Mr Robert Montgumrie requyrit of ane penaltie and his answer: Mr Robert Montgumrie, being requyrit to pay the penaltie contenit in the act of the provinciall assemblie for his absence fra the same inrespect his excuse send thair was nocht fund sufficient as ane act maid thairupone beris, answerit he send ane rassonablle excuse as apperit to him in wret, and farder gif thair be ony penultie of him requirit gif ane law straikis upone him he will obey it quhen he seis it.

Elder for Mukert: Compeirit Henrie Douglas for the kirk of Mukert and accepit plaice of ane elder within the presbytry and solemnitlie promesit in the presens of God be his hand hauldin up that he sould faythfullie use the same to the end of his lyf as God sall blis him with his Holie Spirit.

Electing of the moderatour: It being declairit to the bretherein that the moderatour sould be chosin of new to the nixt provinciall assemblie according to the act of the generall assemblie haldin at Glasquow last, the bretherein having put him in leittis hes electit Patrik Gillaspy moderatour to the nixt synnodall assembly.

That na minister serve at na kirk bot ane: It is ordanit and intimatioun was made be the moderatour that na minister sould accep the chairge of ony kirkis upon thame bot onely of ane according to the act of the generall assemblie.

Complent of Mr Robert Montgumrie: Mr Robert Montgumrie complaynit that he was nocht bruthurlie nor cheritablie handillit be in that thair was summondis direct againis him in name of the eldir-schip he nocht being bruthurlie admonesit of befoir according to the ordur and sua findis fault with the proces led againis him, and desyris gif the brethir will abyd be the same. Answerit thairunto Patrik Gillaspy that he was admonesit personallie be him in name of the brethir that thai fand fault with his necligence in his offeice and nocht awaytting on his chairge, and thairfor desyrit him to compeir befoir the bretherein the xij of September last to mak his awin excuse. And inrespect he comperit nocht personally bot send his wreting quhilk was generall and conteinit na speciall caus of his absence, the said Patrik in name of the brethir affermit that thair was na wrang done to him bot the proces deducit againis him was lauchfullie led.

The bretherenis petitioun againis Mr Robert Montgumrie and his answer thairto: The brethering, considdering Maister Robert Montgumreis allegence and Patrik Gillaspeis answer thairunto, desyris the said Mr Robert yit as of befoir to schaw the speciall causis of his absence fra his chairge everie uthir Sonday and the haill oulk dayis excep the [*blank*] day of [*blank*] last fra doctrein, diseplein and exerceis sen the x day of August besyddis his uther absence of befoir. He answeris he keipit all the Sabbothe dayis few exceptit, and gif he haid bein requyrit athir be word or wret of the bretherein he wald willinglie obey it, and sayis that he haid sic rassonablle bissines ado for him self and for freindis that movit his absence the tyme of his absence as he will mair speciallie declair heireftir.

Approving of the former ordinance againis Mr Robert: The said Mr Robert being removit, the bretherein present approvis the ordinance and citatioun deducit againis him and findis the proces formallie led.

Also thay find his answer to thair formar petitioun as yit generall and thairfor ordanis him presentlie to declair the causis of his absence mair speciall.

Mr Robertis answer thairto: The said Mr Robert answeris tuiching ane mair speciall answer and the approbatioun of the absentis allwing the thing that was done be the presentis tuiching his citatioun, it appeiris to him he hes gevin sufficient answer and refarris the samin to be considderit be the generall assemblie of the kirk and promesis thair to declair the speciall causis of his absence as he salbe requyrit.

Ane desyr of the toun of Stirling and answer thairto maid be Mr Robert: Compeirit Williame Norwall in name of the provest, bailleis and counsell of the toun of Striviling and desyrit Mr Robert Montgumrie, thair minister, to declair unto thame gif he wald remane with thame or nocht to the effect thay micht provyd for thame selffis incaice he left thair kirk. He answeris it plaisit God to call him to be minister thair and hes schawin his diligence in the offeice to Goddis glorie and the weill of his kirk, and for his part sall nocht lave thame destitut to sic tyme that with thair awin avys thai be provydit and sall assist thame alwayis according to his power to Goddis glorie and the weill of his kirk. The said Mr Robertis answer being considderit be the brethir was fund doutsum and nocht direct and plaine to the desyr of the said William and thairfor ordanis him to gif ane plaine answer quhethir he will remane or nocht. Answerit the said Mr Robert, and promesit to gif ane plaine answer to the provest, bailleis and counsell betuix and Sonday nixt to cum quhethir he wald remane with thame him self or nocht.

Ultimo Octobris, 1581

Presentes: Robert Mentayth, Mr Andro Yung, Alexander Fargy, Mr James Pont, Patrik Layng, Mr Alexander Yulle.

The moderatour reportit the ordinance concerning the appellatioun of Dunblane concludit in the generall assemblie quhairof the tennour follwis:

Apud Edinburgh, the xix day of October, 1581

The act of the generall assemblie concerning Dunblane: The generall assemblie of the kirk ordanis the brethir upon the billis to considdir the appellatioun of Dunblane and the proces of the elderschip of Striviling deducit againis thame and to report thair jugement thairin agan to the assemblie.

Apud Edinburgh, xx *Octobris*, 1581

The brethir nominat upone the billis thinkis that the bretherein of Striviling hes lauchfullie procedit according to the act of the generall assemblie and jugis the brethering of Dunblane refusaris nocht to have done obedientlie and in the mentyme thinkis that the ministeris of Dunblane aucht to entir thame selffis in the presbytery of Striviling, and quhen greter zeall, diligence and sinciritie salbe tryit in the ministeris of Dunblane in executing of disceplein and utheris pointtis of thair offeice, that upone thair sute eftir incres of baithe thair numberis, the generall assemblie may be movit to grant that ane new presbytery may be erectit also in Dunblane.

Quhilk ordinance of the bretherein upone the billis was approvit be the haill assemblie and subscryvit be the clark thairof.

James Dalmahoy: Beressone of sum complenttis gevin in againis James Dalmahoy, minister of Cambuskynneth, the brethir ordanis the said James to be summond to the vij of November nixt to answer to sic thingis as salbe layit unto his chairge.

The vij day of November, 1581

Presentes: Patrik Gillaspie, Mr Andro Yung, Thomas Swentoun, Alexander Fargy, Mr Alexander Yulle.

James Dalmahoy: Ane summondis beand producit upone James Dalmahoy, minister, deulie execute and indorsit, comperit the said James and being accusit for mareing of Mr Johnne Forbes and Issobell Miln, parrochinaris of the kirk of Striviling, without testemoniall of the minister or redar thairof, confessit the same. Secundlie, being accusit for mareing of Henrie Strachane and Janet Moir, parrochinaris of Tullibody, nochtwithstanding thair was chalenging made of the man be ane uthir woman, and als without testemoniall or lycence of the elderschip againis the act of the generall assemblie, seing that nane of the parteis was parrochinaris to him, the said James confessit the mariage and also the oppositioun made againis the persone of the mane, bot allegit that the opponar refarrit the mater to the manis aithe quha purgit him self thairby.

Secundlie [*sic*], the said James allegit him self to be minister at the kirk of Tullibody and the parteis to have bein lauchfullie proclamit be him and swa neidit na testemoniall nor lycence of the elderschip. Thridlie, being accusit for mareing of ane Agnes Kidstoun (hir husband [*blank*] beand on lyf and na divorcement passit betuix thame) with ane Johnne Broun, the said James confessit the mariage, bot denyit that he knew hir first gudman to be on lyve. Ferdlie, being accusit for baptesing of ane bairne of Johnne Huttoun, gottin in adultrie and incest upone ane Ellein Maleice in Striviling, confessit the same bot allegit he did it at command of Mr Robert Montgumrie, minister at Striviling.

The brethir contenwis the avysment of James Dalmahoyis accusationis and his answeris gevin thairunto to ane fuller sessioun.

Patrik Layng: The bretherein ordanis ane testemoniall to be gevin to Patrik Laing of his habilitie to entir in the ministrie becaus he hes bein tryit bayth be the brethir of the exerceis of Dumfarmling as David Fargusonis testemoniall gevin thairupon beris, and also be us bayth in exerceis and publict doctrein and fund ablle to proffeit the kirk of God be his doctrein, and als for his lyf and conversatioun seing we have ressavit sure knawlege of the honestie thairof, bayth be ane testemoniall of the gentilmen of Clakmannan quhair he dwellis, and als be report of our brothur Thomas Swintoun send be us thair to that effect.

Ordanis the brethir of Dunblane to be summond conform to the act of the general assembly.

The xiiij day of November, 1581

Presentes: Patrik Gillaspie, Mr Andro Yung, Mr Alexander Yulle, Umphra Cunynghame.

Brethir of Dunblane: Ane summondis beand producit dewlie execute and indorsit upone Mr Andro Grahame, Mr Duncan Nevein and Michaell Lermonthe, compeirit the said Michaell and being desyrit presentlie to adjone him self to the presbytery of Striviling, conforme to the act of the generall assemblie, ansorit that he knew nocht the ordinance of the generall kirk concerning the adjoning of the bretherein of Dunblane to Striviling, and thairfor tuke him to avys to the xxj day of November instant, at quhat tyme he sould gif

ane resulat answer thairanent. And as to Mr Andro Grahame and Mr
Duncan Nevein albeit thai send thair excuisis yit the kirk findis
thame nocht ressonablle, and thairfor ordanis thame to be summond
to the xxj of November instant undir the paine of excommunicatioun.

The xxj day of November, 1581

Presentes: Patrik Gillaspie, Mr Robert Montgumrie, Mr Andro
Yung, the laird of Garden, Mr James Pont, Mr Alexander Yulle
and Umphra Cunynghame.

Mr Robert Montgumrie: The moderatour producit ane wreting
send to the brethir fra Mr Johnne Craig, moderatour in the last
generall assemblie, togethir with ane act of the said assemblie
concerning the tryell of sum accusationis to be gevin in againis Mr
Robert Montgomrie tuiching his lyf and conversatioun, and his
residence at the kirk of Striviling, etc. Quhilk wreting and act being
sein and considderit be the brethrein, the moderatour at thair
command made intimatioun of the said act to the said Mr Robert
and delyverit him ane copie thairof in presens of the sessioun. The
said Mr Robert being requyrit, according to the desyr of the
moderatouris bill, gif he hade ressavit intimatioun of the said act of
befoir fra the said moderatour of the generall asemblie ansorit that
the intimatioun made to him of the said act be Mr Johnne Craig,
moderatour of the generall asemblie, was sufficient and grantit the
samin deulie intimat, albeit all circumstancis was nocht observit.
Farder, the said Mr Robert being requyrit upone the heddis of the
act: first gif he wald be content to abyd the tryell of the elderschip
of Striviling in his lyf and conversatioun and accusatiounis to be
gevin in thairanent, ansorit he was content to abyd tryell befoir the
said presbytery quhatsoevir sould be layit unto his chairge athir in
lyf or doctrein. Secundlie, being inquyrit gif he wald remane
minister at Striviling, ansorit that he wald remane at Striviling, God
willing, to the nixt generall assemblie and langer as the kirk wald
command him. Thridlie, being desyrit that he sould nocht mell with
na uthir functioun nor offeice and namelie that he sould nocht aspyr
to the bischoprie of Glasgw nor trubble his brethir with his admissioun thairto, ansorit that the mater was wechtie and thairfor

desyrit ane ressonablle day to advis with his answer. The assemblie appointtis him the xxviij of this instant to gif ane resulat answer thairunto, to the quhilk he aggreit. Ordanis ane answer to be send to Mr Johnne Craig of his bill, conform to Mr Robert Montgumreis answeris.

Minister of Kilbryd adjonit: Comperit Michaell Lermonthe and submittis him self to the presbytery of Striviling, conform to the ordinance of the generall assemblie.

Mr Andro Graham, Mr Duncan Nevein: Ane summondis producit the secund tyme deulie execut and indorsit upone Mr Andro Grahame and Mr Duncan Nevein at thair dwelling placis, the assemblie undirstandand Mr Andro Grahame to be furth of the cuntrie, contenwis farder proces againis him to his returning and als superseiddis farder proces againis Mr Duncan Nevein to the xxviij of this instant and ordanis the copie of the act of the generall assemblie to be send to him and he to gif resulat answer thairunto the said day with certeficatioun and he failze the sentence of excommunicatioun wilbe ordanit to be pronuncit againis him.

Concerning adulteraris: Ordanis all ministeris within the presbytery to gif up the naimis of adulteraris within thair boundis that has nocht satisfeit the kirk that ordur may be tane thairwith.

The xxviij day of November, 1581

Presentes: Patrik Gillaspie, Michaell Lermonthe, Alexander Fargy, the laird of Garden, Adame Spittell of Blairlogy, Mr James Pont, Umphra Cunnynghame, commissaris of Dunblane and Striviling, and Mr Alexander Iulle.

Mr Robert Montgumrie: The quhilk day being assignit to Mr Robert Montgumrie with his awin consent to gif ane resulat answer to the last part of the act of the generall asemblie, that is to say, that he sould nocht mell with onie functioun or offeice in the kirk bot the offeice of the ministrie at the kirk off Striviling and, namelie, that he sould nocht aspyr to the bischoprie of Glasgw nor trublle his brethir with his admissioun thairto, James Duncanson, scryb to the assemblie, producit ane wreting of the said Mr Robertis direct presentlie to the said assemblie quhairof the tennour follwis.

Tennour of Mr Robertis Montgumreis wreting: Brothur James, becaus I am chairgit schortlie by my expectatioun to ryd for sum bissynes quhilk I sall schaw bayth the brethrein of the presbytery, the magistrattis, elderis and deacunis of our congregatioun, I pray you excuse my absence a[t] all thair handis, for I intend, by Goddis graice, schortlie to return and to awate as becumis me upone my chairge praying you to request the magistrattis and bretherein to request my brothur Patrik Gillaspy to support my absence as I salbe reddie agane in the lyk maner as becumis brethrein nocht doutting bot he will do the samin bayth for thair request and myne and the Lord preserve you and thame in the Lord, at Striviling the 23 of November 1581. *Sic subscribitur,* your brothur in the Lord, Maister Robert Montgumrie, minister at Striviling.

Mr Robert Montgumrie: Quhilk wreting being considderit be the brethrein was fund to report na answer of that part of the act abone specefeit, conform to his promeis, nather yit ony ressonablle excuse of his absence and thairfor ordanis ane summondis to be direct, chairgeing him to compeir befoir the sessioun of the elderschip the fyft day of December nixt to gif resulat answer to that part of the act befoir specefeit with certeficatioun and he compeir nocht the assemblie will proceid againis him according to the act of the generall assemblie.

Mr Duncan Nevein: Compeirit Mr Duncan Nevein and being requyrit to adjone him self to the presbytery of Striviling and to accep plaice thair with the bretherein thairof, conform to the act of the generall assemblie, the said Mr Duncan for answer producit ane wreting, as it beris in the self, quhairof the tennour follwis.

At Striviling the xxviij day of November, 1581

Mr Duncan Neveinis answer: The same day in the terme assignit be the brethrein off Striviling to Mr Duncan Nevein, schoilmaister of Dunblane, to gif resolute answer to the act of the generall assemblie maid at Edinburgh the xx day of October 1581, berand in effect that the brethrein of Striviling had procedit lauchfullie according to the act of the generall assemblie and that the brethrein of Dunblane, refusaris, hade nocht done obedientlie and thairfor thocht that in the mentyme the ministeris of Dunblane aucht to entir thame selffis in the presbytery of Striviling etc., compeirit the said Mr Duncane undir protestatioun nocht admittand the elderschip of Striviling to be jugis to him bot insafar as law will and als undir protestatioun that he confessis nocht that he at ony tyme hade refusit to obey the actis and ordinancis of the kirk safar as thai micht be extendit to himwart, and adherand thairto allegis that he on nawayis is obleist to entir and adjone him self to the presbytery of Striviling in exerceis and offeice of elderschip be vairtew of the act affoir mentionat, and that becaus the said act was made for thame that was ministeris at Dunblane and chairgit be the brethering of Striviling to have adjonit thame to the presbytery of Striviling according to the tennour of the act of the generall assemblie maid at Glasgw and had refusit. And it is of veretie that the said Mr Duncan Nevein is nocht ane minister and thairfor was nocht chairgit to adjone him to Stirling befoir the last generall assemblie. Nathir yit was thair evir ony intimatioun of that act made to him, and swa he can nocht be jugit to haif bein ane refusar to gif obedience to the voce of the kirk, he nevir being chairgit to obey the same act, as said is, nocht grantand that it concernit the foirsaid Mr Duncane in ony part thairof. And quhair it may appeir and be objectit that this act of the last generall assemblie concernis the said Mr Duncane becaus it is of veretie that he hes usit the first and secund plaice in the exerceis of Dunblane thir dyveris yeiris bygane quhen his cours come in ordur amang the brethrein and becaus he is jugit worthie be thame to be ane minister and hes consentit to accept that offeice. And thairfor he is obleist to entir in Striviling to the exerceis. Thairto, this it is ansorit, that the said Mr Duncan consentit to accept the offeice of ministrie gif thair war fund ane kirk vacand neirby Dunblane and he provydit of ane sufficient stipend for his serveice thairat, quhilk as yit is nocht done. And althocht that he of his awin fre will for love that he hade to the Word of God, and becaus the kirk was within ane stane cast to his scholle usit the exerceis in Dunblane, it follwis nocht that he sould be compellit to laif his schoill and the prayeris onsaid upone ane prayer day and gang four myll to ane exerceis and swa tyne the proffeit and commodetie that he hes for his scholle and prayeris, he nathir beand ane minister, as said is, nor yit provydit to ane sufficient stipend. And for thir ressonis and utheris contenit in the uther two wretingis producit for the part of the said Maister Duncane in presence of the brethrein heir and in respect that the

generall assemblie hes fundin na inobedience with him thair act unnawayis can straik upone him, and swa na farder proces sould be led
againis him befoir the brethrein of Striviling in this caus, and gif
ony farder beis deducit againis him, he protestis for remade.

The bretherein eftir sicht of the said answer contenwis thair
avysment thairwith to thai have the interpretatioun of the act of the
generall assemblie fra Mr Johnne Craig, moderatour in the last
generall assemblie.

The fyft day of December, 1581

Presentes: Patrik Gillaspy, Mr Andro Yung, Alexander Fargy,
Adame, commendatar of Cambuskynneth, David, commendatar of
Drybrugh, Alexander Forester of Garden, Adame Spittell of Blair
Logy, Johnne Schaw of Bruicht, Umphra Cunynghame, Duncane
Narne, Mr Alexander Iule, Robert Alexander and Johnne Aucht-
mutty, bailleis, Duncane Leischman, den of gild, and William
Norwall, maister of wark.

Mr Robert Montgumrie: It being askit gif Mr Robert Montgumrie
was summond according to the act of the last sessioun, it was
ansorit be the moderatour and scrybe of the sessioun that the
summondis was formit and delyverit with the copie thairof to
Gilbert Crystesone, quha eftir the ressett of the same neglectit the
executioun thairof and thaireftir. The brethrein, being avysit with
the ordinance maid befoir thame the xxj day of November last
concerning Mr Robert Montgumrie his residence at Striviling in
serving the ministrie thairof and that he sould nocht aspyr to ony
uthir functioun, namelie, the bischoprie of Glasgw nor trublle his
brethrein with his admissioun thairunto according to the act of the
generall assemblie than intimat to him, findis that the said Mr Robert
hes nocht made residence at the kirk of Striviling conform to his
promeis than made befoir tham bot hes bein contenuallie absent
sensyne and swa hes brokin that part of the act of the generall
assemblie, and also hes nocht gevin answer to the uthir part of the
said act concerning his aspyring to the bischoprie off Glasgw and
trubling of his brethrein with his admissioun thairunto according
as it was thane ordenit with his awin consent, and swa hes disobeyit
that part also of the act of the generall asemblie, quhairfor ordanis

the said Mr Robert to be summond befoir tham to the xix day of December instant to heir and se him self decernit to have contravenit and brokin the heddis foirsaidis of the act of the generall assemblie and thairfor to be subject to the censuris of the kirk conteinit in the said act with certificatioun quhiddir he compeir or nocht thay will ordane the sentence of excommunicatioun to be pronuncit againis him with the avys of the brethir conteinit in the act of the generall assemblie foirsaid.

The same day the brethir creat William Stevinsone officer to the presbytery quha presentlie gaif his aithe to use the samin faythfullie.

The xix day of December, 1581

Presentes: Patrik Gillaspy, Mr Robert Montgumrie, Michaell Lermonthe, Alexander Fargy, Mr Alexander Chisholme, ministeris; Alexander Forester of Garden, Umphra Cunynghame, commissar of Striviling, Mr James Pont, commissar of Dunblane, Mr Alexander Iule, maister of the grammir scholle, Johnne Schaw of Bruigh and Johnne Bruce of Auchinbowey.

Mr Duncane Nevein: The samin day the moderatour presentit the answer and interpretatioun of the act of the generall assemblie concerning Mr Duncan Nevein, scholemaistir and reder of Dunblane, bering in effect that he sould make the exerceis in Striviling being within the boundis now appointit within the presbytery erectit thair becaus he is teicher of the youthe, reder of the kirk, and hes made it befoir in Dunblane.

Mr Robert Montgumrie: Quhilk day ane summondis beand producit lauchfullie execute and indorsit upone Mr Robert Montgumrie to heir and se him decernit to have contravenit the act of the generall assemblie in nocht satisfeing the desyr thairof upone the xxviij of November last bypast conform to his promeis, compeirit the said Mr Robert and confessit that the caus quhy he keipit nocht the day appointit was upone occasioun that he was desyrit to cum to Edinburgh for ressonablle bissines that he hade ado and meinit na contemp of the kirk. And quhair as he was accusit for absence fra his flok upone ordinar preiching dayis and assemblie promesis in tyme cuming nocht to depart fra his kirk befoir he schaw thame and obtein athir lycence of his awin kirk or than of the elderschip. Secundlie, as tuiching the part of the act concerning his aspyring to ane uthir functioun, namelie the bischoprik of Glasgw, and trubling of his brethrein with his admissioun thairunto, he answeris that he meinis nocht nor will, nor sall be ony uthir bischop bot sic ane bischop as Paull teichis in his epistillis to Titus and Timothie, that is, a minister and preichour of the Word of God and promesis nevir to trublle or vex his brethrein with his admissioun to the bischoprik of Glasgw.

Margaret Drummond: It is lattin the brethir to undirstand that Margaret Drummond, relict of umquhill Robert Forester of Boquhen, is nocht mareit to Lowrence Barclay and that the bairne that scho was last delyverit of is nocht the said Lowrence bairn and that the same bairn was baptezit be ane that beris na offeice in the kirk, and for this same purpois Patrik Gillaspie, minister at S. Ninianis kirk, producit ane wreting send to the sessioun of his kirk be Johnne Cairnis, reder and minister in Edinburgh, quhairfor the brethir ordanis hir to be summond to compeir befoir the bretherein to schaw gif the mariage be of treuth, quha is fathir of the bairne, quhair it was baptesit and quhome be.

The xxvj day of December, 1581

Presentes: Patrik Gillaspie, Johnne Duncanson, Alexander Fargy, Michaell Lermonthe, Mr James Pont, Mr Alexander Iule, Johnne Broun, Alexander Forester of Garden, James Edmestoun of Duntreyth, Umphra Cunynghame, Duncane Narne.

James Dalmahoy: James Dalmohoyis accusationis and his confessioun thairupon being consedirit be the brethrein, ordanis the actis of the generall assemblie made tuiching baptisme and mariage to be socht out.

Mr Robert Montgumrie: The brethir thocht gude that Mr Robert Montgumreis lyf and conversatioun sould be tryit be thame conform to the act of the generall assemblie. And it beand ressonit gif ony sclandir was thairin, it wes fund be the brethrein that he was bruttit with intemperance of his mouthe sa that sumtymis eftir meikill drink his sensis wald feall him. And lykwys the brethir findis that his doctrein is nocht formall nor sensablle to the commone pepill, and that his jestur in pulpet is nocht decent at sum tymis. Thairfor ordanis him privellie to be conferrit with tuiching the heddis abone specefeit.

E

The secund day of Januar, 1581

Presentes: Patrik Gillaspie, Mr Robert Montgumrie, Alexander Fargy, Michaell Lermonthe, Mr Alexander Iule, Johnne Broun, Alexander Forester of Garden, Alexander Patersone, Umphra Cunyngham, Mr James Pont and Duncane Narne.

Mr Robert Montgumrie: The brethir nominattis and ordanis Mr James Pont, Mr Alexander Iule, Alexander Fargy and Patrik Gillaspie to confer privallie with Mr Robert Montgumrie concerning thais thingis quhairof he is bruitit concerning his lyf and als quhairin thai find fault concerning his doctrein and ordanis thame and him to convein to that effect in the said Mr Roberttis hous the fyft of Januar instant at x houris befoir none and to report his answer to the nixt sessioun.

Becaus the exerceis is nocht weill observit be the brethir appointit upone the same, ordanis the haill brethir to be warnit to the ix of Januar nixt that with consent of the haill besyd the ordinance of the act of the generall assemblie with thair awin consenttis ane penaltie may be appointit for sic as keipis nocht thair awin ordinarie plaice.

The ix day of Januar, 1581

Presentes: Patrik Gillaspie, Mr Robert Montgumrie, Robert Mentayth, Mr Andro Yung, Patrik Layng, Mr William Stirling, yunger, Mr James Pont, Alexander Forester of Garden, Alexander Patersone, Mr Alexander Iule, Johnne Broun.

Margaret Drummond: Ane summondis producit lauchfullie execute and indorsit upone Margaret Drummond conform to the act of the last sessioun maid thairanent, compeirit the said Margaret and allegit that scho haid na recidence nor duelling plaice within the elderschip of Striviling and that hir recidence (gif ony scho hade) was within the toun of Edinburgh, and thairfore was nocht bund to answer befoir the elderschip of Striviling bot befoir the elderschip of Edinburgh. Quhilk allegence being considderit be the brethir, it was fund hir maist recidence to be in Edinburgh and thairfore remittis hir thairunto as hir juge ordinar and ordanis the kirk of Edinburgh to be advertesit heirof.

Ane penaltie appointit for keping of the exerceis: It is appointit and ordeinit with consent of the haill ministeris of the elderschip and brethir of exerceis undir subscryvand that quhatsoevir minister or brothur of exerceis sall faill in making of the exerceis on his ordinar day sall pay ten schillingis mony, and gif he faill in making of additioun or speiking in the secund plaice upone his ordinar day, viz., the day of exerceis immediatlie preceding the day of his awin ordinar exerceis sall pay fyve schillingis mony as for the first faulttis and thir penulteis the secund tyme to be dubillit and the thrid tym trepleist and applyit *ad pios usus*.

[*Signatures*:] Maistyr Robert Montgumrie [*deleted*], Mr James Pont, James Anderson, Mr William Striviling, Patrik Gillaspie, Alexander Fargy, Robert Menteht, Johne Broun, Mr Alexander Iule, Mr Andro Young, Mr William Stirling, Michael Lermonth, Patrik Layng, Mr Alexander Cheisholm, Androw Grayme, Mr Arthour Futhie, Mr Adam Merschall.

Mr Robert Montgumreis complent on the sessioun of his awin kirk: Mr Robert Montgumrie complainit upone Duncane Leischman, schawing that at the ministratioun of baptisme he reprovand the said Duncan and utheris witnessis to ane bairne baptezit becaus thai gaif dyvers namis to the sonne [bairne, *deleted*] sayand thai war in the wrang. The said Duncan ansorit sayand he was in the wrang. The brethir ordanis the said Duncan to be summond to the xvj day of Januar instant to answer to the said complent undir the paine of disobedience. Lykwys the said Mr Robert complanit that the elderis of his kirk keipit nocht oulklie assemblie with him thairfoir ordanis Mr James Pont, Patrik Gillaspie and Mr Alexander Iule to confer with thame that thair ordinar assemblie may be observit and that thingis that ar out of ordur amangis thame may be reformit.

Report of the privie confirrence had with Mr Robert Montgumrie: The brethrein appointit to confer with Mr Robert Montgumrie reportit that in confirrence hade with him concerning his doctrein he confessit that sumtymis thruch laik of memorie and negligence in his studie and awaytting on his buik, being occupyit in uthir effairis he keipit nocht sic furmalitie and sensibilnes in doctrein as become him, quhilk he promesit Godwilling to mend in tymis cuming. And as to his lyf and conversatioun, first quhair he is bruittit with intemperence, confessit that he hes bein sumtymis langer deteinit in cumpany than become him, quhilk Godwilling he promesis to mend in tymis cuming. Bot his conscience buir him witnes that he was nevir swa ovircumit with drink that his sencis faillit him. Secundlie, quhair he is bruittit of greid and avarice in taking xj merk for the hundir contrarie to the commone ordur in the cuntrie, he did nocht preceislie deny the same bot said the mony that he haid layd on hand he hade gevin mair for viij merk nor for x. Thridlie, being askit quhow he could of saif conscience intromet and mell with the patrimony of the bischoprie of Glasgw, seing he servit at the kirk of Striviling and hade ane stepend thairfore, and swa nathir servit the cure of the kirk of Glasgw nathir yit bestowit ony part of the said patrimony upone sic causis as the same was ordeinit for, he ansorit that gif the kirk fand that he could nocht bruke the said patrimony of saif conscience he sould demit the same. Quhilk answer being considirit be the brethrein becaus the said Mr Robert denyit the vyce of intemperance quhairwith he was bruittit, thay thocht gude and ordeinit Alexander Forester of Garden, Patrik Gillaspy, Mr James Pont, Umphra Cunynghame and Mr Alexander Iule or ony thre of thame to tak privie inquisitioun of the said brute and quhat thai find thairby to report agane.

The xvj day of Januar, 1581

Presentes: Patrik Gillaspy, Mr Robert Montgumrie, Mr William Stirling, elder, Robert Mentayth, Mr Alexander Chisholme, Alexander Fargy, Mr James Pont, Mr Alexander Iule, Johnne Broun, Umphra Cunynghame, Robert Alexander and William Norwall.

The catalog of the brethir of the exerceis and ordur to be observit be thame in follwing uthir in exerceis: Mr Robert Montgumrie, minister at Striviling [*deleted*]; James Andirson, minister at Striviling [*substituted*]; Mr James Pont, commissar of Dunblane; Mr Andro Grahame, Mr Andro Yung, ministeris at Dunblane; Mr William Stirling, m[inister] at Abirfull; Patrik Gillaspy, m[inister] at S. Ninianis kirk; Mr Alexander Iule, maister of grammir schole in Striviling; Alexander Fargy, m[inister] at Logy; Robert Mentayth, m[inister] at Alvayth; Johnne Broun [*deleted*]; Michaell Lermonthe, m[inister] at Kilbryd; Patrik Layng, m[inister] at Clakmannan; Mr William Stirling, yunger at Kilmadok [*deleted*]; Mr Duncan Nevein, reder at Dumblane; William Stirling, exhortar at the Port;

Mr Alexander Chisholme m[inister] at Muthill; Mr Arthur Futhie, minister at Airthe; Mr Adame Merschell, minister at [Fossoway].

Ane penaltie appointit for absenttis ilk day of exerceis: It is appointit and ordenit with consent of the haill ministeris of the elderschip and brethir of exerceis undirsubscryvand that gif ony minister or brothur of exerceis be absent fra the elderschip the day of exerceis sall pay for the first fault twa schillingis, secund fault dubillit and the thrid fault trepleit, and gif ony reder be absent he sall pay the first fault xii d., secund fault dubillit and the thrid fault trepleit without ane ressonablle excuis.

[*Signatures*:] Robert Menteht, Maistyr Robert Montgomrye [*deleted*], Patrik Layng, James Andersone [*inserted*], Mr James Pont, Mr Alexander Cheisholme, Mr William Striviling, Mr Adam Merschell, minister of Fosawy, Mr Alexander Iule, Androw Grayme, Johnne Broun, Mr Arthour Fethie, Patrik Gillaspie, M[ichaell] Lermonth, Alexander Fargy, Mr Andro Young, Mr William Striviling.

[*Added in margin*: xijo *Martii* 1582. The brethir aggreis that Mr Adame Merschell be astricted only to keip the exerceis ilk xx dayis in somir and in wintir ilk xl dayis allanirlie nochtwithstanding of this act.]

Minister of Abirfoull adjonit to the presbytery: Compeirit Mr William Stirling, minister at Abirfull and accepit upone him offeice and plaice in this presbytery be solem promeis in the presens of God, his hand beand haldin up promesing faithfullie to exerceis his offeice thairin conform to the Word of God unto the end of his lyf, as it sall plais God to blis him with his Holie Spirit, provyding that gif ane presbytery be heireftir placit be the kirk in Dunblane he mycht be fre of his said consent made to this presbytery.

Elderis adjonit for Striviling: The quhilk day compeirit Robert Alexander, baillie, and William Norwall, thesaurar, chosin be the kirk of Striviling to ber the offeice of elderis within the presbytery for the said kirk off Striviling with thais appointit of befoir, quha be halding up of thair handis and solem promeis in the presens of God promesit faythfullie to exerceis thair officis thairin unto the end of thair lyvis and God sall minister to thame the giftis of his Spirit.

Elezabeth Millaris dilatioun of adultrie againis Henrie Grahame: Compeirit Elezabeth Millar in Gargunnok and grantit hir self to have ane bairne vij oulkis syne or thairby to Henrie Grahame in Meikil Wod, quha as scho allegis denyis the said bairne and swa refusis to caus bapteis the same, and scho, being askit of the tyme and plaice the said Henrie haid to do with hir, confessit the first tyme to be a lytill befoir Mertimes *anno* etc., lxxx yeiris in his awin corne barn afternone; uthir tymis scho rememberit nocht weill excep a lytill befoir Witsonday last in his awin hall. The brethir ordanis the said Henrie to be warnit to answer to the said accusatioun.

The xxiij day of Januar, 1581

Presentes: Patrik Gillaspie, Mr Andro Yung, Michaell Lermonthe, Mr William Stirling, elder, Mr William Stirling, younger, Robert Mentayth, Alexander Fargy, Mr Alexander Iule, Mr James Pont, Johnne Broun, Alexander Forester of Garden, Umphra Cunynghame and William Norwall.

Jonet Crystesonis complent on Johnne Muschett: Compeirit Jonet Crysteson dwelland in Kincardin and complainit upone Johnne Muschett thair alleging that scho could nocht be quyt of the said Johnis trublle, bot that he lay in wait for hir at all tymis to deforce hir. The brethir ordanis the said Johnne to be summond to answer to the said complent.

Penultimo Januarij, 1581

Presentes: Patrik Gillaspie, Mr Robert Montgumrie, Mr Alexander Chisholme, Johnne Broun, Mr James Pont, Alexander Forester of Garden, Robert Alexander, William Norwall, Umphra Cunynghame, Mr Alexander Iule.

Muschett, Crystesoun, adulteraris: Johnne Muschet dwelland in the parrochin of Kincardin being lauchfullie summond conform to the ordinance of the last sessioun at the instance of Jonet Crystesone thair, compeirit the saidis personis and bayth thair allegencis being hard and consider it ordanis the said Johnne and Jonet to compeir befoir us the sext day of Fabruar nixttocum and to bring with thame sufficient cautioun and souerty that nane of thame sall trublle, molest nor intys uthir to wickitnes in tymis cuming undir sic painis as the kirk sall lay unto thair chairge.

Adulteraris in Port: Ane summondis beand producit upone Elezabeth Moir, Thomas McIlchreist, Johnne McWilliame, Elezabeth Blare, Johnne McIlmichell and Jonet Metclathlem, adulteraris within the parrochin of the Port, deulie execute and indorsit chairgeing thame to answer at the instance of the kirk to the cryme of adultrie allegit committit be thame as the said summondis in the self beris, quhilkis personis being oft tymis callit and nocht compeirand, the brethir ordanis thame to be summondis the secund to the effect foirsaid undir the pane of excommunicatioun, and ane summondis to be direct thairupone.

The sex day of Fabruar, 1581

Presentes: Patrik Gillaspie, Mr Robert Montgumrie, Johnne Duncanson, Mr Alexander Chisholme, Mr Andro Yung, Robert Mentayth, Mr Alexander Iule, Mr James Pont, Alexander Fargy, Mr William Sterling, yunger, Patrik Layng, Johnne Broun, Alexander Forester of Garden, Adame Spittell of Blairlogy, Robert Alexander, William Norwall, Umphra Cunynghame.

It was thocht gude be the brethrein that everie minister within the elderschip sould declair quhat text thai trettit in thir kirk and quhat autheris thai follwit. Sa mony as was present declairit as follwis.

Ministeris texttis: Mr Robert Montgumrie the first buke of Moses callit Genesis and first chaptur thairof and the xiiij Sonday of the cathechis, his commentaris [*blank*]. Mr Andro Yung is presentlie to begin the harmony of the 3 evangelistis and the [*blank*] Sonday of the cathechis, his commentaris Calvein, Beza and Gualteir on Louk. Patrik Gillaspie the first epistill of S. Johnne the v. chaptur and beginning thairof, his commentaris, Beza, Calvein, Gualteir. Alexander Fargy the xiiij chaptur of the evangelist Mark the 17 vers, his commentaris Marlorot, Calvein and Musculus. Robert Mentayth the actis of the Apostillis the v. chapter, his commentar, Brentius. Mr William Stirling, yunger, is ordeinit to begin the cathechis, his commentar [*blank*]. Patrik Layng is ordeinit to begin the artickillis of the beleve, his commentar [*blank*].

Jonet Crysteson, adulterarris cautioner: Compeirit Jonet Crysteson in Kincardin and her cautioner, conform to the ordinance of the last sessioun. The sessioun ordanis hir to caus hir cautioner becum actit in the commissaris buikis of Dunblane that scho sall nocht perswad, trublle nor intys Johnne Muschet in Kincardin to adultrie with hir (as scho hes done of befoir) undir the pane of xl libis.

Muschet, disobedient: Inrespect Johnne Muschet brocht nocht his cautioner conform to the ordinance of the last sessioun, ordanis him to be summond to do the samin undir the paine of excommunicatioun.

Waltir, adulterar: Johnne Waltir in Touchadame, adultrar with Jonett Clark, being lauchfullie summond to answer quhy he hade nocht fulfillit his injunctionis gevin to him for the said adultrie compeirit the said Johnne and granttis that he had nocht satisfeit the ordinance of the synnodall assemblie in presenting him self to the stule of repentence everie Sonday and promesis to obey and do the sam in tymis cuming. Ordanis him to entir to the plaice of repentence the nixt Sonday and swa to continew, conform to the ordinance of the synnodall [generall, *deleted*] assemblie undir the paine of excommunicatioun.

Mr Robert Montgumrie: Compeirit Mr Robert Montgumrie and complainit of the previe inquisitioun takin of his lyf and conversatioun as ane wretein gevin in be him bearis, quhairof the tennour follwis. *The tennour of Mr Robert Montgumreis wreting producit*:

Grace, mercie and peace from God the fathir of our Lord Jesus Chryst. So be it.

Seing, brethrein, I have obeyit the ordinance of the generall assemblie and your desyris thairanent, and lykwys your previe admonitionis to me hes bein tane in gud partt, and our mutuall confirrencis bayth towardis doctrein and conversatioun (be Goddis graice to be amendit quhairof we haif all neid), it appeirit to me ye war weill satisfeit and that ye wald report the samin brotherlie and faythfullie to the presbytery (and gaif thankis to God thairfoir); how is it that ye haif enterit and be quhat rewll of the scripturis lauchfull and formall proceiding hes tane and intendis to tak privie inquisitioun of certane personis as ye plais (nocht fundit) againis me athir of doctrein or conversatioun, I nocht beand warnit nor callit for my entres to say for my self and my lauchfull defenss admittit gif neid war againis the juge, the inquest, the witnessis, the forme and memberis of ane informall proces, for na lauchfull proces can be bot quhair thair is ane lauchfull juge, ane persewar and defender, caus and circumstancis requisit, tyme, plaice and ordur aggreing with the law, that is, gif it be ane inquest thai man be lauchfullie summondit and the partie hard and his lauchfull defenss, quhat may be said agains thame of the law (thir nottis) as partiall counsell, gevaris up of dilationis, ingyraris of thame selffis to be examinat, hes bein accusaris of the partie, hes schawin thame selffis ennemeis be word and deid uttering thair maleice and invy alwayis be certane signis of heich contemptis, awcht nathir to be juge, inquest, witness nor ony lauchfull membir of a lauchfull proces agains the persoun defender quhair ony of thir is trew and may be varefeit nor yit can ony accusatioun be lauchfullie deducit and usit, bot quhair the defender is first hard and his lauchfull defensis, nathir yit aucht ane elder (that is ane prechur) to be accusit bot be the witness of twa or thre witnessis. Nane of thir is observit be you that I knaw and thairfor wald be teichit, thairfor na lauchfull proces can be usit meikilles ane lauchfull sentence pronuncit, and prayis you brethrein in the name of God to be war that ye oppin nocht ane dur to the wickit in the kirk of God be privie inquisitionis agains ony minister of his doctrein and conversatioun be certane previe personis, quha of maleice agains the ministeris zealle in doctrein and disceplein will speik sclanderuslie of him (yea of the maist godlie) unrequyrit meikill mair quhen thai ar requyrit, speacially quyetlie, he is a proud man, he is a gredie man, a partiall man, a flytter, a drunkard, a commone companioun at cairttis tabillis, the four houris pennie, and siclyk, for ma nor anew of sic slanderus and wickit personis is in everie congregatioun that regairdis nathir preiching nor disceplein, admonitioun nor correctioun ony way, and gif a ministeris preiching, conversatioun or disceplein salbe offerit to this previe inquisitioun without his knawlege, I dout nocht bot witnessis salbe fund agains him to condam him, and thairfor brethrein yit be war in tyme of sic prettickis, ye use with me that ye trubble nocht the maist part of the brethrein. Bot quhat ye can do to me aggreing with the scripturis be lauchfull and formall ordur cheritablie and brothurlie handillit (as ye wald be done to) I am contenttit thairwith as I schew you in the beginning that I wald obey the kirk in all thingis that I aucht and that appertenit to the kirk. And of this I mervell quhairfra thir new accusationis or inquisitionis cumis now (of new thingis or of auld thingis) mair nor affoir this lang tyme bygane, quhilk gif ony was of a trewthe thai can nocht to my knawlege, for gif ony personis had had ony thing againis me particular or yit the kirk ony way thay haide plaice, and I was reddie to answer nocht doutting brethrein (of our auld brutherlie familiaritie in God) bot ye will admit my lauchfull petitionis, that is, that I may be hard and my lauchfull defensis affoir ye conclude or pronunce ony act quhilk ye promesit to do, and that na accusar, witness, nor inquisitioun sould be againis me, bot sic as I sould knaw and to haif plaice to say againis thame according to equitie, gif ye say ye ar commandit be the kirk, the ordinance makis na mentioun of inquisitioun, bot of tryell of conversatioun, I undirstand be lauchfull meinis, as I have said, gif ye say the moderatour hes commandit be inquisitioun he is nocht abone the ordinance of the generall assemblie nor yit interpretour thairto. Gif ye stand at the word inquisitioun, ye haif na mair for you bot be ane inquest. Bot quha sall cheis thame, quhat nummir, quhat personis, quhat forme, quhat circumstancis, tyme, plaice and ordur, quhidder privellie or publictlie, quhiddir be the haill presbytery or be ane part, and quha sall cheis that part, nane of thir circumstancis is prescryvit to you in wrett for your warrand, and thairfor, bretherein, ye haif passit or intendis to pas farther nor is prescryvit to you. Thismekill brothurlie that ye haif forder respect to the offeice I bair and the sclandir of the Word in my waik persone (as we ar all) nor to serce forther nor ye wald be sercit upone ony occasioun quhair ye have nocht the reull of the scriptouris and ane lauchfull and formall proceiding as becumis brethrein in Chryst. I prays God that in my persone I am callit to the lycht for tryell of my doctrein, quhilk is darrer to me nor my lyf and examinat of my conversatioun quhairunto trewlie I have ansorit, praying God that the kirk may be purgit in us all (speciallie ministeris) for thair is ma faulttis allegit againis me within this schort tyme nor all the tyme I have travellit the ministry this xx yeiris bygane to Goddis glorie, the weill of his kirk and to the confort of thame to quhom I was appointit, as my conscience beris me witnes, and the faythfull report of the faythfull nocht dowting bot ye will tak this in gude part my brethir be rememberence simplie proponit and pondir the same as the mater cravis being ane commone caus amangis brethrein, and interpret all thingis in the best part, and quhair ye dout and speiris, I sall faythfullie declair, or quhair ambiguitie appeiris, I sall expone and declair my mynd as I can cheritablie and the Lord blis you and your assemblie. Amen.

Quhilk wreting being red and considderit the brethrein promesit to answer thairto the nixt sessioun day, viz., the xiij of this instant. The same day Mr Robert Montgumrie desyris certane actis concerning him to be extract to him. The brethrein ordanis the said Mr Robert to mak ane catholog of sic actis as he desyris and thai sall gif answer thairto.

Margaret Cairtour allegit fornicatour: Compeirit Margaret Cairtour and being accusit of adultrie with James Forester in Kipmade, scho denyis the adultrie bot grantis hir with bairne gottin in fornicatioun as scho allegis be Henrie Cunynghame, now in Dunbartane, and that in Murrayis wod within the parrochin of Sanct Niniane. The sessioun ordanis the said Margaret to caus the said Henrie to compeir befoir thame the xx day of this instant to confes the said bairne or than gif he may nocht cum him self that he compeir befoir the sessioun of the kirk of Dunbartane and confes the same and bring to us the said day ane act of the said sessioun upone his confessioun subscryvit be the minister of Dunbartane and be the said Henry together with the clark of the said sessioun.

The xiij day of Fabruar, 1581

Presentes: Patrik Gillaspie, Mr Robert Montgumrie, Michaell Learmonthe, Patrik Layng, Alexander Fargy, Robert Mentayth, Mr James Pontt, Mr Alexander Iule, Johnne Broun, Alexander Forester of Garden, Johnne Schaw of Bruigh, Adame Spittell of Blair Logy, Umphra Cunynghame, Robert Alexander and William Norwall.

The quhilk day being appointit to gif answer to Mr Robert Montgumreis wreting gevin in befoir the brethrein in the last sessioun, the brethrein ansorit as follwis in wrett:

Answer to Mr Robert Montgumreis wreting: Gif the ordinance of the generall assemblie be obeyit or nocht lat the generall assemblie be juge. We sall treulie report quhat is done. As to our privie inquisitioun, we will answer to the assembleis provinciall or generall. Quhair ye say that, that manir of inquisitioun is dangerus, lat him that is giltie feir. As to ony proces deducit befoir us, athir tuiching your lyf or doctrein, thair is nane intentit as yit and sasone as ony beis intentit (according to our promeis) ye sall have plaice to use your lauchfull defenss againis athir juge, partie or witness. We thank you of your admonitionis and promesis to serce you na farther nor we wald be sercit.

Henrie Graham: The same day ane summondis lauchfullie execute and indorsit beand producit upone Henrie Grahame as the same beris, compeirit the said Henrie and being accusit of adultrie committit be him with Elezebeth Millar denyit the same and affermit that he had nevir carnall dell with the said Elezebeth. The brethir remittis the said Henrie to farther tryell and ordanis the said Elezebeth to be summond to mak gude hir delatioun gevin in againis the said Henrie.

Adulteraris in S. Ninianis parrochin: The quhilk day ane summondis lauchfullie execute and indorsit producit upone Johnne Home in Toucht, Robert Millar thair, Margaret Coir thair, incesteus and adulteraris within S. Ninianis parrochin, to answer at the instance of the kirk quhy thai haid nocht fulfillit thair injunctionis ressavit fra the synnodall assemblie for the saidis crymis, the saidis personis being oft tymis callit, compeirit nocht, and thairfor ordanis thame to be summond the secund tyme to the effect foirsaid undir the pane of excommunicatioun.

James McKie: The quhilk day compeirit James McKie in Doun of Mentayth and desyrit his bairne gottin, as he allegit, in fornicatioun with Jane Stewart [Jonet Sandelandis, *deleted*] to be baptezit, promesing to mak his repentence as he salbe commandit. The brethir, undirstanding a brute to be rissin of the said James that his wyf callit Jonet Sandelandis was levand the tyme he begat the bairne upone the said Jane, could nocht weill prescryve repentence unto him unto the tyme thai knew quhethir it was adultrie or fornicatioun, and thairfor ordanis him to bring testemoniall of the deathe of his wyf betuix and the vj day of Merche nixt, and also ordanis Michaell Lermonthe to bapteis the said bairne, takand sufficient cautioun of the said James that he sall obey sic disceplein of the kirk as salbe appointit to him undir the paine of x libis.

Lowrence Barclay, Margaret Drummond: Compeirit Lowrence Barclay and Margaret Drummond and ernistlie desyrit that the sclandir rissin of thame bayth towardis thair mariage, the baptesin of thair last bairne, and the brute rasit towardis the fathir thairof mycht be tryit befoir us. The brethrein ansurit that that actioun at the said Margarettis desyr was refarrit to the tryell of the presbytery of Edinburgh, and swa thai could be na juge thairto unles the same war remittit agane be the said presbytery of Edinburgh to thame. The said Lowrence replyit that that was done without his knawlege and allegit that the caus quhairfor the said Margaret desyrit the mater to be tryit befoir the said sessioun of Edinburgh was becaus scho had thane presentlie ado in the law befoir the lordis of sessioun and swa mycht nocht keip thair sessioun and ouris bayth, bot now hir actionis befoir the lordis being continewit to *Junij* and scho myndit to remane heir, bayth the said Lowrence and scho willinglie submittit thame self to the jurisdictioun of this presbytery, and ernistlie desyris ane wreting to be made in name of the presbytery to the presbytery of Edinburgh that the said actioun may be remittit hethir inrespect also the said Margaret is grit with bairne and may nocht weill travell. The brethrein ordanis ane wreting to be made in thair name and direct to the said presbytery of Edinburgh to the effect foirsaid.

The quhilk day Mr Robert Montgumrie gaif in, in catholog, certan actis desyrit of him of befoir to be extractit. The brethrein ordanis Mr James Pont, Umphra Cunynghame and Patrik Gillaspie to vesie the saidis actis and being fund to appertein to him ordanis thame to be extract.

The xx day of Fabruar, 1581

Presentes: Patrik Gillaspie, Mr William Stirling, Mr Andro Yung, Alexander Fargy, Robert Mentayth, Mr William Stirling, yunger, Patrik Layng, Andro Forester, William Stirling, Mr James Pont, Johnne Broun, William Norwall, Mr Alexander Iule, Robert Alexander, Johnne Schaw of Bruigh, William Drummond, minister of Creif.

Ministeris texttis: Mr William Stirling, elder, and William Stirling in Port being askit quhat text thai teiche and quhat commentaris thai follw, answer as follwis. Mr William Stirling, elder, teichis the artickillis of the beleif, his commentar Calveinis

Institutionis. William Stirling teichis the commandementtis; commentar, Institutionis of Calvein and Petir Verott.

Marione Stalkaris complent on hir husband: Compeirit Marione Stalkar and complanit that Johnne Huchoun, hir husband, wald nocht ressave hir in hous with him and interteny hir as becumis him to do to his wyf. The brethrein ordanis the said Johnne to be summond to answer at the instance of the kirk to heir and se him self decernit to ressave in hous with him the said Marione Stalkar and interteny hir, as becumis him of Goddis law to do to his wyf, or ellis to schaw ane ressonablle caus quhy, undir the paine of disobedience.

Margaret Cairtour: The quhilk day being assignit to Margaret Cairtour to caus Henrie Cunynghame compeir befoir us to gif his declaratioun quhethir scho was with bairne to him as scho allegit or nocht or than to produce ane act of the sessioun of Dunbartane conteining his declaratioun foirsaid, and the said Margaret being oft tymis callit compeirit nocht, and thairfor ordanis hir yit as of befoir to be summond to caus the said Henrie Cunynghame compeir befoir us the xxvij day of Februar instant to the effect foirsaid or thane to bring ane act fra the sessioun of Dunbartane, as said is, with certificatioun and scho failze, we will proceid to the tryell of adultrie againis hir.

Henrie Grahame and Elezabeth Millaris: The same day the sessioun ordanis Henrie Grahame in Meikillwod and Elezabethe Millar to be summond to heir farther tryell tane in the accusatioun of adultrie gevin in be the said Elezabeth againis him undir the paine of disobedience.

Complent of Mr Andro Yung: The same day Mr Andro Yung, minister at Dunblane, complainit that certane of his parrochinaris refusit to subscryve the kingis confessioun of faithe, thairfor ordanis all thais that refusis the same to be summond befoir us to heir and se thame selffis decernit to subscryve the same undir the pane of the sensuris of the kirk.

The xxvij day of Februar, 1581

Presentes: Patrik Gillaspie, Mr Andro Yung, Mr William Stirling, elder, and Mr William Stirling, yunger, Patrik Layng, Johnne

Broun, Mr Alexander Iule, Alexander Fargy, Alexander Forester of Garden.

Text of the exerceis: The brethir thinkis gude and hes ordeinit (that the secund epistill wrettin to the Corrinthianis beand endit, quhilk now is trettit in the exerceis), the epistill to the Gallathianis salbe intreattit nixt.

Adulteraris in the parrochin of S. Niniane: The quhilk [day] ane summondis producit lauchfullie execute and indorsit upone Thomas Johneson in Poppiltreis and Jonet Murray, dochtir to William Murray in Touchadame, adulteraris, to compeir this day to heir and se thame selffis decernit adulteraris and to be subject to the disciplein of the kirk thairfoir, compeirit the saidis Thomas and Jonet and confessit thame selffis adulteraris and submittis thame selffis to the disceplein of the kirk thairfoir. The brethir ordanis thame to compeir befoir the sinnodall assemblie of Lothian, Mers and Striviling scheir to be haldin in Edinburgh the iiij day of Apryll nixttocum to ressave thair injunctionis, conform to the ordinance of the generall assemblie.

Johnne Huchoun chairgit for adherens: The same day ane summondis producit dewlie execute and indorsit upone Johnne Huchoun, chairgeing him to answer at the instance of the kirk quhy he will nocht ressave Marione Stalkar, his wyf, in hous with him and interteny hir as becumis him, and farder to heir and se him self decernit to do the same, compeirit the said Johnne and allegit he aucht nocht to ressave the said Marione, his allegit spous, in hous with him nor interteny hir as his wyf becaus scho hes wickitlie passit away fra him againis his will and playit the harlet sensyne and gottin ane bairn by him with ane uther man. *Marione Stalkar*: Quhairof the said Marione being accusit, grantit that scho was deforcit againis hir will be ane man quhome scho knawis nocht and hade born ane bairne to him and thairfor allegit the same to be na adultric becaus scho was forcit againis hir will. The brethir undirstanding that the mater of the said Marione hes bein tryit befoir the brethrein of Dunblane thairfor ordainis the proces led befoir thame to be producit befoir us be the said Margaret for farder tryell in the mater.

Adulteraris in the parrochin of Clakmannan: The quhilk day ane summondis beand producit deulie execute and indorsit upone James

Tailzour, Jonet Aickein, Johnne Seath, Jonet Wallace, David Burn, adulteraris within the parrochin of Clakmannan, to heir and se thame self decernit to have committit adultrie and to obey the disceplein of the kirk thairfoir undir the paine of disobedience, quhilk personis being oft tymis callit compeirit nocht, thairfor ordanis thame to be summond of new undir the paine of excommunicatioun.

Lowrence Barclay, Margaret Drummond: The quhilk day ane wreting of the presbytery of Edinburgh beand producit contening ane answer of our wreting send unto thame tuiching the sclandir rasit of Lowrence Barclay and Margaret Drummond be the quhilk wretein the said brethir of Edinburgh remittit agane the said sclandir to be tryit befoir us as the sam in the self beris. The same day the said Lowrence and Margaret being askit gif thai war mareit or nocht andsorit [sic] that thair is promeis of mariage betuix thame and thair bannis lauchfullie proclamit bot was nocht mareit as yit, and promesis to compleit mariage betuix and the xv day of Apryll. The brethrein ordanis thame bayth to mak publict repentence in the kirk of Striviling for fornicatioun committit be thame befoir the compleiting of thair mariage. Secundlie, the said Lowrence being askit gif he was fathir to the bairn, quhairof the said Margaret was last delyverit, or nocht, he confessit he was fathir to the same. Thridlie, the saidis Lowrence and Margaret being askit quha baptesit the said bairne and in quhat plaice the same was baptezit, ansorit the said Lowrence that he knew nocht quhair or quhom be the said bairn was baptezit becaus he was nocht in thir parttis for the tyme. The said Margaret ansorit that the said bairne was baptezit in hir awin hous be ane mane brocht thair be hir brethir, William and David Drummondis, quhais name scho knew nocht. The brethir ordanis the said Margaret to gett tryell of the manis name and quhair he dwellis and also ordanis the minister of Incheaffray to be adverteisit to seik tryell of the said man be the saidis William and David Drummondis, his parrochinaris.

Margaret Cairtour: Ane wreting beand producit in Margaret Cairtouris name send fra the minister and eldaris of Dunbartane schawand that Henrie Cunynghame confessit the said Margaret to be with bairne to him as the same in the self beris. The brethir tuke to advys heirwith to the nixt sessioun.

Mr Robert Montgumrie: The same day the brethrein was advertesit be ane wreting send fra the brethrein of Edinburgh befoir specefeit that thair was letters alreddie directit furth at the desyr of Mr Robert Montgumrie to chairge the brethrein of Glasgw to admit him to the archebischoprik thairof, quhilk thing the brethrein undirstanding to be contrarie to the act of the generall assemblie, and also his awin promeis made befoir thame, ordanis that sasone as the saidis letters salbe put to executioun chairgeing the brethrein of Glasgw thairwith that ane summondis be direct to chairge the said Mr Robert to compeir befoir thame to heir and se him self decernit to be excommunicat becaus that he wittinglie and willinglie hes brokin the said act of the generall assemblie concerning the trublein of the brethrein of Glasgw with his admissioun to the archebischoprik thairof, and falsefeing of his awin promeis foirsaid made befoir thame, with certificatioun that the brethrein will decern the sentence of excommunicatioun to be pronuncit againis him with advys of the brethrein conteinit in the act of the generall assemblie befoir specefeit in caice he laif nocht the sute of the said archebischoprik and trubling of his brethrein with his admissioun thairunto and als refuse to accep the said archebischoprik upone him, becaus the sam is ane functioun quhilk hes na warrand in the Word of God.

The vj day of Merche, 1581

Presentes: Patrik Gillaspie, Mr Andro Yung, Thomas Swintoun, Michaell Lermonthe, Patrik Layng, Robert Mentayth, Alexander Fargy, Johnne Broun, Mr Alexander Iule, Mr William Stirling, yunger, William Stirling, Alexander Forester of Garden, Johnne Schaw of Bruigh, Alexander Patersoun [William Stirling, *deleted*], William Norwall, Robert Alexander.

Huchoun, Stalkar: The brethrein continewis the avysment of the actioun betuix Johnne Huchoun and Marione Stalkar to the sicht of the proces led thairintill befoir the brethrein of Dunblane.

Henrie Graham and Elezabeth Millar: The quhilk day ane summondis beand producit lauchfullie execute and indorsit upone Henrie Graham and Elezabeth Millar to haif hard farther tryell tane in the actioun of adultrie allegit and persewit be the said Elezabeth *contra* him, the said Henrie being oftintymis callit, compeirit nocht.

F

Ordanis him to be summond of new undir the pane of excommunicatioun and the said Elezabeth to be wairnit thairto.

Adulteraris in S. Ninianis parrochin: The quhilk day ane summondis beand producit lauchfullie execute and indorsit upone Robert Millar, adulterar, Johnne Home and Margaret Coir, incesteus, within S. Ninianis parrochun to answer quhy thai satisfeit nocht the kirk for adultrie and incest committit be thame undir the paine of excommunicatioun, quhilk personis being oftin tymis callit and nocht compeirit, ordanis thame to be summond of new to heir and se thame selffis decernit to be excommunicat for thair contemp.

Adulteraris in Tillicultrie and Alvayth: The quhilk day ane summondis beand producit upone James Hudsone in Aluathe, husband to Issobell Craig, Issobell Fargy, adulteraris, William Watt in Dillecultrie [*sic*] and Jonet Dugy, incesteus, to heir and se thame self decernit to satisfie the kirk for adultrie and incest committit be thame undir the paine of disobedience, compeirit the said James Hudsoun and grantis adultrie committit be him with Issobell Fargy, quhairfor the brethrein ordanis him to compeir befoir the synnodall assemblie in Edinburgh the iij day of Aprill nixtocum to ressave his injunctionis for the said adultrie. The remanent personis foirsaidis being oft tymis callit and nocht compeirit, the brethrein ordanis thame to be summond of new undir the pane of excommunicatioun. The quhilk day Patrik Bauchok become cautioner and souertie that Margaret Cairtour sall satisfie the kirk of S. Niniance for fornicatioun committit be hir with Henrie Cunynghame in the said parrochin. Thairfor the brethrein ordanit the minister of the said kirk to bapteis the bairne gottin betuix thame.

Complent on Mr Robert Montgumrie: The quhilk day compeirit William Norwall, ane of the elderis of the kirk of Striviling, and in name of the particuler eldership thairof havalie complainit of Mr Robert Montgumreis oft and frequent absence fra his chairge without lycence obteinit contrarie to his awin promeis and of his intollarablle negligence in preiching of the Word, ministratioun of the sacramentis and using of disceplein quhairof albeit he was oft tymis admonesit, yit thair was na amendiment made, and quhairfor desyris that ordur may be tane with him be the brethrein that thair kirk be nocht neglectit in tymis cuming.

At Striviling the xiij day of Merche, 1581

Presentes: Patrik Gillaspie, Mr Andro Yung, Mr William Stirling, elder, Mr William Stirling, yunger, Alexander Fargy, Michaell Lermonthe, Patrik Layng, ministeris; Mr James Pont, Mr Alexander Iule, Johnne Broun, Alexander Forester of Garden, Robert Alexander, William Norwall, Duncane Narne and William Scott, exhortar at Callender.

Suspentioun of Mr Robert Montgumrie: The quhilk day the brethrein having deiplie considderit and diligentlie wyit the havie complent of the elderis of the kirk of Striviling concerning the frequent absence of Mr Robert Montgumrie frome his chairge without ony lycence askit or gevin, and his intollarablle negligence in preiching of the Word, ministratioun of the sacramentis and usein of disciplein, quhairof being oftin tymis admonesit hes nevir pressit to amend nor keipit ony promeis made thairanent, bot be the contrar dois occupy him self contenwallie in warldlie effairis and ungodlie suittis of unlauchfull honouris, preeminence and riches expres againis the Word of God, the actis of the generall assemblie and dewatie of ane trew pastour, yea, and his awin promeis made bayth privatlie and oppinlie in our assemblie as ane act made thairupone at mair lynthe bearis and thairby to satisfie his insatiablle greid and stinking pryd dois quhat lyis in him to wraik his brethrein to steir up ane lamentablle schisme and trublle in the kirk of God and this commone wealthe, and to inflame the hairttis of our souverane lord and his cheif nobilitie againis his maist faythfull subjectis, quhilk to performe he daylie mair and mair insistis and hade alreddie performit war nocht the ardent zeall and singular love his majestie beris to the undoutit trewthe of God and professuris thairof. Thir wickit attemptis being mair thane manifest and in that be mony and sindrie experiencis it may weill appeir that he hes lytill or na regaird of faithe, promeis or offeice without cair, love and zeall toward the kirk of God and professioun of his Word, sclanderus in lyf and conversatioun without feilling of conscience in his calling, quhairof proceding na apperance of amendement swa that the slandir daylie incressis in his persone to the gret greif of all gude men, and joy to the commone ennemeis of the cros of Christ, and that he in the meane sasone ather contenuallie absentis him self in runing furth his cours, or thane be indirect meinis geis about to stay all proceding againis him for sic enorme vycis. Thairfore the brethrein myndfull quhat sould be thair dewattie in removing sic oppin sclandir and punesing sa abominablle faultis partlie alreddie tryit and publeist partlie to be detectid and schawin in the awin tyme according to the powar committit to thame be the Word of God thocht the said Mr Robert worthie to be suspendit and suspendis him from all functioun in the kirk of God and exerceis of ony part of the ministrie thairof ay and quhill be humbill repentence he satisfie for the said crymis to the contentment of the kirk of God and faithfull in the same quhome he hes grevouslie offendit and ordanis him to be summond to compeir befoir the generall assemblie to be haldin in Sanctandrus the xxiiij day of Aprill nixttocum the thrid day of the said assemblie, viz., the xxvij day of Aprill foirsaid to se this sentence approvit or inlairgit incaice he perseveir in his wickit mynd and purpos and alsua ordanis intimatioun to be made to him of this suspentioun as effeiris.

Adulteraris in Tullicultrie: The quhilk day ane summondis beand producit lauchfullie execute and indorsit upone William Watt in Tullicultrie and Jonet Dugy, adulteraris and incesteus personis, chairgeing thame to answer this day at the instance of the kirk and to heir and se thame selfis decernit to satisfie the kirk for incest and adultrie committit be thame undir the paine of excommunicatioun, quhilkis personis being oft tymis callit and nocht compeirit, thairfor ordanis thame to be summond of new to heir and se thame selfis decernit to be excommunicatt for thair contemp with certificatioun gif thay compeir nocht we will proceid to the sentence of excommunicatioun againis thame.

Adulteraris in Clakmannan: The same day ane summondis beand producit lauchfullie execute and indorsit upone James Tailzour, Jonet Aickein, Johnne Seath, Jonet Wallace and David Burn, dwelland within the parrochin of Clakmannan, chairgeing thame to compeir this day to answer at the instance of the kirk and to heir and se thame selffis decernit to have committit adultrie and to obey the disceplein of the kirk thairfoir undir the paine of excommunicatioun, quhilkis personis being oft tymis callit and nocht compeirit, thairfore ordanis thame to be summond of new to heir and se thame selffis respective decernit to be excommunicat for thair contemp, with certificatioun gif thai compeir nocht we will proceid to the sentence of excommunicatioun againis thame.

At Striviling the xx day of Merche, 1581

Presentes: Alexander Fargy, Mr William Stirling, yunger, Michaell Lermonthe, Patrik Layng, ministeris; Johnne Durie, minister at Edinburgh, David Fargusone, minister at Dunfarmling, Johnne Dikis, minister at Culros, Mr Duncane Nevein, Johnne Broun, William Stirling, William Scott, Mr James Pont, Alexander Forester of Garden, Adame Spittell of Blair Logy, Umphra Cunynghame, commissar of Striviling, Alexander Patersone, Duncane Narne at Bannaburne and William Norwall.

Mr Robert Montgumrie: The quhilk day ane summondis beand producit lauchfullie execute and indorsit upone Mr Robert Montgumrie chairgeing him to compeir this day to heir and se him self decernit to be excommunicat as the summondis beris in the self, the said Mr Robert being oft tymis callit and nocht compeirit, the brethrein findis that justlie thai mycht proceid againis him, yit becaus that ane gude part of thair numbir was absent and speciallie Johnne Duncanson, ane appointit be the act of the generall assemblie to that effect, thocht gude that the day of farther proceiding againis the said Mr Robert sould be continewit that the kingis majestie mycht be advertesit of thair unreverent handling be the said Mr Robert and that eftir the knawlege of his hienes gudewill and mynd thairintill ordanis the said Mr Robert to be summond *de novo* unto the synnodall assemblie of the elderschippis of Edinburgh, Dalkayth, Linlythquo and Striviling to be haldin in Edinburgh the iiij day of Aprill nixtocum to heir and se him self decernit to be excommunicat for his wilfull and contempteus breking of the actis of the generall assemblie contravening of his awin promeis made befoir us and utheris notorius crymis that the said assemblie hes to lay unto his chairge or thane to schaw ane ressonablle caus quhy the samin sould nocht be done with certificatioun and he compeir nocht the said assemblie will decern and ordane the sentence of excommunicatioun to be pronuncit againis him.

At Striviling the xxvij day of Merche, 1582

Presentes: Patrik Gillaspie, Johnne Duncansone, Mr Andro Yung, Mr William Stirling, elder, Patrik Layng, Michaell Lermonthe, Robert Mentayth, Thomas Swintoun, Andro Forester, ministeris; Mr William Stirling, yunger, Mr Alexander Iule, William Scot, Mr Duncane Nevein, Adame, commendatar of Cambuskynnethe, Alexander Forester of Garden, Adame Spittell of Blair Logy, Umphra Cunynghame, commissar of Striviling, Duncane Narne, Mr Johnne Stewart, provost off Striviling, and Robert Alexander.

Mr Robert Montgumrie: The quhilk day the brethrein being advertesit of the kingis majesteis [mynd, *deleted*] gude will concerning thair procedingis againis Mr Robert Montgumrie bayth be ane wreting send to thame be Johnne Dury and als be Johnne Duncansonis awin report thocht gude and ordanis ane summondis be direct to summond the said Mr Robert to compeir befoir the synnodall assemblie at Edinburgh the iij day of Aprill nixt according to the ordinance conteinit in the act made thairanent in thair last sessioun.

At Striviling the x day of Aprill, 1582

Presentes: Patrik Gillaspie, Michaell Lermonthe, Alexander Fargy, Patrik Layng, Mr Alexander Chisholme, ministeris; Mr James Pont, Mr Alexander Iule, Mr William Stirling, yunger, Alexander Forester of Garden, Umphra Cunynghame, Alexander Patersone, William Norwall and Robert Alexander.

Commissionaris to the nixt generall assemblie: The brethrein of the presbytery of Striviling electit and nominat Patrik Gillaspie, Mr Andro Yung and Mr William Stirling ministers; Alexander Bruce of Airthe or his sone Mr Robert Bruce, James Kinros of Kippenros, Umphra Cunynghame, commissar of Striviling and Mr James Pont, commissar of Dunblane, barronis and gentill men, commissionaris to the nixt generall assemblie to be haldin in Sanctandrus the xxiiij day of Aprill instant for the said presbytery to concur with the said assemblie for treatting of thais thingis concerning the weill and gude ordur to be observit within the kirkis of the said presbytery and als quhatsumevir thingis salbe trettit in the said assemblie that may tend to the glorie of God and weill of his haill kirk plantit of his mercie within this realme.

Mr Andro Grahame: The same day ordanis Mr Andro Grahame, minister at Dunblane, to be summond to the nixt generall assemblie for negligence in his offeice and sic uthir thingis as the said assemblie wald lay unto his chairge conform to the ordinance of the provinciall assemblie.

Johnne Huchoun: The same day the brethir ordanis ane summondis to be direct to chairge Johnne Huchoun in Alvayth to compeir befoir thair sessioun to heir and se him self decernit to adheir to Marione Stalkar, his spous, or ellis to intent actioun of divorcement againis hir befoir the commissaris of Edinburgh.

At Striviling the xvij day of Aprill, 1582

Presentes: Patrik Gillaspie, Johnne Duncansone, Mr Johnne Porterfeild, Alexander Fargy, Mr William Stirling, elder, Mr William Stirling, yunger, Patrik Layng, Mr Alexander Iule, William Stirling, Johnne Broun, Alexander Forester of Garden and Duncane Narne.

Huchoun and Stalkar: The quhilk day ane summondis beand producit lauchfullie execute and indorsit upone Johnne Huchoun in Tullicultrie chairgeing him to compeir this samin day to heir and se him self decernit to adheir to Marione Stalkar, his spous, and to interteny hir as his lauchfull wyf as becumis him or ellis to intent actioun of divorcement againis hir befoir the commissaris of Edinburgh, compeirit personallie the saidis Johnne Huchoun and Marione Stalkar, the brethir being weill avysit with the allegencis made be ather of the saidis parteis decernis and ordanis the said Johnne Huchoun to ressave the said Marione in hous with him and to adheir unto hir as becumis ane faithfull husband to his wyf or ellis to produce sufficient testemoniall befoir the brethrein betwix and the xv day of May nixt that he hes intentit actioun of divorcement againis hir befoir the commissaris of Edinburgh.

Intimatioun of the act of suspentioun made to Mr Robert Montgumry: The quhilk day William Stevinsone being askit gif he hade made intimatioun to Mr Robert Montgumrie of the act of suspentioun pronuncit againis him the xiij of Merche last conforme to the command gevin to the said William thairanent, the said William affermit that he made intimatioun thairof to the said Mr Robert personallie apprehendit and delyverit him ane copie of the said act of suspentioun quha ressavit the samin and that upone the penult of Merche *anno* 1582 in presens of Johnne Murray, Patrik Kinros, Johnne Hodge and [*blank*] McLintok.

Cautioner for Elezabeth Millar: The samin day compeirit Elezabeth Millar and ernistlie desyrit hir bairne to be baptezit promesing to satisfie the kirk eftir tryell of hir fault athir as adultrix or fornicatrix and thairupone Robert Alexander, baillie, become cautioner inrespect quhairof the brethir ordanis the said Elezabethis bairne to be baptezit.

Excommunicatioun decernit agaïnis adulteraris in Clakmannan: The quhilk day ane summondis producit lauchfullie execute and indorsit upone James Tailzour, Jonet Aicken, Johnne Seath, Jonet Wallace and David Burne, adulteraris, within the parrochin of Clakmannan chairgeing thame to compeir the said day to heir and se thame selffis and ilk ane of thame decernit to be excommunicat for thair contemp and disobedience to the voice of the kirk, quhilkis personis being oft tymis callit and nocht compeirid, and the brethrein having diligentlie wyit and deiplie consederit thair grit obstinacie and manifest contemp of the lauchfull chairgis of the kirk besyd the odius cryme of adultrie committit be thame ordanis and decernis the saidis personis to be excommunicat and cuttit of fra the societie of Christis kirk and to be delyverit into the handis of the devill for the destructioun off thair flesche that thair saullis may be saif in the day of the Lord Jesus.

At Striviling the viij day of May, 1582

Presentes: Patrik Gillaspie, Mr William Stirling elder, Mr Andro Yung, Alexander Fargy, Robert Mentayth, Michaell Lermonthe, Thomas Swintoun, Patrik Layng, ministeris; Mr James Pont, Mr William Stirling, yunger, Johnne Broun, William Norwall and Robert Alexander.

Exerceis beginnis at ix houris: The same day the brethir ordanis the exerceis to begin fra this furthe at ix houris.

At Striviling the xv day of May, 1582

Presentes: Patrik Gillaspie, Mr Andro Yung, Thomas Swintoun, Mr Adame Merschell, Patrik Layng, Alexander Fargy, Mr Alexander Iule, Mr James Pont, Johnne Broun, Umphra Cunynghame. *Moderatour chosin*: The quhilk day Mr Andro Yung be vot of the brethrein was chosin moderatour to the nixt provinciall of assemblie.

Hudsone, adulterar in Alvaythe: The quhilk day compeirit James Hudson in Alveythe and grantit his offence and negligence in nocht compeiring befoir the last provinciall assemblie according to his promeis and promesis to present him self befoir the nixt provinciall assemblie of Edinburgh and obey the injunctionis of the said assemblie for the cryme of adultrie committit be him with Issobell Fargy. Farther, the said James desyrit the bairn gottin in adultrie be him to be baptezit. The brethir ordanis the said James to find cautioun actit in the commissaris buikis of Striviling for obeying of the premisis undir the pane of xl libis., and thaireftir his bairne to be baptezit.

Robert Cousland, sclanderus: The quhilk day it being complainit to the sessioun be the brethir of the particular elderschip of the kirk of Striviling that Robert Cousland, burges of Striviling, hade reteinit in hous with him Issobell Olephant, nochtwithstanding that he was ordeinit be thame to have put hir away a lang tyme syne berassone thair being togethir was varie sclanderus to the haill toun, the said Robert being personallie present, the brethir ordanis him to remove the said Issobell *simpliciter* fra his hous betuix and the xx day of May instant, and to have na mair cumpany nor familiarity with hir, nathir ony manir of societie in eatting, drinking or talking in tymis cuming with certificatioun and he failze, the brethir will ordane the sentence of excommunicatioun to be pronuncit againis him.

At Striviling the xxij day of May, 1582

Presentes: Patrik Gillaspie, Johnne Duncanson, Alexander Fargy, Robert Mentayth, Michaell Lermonthe, Patrik Layng, ministeris; Mr James Pont, Mr Alexander Iule, Johnne Broun, Adame, commendatar of Cambuskynnethe, Umphra Cunynghame, commissar of Striviling, and Robert Alexander, bailly; Mr William Moreson quha exercesit.

Generall fast: The same day Patrik Gillaspie, moderatour, this day made intimatioun to the brethrein that thair was appointit be the generall kirk ane generall fast thruch this haill realme to be keipit on the first and secund Sondayis of *Junij* nixt. Thairfor exhortit the haill brethrein that thai caus the samin to be observit ilk ane within thair awin parrochin thruch the boundis of this elderschip and that doctrein be teichit meit and expedient thairfoir.

At Striviling the xxix day of May, 1582

Presentes: Mr Andro Yung, Johnne Duncanson, Thomas Swintoun, Alexander Fargy, Mr William Stirling, elder, Patrik Gillaspie, ministeris; Mr James Pont, Mr Alexander Iule, Johnne Broun, Mr William Moreson, Alexander Forester of Garden and Umphra Cunynghame, commissar of Striviling.

Mr Andro Grahame: The brethir, considdering the lang absence of Mr Andro Grahame fra his kirk of Dunblane and negligence of his flock, ordanis the said Mr Andro to be summond to compeir befoir thame for the samin and sic uthir thingis as the kirk hes to lay unto his chairge and ane summondis to be direct heirupone.

At Striviling the xij day of *Junij*, 1582

Presentes: Mr Andro Yung, Johnne Duncansone, Patrik Gillaspie, Alexander Fargy, Michaell Lermonthe, Robert Mentayth, Patrik Layng, ministeris; Mr Alexander Iule, Mr Johnne Broun, Mr William Moreson and Robert Alexander.

The same day James Dundas made the exerceis.

James Dalmahoy: The brethrein having considderit and diligentlie wyit the accusationis alreddy layit againis James Dalmahoy, minister, and his answeris made thairto, ordanis ane summondis to be direct for summonding of the said James to compeir befoir thame to answer to sic uthir thingis as the kirk hes to lay unto his chairge and to heir and se thair avysment pronuncit upone the haill undir the paine of disobedience.

James McKie: The quhilk day ane summondis beand producit lauchfullie execute and indorsit upone James McKie in Doun of Mentaythe, allegit adulterar with Jane Stewart, chairgeing him to answer this day at the instance of the kirk for the samin and to heir and se him self decernit to obey and satisfie the disceplein of the kirk thairfoir undir the paine of disobedience, quhilk James being oft tymis callit and nocht compeirit, thairfor ordanis him to be summond of new to the effect foirsaid undir the paine of excommunicatioun with certificatioun and he failze, we will proceid againis him according to the Word of God and disceplein of the kirk havand the warrand thairin.

At Striviling the xix day of *Junij*, 1582

Presentes: Mr Andro Yung, Patrik Gillaspie, Robert Mentayth, Patrik Layng, ministeris; Mr Alexander Iule, Mr James Pont, Mr Johnne Broun, Adame, commendatar of Cambuskynnethe, Umphra Cunynghame, commissar of Striviling, and Robert Alexander, bailly.

James Leckie, Marjorie Erskein: The quhilk day ane summondis beand producit lauchfullie execute and indorsit upone James Lecky and Marjorie Erskein chairgeing thame to haif compeirit this day to have hard and sein thame selffis decernit to have committit adultrie and to undirly and obey the ordinance of the kirk thairfoir undir the paine of disobedience, quhilk personis being oft tymis callit and nocht compeirit, thairfor ordanis thame to be summond of new to the effect foirsaid undir the paine of excommunicatioun with certificatioun and thai failze we will proceid againis thame according to the Word of God and disceplein of the kirk havand the warrand thairin.

Commissionaris to the generall assemblie: The brethrein of the presbytery of Striviling electit and nominat Patrik Gillaspie and Mr Andro Yung, ministeris, commissioneris to the nixt generall assemblie to be haldin in Edinburgh the [*blank*] day of *Junij* instant for the said presbytery to concur with the said assemblie for treatting of thais thingis concerning the weill and gude ordur to be observit within the kirkis of the said presbytery and als quhatsumevir thingis salbe trettit in the said assemblie that may tend to the glorie of

God and weill of his haill kirk plantit of his mercie within this realme.

At Striviling the iij day of July, 1582

Presentes: Mr Andro Yung, Mr Petir Blakburne, Mr Alexander Chisholme, Patrik Gillaspie, Patrik Layng, Alexander Fargy and Robert Mentayth, ministeris; Michaell Lermonthe, minister; Mr Alexander Iule, Mr Johnne Broun, Umphra Cunynghame, William Norwall.

Mr Alexander Chisholme adjonit: The quhilk day compeirit Mr Alexander Chisholme, minister at Muthull, and willinglie adjonit him self to this presbytery ay and quhill ane presbytery war erectit in Strathern quhome the brethrein acceptit.

Robert Ramsay, notar: The samin day ane summondis beand producit lauchfullie execute and indorsit upon Robert Ramsay, notar, Stein Aikman and Gilbert Crysteson, chairgeing thame to compeir befoir the brethrein the said day to answer at the instance of the kirk for sic caussis as eftir follwis, compeirit the said Robert Ramsay personallie quha, being accusit for confering and talkein with Mr Robert Montgumrie being lauchfullie excommunicat be the kirk and lauchfull intimatioun thairof made to the parrochinnaris of the brugh of Striviling in the pulpet thairof, ansorit that he saw nocht the said Mr Robert quhill he tuke him be the hand and than only cravit fra him sum silvir that he was awand to him, nocht knawand the said excommunicatioun becaus he was at Dunune the tyme of the intimatioun of the said excommunicatioun of the said kirk. Farder, being inquyrit gif he drank with the said Mr Robert, the said Robert denyit the samin *simpliciter*. The brethir admonesis the said Robert Ramsay nocht to entir in the said Mr Robert Montgumreis cumpany nor in confirrence with him at na tyme fra this furthe salang as he was undir the said sentence of excommunicatioun, nathir yit crave ony silver fra him excep he obtein lycence fra sum of the brethrein of befoir undir the paine of the censuris of the kirk.

Stein Aikman: Compeirit Stein Aikman personallie, and being accusit for ressaving of Mr Robert Montgumrie, being excommunicat, in his hous and interteneing of him thairin, ansorit that he navir ressavit him in his hous nor yit spak with him thairin sen he was excommunicat. The brethir thairfore admonesis him fra this furth salang as the said Mr Robert is undir the said sentence of excommunicatioun nocht to eat, drink, confer, nor talk with him etc.. undir the paine of the censuris of the kirk.

Gilbert Crysteson, satisfeit: Compeirit Gilbert Crysteson *alias* Thome and being accusit for drinking with Mr Robert Montgumrie, being lauchfullie excommunicat and intimat as said is, and talking with him and leding of his hors fra the toun end of Striviling to the parkyet, the said Gilbert confessit the haill premisis and thairfor was ordeinit be the brethrein to mak publict repentence at the publict plaice in the parroche kirk of Striviling on Sonday the xv day of July nixt.

At Striviling the x day of July, 1582

Presentes: Mr Andro Yung, Robert Mentayth, Alexander Fargy, Michaell Lermonthe, Mr Alexander Chisholme, ministeris; Mr Alexander Iule and Mr Johnne Broun.

James Dalmahoy: The quhilk day ane summondis beand producit laufullie execute and indorsit upone James Dalmahoy, minister, chairgeing him to compeir the said day to answer at the instance of the kirk and to sic thingis as salbe layit unto his chairge, compeirit the said James personallie and being desyrit be the moderatour gif he wald continew in the functioun and offeice of the ministrie to the day of his dayth, ansorit that he wald co[nt]inew in the samin and promesit solempnitlie be his gret aithe to go forward in the samin, as said is. The said James beand accusit gif he tuke mony for solemnizatioun of ane mariage in Tullibody on Sonday last, ansorit that he ressavit nane bot ane fourtie penny peice for making of thair contract of mariage. The said James beand accusit for compleiting mariage betuix Johnne Cousland and Hellein Cunynghame in the kirk of Cambuskynnethe, thay beand fornicaturis nocht makand thair repentence of befoir in S. Ninianis kirk in the parrochin quhairof the said fornicatioun was committit, ansorit that he confessit the mariage of the saidis personis in the said kirk of Cambuskynneth befoir vj houris in the morning bot allegit that thai hade made thair repentence of befoir, quhilk the brethir ordeinit him to preve sufficientlie befoir thame the xvij day of July instant. The brethir continewis farther accusatioun of the said James and thair avysment heirwith to the nixt sessioun, he beand warnit thairto *apud acta* undir the paine of disobedience.

At Striviling the xvij day of July, 1582

Presentes: Mr Andro Yung, Mr Alexander Chisholme, Patrik Gillaspie, Alexander Fargy, Patrik Layng, Michaell Lermonthe, Robert Mentayth, ministers; Mr James Pont, Mr Johnne Broun, Mr Alexander Iule, Mr William Stirling, yunger, Duncane Narne and Robert Alexander.

James Dalmahoy: The quhilk day James Dalmahoy being oft tymis callit and nocht compeirit as he was lauchfullie summond at the last act bot Alexander Fargy in his name compeirit and declairit ane excuse of his absence, continewis his mater quhill the said excuse be tryit and ordanis him to be summond of new undir the paine of disobedience.

Robert Wilson: The samin day ane summond beand producit lauchfullie execute and indorsit upone Robert Wilsone, tailyour, Alexander Yung, baxter, Andro Squyer and Margaret Bavarage, spous to James Castellaw, chairgeing thame to compeir befoir the brethrein the said day to answer at the instance of the kirk for the causis eftir follwing and specefeit in the said summondis, compeirit personallie the said Robert Wilsone and being accusit for ressaving of Mr Robert Montgumrie in his hous, being excommunicat and lauchfull intimatioun thairof made in his parroche kirk, and interteneing at denner thairin, ansorit the said Robert and denyit the samin *simpliciter*. Farder being accusit for conveying of the said Mr Robert doun the gait, confessit the samin bot allegit that he past with him only to crave sum silver he was awand him. The brethir admonesis the said Robert that he fra this furth talk nocht, keip nocht companie in etting, drinking nor ony utherwayis with the said Mr Robert salang as he remainis excommunicat undir the paine of the censures of the kirk and continewis thair avysment with the said accusationis till thai gait farther tryell thairof.

Alexander Yung: Compeirit Alexander Yung, baxter, and being accusit for drinking and talking with Mr Robert Montgumrie, being excommunicat, lauchfull intimatioun thairof beand made as said is, the said Alexander denyit that he drank with him bot confessit that he and Duncane Robertsone was drinkand ane chopein of wyne in Michaell Gairdneris tavern at the quhilk tyme the said Mr Robert come in upone thame and that the said Alexander spak na thing to him bot reprovit him for his contemp of the kirk and that he at his awin tuke up aff the burde thair peice with wyne and drank of it. The brethir admonesit the said Alexander as thai did the said Robert Wilson of befoir.

Andro Squyer, Margaret Bavarage: The same day the saidis Andro Squyar and Margaret Bavarage being oft tymis callit as thai quha war lauchfullie summond according to the summondis and executioun producit this day on thame compeirit nocht. Thairfor the brethir ordanis thame to be summond of new for the causis conteinit in the said summondis producit on thame to compeir undir the paine of excommunicatioun.

Johnne Drummond, Jonet Quhyt: The quhilk day ane summondis beand producit lauchfullie execute and indorsit upone Johnne Drummond, *alias* Denmark, Jonet Quhyt, spous to James France, and the said James for his entires, chairgeing the said Johnne and Jonet to have compeirit the said day befoir the brethir to heir and se thame selffis decernit to have committit adultrie togethir and thairfor to undirly and obey the censuris of the kirk thairfoir undir the paine of disobedience. Quhilk personis being oft tymis callit compeirit nocht. Nochttheles the brethir for dyvers ressonis proponit to thame be thair minister, Mr Alexander Chisholme, tuiching certane circumstancis, quhilk was neidfull to be tryit befoir the said adultrie could be knawin to be of trewthe, quhilk could nocht be esallie done heir inrespect of the far distance of the plaice quhair the saidis personis dwellis, viz., the parrochun of Muthill fra the sessioun plaice of this presbytery, remittit the tryell thairof to the particular elderschip of Muthill, and quhat thai fand thairby to report againe to the brethrein befoir thai pronunce sentence thairintill.

At Striviling the xxiiij day of July, 1582

Presentes: Patrik Gillaspie, Mr William Stirling, elder, Mr Williame Stirling, yunger, Alexander Fargy, Michaell Lermonthe, ministeris; Mr James Pont, Mr Alexander Iule, William Stirling.

James Dalmahoy: The quhilk day ane summondis beand producit lauchfullie execute and indorsit upone James Dalmahoy chairgeing him to have compeirit the said day to the effect conteinit in the said summondis, the said James being oft tymis callit compeirit nocht. Thairfor ordanis him to be summond of new to the effect foirsaid undir the paine of excommunicatioun.

The quhilk day the summondis beand producit lauchfullie execute and indorsit upone Andro Squyer chairgeing him to have compeirit this day to answer at the instance of the kirk for interteneing of Mr Robert Montgumrie being excommunicat, as at mair lynthe is conteinit in the summondis raisit thairupone undir the paine of excommunicatioun, quhilk Andro being oft tymis callit compeirit nocht, the brethrein for gude and rassonabill causis moving thame continewis proces this day againis the said Andro and ordanis him to be summond of new againe in the same form and effect as of befoir.

At Striviling the last day of July, 1582

Presentes: Mr Andro Yung, Patrik Gillaspie, Mr William Stirling, elder, Robert Mentayth, Alexander Fargy, Mr Alexander Chisholme, Michaell Lermonthe, ministers; Mr William Stirling, yunger, Mr Johnne Broun, Mr Alexander Iule, Umphra Cunynghame, commissar of Striviling, and Robert Alexander.

James Dalmahoy: The quhilk day ane summondis beand producit lauchfullie execute and indorsit upone James Dalmahoy, minister, chairgeing him to compeir this day to answer at the instance of to sic accusatiounis as was to lay unto his chairge, compeirit the said James personallie and being accusit be the moderatour in quhat kirk [he mareit, *deleted*] Johnne Cousland and Hellein Cunyngham made thair repentence befoir thair mariage for fornicatioun committit be thame, the said James confessit that thai made it befoir him in the kirk of Cambuskynnethe the tyme of thair mariage viz., at vj houris in the morning. The brethrein findis the said James to have made gret fault, first, in mareing the saidis personis at vj houris in the morning, secundlie, in mareing of thame quhill the said personis hade made thair repentence in Sanct Ninianis kirk in the quhilk parrochin thair had committit the said fornicatioun quhilk was cleirlie knawin to the brethir. Secundlie, the said James being accusit for selling of the sacrament of baptisme to sindrie personis and taking mony thairfor, the said James denyit the taking of silvir for the sacrament, bot that quhilk he tuke, he tuke it for his travelling fra his hous to the kirk quhair he ministrat the samin. Thridlie, the said James being accusit for baptezein of ane bairne in Tillebody, gottin in adultrie be Marione Bennet in Culros by hir husband without ony satisfactioun made to the kirk thairfor and without testemoniall of the minister of Culros thairupone, quhilk the said James confessit. Ferdlie, being accusit for baptezein of ane bairne gottin in adultrie and incest be Thomas Moderall with his brothur dochtir by his wyf within the parrochin of Sanct Niniane without ony repentence or satisfactioun of the kirk thairfoir, the said James confessit the samin, bot allegit command of Patrik Gillaspie, minister at S. Ninianis gevin to him to that effect, quhilk the said James could nocht preve nathir be word or wrett, and thairfor was jugit be the brethrein to be ane fault. Fyftlie, the said James being accusit for abusing of the sacrament of baptisme in ministring the samin to ane bairne off Alexander Schorttis in Blakgrange within his awin barne, the said James confessit the samin bot allegit the occasioun thairof was becaus of the foull wathir that was that day, thrw the quhilk nane mycht travell to the kirk, nochtwithstanding of the quhilk allegence the brethir findis it ane fault inrespect of his awin confessioun.

Depositioun of James Dalmahoy: The brethrein having diligentlie considderit the sindrie and dyvers accusationis layit againis the said James Dalmahoy sindrie dyettis, as the proces beris and his ansuris made thairto being ryplie avysit thairwith, all in ane voice thocht the said James Dalmahoy worthie to be deposit and deposis him frome all functioun in the kirk of God and exerceis of ony part of the ministrie thairof at all tymis fra this furth, quhilk depositioun is presentlie intimat to the said James personallie present.

Andro Squyar: The quhilk day ane summondis beand producit lauchfullie execute and indorsit upone Andro Squyar chairgeing him to have compeirit the said day to answer at the instance of the kirk for interteneing of Mr Robert Montgumrie, being excommunicat, as at mair lynthe is conteinit in the summondis raisit thairupone undir the paine of excommunicatioun, quhilk Andro being oft tymis callit compeirit nocht, thairfor ordanis the said Andro to be summond of new to heir and se him self decernit to be excommunicat for

G

his contemp and disobedience with certificatioun and he obey nocht in satisfeing of the kirk the brethrein will proceid and decern the sentence of excommunicatioun to be pronouncit againis him.

At Striviling the vij day of August, 1582

Presentes: Mr Andro Yung, Patrik Gillaspy, Mr Andro Hay, Johnne Duncanson, Alexander Fargy, Michaell Lermonthe, Mr Alexander Chisholme, Mr Adame Merschell, ministeris; Mr James Pont, Mr Alexander Iule, William Stirling, Alexander Forester of Garden, Umphra Cunynghame and Robert Alexander.

Andro Squyar: The quhilk day ane summondis beand producit lauchfullie execute and indorsit upone Andro Squyer chairgeing him to compeir the said day to heir and se him self decernit to be excommunicat for his former contemp and disobedience, compeirit the said Andro personallie quha being accusit for bering of Mr Robert Montgumrie familiar cumpanie, being excommunicat, and dew intimatioun made thairof and for talking with him, the said Andro confessit that he was his tennent and, at his command, he led doun his hors affoir him to the toun end and denyit that he bure the said Mr Robert ony farder cumpany nather yit drank nor eat with him sen he was excommunicat. Farder being accusit quhy he haid sa lang disobeyit the summondis of the kirk and lauchfull chairgis thairof, to witt, this moneth bypast being four sindrie tymis summond, nather yit send na lauchfull excuse of his absence at na tyme, the said Andro could gif na gude rassone thairfor. Quhairfor the bretherein considdering his gret disobedience swa oft without ony lauchfull excuse ordeinit him to mak publict repentence in the kirk of Striviling at the publict plaice thairof on the nixt Thurisday that thair sould happin ane sermond to be made in the said kirk for his said disobedience as he sould be warnit thairto be the officer.

Jane Stewart, adultrix: The quhilk day ane summondis beand producit lauchfullie execute and indorsit upone Jane Stewart in Lochburne, allegit adultrix with James McKie, chairgeing hir to compeir the said day to answer at the instance of the kirk for the samin adultrie and to heir and se hir self decernit to satisfie the disciplein of the kirk thairfoir, compeirit the said Jane personallie and confessit that it is twa yeiris past sen scho haid carnall dell with the said James McKie, and als confessit that of hir conscience sche could nocht deny bot sche haid carnall dell with the said James befoir his wyffe was ded and thairfor the brethrein decernis hir to have committit adultrie with the said James and ordanis and commandis hir to seperat hir self with all diligence fra the said James and nocht to cum in his cumpany againe undir the paine of excommunicatioun, and ordanis Alexander Fargy, hir minister, to warne the said Jane to the nixt synnodall to ressave hir injunctiounis.

James McKie: The quhilk day the secund summondis producit upone James McKie, adulterar with Jane Stewart, deulie execute and indorsit chairgeing him to compeir the said day to answer at the instance of the kirk for the said adultrie and to heir and se him self decernit to obey and satisfie the disciplein of the kirk thairfoir undir the paine of excommunicatioun. Quhilk James being oft tymis callit compeirit nocht, thairfor ordanis him to be summond to heir and se him self decernit to be excommunicat for his contemp and disobedience with certificatioun and he failze the brethir will proceid to the pronunceing of the said decreit againis him.

James Galbrayth, adulterar, intimat to Mr Andro Hay: The quhilk day the act made on the xxvj day of September last tuiching the adultrie committit be James Galbrayth of Culcruch with Margaret Leiche was intimat to Mr Andro Hay beand personally present and ane copy thairof delyverit to him.

At Striviling the xiiij day of August, 1582

Presentes: Mr Andro Yung, Patrik Gillaspie, Mr William Stirling, elder, Alexander Fargy, Robert Mentayth, Patrik Layng, ministeris; Mr Alexander Iule, William Stirling.

James McKie decernit to be excommunicat: The quhilk day ane summondis beand producit lauchfullie execute and indorsit upone James McKie, adulterar with Jane Stewart, chairgeing him to have compeirit the said day to have hard and sein him self decernit to be excommunicat for his contemp and disobedience to the voice of the kirk, quhilk James being oft tymis callit compeirit nocht and the brethrein having diligentlie wyit and deiplie considderit his gret obstinacie and manifest contemp of the lauchfull chairgis of the kirk besyd the odius cryme of adultrie committit be him ordanis and decernis the said James to be excommunicat and cuttit of fra the societie of Christis kirk and to be delyverit into the handis of the devill for the destructioun of his flesche that his saull may be saif in the day of the Lord Jesus.

At Striviling the xxj day of August, 1582

Presentes: Mr Andro Yung, Johnne Duncanson, Patrik Gillaspie, Robert Mentayth, Alexander Fargy, Patrik Layng, ministeris; Mr Alexander Iule, William Stirling and Duncane Narne.

Mr Duncan Nevein: The quhilk day ane summondis beand producit lauchfullie execut and indorsit upone Mr Duncane Nevein chairgeing him to have compeirit the said day to heir and se Mr Johnne Craigis interpretatioun of the act of the generall assemblie made anentis the adjoning of the brethrein of Dunblane to this presbytery declarit and the brethreinis sentence and decreit pronuncit in the said matter, quhilk Mr Duncan being oft tymis callit compeirit nocht personallie, bot Mr Andro Yung declairit to the brethrein in name of the said Mr Duncan ane excuis for his absence and thairfor the brethrein continewit the said mater quhill thai be farder avysit.

Andro Squyer: The quhilk day ane summondis beand producit lauchfullie execut and indorsit upone Andro Squyar chairgeing him to have compeirit the said day to answer at the instance of the kirk and to underly the censuris thairof for his disobedience to the lauchfull ordinancis of the samin, quhilk Andro beand oft tymis callit compeirit [nocht, *deleted*] personallie quha being accusit for his disobedience, it wes fund be the brethrein that the said Andro was na thing mendit bot continewit still obstinat and disobedient as of befoir, thairfor ordeinit to delait to the civill magistrattis, viz., to the provest and bailleis of Striviling the said Androis contemp and disobedience to the kirk, desyring thame to adjone thair auctoritie to the auctoritie of the kirk in punesing of the said Andro quhill he be movit with repentence and offir him self to the kirk and obey the disceplein thairof.

Thomas Johneson, adulterar: The quhilk day ane summondis beand producit lauchfullie execute and indorsit upone Thomas Johnneson in S. Ninianis parrochin, adulterar with Jonet Murray, chairgeing him to compeir befoir us the said day to declair quhy he hes nocht fulfillit his injunctionis gevin to him for the said adultrie be the last provinciall assemblie of this province, compeirit the said Thomas and confessis he hes nocht obeyit the injunctiones ressavit be him fra the said assemblie. The brethir ordanis him to entir to the plaice of repentence the nixt Sonday in the said kirk of S. Niniane and thair mak publict repentence and swa furth to continew ilk Sonday quhill the xxj day of Fabruar nixt undir the paine of excommunicatioun.

Margaret Bruce: The quhilk day ane summondis lauchfullie execute and indorsit being producit upone Margaret Bruce dwelland within the parrochin of Clakmannan chairgeing hir to have compeirit the said day to answer at the instance of the kirk and to heir and se hir self decernit to have committit adultrie with Robert Bruce of Clakmannan and thairfor to underly the censuris of the kirk, quhilk Margaret, being oft tymis callit, compeirit nocht, thairfor the brethrein ordanis hir to be summond of new undir the paine of excommunicatioun.

Johnne Cuthbert for nonadherence: The quhilk day ane summondis beand producit lauchfullie execute and indorsit upone Johnne Cuthbert in Brumrig chargeing him to compeir the said day to answer at the instance of the kirk quhy he adheiris nocht to Issobell Ellesone, his spous, and interteneis hir as Godis law prescryvis, and to heir and se him self decernit be our decreit to adheir and interteine his said spous, as said is, undir the paine of disobedience, quhilk Johnne being oft tymis callit compeirit nocht thairfor ordanis him to be summond of new to compeir to the effect foirsaid undir the paine of excommunicatioun.

James McKie: The quhilk day compeirit James McKie personallie eftir the first admonitioun gevin be Alexander Fargy, his minister, according to the ordur befoir the pronunceing of the sentence of excommunicatioun againis him according to our decreit gevin thairanent and offerit him self to obey quhat the brethir wald command him. The brethrein being ryplie avysit with the odius cryme of adultrie committit be him with Jane Stewart decernis and ordanis him with all diligence to seperat him self fra the said Jane Stewart *simpliciter* and nocht to cum in hir cumpanie agayne undir the paine of excommunicatioun, and als commandis him to pas to the nixt provinciall assemblie of Edinburgh, Dalkayth, Striviling and Linlythquow to be haldin in Edinburgh on sic day as he salbe warnit to, be his said minister undir the said paine of excommunicatioun to ressave his injunctionis for the said adultrie.

At Striviling the xxviij day of August, 1582

[*Presentes*:] Patrik Gillaspie, Alexander Fargy, ministeris; Mr Alexander Iule, Duncane Narne and Umphra Cunynghame.

Adulteraris in Kippen: The quhilk day ane summondis beand producit lauchfullie execute and indorsit upone Duncane Carrik in Kippen and Issobell Finlasone, allegit adulteraris, chairgeing thame to have compeirit the said day to answer to the cryme of adultrie allegit committit be thame and to heir and se thame selffis decernit to obey and satisfie the disceplein of the kirk thairfor, undir the paine of disobedience, quhilk personis being oft tymis callit comperit nocht, thairfor the brethir ordanis the saidis personis to be summond of new to the effect foirsaid undir the paine of excommunicatioun.

Johnne Cuthbert: The quhilk day ane summondis beand producit lauchfullie execute and indorsit upone Johnne Cuthbert in Brumrig within the parrochin of Sanct Niniane, chairgeing him to have compeirit befoir us the said day to answer at the instance of the kirk quhy he adheris nocht to Issobell Ellesone, his spous, and interteneis hir as Godis law prescryvis, and to heir and se him self decernit to do the samin undir the paine of excommunicatioun, quhilk Johnne being oft tymis callit compeirit nocht, thairfor the brethir ordanis the said Johnne to be summond of new to heir and se him self decernit to be excommunicat for his contemp and disobedience with certificatioun and he obey nocht in satisfeing of the kirk, the brethrein will proceid and decern as said is.

At Striviling the iiij day of September, 1582

Presentes: Mr Andro Young, Mr Alexander Chisholme, Patrik Gillaspie, Robert Mentayth, Michaell Lermonthe, Patrik Layng, ministeris; Mr Alexander Iule, Mr James Pont, Mr Robert Rollok, Robert Alexander, Mr Richard Wricht, Mr Johnne Stewart, provest, and Malcolme Wallace, baillie.

Adulteraris in Tullicultrie excommunicat: The quhilk day ane summondis beand producit lauchfullie execute and indorsit upone William Watt in Tullicultry and Jonet Dugy, adulteraris and incesteus personis, chairgeing thame to have compeirit this day to heir and se thame selffis and ilk ane of thame decernit to be excommunicat for thair contemp and disobedience to the voice of the kirk, quhilkis personis being oft tymis callit compeirit nocht and the brethrein having diligentlie wyit and deiplie considderit thair grit obstinacie and manifest contemp of the lauchfull chairgis of the kirk besyd the odius cryme of adultrie and incest committit be thame ordanis and decernis the saidis personis to be excommunicat and cuttit of fra the societie of Chrystis kirk and to be delyverit into the handis of the devill for the destructioun of thair flesh that thair saullis may be saif in the day of the Lord Jesus.

At Striviling the xj day of September, 1582

Presentes: Mr Andro Young, Patrik Gillaspie, Alexander Fargy, Robert Mentayth, Michaell Lermonthe, ministeris; Mr James Pont, Mr Alexander Iule, Mr Robert Rollok and Umphra Cunynghame, commissar of Striviling.

Mr Duncan Nevein: The quhilk day ane summondis beand producit lauchfullie execute and indorsit upone Mr Duncane Nevein, scholmaistir in Dunblane, chairgeing him to have compeirit this day to have hard and sein Mr Johnne Craigis interpretatioun of the act of the generall assemblie made anentis the adjoning of the brethrein of Dunblane to this presbytery declairit, and the brethreinis sentence and decreit pronuncit in the said mater, quhilk Mr Duncan being oft tymis callit compeirit nocht thairfor the brethrein ordanis him to be summond of new to the effect foirsaid undir the paine of excommunicatioun.

Disobedientis in Dunblane: The quhilk day ane summondis beand producit lauchfullie execute and indorsit upone James Duthy in Dunblane, cautioner and souertie for James Walkar and Issobell Porteus, Johnne Tailyour, millar in Kinbuk, Marione Michell, servand to Johnne Scot in Dunblane, and Marione Forfer thair, chargeing thame to have compeirit befoir us the said day to answer at the instance of the kirk for disobedience to the lauchfull chairgis of the sessioun of thair awin parroche kirk of Dunblane and to underly the censuris of the kirk thairfor undir the paine of disobedience, quhilk personis being oft tymis callit compeirit nocht, thairfor the brethrein ordanis thame to be summond of new undir the paine off excommunicatioun.

Johnne Cuthbert: The quhilk day ane summondis beand producit lauchfullie execute and indorsit upone Johnne Cuthbert chairgeing him to have compeirit the said day to have hard and sein him self decernit to to [*sic*] have bein excommunicat for his contemp and disobedience, compeirit the said Johnne Cuthbert personallie and being accusit quhy he contempnit and disobeyit the lauchfull summondis of the presbytery, being swa aft summond, could gif na gude rassone thairfoir, and thairfor was ordeinit be the brethir to mak publict repentence the nixt [Sonday] in his parroche kirk of Sanct Niniane in the publict plaice thairof undir the paine of disobedience, and farder being accusit quhy he adheris nocht to Issobell Ellesone his [spouse] and interteneis hir in hous with him as Goddis law prescryvis, the said Johnne could allege na ressonablle caus quhy he sould nocht do the samin and thairfor was decernit and ordeinit be the brethir to ressave the said Issobell, his spous, agane in hous with him and intertenis hir as Godis law prescryvis and nocht to put hir fra him agane undir the paine of excommunicatioun.

Andro Squyer, satisfeit: The quhilk day the bailleis of the brugh of Striviling reportit to the brethir that thai for contemp and disobedience of Andro Squyer to the brethreinis ordinance hade causit thair officeris lay handis on him quha hade promesit to thame to obey the brethrein quhom thay presentit personallie to satisfie for his said contemp. The brethrein having diligentlie wyit his lang disobedience and contemp of his refuse to satisfie the ordinance of the kirk made thairanent decernit and ordeinit him to mak publict repentence in the kirk of Striviling the nixt Sonday that thair sould happin ane preiching to be thair undir the paine of excommunicatioun.

At Striviling the xviij day of September, 1582

Presentes: Mr Andro Yung, Mr Alexander Chisholme, Patrik Gillaspie, Thomas Swintoun, Robert Mentayth, Michaell Lermonthe, ministeris; Henrie Colvill, minister at Forfar, Mr Robert

Rollok, Mr Alexander Iule and Mr James Pont, commissar of Dunblane.

Mr Duncane Nevein adjonit: The quhilk day ane summondis beand producit lauchfullie execute and indorsit upone Mr Duncane Nevein, chairgeing him to have compeirit befoir the brethir the sed day to have hard and sein Mr Johnne Craigis interpretatioun of the act of the generall assemblie made anenttis the adjoning of the brethrein of Dunblane to this presbytery declairit, and the brethreinis sentence and decreit pronuncit thairintill, compeirit the said Mr Duncan personallie. The brethrein beand ryplie avysit with the said act and interpretatioun of the said Mr Johnne Craig togethir with the said Mr Duncanis haill allegeance made in the contrar decernis and ordanis the said Mr Duncane to adjone him self to the said presbytery and exerceis thairin undir the paine off disobedience becaus he is a teicher of the youthe, reder at the kirk of Dunblane, and hes made the exerceis of befoir in Dunblane, nochttheles inrespect of the said Mr Duncanis small stepend and utheris motevis moving the brethrein, thay grant *ex gratia* to the said Mr Duncane that he sall nocht be astrictit to convein ilk day of exerceis with the brethrein bot only on the dayis that it sall fall him to mak the exerceis and to ad in the secund plaice on the quhilkis he sall teiche according to the ordur and to convein with the brethir ilk day of exerceis that it sall happin him to be in Striviling.

Robert Fogo: The quhilk day ane summondis beand producit lauchfullie execute and indorsit upone Robert Fogo in Doun chairgeing him to have compeirit the said day to answer at the instance of the kirk for sic thingis as salbe layit unto his chairge undir the paine of disobedience, quhilk Robert being oft tymis callit compeirit nocht thairfor the brethrein ordanis the said Robert to [be] summond of new undir the paine of excommunicatioun to compeir to the effect foirsaid.

Disobedientis in Dunblane: The quhilk day ane summondis beand producit lauchfullie execute and indorsit upone Johnne Tailyour in Kinbuk and Marione Forfar in Dunblane chargeing thame to have compeirit the said day to answer at the instance of the kirk for disobedience to the lauchfull chairgis of the sessioun of thair awin parroche kirk of Dunblane and to undirly the censuris of the kirk thairfoir, undir the paine of excommunicatioun, quhilk personis being oft tymis callit compeirit nocht, thairfor the brethrein ordanis the saidis personis to be summond to heir and se thame selffis decernit to be excommunicat for thair contemp and disobedience with certificatioun and thai failze we will proceid and decern, as said is, according to the Word of God and disciplein of the kirk havand the warrand thairof thairin.

At Striviling the xxv day of September, 1582

Presentes: Mr Andro Yung, Mr Alexander Chisholme, Robert Mentayth, Patrik Gillaspie, Patrik Layng, Mr William Stirling, elder, Michaell Lermonthe, Thomas Swintoun, Mr Adame Merschell, Alexander Fargy, ministeris; Mr James Pont, Mr Alexander Iule, William Stirling, Mr Robert Rollok.

Marione Forfar decernit to be excommunicat: The quhilk day ane summondis beand producit lauchfullie execute and indorsit upone Marione Forfar in Dunblane chairgeing hir to have compeirit befoir the brethrein the said day to have hard and sein hir self decernit to be excommunicat for hir contemp and disobedience to the voice of the kirk as the said summondis at mair lynthe beris, quhilk Marione being oft tymis callit compeirit nocht and the brethrein having diligentlie wyit and deiplie considderit hir gret obstinacie and manifest contemp of the lauchfull chairgis of the kirk alsweill hir awin kirk as the voice of the elderschip, ordanis and decernis the said Marione to be excommunicatt and cuttit of fra the societie of Chrystis kirk and to be delyverit in the handis of the devill for the destructioun of hir flesche that hir saull may be saif in the day of the Lord Jesus.

At Striviling the penult day of October, 1582

Presentes: Mr Andro Yung, Patrik Gillaspie, Robert Mentaythe, Alexander Fargy, ministeris; Mr James Pont, Mr Alexander Iule, Robert Alexander, Umphra Cunynghame, Sir James Stirling of Keir, knycht, provest; James Anderson and Mr Williame Edmestoun, ministeris.

Commissionar to Edinbrugh: The quhilk day the brethrein present with universall consent nominat and ordeinit Patrik Gillaspie commissionar for this presbytery to pas to Edinburgh thair to travell with the lordis modefearis of stependis for the weill of the haill brethrenis stipendis and to crave augmentatioun to the brethrein that hes neid.

The brethrein sustein the commissionaris expensis: The same day the brethering calling to remembrance and considderand the gret and lairge expensis sustenit be sum of the brethrein nominat commissionaris to travell for the haill in tymis past besyd thair awin travellis and wiling that the samin salbe helpit in tymis cuming all with ane voice consenttis and aggreis that the brethrein havand stependis be commone contributioun ilk ane according to his stepend to be valurit sall sustein and pay the said commissionaris expensis to be sustenit be him in his said jurnay to Edinbrugh.

Exerceis beginnis at x houris: The brethrein inrespect of the schortnes of the day presentlie ordanis the exerceis to begin at x houris in tymis cuming.

At Striviling the xiij day of November, 1582

Presentes: Mr Andro Yung, Patrik Gillaspie, Mr William Stirling, Mr Alexander Chisholme, Michaell Lermonthe, Alexander Fargy, Robert Mentayth, ministeris; Mr Alexander Chisholme [*recte*, Iule], Umphra Cunynghame and William Norwall.
[No minutes.]

At Striviling the xx day of November, 1582

Presentes: Mr Andro Yung, Patrik Gillaspie, Alexander Fargy, Mr Alexander Chisholme, Robert Mentayth ministeris; Mr Alexander Iule, Williame Stirling, Umphra Cunynghame, Maisteris Richard Wricht and Johnne Broun.

James Lecky, Merjorie Erskein: The quhilk day ane summondis producit lauchfullie execute and indorsit upone James Lecky and Merjory Erskein dwelland in Sanct Ninianis parrochin, allegit adulteraris, chairgeing thame to have compeirit the said day to have hard and sein thame selffis decernit to have committit adultrie and to undirly and obey the ordinance of the kirk thairfoir undir the paine of excommunicatioun, compeirit the said James Lecky personally

and being accusit be the moderator that [gif, *deleted*] he haid committit adultrie with Merjorie Erskein, having carnall copulatioun
with hir, becaus it is [was, *deleted*] allegit that he was mareit with
Jonet Leckie, relict of umquhill William Michell in Gait syd quha is
yit alyve, the said James denyit that he committit ony adultrie with
the said Merjorie becaus, as he allegit, he was nevir mareit with the
said Jonet Leckie nor na uthir woman, bot confessis fornicatioun
with the said Jonet Leckie and Merjorie Erskein, for the quhilk he
offeris to satisfie the kirk as he salbe commandit. The brethrein being
avysit with the said James allegence contenuis thair sentence thairin
quhill the xxvij day of November instant that thai may accuse the
said Jonet Leckie gif the said mariage was in veritie or nocht, the
said James being warnit thairto *apud acta*. The said Merjorie Erskein
being oft tymis callit compeirit nocht. Thairfor the brethir ordanis
hir to be summond to heir and se hir self decernit to be excommunicat for hir contemp and disobedience withe certificatioun and
sche failze we will proceid and decern, as said is, according to the
Word of God and disceplein of the kirk havand the warrand thairof
thairin.

Duncane Carrik: The quhilk day ane summondis beand producit
lauchfullie execut and indorsit upone Duncane Carrik in Kippen
chairgeing him to compeir befoir us the said day to answer at the
instance of the kirk to the cryme of adultrie allegit committit be him
with Issobell Finlason and to heir and se him self decernit to obey
and satisfie the disceplein of the kirk thairfoir, undir the paine of
excommunicatioun, quhilk Duncane being oft tymis callit compeirit
nocht, thairfor the brethir ordanis to summond the said Duncane to
heir and se him self decernit to be excommunicat for his contemp
and disobedience with certificatioun and he failze we will proceid
and decern, as said is, according to the Word of God and disceplein of
the kirk havand the warrand thairof thairin.

James McKie, Jane Stewart: The quhilk day it was schawin and
complainit to the brethir be Alexander Fargy, minister at Logy, that
he, according to our ordinance, lauchfullie warnit James McKie and
Jane Stewart personallie to compeir befoir the last synnodall
assemblie haldin at Edinburgh the [*blank*] day of October last
bypast, thair to have ressavit thair injunctionis for adultrie committit be thame undir the paine of excommunicatioun, quhilk

personis hathe baithe contempuandlie disobeyit the said chairge and nocht to thair to the effect and lykwys declairit that the saidis personis haid nocht seperat thame selffis fra uthir according to the ordinance and command gevin to thame be the brethir, bot lykwys disobeyit the samin and remanit still and now presentlie is remanand in hous togethir. The brethir ordanis to summond bayth the saidis personis to heir and se thame selffis decernit to be excommunicat for thair contemp and disobedience with certificatioun and thai failze we will proceid and decern, as said is, according to the Word of God and disceplein of the kirk havand the warand thairof thairin.

At Striviling the xxvij day of November, 1582

Presentes: Mr Andro Yung, Patrik Gillaspie, Alexander Fargy, Mr William Stirling and Michaell Lermonthe, ministeris; Mr Alexander Iule, Mr James Pont, William Stirling, Umphra Cunynghame and Robert Alexander.

The text of the exerceis: The brethrein hes thocht gude and ordeinit that the epistill of Paull wrettin to the Ephesianis be teichit in the exerceis immediatlie eftir the epistill wrettin to the Gallatianis be endit.

James McKie and Jane Stewart decernit to be excommunicatt: The quhilk day ane summondis beand producit lauchfullie execute and indorsit upone James McKie and Jane Stewart, parrochinnaris in Logy, chairgeing thame to have compeirit befoir the brethrein the said day to have hard and sein thame selffis decernit to be excommunicat for thair contemp and disobedience as the said summondis at mair lynthe beris, quhilkis personis being oft tymis callit compeirit nocht and the brethrein having diligentlie wyit and deiplie considderit thair gret obstinacie and manifest contemp of the lauchfull chairgis of the kirk besyd the odius cryme of adultrie committit be thame, ordanis and decernis the saidis James and Jane to be excommunicat and cuttit off fra the societie of Chrystis kirk and to be delyverit into the handis of the devill for the destructioun of thair flesche that thair saullis may be saif in the day of the Lord Jesus.

James Leckie, Jonet Leckie: In the terme assignit be the brethrein to pronunce sentence in the allegit cryme of adultrie layit to the chairge of James Lecky, brothur to Walter Lecky of that Ilk, allegit committit be him with Merjorie Erskein inrespect he is allegit to have bein mareit on Jonet Lecky, relict of umquhill William Michell in Gaitsyd, the said James and Jonet Lecky comperand personally, the said Jonet is accusit be the moderator gif scho was at ony tyme mareit with the said James, denyit the samin *simpliciter*, bot confessit that upone xiij yeir syne or thairby on ane fasternisevin at nycht, eftir supper in the auld lady Leckeis hous in presens of the said laird of Lecky and utheris thair freindis thair conveinit and in presens of William Stirling, reder att Kippen, the said James and scho promesit mutuallie to compleit mariage on Sonday immediatlie eftir the fest of peace nixt thaireftir and lykwys confest that scho bure ane bairne to the said James and swa hade carnall copulatioun with the said James and cohabitatioun with him eftir the said promeis dyveris yeiris, for the quhilk carnall copulatioun with the said Jonet Lecky (as is confessit) the brethrein ordanis the said James and Jonet to mak publict repentence in the parroche kirk of the parrochin quhair the said offence was committit, viz., in the kirk of Kincardin on Sonday the ix day of December nixt befoir Alexander Fargy, minister at Logy, appointit be the brethrein to that effect, and lykwys for fornicatioun committit be the said James with the said Merjorie (as the brethrein presentlie understandis), ordanis him to mak publict repentence in the parroche kirk of the parrochin quhair the said fornicatioun was committit, viz., in the kirk of Sanct Niniane befoir the minister thairof on Sonday the secund day of December nixt and attour commandis and ordanis the said James to separet him self in societie fra the said Merjorie Erskein and frathynefurth to remane fra hir undir the paine of the censuris of the kirk.

At Striviling the iiij day of December, 1582

Presentes: Patrik Gillaspie, Mr Alexander Chisholme and Alexander Fargy, ministeris; Mr Duncane Nevein, Mr James Pont, Mr Alexander Iule, Umphra Cunynghame, commissar of Striviling, Robert Alexander, William Norwall, and Mr Johnne Stewart.

James Andirsone plessit ane brothur in the presbytery: The quhilk day compeirit Malcolme Wallace, Duncane Leischman, bailleis of

Striviling and elderis in the kirk thairof, William Norwall and
Robert Alexander, elderis in the presbytery, in name and behalf of
the haill kirk of the said brugh, quha exponit and declairit to the
brethrein that the parrochinnaris of Striviling haid lauchfullie electit
and chosin James Andirson to be thair minister according to the
powar gevin to thame be ane act of the generall assemblie of the dett
at Edinburgh the xx day of October last bypast, and lykwys was
publictlie plaicit minister to thame on Sonday the secund day of
December instant be Johnne Duncansone, minister, as ane act thairof
in the buikis of the particular elderschip of the kirk of Striviling at
mair lynth beris, and thairfor desyrit the brethrein to accep and
ressave him as thair minister to be ane brothur with thame in this
presbytery according to the ordur tane be the generall kirk thairanent. Quhilk James Andirson compeirit personallie and accepit
plaice and offeice in this presbytery and promesit solemnitlie be
uphaulding of his hand faythfullie to execute his offeice in teiching
of the Word, ministratioun of the sacramenttis and executioun of
disceplein according to the Word of God at the said kirk of Striviling
as alswa in exercesing with the brethrein and concuring with thame
be his avyse and jugement for tryell of sic thingis as salbe treattit in
the presbytery unto the end of his lyf as it sall plais God to minister
to him the giftis of his Holie Spirit.

Adulteraris in S. Ninianis parrochin: The quhilk day Patrik
Gillaspie, minister at S. Ninianis kirk, complainit that albeit Johnne
Waltir in Touchadame, adulterar with Jonet Clark, and Thomas
Johneson, adulterar with Margaret Murray, dwelland within the
said parrochin, was decernit and ordeinit be us to entir to the plaice
of repentence within the said kirk on the nixt Sondayis thaireftir and
swa to have continewit ilk Sonday according to the ordinance
ressavit be thame fra the synnodall assemblie of this province and
our said ordinancis made thairanent undir the paine of excommunicatioun, nochttheles the said Johnne and Thomas hes nocht obeyit
our saidis ordinancis in making of thair repentence, as said is, bot hes
contemnit the same, thairfor the brethrein ordanis the saidis personis
to be summond to heir and se thame selffis decernit to have contravenit our saidis ordinancis and thairfor decervis to be execute and
pronuncit againis thame the paine thairin contenit, viz., excommunicatioun with certificatioun and thay failze, we will proceid and

decern thame to have contravenit the samin according to the Word of God.

At Striviling the xj day of December, 1582

Presentes: Mr Andro Yung, Mr Andro Grahame, Patrik Gillaspie, James Andirson, Mr Alexander Chisholme, Alexander Fargy and Michaell Lermonthe, ministeris; Mr James Pont, Mr Alexander Iule and Umphra Cunynghame, commissar of Striviling, elderis.

Moderatour electit: The quhilk day James Andirson, minister at Striviling, be voit of the brethrein was chosin moderator to the nixt provinciall assemblie.

The brethrein that hes bein oft absent: The brethrein, undirstandand the lang and frequent absence of the brethrein eftir follwing fra the exerceis and elderschip, to wit, Robert Mentayth, Mr Adame Merschell, Patrik Layng, William Stirling and William Scott, ordanis thame to be summond to heir and se thame selffis decernit to pay the penalteis conteinit in our actis made thairanent and to sustein and underly the censuris conteinit in the actis of the generall assemblie under the paine of disobedience.

James Andirsonis text: The brethrein thinkis gude and ordeinis James Andirson, minister at Striviling, to teiche in his kirk the harmony of the Evangelistis, his commentaris to be Calveinis harmony, and Gwalteir on Louk with sic uther godlie and lernit wretaris as wrettis thairupone. Compeirit Mr Andro Grahame, minister at Dunblane, and acceptit on him offeice and plaice in this presbytery be solem promeis in the presens of God, his hand haldin up faythfullie to execute his offeice in teiching of the Word of God, ministratioun of the sacramentis and executioun of disciplein according to the same Word as alswa in exercesing with the brethrein and concuring with thame be his avys and jugement for tryell of sic thingis as salbe treattit in the presbytery unto the end of his lyf as it sall plais God to minister unto him the giftis of his Holie Spirit.

The act of the generall assemblie tuiching bischoppis intimat: The quhilk day ane act of the last generall assemblie was intimat to the brethrein gevand thame commissioun to accuse the bischoppis of Dunblane and Iyllis of certane offencis conteinit thairin as the samin at lynthe beris.

Mr Andro Grahame: Quhilk act beand red to the brethrein in presens of Mr Andro Grahame, the said Mr Andro was summond *apud acta* to compeir befoir the brethrein the xxv day of December instant in the parroche kirk of Striviling befoir none to answer to the accusatiounis conteinit in the said act and everie ane of thame as he salbe demandit undir the paine of disobedience and ordeinit the scryb to gif the copie of the said act to the said Mr Andro, to the quhilk ordinance the said Mr Andro aggreit and grantit his said wairning to be lauchfull.

Bischop off Iyllis: The brethrein ordanis that Johnne Campbell, bischop of the Iyllis, sasone as he may be apprehendit be summond to compeir befoir thame to answer to the accusationis conteinit in the said act of the generall assemblie and everie ane of thame as he salbe demandit undir the paine of disobedience and that becaus he is nocht presentlie in thir boundis.

James Leckie: The quhilk day compeirit James Leckie, brothur germane to Waltir Leckie of that Ilk, and confessit that promeis of mariage was made betuix him and Merjorie Erskein, and thairfor desyrit the brethrein to gif command to Patrik Gillaspie, thair minister, to proclame the said promeis lauchfullie, as effeiris, in thair parroche kirk of Sanct Ninian to the effect that mariage may be solemnizat betwix thame according to the ordur. It was askit at the said James gif he satisfiet ane formar ordinance of the bretherin in making of repentence as he was commandit. He answerit that he hade satisfeit the samin in all pointtis quhilk was varefeit be Patrik Gillaspie and Alexander Fargy, ministeris and ressavaris of the samin. The brethrein tuke to avys with thair answer to the said James desyr to the xviij December instant, the said James wairnit thairto *apud acta*.

At Striviling the xviij day of December, 1582

Presentes: James Andirson, Mr Andro Yung, Mr Andro Grahame, Alexander Fargy, Michaell Lermonthe and Mr Alexander Chisholme, ministeris; Mr Alexander Iule; Duncane Narne, elder; Mr Airthur Futhie and Mr Andro Knox, ministeris.

Mr Andro Grahame: The brethrein, understanding that on the nixt day of exerceis, viz., the xxv of this instant, is appointit to Mr Andro

H

Grahame to answer to the accusatiounis conteinit in the act of the generall assemblie that the brethrein may juge thairon, thinkis gude and ordeinis the said Mr Andro to mak the exerceis the said day to the effect the brethrein may juge on his doctrein alsweill as uthirwayis conforme to the said act.

Mr Arthur Futhie: Compeirit Mr Arthur Futhie, minister at Airthe, and acceptit on him offeice and plaice in this presbytery be solem promeis in the presens of God, his hand haldin up faythfullie to execute his offeice in teching of the Word of God, ministratioun of the sacramentis and executioun of disceplein according to the same Word unto the end of his lyf, as alswa in exercesing with the brethrein and concuring with thame be his avys and jugement for tryell of sic thingis as salbe trettit in the presbytery as it sall plais God to minister unto him the giftis of his Holie Spirit.

William Scott: The quhilk day William Scott, allegit to be admittit minister at the kirk of [*blank*], was desyrit gif he wald gif ane pruf of his doctrein to the brethrein quhairbe thai mycht knaw gif he could proffeit the flok quhomunto he was committit in teiching of the Word [of] God or nocht, answerit that glaidlie he wald gif thame ane prufe of his doctrein on sic text as thai wald appoint to him. The brethrein ordanis him to teiche privellie in the minister of Strivilingis chalmir on the xxix day of Januar nixt tocum, and that on the last part of the last chaptur of the evangelist Mathow.

Adulterar in Muthill: The quhilk day compeirit Andro McIlroy, parrochinnar in Muthill, and confessit him self mareit with Marione Gallway quha levis yit and that he hes gottin ane bairne by hir in adulterie with Agnes Sword, quhilk bairne was borne in November last, for the quhilk fault the brethrein ordanis the said Andro to pas to the nixt synnodall assemblie of this province to be haldin in Edinburgh the secund day of Aprill nixt, and in the mentyme ordanis and commandis the said Andro to separat him self fra the said Agnes Sword and remane fra hir societie and company under the paine of excommunicatioun.

Adulteraris in S. Ninianis parrochin: The quhilk day ane summondis producit lauchfullie execute and indorsit upone Thomas Johneson, adulterar with Margaret Murray, and Johnne Waltir, adulterar with Jonet Clark, chairgeing thame to compeir the said day to answer at the instance of the kirk and to heir and se thame selffis decernit to have contravenit the ordinanc of the brethrein, as at mair lynthe is conteinit in the summondis producit thairupone, compeirit the said Thomas Johnesone and confessit his disobedience and contravening of the ordinance befoir specefeit, and thairfor is ordeinit be the brethrein to entir to the plaice appointit for penitenttis within his parroche kirk of Sanct Niniane the nixt Sonday, and swa to continew ilk Sonday thaireftir to the nixt synnodall assemblie of this province, viz., the secund day of Aprill nixt undir the paine of excommunicatioun with certificatioun and he failze we will direct summondis *simpliciter* for pronuncing of the sentence [of] excommunicatioun againis him. The said Johnne Waltir, being oft tymis callit, compeirit nocht. Thairfor the brethrein decernis him to have contravenit the said ordinance and thairfor decervis to be execute and pronuncit againis him the paine thairin conteinit, viz., the sentence of excommunicatioun, and ordanis him to be summond to heir and se him self decernit to be excommunicat for his contemp and disobedience, with certificatioun and he failze, we will proceid and decern him to be excommunicat, as said is, according to the Word of God and disceplein of the kirk, havand the warrand thairof thairin.

At Striviling the xxv day of December, 1582

Presentes: James Andirson, Mr Andro Yung, Mr Andro Grahame, Mr Alexander Chisholme, Mr William Stirling, Patrik Gillaspie and Michaell Lermonthe, ministeris; Mr Duncane Nevein, Mr James Pont, Mr Alexander Iule, Alexander Forester of Garden, Umphra Cunynghame, commissar of Striviling, Robert Alexander, William Norwall and Duncane Narne, elderis.

Mr Andro Grahame: The quhilk day Mr Andro Grahame made the exerceis according to the ordinance in the last sessioun on the ordinarie text of exerceis, quhilk begouthe in the first chaptur of the epistill wrettin to the Ephesianis at the 13 vers and red to the xv vers of the samin exclusive, and inquisitioun of his doctrein being tane was fund sound and proffitabllle, and was admonesit to exerceis him self mair diligentlie in tyme cuming nor he did befoir, quhilk he promesit to obey.

Mr Andro Grahame: In the terme assignit to Mr Andro Grahame to answer to the heddis conteinit in the act of the generall assemblie, the said Mr Andro compeirand personallie and being accusit thairupone as eftir follwis particularlie, viz., for non preiching of the Word and administratioun of the sacramentis, negligence of doctrein and disceplein, hanting and frequenting the cumpany of excommunicat personis and namelie the excommunicantis in Dunblane and Mr Robert Montgumrie, geving collatiounis of beneficis againis the actis of the generall assemblie, for geving sclandir ony wayis in lyf and conversatioun and finellie for wasting and delapidatioun of the patrimony of the kirk and setting of takis thairof againis the saidis actis of the generall assemblie, as in ane act of the last generall assemblie direct to the brethrein of this presbytery for tryell of the said Mr Andro and bischop of Iyllis at mair lynthe is conteinit of the det at Edinburgh the xiij day of October, the yeir of God, etc., lxxxij yeiris. The said Mr Andro answerit as follwis. *In primis*, to the first, quhair he is accusit for non preiching of the Word and administratioun of the sacramentis and siclyk for negligence of doctrein and disceplein, ansorit that he hade nocht preichit the Word nor made ministratioun of the sacrementis nather exercesit disceplein in the kirk of Dunblane, as his propir kirk appointit to him to serve at, the speace of ane yeir bypast, excusand his absence and negligence in the premisis be ther twa occasionis, first for taking ordur with ane certane portioun of landis and leving quhilk he hade in the northe parttis that thairthrw heireftir he sould nocht be abstractit from his foirsaid cure in thir parttis. The uthir occasioun was the lang seiknes of his wyf in the northe partis quha thair departit this lyf. Secundlie, being accusit for hanting with excommunicat personis and speciallie the personis foirsaidis, he denyit the samin *simpliciter* and refarrit him to the testimony of the brethrein of Dunblane quha beand present testefeit him to be innocent of that hed of accusatioun. Thridlie, being accusit for geving of collationis of beneficis againis the actis of the generall assemblie, ansorit he nevir gaif ony collatioun of beneficis to na persone sen his admissioun to the foirsaid bischoprie, as the foirsaid bretherein in Dunblane present knew and being demandit thairof affermit the same. Ferdlie, being accusit of his lyf and conversatioun answerit that as he undirstude he hade gevin na occasioun of sclandir thairin and refarrit the testimony thairof to his brethrein foirsaid. The said Mr Andro beand removit and the brethrein of Dunblane in speciall beand requyrit on thair conscience to testefie the trewthe thairintill answerit all in ane voice thai knew na thing in his lyf bot godlienes and honestie. Fyftlie, being accusit for wasting and delapidatioun of the patrimony of the kirk and setting of takis thairof againis the actis of the generall assemblie, the said Mr Andro desyrit to knaw quhat was dilapidatioun of the patrimony, to quhom it was ansorit that setting of fewis or takis of landis or teindis with diminutioun of the auld dewatty, setting of victuell for small pricis of silvir, geving of pentionis, namelie, to unqualefeit personis and siclyk was delapidatioun, quhairupone he requyrit the first day of Januar to be advysit with sic thingis as he hade done thairanent sen his entrie to the said bischoprie quhilk was grantit unto him, and he ordenit to gif in particularlie in wrett, all fewis, takis of teindis, utheris settis and pensionis made and gevin be him, quhome to, quhow lang, for quhat dewatty, the said day.

The quhilk day ane bill of complent was gevin in be Johnne Drummond of Petzallany againis the said Mr Andro Graham in name of the said Johnne and remanent possessuris and tennents of the kirk landis of the bischoprik of Dunblane, makand mentioun that the said Mr Andro, quhome he callis bischop of Dunblane, hes nocht onelie to the grit hurt, damnage and skayth of his successuris bot alswa to the extreim hurt of us, possessuris and tennentis of the saidis kirk landis, sauld, delapidat and put away the haill leving of the said bischoprie or at the lest ane gret part thairof in gret menis handis by us, the saidis possessuris and kyndlie tennentis, as at mair lynthe is conteinit in the bill gevin in thairupone. The brethrein assignis the first day of Januar to the said Mr Andro Grahame to answer thairto *partibus apud acta citatis*.

Elezabeth Chisholme: Anent ane bill of complent gevin in be Elezabethe Chisholm, relict of umquhill Alexander Drummond of Megur, makand mentioun that quhair hir said umquhill spous and scho had, lyk as thay have, in tak the teindis of the landis of Kinbukis pertening to my lord Drummond in heritage and albeit the said Elezabeth hade dyvirs tymis requyrit Andro, bischop of Dunblane, to renew hir saidis takis quha onnawayis will do the samin bot maist ungodlie intendis to set the samin to utheris ovir hir hed, as scho allegis, as at mair lynthe is conteinit in the said bill gevin in be hir thairupone, the said Andro, bischop of Dunblane, compeirand

personallie promesit solemnitlie nocht to do na wrang to the said
Elezabeth in setting of ony tak of the teindis foirsaidis to na persone
nor personis ovir the said Elezabethis hed without the advys and
consent of the kirk hade and obteinit be him thairto.

Marione Forfar: The brethir undirstanding that forsamekill as
upone the xxv day of September last bypast Marione Forfar in
Dunblane was decernit be thame to be excommunicat for hir contemp and disobedience to the voice of the kirk, as at mair lynthe is
conteinit in our said decreit of the det foirsaid, nochttheles the
brethrein undirstanding na executioun to have follwit as yit on thair
said decreit, thairfoir the brethrein ordanis and commandis Maisteris
Andro Grahame and Andro Yung, ministeris at Dunblane, or ony
of thame to proceid this nixt Sonday publictlie to the first admonitioun againis the said Marione Forfar and to report thair executioun
thairof to us in the nixt sessioun as thai will answer thairupone.

At Striviling the first day of Januar, 1582

Presentes: James Andirsone, Patrik Gillaspie, Mr Alexander
Chisholm, Michaell Lermonthe, Mr William Stirling, Mr Andro
Graham, ministeris; Mr James Pont, Mr Alexander Iule, Umphra
Cunynghame, Duncane Narne and Robert Alexander, elderis.

Robert Mentayth: The quhilk day ane summondis beand producit
lauchfullie execute and indorsit upone Robert Mentayth, minister,
chairgeing him to have compeirit the said day to answer at the
instance of the kirk for his absence fra the exerceis, as at mair lynthe
is conteinit in the saidis summondis producit thairupone, compeirit
[*blank*] Mentayth, his sone, and producit ane wreting of the said
Robert Mentaythis declairand that he was veseit be God with seiknes
that he mycht nocht be present. Quhilk excuse was fund ane ressonablle [*sic*] be the brethrein, and thairfoir remittit the said Robert for
his absence.

Mr Adame Mairschell: The quhilk day ane summondis producit
deulie execute and indorsit upone Mr Adame Merschell, chairgeing
him to have compeirit the said day to answer at the instance of the
kirk for his frequent absence fra the exerceis, as at mair lynthe is
conteinit in the said summondis, quhilk Maister Adame being oft
tymis callit compeirit nocht, thairfor the brethrein ordanis the said

Mr Adame to be summond of new to the effect foirsaid undir the paine of excommunicatioun.

Mr Andro Grahame: The quhilk day being assignit be the brethrein to Mr Andro Grahame to gif in, particularlie in wrett, all fewis, takis of teindis, utheris settis and pentionis made and gevin be him sen his entrie to the bischoprik of Dunblane to be veseit be the brethrein, compeirit the said Mr Andro Grahame and producit ane inventer of the fewis and takis sett be him, as it beris in the self, declairand that gif ony thing was omittit furth of the said inventar the samin was only inrespect of immemorie, quhairof gif he him self rememberit heireftir or gif ony faythfull brothur wald call him to rememberance of ony thing omittit, he wald glaidlie gif it in to the brethrein as he hes done presentlie, with the quhilk inventar producit the brethrein tuke to avys to the viij day of Januar instant, the said Mr Andro warnit thairto *apud acta*. The quhilk day being assignit be the brethrein to Mr Andro Grahame to answer to ane bill of complent producit be Johnne Drummond of Petzallany againis him compeirit the said Mr Andro and producit ane answer thairto, as it beris in the self. The brethrein at the desyr of the said Johnne Drummond assignis to him the viij day of Januar instant to reply to the said answer producit be the said Mr Andro *partibus apud acta citatis*.

Johnne Drummond off Petzallany: The quhilk day James Andirsone, moderatour, in the name and at command of the brethrein declairit and exponit to the said Johnne Drummond of Petzallany that forsamekill as he hade producit befoir thame ane bill of complent againis Mr Andro Grahame to the quhilk he hade ansorit as the proces beris, in the quhilk matter the brethrein wald tak sic tryell as becumis thame and minister ecclesiasticall disceplein to ather of thame according to Goddis Word, and seing that the said Mr Andro Grahame be the ordinance of the generall kirk was subject to the censuris and disceplein to be pronuncit be thame, thairfor desyrit the said Johnne Drummond of Petzallanie to declair thame gif he wald willinglie submit him self to the jurisdictioun of the presbytery of Striviling in this caus and sustein the censuris of the kirk to be pronuncit be thame. Ansorit that glaidlie he wald submit him self to thair jurisdiction in censures and disceplein in this caus and obey the same as he sould be commandit. The same day compeirit the said Johnne Drummond of Petzallany and for instructioun of the bill of complent producit be him aganis the said Mr Andro Grahame he producit ane inventar of the yeirlie dewattie pertening to the bischoprik of Dunblane (as he undirstude), as it beris in the self.

Johnne Waltir, adulterar in S. Niniane parrochin: The quhilk day compeirit Johnne Waltir in Touchadame, adulterar with Jonet Clark, the man mareit, and confessit his lang disobedience to the kirk and contravening of our ordinance and injunctioun gevin to him on the vj day of Fabruar last bypast and thairfoir submittis him self in will of the brethrein and promesit to obey the same in tymis cuming. The brethrein, having diligentlie wyit and considderit his lang disobedience and cryme of adulterie committit be him, decernis and ordanis him to mak publict repentence at the plaice appointit for penitenttis in his parroche kirk of S. Niniane ilk Sonday quhill the brethrein be satisfeit thairwith undir the paine of excommunicatioun with certificatioun and he failze we will direct summondis *simpliciter* for pronunceing of the sentence of excommunicatioun againis him.

At Striviling the viij day of Januar, 1582

Presentes: James Andirsone, Patrik Gillaspie, Mr Andro Grahame, Mr William Stirling, Michaell Lermonthe, Mr Arthur Futhie, Mr Andro Yung, Alexander Fargy, ministeris; Mr James Pont, commissar of Dunblane, Umphra Cunynghame, commissar of Striviling, Mr Alexander Iule, Robert Alexander, William Norwall, elderis; William Striviling; William Drummond of Miln of Nab, minister; Sir James Stirling of Keir, knycht, provest.

William Stirling: The quhilk day ane summondis beand producit lauchfullie execute and indorsit upone William Stirling, reder, chairgeing him to compeir this day to answer at the instance of the kirk for his absence fra the exerceis certane dayis conteinit in the said summondis, compeirit the said William Stirling, and, being desyrit be the moderatour to declair the caus of his absence fra the exerceis and nocht awaitting to teiche in the secund plaice on the iiij day of December last bypast and lykwys for his absence on the xj day of the said moneth and nocht making of the exerceis on the samin day as he aucht to have done, answerit that ane lytill befoir the first day of his absence he fell and hurt his leg that he mycht nocht keip nane of the saidis dayis, quhilk excuse the brethrein fand ressoablle. Secundlie,

being accusit for mareing of Jonet Crystesone on William Michell
in Coustrie, the said Jonet havand ane uthir husband as yit alyve
callit Andro Wilsone in Waster Lainrik, quha lykwys hade committit adultrie in getting of ane bairne with Johnne Muschet in the
parrochin of Kincardin, the said William denyit the said accusatioun
simpliciter. Thridlie, being accusit for mareing of James Leckie,
brothur to Waltir Leckie of that Ilk, and Jonet Leckie togethir in ane
barne albeit he denyit the samin of befoir, and thairfoir was desyrit
to declair the trewthe thairof, the said William, yit as of befoir,
denyit that he compleitit ony mariage betuix the said James and
Jonet, bot grantis that in his presens mutuall promeis was made be
the said James and Jonet to utheris to compleit mariage togethir on
Sonday nixt eftir the fest of peace nixt thaireftir, according to the
said Jonettis confessioun thairof made befoir the brethrein on the
xxvij day of November last bypast. Fourtlie, the said William being
accusit for selling of the sacrament of baptisme in taking of silvir
thairfoir and siclyk for mariagis, the said William denyis the samin
simpliciter. For the bettir tryell of the said accusatiounis layit to
the chairge of the said William, the brethrein ordanis and gevis
commissioun to Mr William Stirling and Michaell Lermonthe, ministeris, to tak privie inquisitioun tuiching the saidis accusationis in
sic plaicis and of sic personis as thai may have the best tryell thairof,
and quhat thai find thairby to report againe to the sessioun.

Duncane Carrik decernit excommunicat: The quhilk day ane summondis beand producit lauchfullie execut and indorsit upone
Duncane Carrik in Kippen chairgeing him to have compeirit befoir
the brethrein the said day to have hard and sein him self decernit to
be excommunicat for his contemp and disobedience, as the said
summondis at mair lynthe beris, quhilk Duncane being oft tymis
callit, compeirit nocht, the brethrein, having diligentlie wyit and
deiplie considderit the said Duncanis gret obstinacie and manifest
contemp of the lauchfull chairgis of the kirk besyd the odius cryme
of adultrie allegit committit be him, ordanis and decernis the said
Duncane to be excommunicat and cuttit aff fra the societie of Chrystis kirk and to be delyverit into the handis of the devill for the
destructioun of his flesche that his saull may be saif in the day of the
Lord Jesus. The brethrein ordanis and commandis William Stirling
to proceid the nixt Sonday in geving of admonitioun according to

the ordur of the kirk to Duncane be the nixt Sonday that he obey
the voice of the kirk and satisfie the command thairof undir the
paine of excommunicatioun and the said William to report his
executioun againe to the sessioun.

Mr Andro Graham: The quhilk day being assignit to [be, *deleted*] the
brethrein to pronunce thair avysment on the inventar of the fewis
and takis sett be the bischop of Dunblane of the bischoprie thairof
producit be him, the brethrein being ryplie avysit thairwith findis
the samin nocht sufficient nathir in generall nor particular. First,
tuiching the generall, quhair all delapidatioun of the patrimony of
the kirk is devydit be him in twa heddis, viz., in setting of landis in
few and in setting of teindis in tak within the just availl, quhilk
divisioun is fund be the brethrein nocht to comprehend the haill
pointis of dilapidatioun becaus dilapidatioun may be in setting of
lang takis of landis within the just availl or lyverentis alsweill as
fewis, and in geving of pentionis in lyverentis out of the patrimony
to temporall personis. Secundlie, as tuiching the particularis, the said
Mr Andro in the inventar producit be him confessis that thair is mony
landis and teindis of the said bischoprie set be him sen his entrie bot
specefeis nocht quhw lang speace the takis ar sett nor for quhat
yeirlie dewatty nor for quhat pricis ilk boll of victuell is sett for,
alsweill of the few landis as of the takis of teindis, nather yit quhat
was the auld dewatty befoir the setting sett be him, lykwys nocht
specefeand qua possessit the landis and teindis of befoir and quhome
to thai ar sett now, and thairfoir the brethrein ordanis the said Mr
Andro to gif in and produce befoir thame the xv day of this instant
ane new inventar concerning the haill fewis and takis alsweill of
landis as of teindis set be him and pentionis gevin be him to quhatsumevir persone sen his entrie with direct answer in everie ane of
thame to everie ane of the heddis abone writtin. The said Mr Andro
Grahame being desyrit to declair gif he hes sett ony of the assumit
thrid of the bischoprik of Dunblane to ony persone or personis, the
said Mr Andro confessis he hes set nane thairof and promesis to sett
nane of the samin in tymis cuming. The said Mr Andro is admonesit
nocht to styll him self bischop in tymis cuming nather be word nor
wrett according to the ordinance of the generall assemblie.

Buikis of disceplein: It is thocht gude and ordeinit be the brethrein
that ilk minister within the boundis of this presbytery bring and

produce befoir the brethrein thair buikis and proces of the disciplein usit be thame in thair particular sessionis on the xix day off Fabruar nixt to be sein and considderit be thame to the effect ane uniform and generall ordur of disceplein may be establischit, usit and execute within the boundis of this presbytery without ony discrepance in tymis cuming.

Petzallany contra *Mr Andro Graham*: In the terme assignit to Johnne Drummond of Petzallany to reply to ane answer producit be Mr Andro Grahame to ane bill of complent gevin in be the said Johnne Drummond againis the said Mr Andro, compeirit the said Johnne Drummond and producit ane reply to the said answer, as it beris in the self, and for verefeing of certane allegencis conteinit thairin producit ane instrument undir signe and subscriptioun of Andro Drummond, notar publict, of the dett the xxj day of *Junij anno* etc., lxxix, testefeand that the said Mr Andro faythfullie promesit to caus my lord of Montrois lett the rowmis and possessionis of the kyndlie tennentis and possessuris to be possessit be thame as of befoir, as at mair lynthe is conteinit thairin, and lykwys producit the copie of ane oblegatioun made be the said lord of Montrois to the said Mr Andro, as the samin beris in the self. The brethrein at the desyre of the said Mr Andro assignis to him the xv day of this instant to answer to the said reply producit be the said Johnne *partibus apud acta citatis*.

At Striviling the xv day of Januar, 1582

Presentes: James Andirsone, Mr Andro Grahame, Mr Andro Yung, Mr William Stirling, Robert Mentayth, Mr Arthur Futhie, Patrik Gillaspie, Michaell Lermonthe, Alexander Fargy, ministeris; Mr Alexander Iule, ane brothur of exerceis, Adame commendatar of Cambuskynneth, Mr James Pont, Umphra Cunynghame, elderis; and Mr Johnne Broun.

James McKie, Jane Stewart: The brethir undirstanding that forsamekill as upone the xxvij day of November 1582 James McKie and Jane Stewart war decernit be thame to be excommunicat for thair contemp and disobedience to the voice of the kirk, as at mair lynthe is conteinit in our said decreit of the dett foirsaid, nochtwithstanding the brethrein understanding na executioun to have follwit as yit on thair said decreit, thairfor the brethrein ordanis and commandis Alexander Fargy, minister to the saidis personis, to proceid this nixt Sonday publictlie to the first admonitioun againis the said James and Jane and to report his executioun thairof to us in the nixt sessioun as he will answer thairupone.

Adulteraris in Tullicultry: Robert Mentayth, minister at Alvayth, beand requyrit gif he hade admonesit lauchfullie according to the ordur William Wat in Tullicultrie and Jonet Dugy (quha ar decernit to be excommunicat) to obey the kirk and disceplein thairof befoir the pronunceing of the sentence of excommunicatioun againis thame, the said Robert Mentayth ansorit that he hade admonesit lauchfullie the saidis personis twa sindrie Sondayis and saw na repentence of thair disobedience nor fault. Thairfor the brethrein ordanis the said Robert to proceid according to the ordur and report his executionis to the brethrein.

Mr Andro Graham: The quhilk day Mr Andro Grahame being desyrit to produce ane new inventar contening the haill fewis and takis, alsweill of landis as of teindis, sett be him of the bischoprik of Dunblane conform to the ordinance made in the last sessioun, the said Mr Andro compeirand personallie and declairit that inrespect of schortnes of tyme he had nocht as yit rememberit sufficientlie on all sic things as he was ordeinit to specefie in the said inventar and thairfor promesit to avys farther and produce the said inventar the xxij day of Januar instant.

Petzallany contra *Mr Andro Grahame*: In the terme assignit to Mr Andro Grahame to answer to ane reply produced be Johnne Drummond of Petzallany compeirit the said Mr Andro and producit ane answer thairto, as it beris in the self, with the quhilk and remanent proces deducit betuix the saidis parteis the brethrein will advys, as thai find occasioun.

Bischop off Iyllis: The quhilk day ane summondis beand producit lauchfullie execute and indorsit upone Mr Johnne Campbell, bischop of Iyllis, chairgeing him to compeir the said day to answer upone the heddis conteinit in ane act of the generall assemblie, as at mair lynthe is conteinit in the said summondis, compeirit the said Mr Johnne personallie at quhais desyr the brethrein assignit to him the xxij day of Januar instant to answer to the heddis conteinit in the said act and everie ane of thame as he salbe particularlie demandit, on the quhilk day he is ordeinit to mak the exerceis that the brethrein may have ane pruif of his doctrein also.

Follwis the tennour of the said act of the generall assemblie.

Act of the generall assembly tuiching bischoppis:

Acta sessionis 9a xiijo Octobris, 1582

Anent bischopis, seing the gret sclandir and offence rissin to the haill kirk of this realme be thair impunitie and ovirsicht to the greif of gude menis consciencis, the haill assemblie hes gevin and gevis commissioun to the particular presbyteriis under specefeit with all possiblle and convenient diligence to summond and call befoir thame everie ane as thai be particularlie divydit in manir follwing, that is to say, the presbyterie of Perthe, the bischop of Murray; the presbytery of Edinbrugh, the bischop of Abirdein; the presbytery of Mernis, the bischop of Brechin; the presbyterie of Dundy, the bischop of Dunkell; the presbyterie of Glasgw, the bischop of Sanctandrus; the presbiterie of Striviling, the bischoppis of Dunblane and Iyllis; and to accuse thame and everie ane of thame of the offencis follwing, all or part, as thai ar giltie, viz., of non preiching and ministratioun of the sacramentis, of negligence of doctrein or disceplein hanting and frequenting the cumpanie of excommunicat personis, waisting of the patrimony of the kirk, setting of takis againis the actis of the kirk geving collationis of beneficis againis the tennour of the same actis and finallie for geving sclandir ony wayis in lyf and conversatioun and eftir dew tryell, proces and convictioun to put ordur to everie ane of thame according to the qualetie of thair offencis and actis of the assemblie betuix and the nixt meitting of the haill kirk as thai will answer thairto. Extract, etc.

At Striviling the xxij day of Januar, 1582

Presentes: James Andirsone, Mr Andro Grahame, Mr William Stirling, Mr Alexander Chisholme, Alexander Fargy, Michaell Lermonthe, Mr Andro Yung, Patrik Gillaspie, Johnne Duncansone, ministeris; Mr Alexander Iule, ane brothur of the exerceis; Umphra Cunynghame, William Norwall, elderis; and Sir James Stirling of Keir, knycht, provest.

Bischop of Iyllis: The quhilk day Mr Johnne Campbell, bischop of the Iyllis, made the exerceis according to the ordinance made in the last sessioun on the ordinarie text of exerceis, quhilk begouthe in the 2 chaptur of the epistle wretin to the Ephesians at the 8 vers and red to the 14 vers of the samin exclusive, and inquisitioun of his doctrein being tane, the brethrein findis the samin generall aggreing with the grundis of religioun bot nocht sufficient in opning up the sence and mening of the said text. The said Mr Johnne, being admonesit thairof, declairit the caus thairof was in him self that tuke sa schort ane day to teiche, in the quhilk tyme he was swa occupyit in aggreing of certan his freindis in Glasgw that he hade ovir schort tyme to study. The moderatour, in name of the brethrein, admonesit him to be mair diligent in exercesing him self in teiching nor he hade bein of befoir, quhilk he promesit to do.

Marione Forfar: The quhilk day Mr Andro Yung and Mr Andro Grahame being inquyrit be the moderatour gif thay, or ony of thame, hade proceidit in admonitionis againis Marione Forfar, quha is decernit to be excommunicat, as thai war commandit or nocht ansorit the said Mr Andro Yung that he hade admonesit hir publictlie in pulpet this last Sonday, according to the ordur, to obey the voice of the kirk, and that as for the first admonitioun, and fand na obedience in hir as yit. Thairfor the brethrein ordanis him to proceid the nixt Sonday to the secund admonitioun againis hir and to report the samin in the nixt sessioun.

Excommunicantis in Dunblane: The same day the brethrein undirstanding the gret obstinacie and manifest contemp to the kirk done be sindrie personis in Dunblane, excommunicat and separat fra the societie of the faithfull, and in speciall be Sir William B[l]akwod, Sir William Drummond, Elezabeth Carnewethe, Agnes Cowall and Andro Blakwod, quha without all feir of God and the civill magistrat continewis and hes continewit this lang tyme past undir the sentence of excommunicatioun remaning still in cumpanie amangis the faythfull in contemp of the kirk and auctoritie thairof, thairfor the brethrein ordanis and commandis Mr Andro Grahame, bischop thairof, to use all lauchfull meinis he may of his offeice and auctoritie for expelling and removing of the saidis personis and all utheris excommunicantis (gif ony be within the said toun) furthe of the cumpanie of the faithfull thair, as he will answer to the brethrein thairupone.

James McKie: The quhilk day compeirit James McKie personallie quha was decernit be our decreit to be excommunicat for his contemp and disobedience as our decreit of the dett the xxvij day of November last bypast at mair lynthe beris and grantit that he hade offendit God in disobeying the voice of his kirk be the odius cryme of adultrie committit be him with Jane Stewart, for the quhilk he offerit and promesit to obey quhat the brethrein wald command him for his saidis offencis and confessit farder that he hade alreddy separatit him self fra the said Jane Stewart and promesit nevir in tymis cuming to ressave againe hir in cumpany with him. The brethrein decernis and ordanis the said James McKie to pas to the nixt provinciall assemblie of the presbyteriis of Edinburgh, Dalkayth, Lynlithquow and Striviling to be haldin in Edinburgh, the secund day of Aprill nixt tocum thair to ressave his injunctionis for the adultrie committit with the said Jane and to obey thame undir the paine of excommunicatioun, with certificatioun and he failze we will direct our precept *simpliciter* for pronunceing of the sentence of excommunicatioun becaus the samin hes bein twa sindrie tymis decernit againis him alreddy for the said fault and disobedience jonit thairwith, quhilk the said James promesit to obey.

Jane Stewart: The quhilk day Alexander Fargy, minister at Logy, being desyrit gif he proceidit this last Sonday in the first admonitioun againis Jane Stewart, adultrix with James McKie, as he was ordeinit in the last sessioun, the said Alexander answerit that the said Jane was fugeteive furth of his parrochin befoir Sonday last (and as it was allegit to him) that scho was presentlie dwelland in Striviling with Johnne Stewart, servand to the kingis majestie. The brethrein commandis the minister of Striviling to admoneis the said Jane in the sessioun thairof on the xxiiij day of Januar instant to obey the kirk and voice thairof, and to requyr hir gif scho will compeir befoir the brethrein the xxix of this instant and satisfie the brethrein thairanent, quhilkis gif scho will nocht obey or at the lest promeis obedience, as said is, ordanis the said minister to proceid againis hir this nixt Sonday in publict admonitionis according to the ordur.

William Michell, Jonet Crystesone: The brethrein undirstanding ane gret brute to be rissin that William Stirling in Port hes compleitit mariage betuix William Michell in Coustrie and Jonet Crystesone (the said Jonet beand ane adultrix convict) by Andro Wilson, ane uther husband of hiris, quha is yit alyve, nochtwithstanding that the said William hes alreddy denyit the samin, thairfor and for the bettir tryell thairof ordanis the said William and Jonet to be summond to answer at the instance of the kirk for sic thingis as salbe requyrit at thame undir the paine of disobedience.

William Stirling: The quhilk day Mr William Stirling and Michaell Lermonthe, being inquyrit be the moderatour quhat thai hade done tuiching the inquisitioun thai war commandit to tak anent the accusatiounis that was layd againis William Stirling, answerit that sensyne thai hade done na thing thairintill bot promesit to tak inquisitioun thairanent, as thai war commandit and quhat thai fand thairby to report the samin to the brethrein of the fyft day of Fabruar nixt tocum.

Mr Andro Grahame: The quhilk day Mr Andro Grahame being desyrit to produce ane new inventar contening the haill fewis and takis aswell of landis as of teindis set be him of the bischoprik of Dunblane, conform to his promeis in the last sessioun, the said Mr Andro compeirand personallie allegis as yit that inrespect of schortnes of tyme he hade nocht made the said inventar swa perfyt as was requysit and thairfor promesit to produce the samin sufficient on the xxix day of Januar instant according to the brethreinis ordinance made thairanent.

Mr Johnne Campbell: The quhilk day being assignit to Mr Johnne Campbell, bischop of Iyllis, to answer to the heddis conteinit in the act of the generall assemblie of the dett at Edinburgh the xiij day of October 1582 and everie ane of thame as follwis in the said act, compeirit personallie the said Mr Johnne and being accusit thairupone as eftir follwis particularlie, viz., for nonpreiching of the Word and administratioun of the sacramentis, negligence of doctrein and disceplein, hanting and frequenting the cumpany of excommunicat personis, namelie, Mr Robert Montgumrie and Colein Campbell in Glasgw, geving callationis of beneficis againis the actis of the generall assemblie, for geving sclandir onywayis in lyf and conversatioun and finallie for wasting and dilapidatioun of the patrimony of the kirk and setting of takis thairof againis the saidis actis of the generall assemblie, as at mair lynthe is conteinit in the said act of the det foirsaid. The said Mr Johnne answerit as follwis. *In primis*, to the first quhair he is accusit for nonpreiching of the Word and administratioun of the sacramentis and for negligence in doctrein and disceplein answerit that he preichit the Word and ministrat the sacramentis at the kirk of Ycolumkill quhill the beginning of Merche *anno* 1580, at the quhilk tyme my lord McLane discordit with him for reducein of ane certane few set to him be Mr Johnne Carswall, his predicessur, thrw the quhilk discord he was compellit to lave that cuntrie at that tyme and sensyne hes nocht resortit thair, bot eftir he come in Argyll he preichit and ministrat the sacramentis in the kirk of Ardchattane oft tymis quhen he was thair. Farder, the said Mr Johnne confessit that he come to the lawland nocht lang eftir the said discord, as said is, quhair he remainit the speace of half ane yeir in sutting remeddis fra the king and councell for wrangis done to him be the said McLane, during the quhilk tyme he preichit in na plaice. Being accusit for non-executing of disceplein, answerit that quhen he teichit, he executit disceplein as occasioun servit. Secundlie being accusit for hanting with excommunicat personis, namelie, Mr Robert Montgumrie and Collein Campbell in Glasgw, answerit and confessit that Mr Robert Montgumrie send ane wreting to him in the nycht to cum and speik with him, quhilk he refusit *simpliciter* and denyit ony farther with him in confirrence athir be word or wrett sen he was excommunicat. As tuiching the said Collein, he answerit that he nevir spak with him sen he was excommunicat quhill he hade entirat in satisfeing the injunctionis of the kirk and hade bein twys befoir the kirk in secclayth and denyis cumpany and confirrence with all uthir excommunicantis. Thridlie, being accusit for geving of callatiounis of beneficis againis the actis of the generall assemblie, answerit that he gave sum collatiounis befoir the said act, bot nane sensyne. Ferdlie, being accusit of his lyf and conversatioun answerit that as he undirstude he hade gevin na occasioun of sclandir thairin and refarrit the testimony thairof to quhatsumevir brethrein it sould plais the brethrein of this presbytery to inquyr of in hieland or law land. Fyftlie, being accusit for wasting and dilapidatioun of the patrimony of the kirk and setting of takis thairof againis the actis of the generall assemblie, answerit that he hade nathir sett fewis nor takis to na persone of the patrimony thairof bot sen his entires had reducit ane few sett to my lord Macclane be Mr Johnne Carswall his predicessur.

The brethrein, being avysit with the said Mr Johnnis answeris havand na farther testimony thairof bot his awin confessioun, thocht

I

gude and ordeinit publict edickis to be direct to the parroche kirkis of Ycolumkill and Ardchattan, makand intimatioun to all personis of the commissioun gevin to this presbytery be act of the generall assemblie for trying of the said Mr Johnne in the heddis abone specefeit, chairgeing all and quhatsumevir that hes ony thing to object againis the said Mr Johnne in the offencis foirsaidis that thai compeir befoir the said presbytery the xxvj day of Merche nixt, and lykwys that ane edict be direct of the forme foirsaid with the copie of the said act of the generall assemblie to Mr Neill Campbell and remanent brethrein of Argyll, makand intimatioun to thame lykwys of our said commissioun for tryell of the said Mr Johnne, as said is, desyrand thame to report to us faythfullie quhat thai knaw in him concerning the heddis foirsaidis, and everie ane of thame betuix and the xxvj day of Merche foirsaid, as thai will answer to the generall assemblie of the kirk thairupone.

James Leckie: The quhilk day ane summondis beand producit lauchfullie execute and indorsit upone James Leckie chairgeing him to compeir the said day to heir and se the brethreinis avysement and sentence pronuncit anent thair command desyrit be the said James to be gevin to Patrik Gillaspie, his minister, to proclame lauchfullie, as effeiris, ane promeis of mariage made betuix him and Merjorie Erskein and thaireftir to solemneiz mariage betuix thame, the said James compeirand personallie the brethrein as yit nocht being fully avysit thairwith continewis thair jugementis thairin to farthir confirrence that thai may be farther resolvit of all douttis thairintill.

Pyper, William Wricht: The quhilk day ane summondis beand producit lauchfullie execute and indorsit upone Thomas Edmane, pyper, and William Wricht in Nathir Inveralloun to compeir the said day to answer at the instance of the kirk for sic thingis as sould have bein layit to thair chairgis undir the paine of disobedience, quhilk personis being oft tymis callit compeirit nocht, thairfor the brethrein ordanis thame to be summond of new to the effect foirsaid undir the paine of excommunicatioun.

At Striviling the xxix day of Januar, 1582

Presentes: James Andirson, Alexander Fargy, Mr William Stirling, Mr Arthur Futhie, Patrik Gillaspie, Mr Alexander Chisholme, Michaell Lermonthe and Mr Andro Yung, ministeris; William Scott, reder; Mr Alexander Iule, ane brothur of exerceis; Mr James Pont, Umphra Cunynghame, commissar of Striviling and William Norwall, elderis.

Marione Forfar: The quhilk day Mr Andro Yung, being requyrit gif he hade proceidit and gevin the secund admonitioun to Marione Forfar in Dunblane to obey and satisfie the kirk befoir the pronuncein of the sentence of excommunicatioun againis hir as he was ordeinit or nocht, ansorit that the said Marione promesit to compeir this day befoir the brethrein and satisfie the kirk, quha instantlie compeirit personallie and confessit hir to have offendit God in disobeying the voice of the assemblie of hir awin parroche, and lykwys the voice of this presbytery, for the quhilk scho offerit hir self to obey the command of the brethrein, and lykwys confessit hir to have committit fornicatioun with William Quhythed fyve yeir syne or thairby, and lykwys with Johnne Ure twa yeir syne or thairby, and that undir promeis of mariage with the said William and Johnne, for the quhilk fornicatioun committit be hir, as said is, the said Marione offeris hir self to obey the kirk. The brethrein being avysit with the said Marion disobedience to the voice of the kirk decernis and ordanis hir to mak publict repentence thairfor the nixt Sonday in the plaice appointit for penitenttis within hir parroche kirk of Dunblane, according to the ordur, and for the fornicatioun committit be hir, as said is, ordanis hir to mak publict repentence at the plaice foirsaid on Sonday the x day of Fabruar nixt and on the Sonday nixt thaireftir undir all hiest paine and chairge that eftir mycht follw be the censuris of the kirk.

Johnne Tailyour: The quhilk day compeirit Johnne Tailyour in the parrochin of Dunblane and confessit him to have committit a gret fault againis God in disobeying the voice of his awin kirk, for the quhilk he offeris him self in the will of the brethrein. The brethrein being avysit thairwith ordanis the said Johnne to mak publict repentence in his awin parroche kirk according to the ordur the nixt Sonday for his said disobedience and thaireftir to obey the voice of his awin kirk undir the paine of excommunicatioun.

Mr Andro Grahame: The quhilk day being assignit to Mr Andro Grahame to produce ane new inventar contening the haill fewis and takis, alsweill of landis as of teindis, set be him of the bischoprik of

Dunblane conform to his promeis on the xxij day of Januar instant, the said Mr Andro being oft tymis callit compeirit nocht. The brethrein ordanis him to be summond to compeir befoir thame the fyft of Fabruar nixt to produce befoir thame the inventar of the haill fewis, takis and pentionis gevin and set be him of the said bischoprik according to thair ordinance made on the viij day of Januar instant in all pointis undir the paine of disobedience.

Act of the generall assemblie for setting of fewis and takis, etc.: The quhilk day the extract of ane act of the generall assemblie made anent setting of fewis and takis of benefices etc., was intimat be the moderatour to the assemblie quhairof the tennour follwis.

Acta sessione 3a xiio *Julij*, 1578

Anent the penalty of bischoppis, ministeris and utheris berand functioun in the ministrie that settis, fewis and takkis of thair beneficis and ecclesiastik levingis or ony part thairof or ministeris in chapiteris that gevis thair consenttis thairto without the consent of the generall assemblie of the kirk againis the tennour of the actis made in assemblie befoir the kirk and assemblie present hes votit and concludit that the saidis personis quhilk sall happin to contravein the said act salbe depryvit frome thair officis and functiounis in tyme cuming. Extract, etc.

Jane Stewart: The quhilk day compeirit Jane Stewart, quha was decernit be decreit of the brethrein to be excommunicat for hir contemp and disobedience, as the samin of the dett the xxvij day of November last at mair lynthe beris, and grantit hir to have committit ane gret fault be hir said disobedience besyd the odius cryme of adultrie committit be hir with James McKie, for the quhilkis offencis the said Jane offeris hir self in the will of the kirk and promesis to obey thair ordinance, and farder confessit that scho had alreddy separatit hir self fra the said James McKie and sall nevir agane entir in cumpanie with him. The brethrein decernis and ordanis the said Jane to pas to the nixt provinciall assemblie of the presbyteriis of Edinburgh, Dalkayth, Linlythquow and Striviling to be haldin in Edinburgh the ij day of Aprill nixtocum thair to ressave [hir, *deleted*] injunctionis to be adjonit to hir for the adultrie committit be hir with the said James McKie and to obey thame undir the paine of excommunicatioun, with certificatioun and scho failze we will command the said sentence to be pronuncit againis hir according to the decreit alreddy pronuncit becaus the samin sentence hes bein 2 sindrie tymis decernit to be execut againis hir for the said adultrie and disobedience jonit thairwith, inrespect of the quhilkis ordanis the scryb to gif out testemoniall to testefie hir present obedience to the kirk.

Fundlein bairne : The quhilk day it was intimat to the brethrein be James Andirsone, minsiter at Striviling, that thair was ane mane chyld fund on ane gait syd, quhilk passis up fra the fut of Marie wynd to the castell of Striviling, quhilk now is [blank] yeiris of aige or thairby, quhilk nevir was knawin to have bein baptezit. Thairfor, William McNair, nuresar and fosterar of the said mane chyld, presentlie desyrit him to bapteis the said bairne, quhilk the said minister desyrit the brethreinis jugement thairanent. The brethrein being avysit thairwith eftir diligent inquisitioun being tane of the brethrein presentlie conveinit could nocht find quhair the said mane chyld hade bein baptezit befoir, thairfor thocht gude that the said minister of Striviling sould caus warne befoir the sessioun of his awin kirk the said William McNair, fosterar thairof, quhome he sould admoneis to teiche the said bairne the sowme of ane Christiane fayth, viz., the xij articillis of the beleif that he mycht gif ane confessioun thairof the tyme he ressavit the sacrament of baptisme and thaireftir the said minister to proceid and bapteis the said fundlein bairn lauchfullie according to the ordur.

William Scott : The quhilk day being appointit to William Scott, allegit admittit minister at the kirk of Callender, to teiche privallie in the minister of Strivilingis chalmir on the last part of the last chaptur of the evangelist Mathw, compeirit the said William and teichit on the said text with quhais teiching the brethrein of the ministrie present being avysit findis the samin sound and thairfor continewis him, as of befoir, to exhort unto his flok and minister baptisme quhill thai tak farder tryell of him.

At Striviling the fyft day of Fabruar, 1582

Presentes : James Andirsone, Johnne Duncansone, Mr Andro Grahame, Mr William Stirling, Patrik Gillaspie, Mr Alexander Chisholme, Michaell Lermonthe, Mr Andro Young, Alexander Fargy, ministeris; Mr James Pont, Alexander Patersone, William

Norwall, Duncane Narne, elderis; Mr Alexander Iule, ane brothur of exerceis; Sir James Stirling of Keir, knycht, provest; and Mr Johnne Stewart.

Exerceis beginnis at ix houris: The brethrein thinkis gude and ordeinis that the exerceis begin at ix houris befoir none inrespect of the lynthe [schort, *deleted*] of the day presentlie.

Mr Andro Graham: The quhilk day ane summondis beand producit lauchfullie execute and indorsit upone Mr Andro Grahame chairgeing him to compeir the said day and produce befoir the brethrein the inventar of the haill fewis, takis and pentionis gevin and set be him of the bischoprik off Dunblane, as at mair lynthe is conteinit in the said summondis, compeirit the said Mr Andro and producit ane inventar of the fewis, takis and pentionis gevin and sett be him, as it beris in the self, with the quhilk the brethrein tuke to avys to the xix day of Fabruar instant, the said Mr Andro wairnit thairto *apud acta*.

Buikis off disceplein: The quhilk day being appointit to the brethrein to produce thair buikis of disceplein to be veseit according to ane ordinance made thairanent on the viij day of Januar last bypast, it was ansorit that thai hade thame nocht present bot sould produce thame heireftir.

James Drummond: The quhilk day ane summondis beand producit lauchfullie execut and indorsit upone James Drummond, dwelland in the parrochin of Muthill, chairgein him to have compeirit the said day to answer at the instance of the kirk for fornicatioun allegit committit be him with Elezabeth Forsythe and to heir and se him self decernit to have committit the samin and to underly the censuris of the kirk thairfoir, as at mair lynthe is conteinit in the said summondis, the said James being oft tymis callit compeirit nocht. Thairfor the brethrein ordanis the said James to be summond of new to the effect foirsaid undir the paine of excommunicatioun.

William Stirling: The quhilk day Mr William Stirling and Michaell Lermonthe being desyrit to report to the brethrein quhat thai hade tryit be the privie inquisitioun that thai war commandit to tak anent the accusationis layit againis William Stirling, reder, ansorit that thai could nocht gait tryell of na fault in him excep that thair is ane gret bruit that he sould have mareit Jonet Crystesone, devorcit for adultrie fra Andro Wilson, hir husband, with ane uthir mane callit William Michell in Coustrie, and that na witnessis wald testefie to thame nor abyd be the same unles thai war summond befoir the presbytery. For tryell of the quhilk, the brethrein ordanis the said William Michell and Jonet Crystesone to be summond to answer at the instance of the kirk for sic thingis as sould be layit unto thair chairge undir the paine of disobedience.

At Striviling the xij day of Fabruar, 1582

Presentes: James Andirsone, Johnne Duncansone, Mr Andro Grahame, Mr Andro Yung, Michaell Lermonthe, Patrik Gillaspie, Mr Arthur Futhie, Alexander Fargy, ministeris; Mr Duncane Nevein, reder; Mr James Pont, Umphra Cunyngham, elderis; Mr Alexander Iule, ane brothur of exerceis; David, commendatar of Dryburgh; Johne Bruce of Auchinbowie and Mr Johnne Stewart.

Patrik Layng: The quhilk day ane summondis beand producit deulie execute and indorsit upone Patrik Layng chairgeing him to have compeirit the said day to answer at the instance of the kirk for his lang and frequent absence fra our exerceis and assembleis contenuallie sen the fourt day of September last bypast, as at mair lynthe is conteinit in the said summondis, the said Patrik being oft tymis callit compeirit nocht, thairfor ordanis the said Patrik to be summond of new to the effect foirsaid undir the paine off excommunicatioun.

James Lecky: The quhilk day ane summondis beand producit lauchfullie execute and indorsit upone James Leckie chairgeing him to compeir the said day to heir and se the brethreinis avysment and sentence pronuncit anent thair command desyrit be him to be gevin to Patrik Gillaspie, his minister, to proclame ane promeis of mariage made betuix him and Merjorie Erskein and thaireftir to solemneiz mariage betuix thame according to the ordur, the said James compeirand personallie, the moderatour in name of the brethrein declairit to the said James that it is the avys and jugement of the brethrein of the presbytery of Edinburgh that he sall nather be proclamit nor mareit with the said Marjorie for the causis conteinit in ane act maid anent the tryell of adultrie allegit committit be the said James with Jonet Leckie, of the dett the xxvij day of November last bypast, bot the brethrein of this presbytery suspendis thair jugementis and sentence thairin quhill thai be avysit with the brethrein of the nixt synnodall assemblie of this province to be haldin in Edinburgh the secund day of Aprill nixt, and decernis and ordanis the said James Leckie to separat him self fra the said Merjorie with all diligence and nocht to entir in cumpanie agane with hir bot remane fra hir societie quhill the brethreinis sentence be pronuncit thairintill undir the paine of excommunicatioun.

Robert Fogo: The quhilk day ane summondis beand producit lauchfullie execute and indorsit upone Robert Fogo in Doun chairgeing him to have compeirit the said day to answer at the instance of the kirk for sic thingis as sould have being layit unto his chairge undir the paine of excommunicatioun, quhilk Robert being oft tymis callit compeirit nocht. Thairfor the brethrein ordanis him to be summond to heir and se him self decernit to be excommunicat for his contemp and disobedience with certificatioun and he failze the brethrein will proceid and decern him to be excommunicat for the caus foirsaid according to the Word of God and disceplein of the kirk, havand the warrand thairof thairin.

Johnne Stevinsone, reder: The quhilk day Johnne Stevinsone, reder at the kirk of Kincardin, was accusit be the moderatour to declair the trewthe gif he hade proclaimit ane promeis of mariage allegit made betuix William Michell in Coustrie and Jonet Crystesone in the said kirk or nocht, the said Johnne confessit that he hade proclaimit the said promeis in the said kirk thre soverall Sondayis and na impediment was allegit to him in the contrar and thairfoir thaireftir he subscryvit ane testimoniall testefeand the same quhilk he delyverit to the said [*blank*]. The brethrein continewis farther tryell heirin quhill thai be farther avysit.

At Striviling the xix day of Fabruar, 1582

Presentes: James Andirsone, Patrik Gillaspie, Mr Andro Grahame, Mr William Stirling, Mr Alexander Chisholme, Mr Andro Yung, Alexander Fargy, Michaell Lermonthe, Patrik Layng, ministeris; Mr Alexander Iule, Mr James Pont, Umphra Cunynghame, elderis; William Scott, Mr Duncane Nevein and William Stirling, rederis; Sir James Stirling of Keir, knycht, provest; and Mr Johnne Stewart.

William Michell, Jonet Crysteson: The quhilk day ane summondis beand producit lauchfullie execute and indorsit upone William

Michell in Coustrie chairgeing him to compeir the said day to
answer at the instance of the kirk for sic thingis as salbe requyrit at
him, as at mair lynthe is conteinit in the said summondis, compeirit
the said William Michell and confessit him to be mareit with Jonet
Crystesone in the kirk of Kippen on ane Thurisday be William
Stirling, reder thairat, and confessit that thair bannis was lauchfullie
proclaimit in thair parroche kirk of Kincardin be Johnne Steinsone,
reder thairat. Lykwys, compeirit the said Jonet Crystesone and
confessit hir self to have bein mareit on Andro Wilsone, now in
Waster Lainrik, be Alexander Fargy, minister, in hir parroche kirk
of Kincardin fyve yeir syne or thairby quhome scho belevis be yit on
lyve and confessit that scho hade borne ane bairne gottin on hir in
adulterie be Johnne Muschet in Kincardin by hir said husband and
that scho was divorcit fra hir said husband thairfoir be Mr James
Pont, commissar of Dunblane, havand commissioun of the commissaris of Edinburgh to that effect, quhilk Mr James beand personallie present testefeit the samin and that the said Andro Wilsone
hade libertie be the samin decreit to marie in the Lord. Attour, the
said Jonet Crystesone confessit hir mareit at midsomir last bypast or
thairby on the said William Michell in the kirk of Kippen on ane
Thurisday be the said William Stirling, reder thairat, according to
the said William Michell confessioun in all pointtis. Mairattour,
compeirit the said William Stirling and confessit the mareing of the
said William Michell and Jonet Crystesone according to thair
confessionis, albeit he denyit the samin of befoir. The brethrein
continewis thair jugementis anent the mariage made betuix the said
William and Jonett, and anent the said William Stirling, quha made
the said mariage to the fyft day of Merche nixtocum, the said
William Michell, Jonet Crystesone and William Stirling warnit
thairto *apud acta*.

Patrik Layng: The quhilk day ane summondis beand producit
lauchfullie execute and indorsit upone Patrik Layng chairgeing him
to compeir the said day to answer at the instance of the kirk for his
lang and frequent absence fra our exerceis and assembleis contenuallie sen the iiij day of September last bypast, as at mair lynthe
is conteinit in the said summondis, compeirit the said Patrik Layng
and being accusit for his absence the speace foirsaid excusit the samin
for iij rassonis. First, that he hade bot ane small stepend of ane reder

to sustein his chairgis and his kirk and dwelling was fyve myll distant fra this toun and thairfor allegit he mycht nocht gudlie be astrictit to keip the exerceis ilk Tyisday. Secundlie, allegit that thrw the keiping of the exerceis in tymis past he hade tint his schulle thrw the quhilk he gat ane gret part of his leving. Thridlie, that thairthrw he hade tint ane offeice of ane court clark, thruch the quhilk he hade commoditie to leiv upone, and thairfoir desyrit the brethrein to accep his absence in gude pairt and he sould be efter present in tymis cuming. The brethrein being avysit with his saidis excusis accepis thame presentlie as thai ar of availl and ordenis him to ad in the exerceis on the xij of Merche and to mak thame on the xix day of Merche.

William Wingyett: The samin day compeirit William Wingyet in Touchadame and grantis fornicatioun with Jonet Johnesone in Couldinhuis and that as for the fourt fault in thame bayth, and the said William refusis to marie the said Jonet, for the quhilk he is decernit and commandit be the brethrein to pas to the nixt provinciall assemblie of this province to be haldin in Edinburgh the secund day of Aprill nixt thair to ressave his injunctionis for the said fault and to obey thame undir the paine of excommunicatioun with certificatioun and he failze, we will decerne the sentence thairof to be pronuncit againis him and for obedience of this our ordinance commandis the said William to act cautioun in the buikis of the commissar of Striviling betuix and the xxiiij day of this instant that he sall obey and fulfill this our ordinance, as said is, undir the painis conteinit in the actis of parliament and generall assemblie of the kirk.

Johnne Dow: The quhilk day ane summondis beand producit lauchfullie execute and indorsit upone Johnne Dow in Kildeis chairgeing him to compeir the said day to heir and se him self decernit to underly the censuris of the kirk for disobedience to the voice of the sessioun of his awin kirk and tryell tane in fornicatioun allegit committit be him with [*blank*], as the said summondis at mair lynthe beris, the said Johnne being oft tymis callit compeirit nocht, thairfor ordanis him to be summond of new to the effect foirsaid undir the paine of excommunicatioun.

Thomas Quhyt: The quhilk day ane summondis beand producit lauchfullie execute and indorsit upone Thomas Quhyt in Kildeis, allegit adulterar with Agnes Gentill, chairgeing him to compeir the said day to heir and se him self decernit to have committit the said adultrie, as at mair lynthe is conteinit in the said summondis, the said Thomas being oft tymis callit compeirit nocht. Thairfor the brethrein ordanis him to be summond of new to the effect foirsaid undir the pane of excommunicatioun.

Mr Andro Grahame: The quhilk day being appointit be the brethrein to avys with the inventar of the fewis, takis and pentionis gevin and sett be Mr Andro Grahame, bischop of Dunblane, of the bischoprik thairof sen his entrie thairto, the brethrein findis that the said Mr Andro confessis thairin that the fewis and takis sett be him sen his entrie ar set for the auld dewatty withe the pultrie, carrage of pettis and uthir arrage and carrage astrictit of auld to the bischop thairof, and the brethrein nocht being certefeit gif the pultrie, carrage of pettis and uthir arrage and carrage was now payit to the said bischop as thai war of auld or nocht. Thairfor the said Mr Andro, beand requyrit be the moderatour to declair the trewthe thairof, confessit that he hade sett the pultrie, carrage of pettis and uthir arrage and carrage for silvir bot rememberit nocht the speciall sowme thairof and thairfoir confessit thai ar nocht now payit to the plaice as of befoir.

The brethrein being avysit with the said inventar producit be the said Mr Andro Grahame findis, in generall, that be the fewis and takis sett be him of the bischoprik of Dunblane that he hes hurt the patrimony thairof and for tryell of the speciallis thairof appointis and gevis commissioun to James Andirsone, moderatour, Patrik Gillaspie, Mr James Pont, Umphra Cunynghame and Mr Alexander Iule to avys thairupone and to report thair jugementis to the nixt sessioun on the xxvj day of Februar instant, the said Mr Andro warnit thairto *apud acta*.

The brethrein being avysit with Mr Andro Grahamis answer made to that part of the act of the generall assemblie, viz., for nonpreiching of the Word and administratioun of the sacramentis and considderit his excusis thairin findis his saidis excusis nocht sufficient to excuse his absence fra his kirk the speace of ane haill yeir and thairfor decernis him convict of that part of the said act, viz., in nonpreiching of the Word, administratioun of the sacramentis the speace of ane haill yeir according to his awin confessioun.

Farder, the said Mr Andro being accusit gif he hade preichit or ministrat the sacramentis in his awin kirk off Dunblane at ony tyme sen his returning furth of the northe partis that he acceptit plaice in this presbytery, viz., sen the xj day of December last bypast or nocht, answerit that he was swa occupyit with making answer to the act of the generall asemblie to the brethrein that he could have na tyme to studie and thairfor confessit he hade teichit nane nor yit ministrat the sacramentis sensyne. The brethrein, being advysit with the said Mr Andro answer, findis the samin na sufficient excuis, and thairfor convictis him negligent in doctrein sen the xj day of December last bypast.

The brethrein, being avysit with the accusatioun of the said Mr Andro on the secund part of the act of the generall assemblie, viz., for hanting with excommunicat personis and his answer thairto, togethir with the testimonie of the brethrein of Dunblane, pronuncis him innocent thairof inrespect of his answer and testimonie foirsaid. The brethrein, being avysit with the accusatioun layit againis the said Mr Andro Grahame on the thrid part of the act of the generall assemblie, viz., for geving of collationis off beneficis againis the actis of the generall assemblie and his answer made thairto togethir with the testimonie of the brethrein of Dunblane, pronuncis him innocent thairof inrespect of his answer and testimonie foirsaid. The brethrein, being avysit with the accusatioun layit againis the said Mr Andro Grahame on ane uther part of the said act of the generall assemblie, viz., for geving sclandir ony wayis in his lyf and conversatioun, and his answer made thairto togethir with the testimonie of the brethrein of Dunblane, findis na thing in his lyf bot godlines and honestie.

At Striviling the xxvj day of Fabruar, 1582

Presentes: James Andirsone, Patrik Gillaspie, Mr Alexander Chisholme, Alexander Fargy, Mr Arthur Futhie, Mr Andro Yung, Johnne Duncanson, ministeris; Mr Alexander Iule, ane brothur of the exerceis; Mr Duncane Nevein and William Stirling, rederis; Mr James Pont and Umphra Cunynghame, elderis.

Mr Andro Grahame: The quhilk day the brethrein appointit in the last sessioun to try be the inventar producit be Mr Andro Grahame, conteining the fewis and takis set be him of the bischoprik of Dunblane in quhat speciallis the said Mr Andro hes hurt the patrimony of the said bischoprik, reportit to the remanent brethrein that, be thair apperance, the said Mr Andro hes diminisit the auld rentall of the said bischoprik be setting of sum fewis and takis sen his entrie thairto be diminutioun of bollis of victuell yeirlie, and setting of ane grit part thairof for viij s. the boll and including the teindis with the fewis for the sam price quhilkis was separat of befoir fra the landis and the teindis led in in victuell to the plaice of befoir and also that he hes sett ane gret part of landis in few to utheris thane the auld possessuris. The brethrein thinkis gude and ordeinis ane summondis to be direct to summond certane witnessis that best kennis the trewthe [thairof, *deleted*] to beir lell and suthfast witnessing tuiching the rentall of the bischoprik of Dunblane insafar as thai knaw or salbe speirit at thame, ilk persone undir the paine of disobedience and that the said Mr Andro be summond to heir thame ressavit, sworne and admittit, with certificatioun and he failze witnessis salbe ressavit.

At Striviling the fyft day of Merche, 1582

Presentes: James Andirsone, Mr Andro Grahame, Mr Andro Yung, Mr William Stirling, Michaell Lermonthe, Mr Alexander Chisholme, Alexander Fargy, Patrik Gillaspie, Johnne Duncanson, Patrik Layng, ministeris; David, commendatar of Drybrugh; William Stirling, William Scott, rederis; Mr Alexander Iule, ane brothur of exerceis; Umphra Cunynghame, Alexander Patersone, Duncane Narne, elderis.

William Stirling: The quhilk day William Stirling, reder, made the exerceis on the ordinarie text of exerceis, quhilk begouthe in the 3 chaptur of the epistle wrettin to the Ephesians at the 20 vers and red to the 4 vers of the fourth chaptur exclusive, and inquisitioun of his doctrein being tane, the brethrein jugis that the said William undirstude nocht that quhilk he teichit and thocht that apperandlie he hade his said doctrein pennit in wrett and thaireftir cumit the same perqweir.

The brethrein having considderit the travellis and painis sustenit be thair scryb James Duncansone without ony gratitude or payment payit to him thairfoir consenttis and aggreis that for the present necessitie he sall have ten pundis mony of feall thairfoir yeirlie at Witsonday and Mertimes to be payit to him ay and quhill the brethrein obtein to him ane better feall or als gude sum uthir way. For payment of the quhilk feall for his wreting in our sessioun and doing the offeice pertening to ane clark in sic assembleis, the brethrein in the ministrie undirsubscryvand obleisis thame to pay him yeirlie at the termis foirsaidis during the said speace ten schillingis mony for ilk hundir pund thai have assignit to thame for thair serveice in the ministrie and consenttis that he have yeirlie of the elderis in the presbytery as thai will gif of thair gude wills the first terme payment to begin at Witsonday nixt. [*Signed*:] James Andirson, Patrik Gillaspie, M. Androu Grayme, minister at Dunblane, Mr Arthour Fethie, A. Young, M. William Striviling, Alexander Fargy.

Continuatioun: The quhilk day being assignit to the brethrein to pronunce thair jugementis anent the mareing of William Michell and Jonet Crystesone togethir, compeirit bayth the saidis personis personallie. The brethrein will nocht acknawlege the samin as lauchfull mariage presentlie and continewis thair jugementis thairin to the first day of May nixt and commandis the said William and Jonet to separat thame selffis sindrie with all diligence and remane sindrie quhill the brethrein pronunce thair jugementis thairin undir the paine of excommunicatioun.

William Stirling: The samin day being assignit to the brethrein to pronunce thair jugementis anent William Stirling that mareit the said Jonet Crystesoun on the said William, quha was divorcit of befoir fra Andro Wilsone, hir spous, for adultrie committit be hir, compeirit the said William personallie and being demandit of the moderator to declair quhat occasionis movit him to compleit the said mariage, the said William ansorit that he ressavit ane testimoniall subscryvit be Johnne Stevinsone, reder at thair parroche kirk of Kincardin, quhilk testemoniall he producit of the det the xij day of *Junij* 1582, and lykwys becaus thai wantit thane, as thai do yit, ane minister at thair awin parroche kirk to marie thame, quhilk rassonis movit him to compleit the said mariage. Farder, the said William, being demandit gif he ressavit ony gratitude for making of the said mariage, confessis he ressavit twa half merk pecis thairfoir, and that he was nocht thair minister bot that thai war parrochinnaris of Kincardin kirk, with the quhilk parrochin he hade na thing to do concerning his offeice. The brethrein findis that be making of the said mariage the said William hes brokin twa actis of the generall assemblie, ane that na minister sould marie personis divorcit, ane uthir that na minister sould marie personis that dwellis bayth outwith his parrochin without lycence of the elderschip. Farther, the said William being demandit gif he mareit Johnne Gourlay and Cristane Gourlay in the kirk of Kippen on Sonday immediatlie preceiding fasternisevinlast or nocht and quhair thair bannis was proclaimit, the said William confessit that he mareit the saidis personis in the said kirk the said day at 6 houris in the morning or thairby, and that thair bannis was nocht proclaimit and that he said Johnne was ane parrochinnar of S. Lollanis kirk, viz., the parroche kirk of Kincardin, and that he knew nocht in quhat parrochin the woman dwelt. The brethrein continewis thair farther jugementis anent the said William to the xix day of Merche instant, the said William warnit thairto *apud acta*. The brethrein ordanis Johnne Stevinsone, reder at the kirk of Kincardin, to be summond to answer at the instance of the kirk for proclaiming of Jonet Crystesone in the said kirk with William Michell, the said Jonet beand divorcit fra Andro Wilsone, hir husband, for adultrie on hir part of befoir, and farder as he salbe demandit.

Mr Andro Grahame: The quhilk day ane summondis beand producit lauchfullie execute and indorsit upone William Scott, exhortar at the kirk of Callender, and James Stirling in Dunblane chairgeing thame to compeir the said day to beir lell and suithfast witnessing for preving of the just auld rentall of the bischoprik of Dunblane and chairgeing Mr Andro Graham, bischop thairof, to compeir the said day to heir and se the saidis witnessis ressavit, sworne and admittit, as at mair lynthe is contenit in the said summondis, compeirit the said Mr Andro personallie. The saidis witnessis was ressavit, sworne and admittit. The brethrein ordanis utheris witnessis to be summond to the effect foirsaid ilk persone undir the paine of disobedience to the xix day of Merche instant, the said Mr Andro warnit thairto *apud acta*.

Duncane Carrik: The quhilk day compeirit Duncane Carrik in Kippen (beand decernit to be excommunicat for disobedience to the kirk) and offerit him self in the will of the kirk and being accusit be the moderatour for committing adultrie, confessit him self mareit with Agnes Iull and hes gevin ane bairne by hir in adultrie with Agnes Finlasone, for the quhilk he offeris obedience to the kirk, for the quhilk he is decernit be the brethrein to pas to the nixt provinciall assemblie of this province to be haldin in Edinburgh, the secund day of Aprill nixt, thair to ressave injunctionis for his said fault and to obey thame undir the paine of excommunicatioun. The said Duncane ansorit and allegit that he mycht nocht pas to Edinburgh inrespect of ane gret infirmitie and seiknes he hade thruch the gravell berassone quhairof he mycht nocht travell, with the quhilk allegeance the brethren tuke to advys to the xij day of Merche instant that they micht try in the mentyme gif the said Duncanis allegence was of varetie or nocht.

At Striviling the xij day of Merche, 1582

Presentes: James Andirsone, Patrik Gillaspie, Mr Arthur Futhie, Michaell Lermonthe, Mr Andro Yung, Mr Adame Merschell, Mr Alexander Chisholme and Patrik Layng, ministeris; Mr Alexander Iulee, brothur of the exerceis; Mr James Pont, Umphra Cunynghame, Robert Alexander and William Norwall, elderis.

Duncane Carrik: The brethrein, being advysit with Duncane Carrikis allegence, ordanis and decernis him (nochtwithstanding thairof) to pas to the nixt provinciall assemblie the ij day of Aprill nixt tocum to be haldin in Edinburgh to the effect and undir the paine conteinit in thair ordinance made thairanent in the last sessioun, becaus his allegence is nocht varefeit to the brethrein.

Ane act for executioun of summondis: The brethrein undirstanding that sindrie and dyvirs summondis ar directit furth in name of this presbytery for summonding of sindrie personis to compeir befoir thame for tryell of sic offencis as concernis thame to juge, quhilk ar neglectit in the executioun, thrw the quhilk the disceplein of the kirk stayis onexecute againis sclanderus personis, thairfor statuttis and ordanis that ilk minister* for thair awin parttis, and that the minister, ressavar of the said summondis, report the samin againe to the scryb of our sessioun dewlie execute and indorsit in dew and convenient tyme, quhilk minister salbe haldin to answer for the executioun thairof quhensoevir he salbe requyrit, and quhen it sall happin ony summondis to be direct againis ony minister or reder that the minister that dwellis nixt to him quhome againis the summondis is direct caus execute the samin and report it againe, as

* For omission in text, see p. 311

said is, quha salbe haldin to answer for the executioun thairof, as is
befoir writtin, and quhasoevir neglectis the obedience of this act,
as is abone writtin, and to that effect seikis nocht the summondis
sall pay for the first fault xl d., the 2. fault to be doubillit, and the 3.
to be repleit.

Ane act anent absentis the day of exerceis: The brethrein persaving
sindrie ministeris within the boundis of this presbytery to be oft
absent fra the exerceis and sessioun excusand thair absence sumtyme
be baptezein of bairnis and examining of thair congregatioun befoir
the ministratioun of the Lordis Supper, thairfor it is statute and
ordeinit be universall consent of the brethrein that na minister fra
this furth upon the ordinar day of exerceis, viz., ilk Twysday ministrat baptisme, mariage nor exame ony of his congregatioun nor use
na uthir kynd of exerceis that day, that may withhauld him fra the
exerceis undir the paine of [*blank*].

*Ane act that the communioun sall nocht be ministrat in Lenterun nor on
peace day, sa callit*: The brethrein findis that the ministratioun of the
sacrament of the Lordis Supper to the pepill on the day callit of auld
peace day or in the tyme of Lenterun augmentis ane auld superstitioun that is in the hairttis of sum personis, to wit, that the said day
callit peace day or the tyme of Lenterun is ane mair hally tyme nor
uthir tymis of the yeir and thairfor inrespect of the tyme thinkis the
sacrament thane ministrat the holyar, for avoyding of the quhilk
superstitioun the brethrein with ane consent ordanis and commandis
that na minister within the boundis of this presbytery fra the first
day of Aprill nixt tocum furth minister the sacrament of the Lordis
Supper to ony congregationis on the said day callit of auld peace day
nor at na tyme within the speace of Lenterun, sa callit.

Thomas Quhyt, allegit adulterar: The quhilk day ane summondis
beand producit lauchfullie execut and indorsit upone Thomas Quhyt
in Kildeis chairgeing [him] to have compeirit the said day to heir
and se him self decernit to have committit adultrie with Agnes
Gentill and to undirly the censuris of the kirk thairfoir undir the
paine of excommunicatioun, quhilk Thomas being oft tymis callit
compeirit nocht. Thairfor the brethrein ordanis him to be summond
to heir and se him self decernit to be excommunicat for his contemp
and disobedience, with certificatioun and he failze thay wille proceid
and decern him to be excommunicat, as said is, according to the

K

Word of God and disceplein of the kirk, havand the warrant thairof thairin.

At Striviling the xix day of Merche, 1582

Presentes: James Andirsone, Patrik Gillaspie, Mr Alexander Chisholme, Michaell Lermonthe, Mr Andro Grahame, Mr William Stirling, Alexander Fargy, Mr Arthur Futhie, Mr Andro Yung and Patrik Layng, ministeris; Mr Alexander Iule, ane brothur of exerceis; William Stirling, William Scott, rederis; Alexander Forester of Garden, Alexander Patersone, notar, and Robert Alexander, elderis.

Patrik Layng: The quhilk day compeirit David Bruce of Lin Miln, parrochinnar of Clakmannan, quha being desyrit be the moderatour to declair the trewthe anent Patrik Layng gif he usit his offeice in the kirk sufficientlie and gif he was upricht in his lyf and conversatioun nor nocht, the said David ansorit that he was nocht swa upricht in his offeice as became him becaus he knew him to have baptezit bairnis gottin in adultrie and fornicatioun, sum of thame alsweill borne in uthir parrochunis as in his awin parrochun of Clakmannan, the parentis quhairof nocht havand satisfeit the kirk, and ane ressavar of mony for baptezein of thame, and for compleiting of mariage. As tuiching his lyf and conversatioun, the said David knew na thing thairin bot honestie. Off the quhilkis offencis the said Patrik being accusit in generall and in speciall as eftir follws, he ansorit as heireftir is mentionat. First, being accusit for baptesein of bairnis gottin in adultrie thair parentis nocht satisfeing the kirk, the said Patrik denyit the samin *simpliciter*. Secundlie, being accusit for baptesein of bairnis gottin in fornicatioun within his awin parrochun of Clakmannan, the parentis of thame nocht satisfeing the kirk, and ressavit silver thairfoir and swa sellit the sacrament unlauchfullie, the said Patrik denyit that he baptezit ony sic bairnis bot sic as thair parentis ather made repentence or ellis fand cautioun to mak repentence and swa inrespect of cautioun fund be sum personis, and be command of the elderis, he baptezit thair bairnis, and na uthirwayis, and denyis that he ressavit ony mony thairfoir. Thridlie, being accusit gif he baptezit ane bairne gottin in fornicatioun be Archibald Bruce of Kennet on [*blank*] Baxter, quha than dwelt with the said Archibald, the mane nocht havand satisfeit the kirk thairfoir, the said Patrik confessit the baptezein of the same bairne and that the father thairof nathir made repentence thairfoir nor yit presentit his said bairne to baptism bot allegit the mothur thairof made repentence for the samin. Fourtlie, being accusit gif he baptezit ony bairnis gottin furth of his awin parrochun and, in speciall, bairnis of the parrochun of Airthe and gif he ressavit ony silver thairfoir, the said Patrik confessit that he baptezit bairnis lauchfullie gottin of the parrochun of Airthe bot denyit the ressett of ony silvir thairfoir, and denyit that he baptezit ony bairnis of that parrochun nor of ony uthir parrochun nor his awin gottin in adultrie nor fornicatioun. Fy[f]tlie, being accusit for baptezein of ane bairne in the kirk of Allvay gottin in fornicatioun be Mr James Erskein on [blank] Mwbray, dochtir of the laird of Barnbwgall, the said Patrik confessit the same and that nather the fathir nor the mothur made repentence thairfoir bot allegit the said Mr James fand cautioun to satisfie the kirk thairfoir and confessit that the said bairne was borne in Litill Sawchie within the parrochun of S. Niniane. Sextlie, being accusit for taking of silvir for making of mariagis, the said Patrik denyit the samin *simpliciter*. The brethrein admittis the haill accusatiounis foirsaidis denyit be the said Patrik to the said David Bruce probatioun and assignis thairto the xxvj day of Merche instant, the said Patrik warnit thairto *apud acta*.

William Stirling: In the terme assignit be the brethrein to pronunce thair jugementis anent the accusatiounis layit againis William Stirling and his answeris made thairto, the said William compeirand personallie, the moderator requyrit him to declair the trewthe gif he knew that Jonet Crystesone was divorcit fra Andro Wilsone, sumtyme hir husband, for adultrie committit be hir befoir he mareit hir with William Michell in Coustrie or nocht, the said William Stirling confessit that befoir he mareit hir on the said William Michell he knew hir to be divorcit fra hir first husband for adultrie committit be hir, bot inrespect of the testimoniall he ressavit of the proclamatioun of thair bannis bearand that na impediment was opponit in the contrar and that thai hade nocht ane minister in thair awin kirk as befoir he allegit thairfoir, he mareit the said Jonet Crystesone on the said William Michell, as said is.

William Stirling, suspendit: The brethrein, having considderit the accusatiounis layit againis William Stirling, reder, and his answeris made thairin, continewis thair jugementis thairintill quhill thai be farther advysit thairwithe, bot presentlie thinkis the said William worthie to be suspendit and suspendis him from all functioun in the kirk of God and exerceis of ony part of the ministrie thairof to the ix day of Apryll nixt tocum.

Mr Andro Grahame: The quhilk day ane summondis beand producit lauchfullie execute and indorsit upone James Blakwod, William Wricht and Robert Drummond, messinger in Dunblane, chairgeing thame to compeir the said day to beir lell and suithfast witnessing tuiching the rentall of the bischoprik of Dunblane insafar as thai knaw or salbe speirit at thame, as at mair lynthe is conteinit in the said summondis, compeirit Mr Andro Grahame, bischop thairof, and the saidis James Blakwod and William Wricht, witnessis foirsaid, quha was ressavit, sworne and admittit, the said Robert Drummond being oft tymis callit compeirit nocht. Thairfor the brethrein ordanis him to be summond of new to the xxvj day of Merche instant to the effect foirsaid under the paine of excommunicatioun, the said Mr Andro Grahame warnit thairto *apud acta*.

Buikis of disciplein producit: The same day Patrik Gillaspie, Mr Arthur Futhie, Mr William Stirling and Alexander Fargy, ministeris, producit thair buikis of disceplein to be veseit and considderit be the brethrein. The brethir appointtis the moderatour and remanent brethrein of Striviling to vesie the saidis buikis and report thair jugementis to the nixt sessioun.

At Striviling the xxvj day of Merche, 1583

Presentes: James Andirsone, Mr Arthur Futhie, Johne Duncanson, Patrik Gillaspie, Mr Johnne Campbell, Mr Andro Grahame, Alexander Fargy, Robert Mentayth, Mr Andro Yung, Michaell Lermonthe, Mr Alexander Chisholme and Patrik Layng, ministeris; Mr Alexander Iule, ane brothur of exerceis; Mr James Pont, Umphra Cunynghame, Robert Alexander, William Norwallis, elderis in the presbytery of Striviling, and Mr Johnne Stewart.

The quhilk day the moderatour made intimatioun to the brethrein that the provinciall assemblie of this province is to be haldin in Edinburgh on the secund day of Aprill nixt, thairfor admonesis the haill brethrein within the boundis of this presbytery to be present thair the said day, and that ilk minister warne the reder nixt to him to be present thair lykwys, and that ilk minister warne the adulteraris within his parrochun to compeir thair the said day to ressave thair injunctionis, undir the paine of excommunicatioun, and that Patrik Gillaspie warne William Wingzet, fornicatour with Jonet Johnesone, the fourth tyme, to compeir thair the said day to ressave his injunctionis for the said fault, undir the paine conteinit in the last act made thairanent.

Jonet Johneson: The samin day compeirit Jonet Johnesone and grantis fornicatioun with William Wingzet and that as for the foirt fault, quha is ordeinit and commandit to compeir befoir the provinciall assemblie of this province to be haldin in Edinburgh the secund day of Aprill nixt tocum thair to ressave injunctionis to be injonit to hir for the said fault under the paine of excommunicatioun. It is thocht gude and ordeinit be the brethrein that thay sall teiche in the exerceis forward fra the text this day teichit to the end of the epistillis of S. Paull.

Mr Johnne Campbell: The quhilk day compeirit Mr Johnne Campbell, bischop of Iyllis, and producit twa edictis dewlie execute and indorsit be the quhilkis intimatioun was made at the parroche kirkis of Eclmekill and Ardchattan of the commissioun gevin to the brethrein be act of the generall assemblie to summond and call befoir thame the said Mr Johnne and to accuse him of the offencis conteinit in the said act, all or part, as he is giltie and all personis that hes to object or say againis the said Maister Johnne in the heddis conteinit in the said act and mentionat in the said edictis or ony of thame [that] was lauchfullie summond in the saidis kirkis to haif compeirit befoir the brethrein the said day to declair quhat thay hade to oppone againis him quhair ecclesiasticall disceplein sould have bein ministrat according to the Word of God, as at mair lynthe is conteinit in the saidis edictis and executionis producit thairupone and albeit that publictlie all personis that hade to object or say againis the said Mr Johnne in the heddis foirsaidis, was callit to compeir befoir the brethrein instantlie and lauchfull tyme of day biddin, yit nane compeirit nor objectit againis him, and thairfor the moderator, in name of the brethrein, entirit with the said Mr Johnne in tryell of the heddis follwing. First, the said Mr Johnne beand inquyrit gif he hade delyverit to Mr Neill Campbell the copy of the act of the generall assemblie contenand the brethreinis pwar for

trying of the said Mr Johnne, with ane edict direct be thame thairanent and ane wreting direct to him for ressait of the samin and
quhat answer he hade ressavit thairof, the said Mr Johnne answerit
he delyverit the samin wrettis to the said Mr Neill, quha ansorit to
him that he wald send his answer in wrett to the brethrein of this
presbytery in dew and convenient tyme and thairfor he ressavit na
uthir answer nathir be word nor wret. Secundlie, the said Mr Johnne
being requyrit to declair gif he ressavit the bischoprik of the Iyllis
and the abbacie of Ecolmekill conjunct or nocht and gif thai remane
presentlie in his handis as he ressavit thame or nocht, the said Mr
Johnne answerit and confessit that he ressavit the said bischoprik and
abbacie conjunct togethir the tyme of his entres thairto, lyk as Mr
Johnne Carswall his predicessur hade thame of befoir conjunct, bot
grantis that sensyne he hes made resignatioun of the said abbacie in
the kingis gracis handis in favoris of his sone Mr Alexander Campbell
and swa hes denudit his handis thairof. Farder, beand inquyrit gif
thair was ony pactioun and conditioun made betuix him and his sone
anent the said abbacie at the tyme of the said resignatioun the said
Mr Johnne denyit that thair was ony pactioun and conditioun betuix
thame anent the samin. Thridlie, beand requyrit gif he hade sett in
few or be takkis ony of the leving addettit to the bischoprik of Iyllis
and abbacie of Ycolmekill sen his entrie thairto or nocht, the said Mr
Johnne denyis that he hes sett ony thing thairof sen his entrie nather
be few nor tak excep only that he hes confermit ane few of new, sett
be Mr Johnne Carswall, his predicessur, to my lord Erlle of Argyll
of the landis of Skirhingzie in Kintyr. Fourtlie, beand inquyrit gif he
hes ressavit ony few or tak of ony part of the said abbacie of Ecolmekill of Mr Alexander Campbell, his sone, sen his dimissioun of the
samin in his favoris or in favoris of ony of his freindis or nocht, the
said Mr Johnne answerit that he hes nocht ressavit na part of the said
abbacie of his said sone nather be few nor takis sen his dimissioun of
the sam in his favoris nor nane of his freindis. Fyftlie, the said Mr
Johnne beand inquyrit gif the fyve iyllis of Barra be as yit fre unset
or nocht, the said Mr Johnne ansorit that thai ar fre, unset athir in
few or be tak nather be him nor his predicessur.

The said Mr Johnne Campbell is admonesit nocht to styll him self
bischop, nor lord, in tymis cuming, nather be word nor wrett,
according to the ordinance of the generall assemblie. The brethrein

continewis thair jugementis anent the accusationis layit againis the said Mr Johnne to the xvj day of Aprill nixt, the said Mr Johnne warnit thairto *apud acta*, with certificatioun and he failze, the brethrein will pronunce according to the Word of God and disceplein of the kirk, and als summondis the said Mr Johnne to compeir befoir the nixt generall assemblie of the kirk to be haldin in Edinburgh, the xxiiij day of Aprill nixttocum, the secund day of the said assemblie, viz., the xxv day of the said moneth of Aprill to heir and se the brethrein report to the said assemblie of thair obedience to the commissioun of the generall assemblie gevin to thame anentis him and sic uthir thingis as thai have fund concerning him togethir with the said assembleis determinatioun thairanent undir the paine of disobedience.

Robert Drummond, witnes: The quhilk day beand producit ane summondis dewlie execute and indorcit upone Robert Drummond, messinger, chairgeing him to compeir the said day to beir lell and suithfast witnessing tuiching the rentall of the bischoprik of Dunblane insafar as he knawis or salbe speirit at him undir the paine of excommunicatioun (Mr Andro Grahame, bischop thairof, beand personallie present), compeirit the said Robert Drummond quha was ressavit, sworne and admittit, and examinat thairupone as the depositionis beris.

Anent Mr Andro Grahame: The brethrein, being advysit with the depositionis of the witnessis summond for preving of the just rentall of the bischoprik of Dunblane, findis that sufficient tryell of the said rentall can nocht be guidlie hed of witnessis nathir yit can it be weill varefeit quhat parttis of the leving addettit to the said bischoprik ar set in few or be takis be the said Mr Andro Grahame, bischop thairof, sen his entrie thairto or quhat yit remainis in the bischopis handis unsett unles the register of his fewis and settis be producit. Thairfor the brethrein ordanis the said Mr Andro to produce his buikis of register of the haill fewis and settis of the leving of the said bischoprik sett be him sen his entrie thairto befoir thame on the xvj day of Aprill nixt to the effect foirsaid and that James Blakwod in Dunblane, kepar of the register buikis of the auld fewis and takis sett of the said bischoprik befoir the said Mr Androis entrie thairto, be summond to compeir the said day and to bring with him and produce the saidis register buikis contening the haill auld fewis and

takis foirsaidis to the same effect foirsaid undir the paine of disobedience.

Mr Andro Grahame: The samin day the said Mr Andro Grahame
beand accusit gif he hade teichit or ministrat the sacramentis in his
awin kirk of Dunblane at ony tyme sen the xix day of Fabruar last
to this present or nocht, the said Mr Andro answerit that he was swa
occupyit with making answer to the act of the generall assemblie to
the brethrein that he could have na tyme to studie and thairfor
confessit he hade teichit nane nor yit the [*sic*] ministrat the sacramentis sensyne bot promesis to amend in tymis cuming.

Anent thingis to be registrat in the buikis of disceplein: The quhilk day
it is statute and ordeinit that ilk minister caus register in buikis, ane
or ma, all mariagis made be him, all bairnis baptezit be him, all
personis that deis within the parrochun, and the almus collectit for
the puiris at the kirk duir, with the distributioun thairof, and suirey
keipit.

The buikis of disceplein salbe producit: The same day it is ordeinit
that ilk minister produce his buik of disceplein with the register of
the foirsaidis befoir the brethrein of the presbytery at twa sindrie
tymes in the yeir, viz., on the secund Twysdayis of Merche and
September to be veseit and considderit be thame and delyverit againe
to the minister, keipar thairof.

Buikis off disceplein: The quhilk day the buikis of disceplein of the
parrochunis of S. Ninianis kirk, Airthe, Logy and Abirfoull was
veseit and admittit and delyverit againe to the ministeris of the said
parrochunis.

Upone the ij day of Aprill the brethrein was absent at the synnodall assemblie of this province and thairfor na thing was done.

At Striviling the ix day of Aprill, 1583

Presentes: James Andirsone, Johnne Duncansone, Patrik Gillaspie,
Mr Alexander Chisholme, Mr William Stirling, Mr Arthur Futhie,
Robert Mentayth, Mr Andro Yung, Michaell Lermonthe, Alex-
ander Fargy, ministeris; Alexander Forester off Garden, Mr James
Pont, Duncane Narne, Umphra Cunynghame, elderis; and Mr
Alexander Iule, ane brothur off exerceis.

Commissionaris to the nixt generall assemblie: The quhilk day the brethrein of the presbytery of Striviling electit and nominat James Andirsone, Patrik Gillaspie, and Johnne Duncanson, ministeris; Sir James Stirling off Keir, knycht and provest of Stirling, and Alexander Forester of Garden, barronis; commissionaris for thame to pas to the nixt generall assemblie of the kirk to be haldin in Edinburgh the xxiiij day of Aprill instant with full powar to concur with the said assemblie for treatting of thais thingis concerning the weill and gude ordur to be observit within the kirkis of the said presbytery and als quhatsumevir thingis that salbe trettit in the said assemblie that may tend to the glorie of God and weill of his haill kirk plantit of his mercie within this realme.

Adulteraris: The quhilk day the brethrein ordanis that all adulteraris that hes past to the synnodall assemblie be warnit to compeir befoir the brethrein the nixt sessioun to heir and se the injunctionis of the synnodall assemblie injoinit to thame for thair offencis be exponit and declairit to everie ane of thame, in speciall, to the effect thai pretend na ignorance. The brethrein ordanis ilk minister within the boundis of this presbytery to proceid with the censuris of the kirk againis all adulteraris disobedient within the boundis that hes nocht past to the said synodall assemblie of this presbytery as thai war ordeinit, ilk minister for his awin part respective, as thai will answer before the brethrein of this presbytery.

William Stirling suspendit: The brethrein, undirstanding William Stirling, reder, to be suspendit to this day fra all functioun in the kirk in consideratioun of certane accusatiounis layit againis the said William, as at mair lynthe is conteinit in ane act made thairon of befoir, continewis thair jugementis as yit quhill thai be farther advysit anent the accusatiounis layit againis him, bot presentlie suspendis him of new fra all functioun in the kirk of God and exerceis of ony part of the ministrie thairof to the vij day of Merche nixt.

Johnne Wilsone: The quhilk day compeirit Johnne Wilsone in Polmais and grantis him to have gottin ane bairne in fornicatioun withe Agnes Mentayth and grantis lykwys that he committit adultrie with Agnes Broun by his wyf, Elezabeth Bennet, for the quhilk adultrie he confessis that he hes satisfeit the kirk. The brethrein, being advysit with the said Johnnis oft falling in huredom, first in adultrie and now fornicatioun, decernis and ordeinis him to mak publict repentence at the publict plaice appointit for penitentis within his awin parroche kirk of Sanct Niniane sex sindrie Sondayis in tyme of sermonde, beginnand on the nixt Sonday the xiiij day of Aprill nixt, undir the paine of disobedience.

Commissioun to vesy the kirk off Muthill: The brethrein ordanis and gevis commissioun to Mr Andro Yung, Mr William Stirling and Michaell Lermonthe, ministeris, to pas to the parroche kirk of Muthill betwix and the first Twysday of *Junij* nixt and vesie the samin *pro re nata* and tak inquisitioun and tryell of sic thingis in that parrochun as concernis the glorie of God and weill of his kirk and farther to travell with the congregatioun thairof and desyr thame to provyd a sufficient dwelling for Mr Alexander Chisholme, thair minister, with certificatioun gif thai failze thair wilbe libertie gevin to the said Mr Alexander to pas to ane uthir kirk, and quhat the saidis ministeris findis be thair said visitatioun to report to the brethrein heir on the said first Twysday of *Junij*.

Questionis proponit to the synnodall assemblie: The quhilk day James Andirsone, moderatour, reportit to the brethrein certane questionis gevin to him in wret to be proponit to the last synnodall assemblie to desyr the jugementis of the brethrein of the said assemblie and resolutioun to everie ane of thame, quhilk questionis and answeris made thairto he producit befoir the brethrein, quhairof the tennour follwis. *Questio*: Ane certane mane and ane woman makis mutuall promeis of mariage in presens of the reder of the kirk be word and in presens of bayth thair freindis conveinit for that purpois on the nycht of auld callit fasternisevin eftir supper xiij yeir syne or thairby and promesit to solemneiz the same befoir the kirk on law Sonday nixt thaireftir, and immediatlie eftir the foirsaid promeis thay hade carnall dell and cohabitatioun the speace of ij or iij yeiris without ony solemnizatioun of the band. Thaireftir the foirsaid mane lavis the said woman and adjonis him self unto ane uthir woman be carnall dell and cohabitatioun with the quhilk secund he wald solemneiz mariage, the first woman refusand to persew the said mane for his first promeis made to hir. *Queritur*: Gif, eftir the said mane hes satisfeit the kirk for the carnall dell with bayth the said wemen (nocht beand mareit, as said is), quhethir gif he may lauchfullie marie the secund woman; gif nocht, gif he and the first woman salbe compellit to compleit amd solemneiz mariage according to thair first promeis.

Thir questionis was all answerit on the iiij day of Aprill, 1583: *40 Aprilis 1583, Respondetur*: The secund mariage stayis and urge for adherence of the first.

Anent mariage: *Questio*: Ane woman committis incest and satisfeis the kirk thairfoir be externall forme of repentence. *Queritur*: Gif the said woman may be mareit with ane uther mane or nocht. *Respondetur*: Affirmative.

Adherence: *Questio*: ane certane man and his wyf committis, ather of thame, adultrie by uthir and pass sindrie without ony durors lauchfullie led. *Queritur*: gif the kirk may compell thame to adheir togethir or nocht. *Respondetur*: affirmative *propter recompensatione*.

Injunctionis to ane fornicatour eftir he hes committit adultrie: *Questio*: Ane certane mane committis adultrie and satisfeis the kirk thairfoir, thaireftir his wyf being ded he fallis in fornicatioun. *Queritur*: Quhat forme of repentence he sall mak quhethir as ane simplle fornicatour or as relaps in fornicatioun. *Respondetur*: Relaps it is, and vj dayis repentence is the ordur.

Malitiosa disertione: *Questio*: ane certane woman laves hir husband *malitiosa desertione* thrw the quhilk hir husband fallis in adultrie and thaireftir ar reconceillit. *Queritur*: Gif ony disciplein salbe usit againis hir inrespect of the reconciliatioun. *Respondetur*: We think les nor the sclandir be all the greter sen reconciliatioun follwis it aucht to be bureit.

Anent mariage: *Questio*: Thair is a certane mane and a woman mareit, the mane committis adultrie and thaireftir passis out of the realme, the woman conteinis hir self without fault the speace of ix or x yeiris thaireftir, and then fallis in adultrie in lyk manir, na divorcement beand led, now his husband is ded. *Queritur*: Gif it be lesum to marie the said woman now with ane mane or nocht. *Respondetur*: Affirmative (the ordur of the kirk being observit).

Anent dilapidatioun: *Questio*: Ane beneficit persone berand offeice in the functioun of the kirk settis victuell of his benefeice as maill and beir sum for viij s. the boll, sum for xiij s. iiij d. the boll, etc. Item, settis, pultrie, arrage, carrag of pettis and fewall for small pricis of silvir far within the availl that hes bein in our dayis. Item, landis sett of befoir *decimis non inclusis* now sett in few *decimis inclusis* for viij s. the boll teind. *Queritur*: Gif this be dilapidatioun of the patrimony of the kirk or nocht. *Respondetur*: Affirmative and that the actis of the generall assemblie sould be execut upone him.

Anent dilapidatioun: *Questio*: Ane beneficit persone rassavis ane bischoprie and ane abbacie as ane benefeice unit the tyme of his predicessur and in his awin persone, and thaireftir disjonis the said abbacie fra the bischoprik in favoris of ane certane speciall freind. *Queritur*: Gif this be dilapidatioun of the patrimony of the kirk or nocht. *Respondetur*: We undirstand nocht the questioun nor the manir of the disjoning and thairfor thinkis the personis ye mein of wald be warnit to the generall assemblie, thair to be tryit upone this hed.

Anent buriall: *Questio*: Seing the inner kirk of Dunblane, of auld callit the queir, servis presentlie for preiching of the Word and administratioun of the sacramentis. *Queritur*: Gif the assemblie of Dunblane may suffir sic personis to be bureit in the uttir kirk as will contribute to the reparatioun of the same, and gif thai may mak ane act thairanent. *Respondetur*: This is perilous and thairfoir thocht it not meit to be done. *Queritur*: Quhat ordur sould be takin with ministeris and redaris that ar of na presbyterie. *Respondetur*: To the nixt presbyterie quhill farther ordur be tane.

Mercattis dischairgit on Sondayis: The quhilk day the moderatour made intimatioun to the brethrein that be act of this last synnodall assemblie all marcattis ar dischairgit to be haldin within the boundis of the synnodall upone Sondayis under the painis thairin conteinit, and that be the same act ilk minister is commandit to proceid againis the contravenaris thairof (beand his awin parrochinnaris) with the censuris of the kirk according thairto.

At Striviling the xvj day of Aprill, 1583

Presentes: James Andirsone, Mr Andro Grahame, Patrik Gillaspie, Mr Alexander Chisholme, Mr Arthur Futhie, Mr Andro Yung, Mr William Stiriling, Alexander Fargy, Patrik Layng, Mr Johnne Campbell, Johnne Duncansone, ministeris; Mr James Pont, Umphra Cunynghame and Robert Alexander, elderis; Mr Alexander Iule, ane brothur of the exerceis.

Mr Andro Graham: The quhilk day Mr Andro Grahame beand

desyrit be the moderatour to produce his register buikis of the haill fewis and takis sett be him of the bischoprik of Dunblane sen his enteres thairto according to ane ordinance made be the brethrein on the xxvj day of Merche last bypast, the said Mr Andro answerit and confessit that he hes the register of sum thingis sett be him bot nocht all and in speciall confessis that he hes nocht the fewis and takis sett to my lord Grahame, the Maistir of Mar, nor the Maistir of Levingstoun registrat, bot hoppis to get the copeis of the charturis and takis that he wantis onregistrat, at the lest the substantiall pointis of thame quhen he plesis to requyr for thame and thairfor, seing he hes nocht the register of all presentlie in his handis, desyris the brethrein to appoint him ane convenient day againe the quhilk he sall use diligence to get the register of the haill and produce the samin befoir thame according to thair desyr. The brethrein undirstanding that thai have na farther commissioun to try the said Mr Andro Grahame bot to the nixt generall assemblie of the kirk and that thai have na sessioun day ordinar betuix and thane to appoint to the said Mr Andro for satisfeing of his desyr, thairfor ordanis him to use sufficient diligence betuix and the nixt generall assemblie and produce befoir the brethrein thairof on the xxv day of Aprill instant ane auctentik register of the haill fewis and takis sett be him of the fruictis of the said bischoprik sen his enteres thairto to be sein and considderit be the brethrein of the said assemblie and in speciall the fewis and takis sett to my lord Grahame, the Maistir of Mar and Maistir of Levingstoun and to heir and se thair jugementis pronuncit concerning the haill thingis deducit in proces befoir us againis him and summondis the said Mr Andro thairto *apud acta* undir the paine of disobedience. The same day, the said Mr Andro Grahame being askit gif he hes teichit or ministrat the sacramentis as yit at ony tyme sen his hame cuming in his awin kirk of Dunblane, the said Mr Andro answerit that he teichit on Sonday last befoir none in his said kirk, bot nocht at na uthir tyme sensyne for the causis schawin be him to the brethrein of befoir. The brethrein thinkis gude and ordeinis that the haill proces deducit befoir thame againis Mr Andro Grahame concerning his tryell, according to the act of the generall assemblie, be extractit and producit befoir the nixt generall assemblie be the moderator to be haldin in Edinburgh on the xxv day of Aprill instant. The brethrein thinkis gude that the moderatour report be word to the nixt generall assemblie the proces deducit befoir thame concerning the tryell of Mr Johnne Campbell, bischop of Iyllis, according to the act of the generall assemblie.

Mr Johnne Campbell: The quhilk day being assignit to the brethrein to pronunce thair jugementis anent the accusatiounis layit againis Mr Johnne Campbell, bishcop of Iyllis, the said Mr Johnne beand personallie present the brethrein, yit as of befoir, continewis thair jugementis thairin to the first Twysday eftir Sanct Lowrence day, viz., the xiij day of August nixt, the said Mr Johnne warnit thairto *apud acta* with certificatioun and he failze the brethrein will pronunce according to the Word of God and disceplein of the kirk. The said Mr Johnne promesis keip the said day and compeir befoir the brethrein, according to thair ordinance in all pointis.

Issobell Boyd: The quhilk day it was declairit to the brethrein be James Andirsone, minister at Striviling, that quhair ane woman in this toun callit Issobell Boyd, beand suspectit for adultrie, was summond to have compeirit befoir the sessioun of the kirk of Striviling for tryell of the samin, hes fled furth of this toun for eschwein of disceplein and thairfor desyris the brethrein to tak sic ordur that the said Issobell may sustein disceplein, it is ordeinit that ilk minister tak privie inquisitioun in ilk ane of thair sessiounis for the said Issobell, and also to inquyr for hir publictlie in pulpet laving adoptioun to the minister to use ony of the twa first as he plesis, and quhow son tryell be hade of hir to reveill it to the brethrein and expell hir furth of thair congregatioun.

Margaret McQuhirry: The quhilk day compeirit Margaret McQuhirry in Airthe, unmareit, and grantis hir to have borne ane bairne gottin in adultrie on hir be Alexander Robertsone thair, mareit, and submittis hir in the will of the kirk.

Margaret Stewart: The samin day compeirit Margaret Stewart in Airthe, unmareit, and grantis hir to have borne ane bairne gottin in adultrie on hir be James Smyth, mareit, and submittis hir in the will of the kirk thairfoir.

David Burne: The samin day compeirit David Burne in Clakmannan with Margaret Yung and grantis him to have gottin ane bairne in adultry by his wyf on Agnes Alexander in Allway for the quhilk he submittis him in the will of the kirk.

The xxiiij and last dayis of Aprill the brethrein was absent at the generall assemblie and thairfor thair was na thing done.

At Striviling the vij day of May, 1583

Presentes: James Andirsone, moderatour, Mr Andro Grahame, Mr Arthur Futhie, Mr William Stirling, Mr Alexander Chisholme, Robert Mentayth, Mr Andro Yung, Johnne Duncanson, Alexander Fargy, Michaell Lermonthe, Patrik Layng, Andro Forester, ministeris; William Scott, William Stirling, rederis; Mr James Pont, Robert Alexander, Umphra Cunynghame, elderis; and Mr Alexander Iule, ane brothur off exerceis.

Moderatour chosin: The quhilk day Mr William Stirling, minister at the kirk off Abirfoull, be voit of the brethrein was chosin moderatour in this presbytery to the nixt provinciall assemblie.

Anent making off actis: The quhilk day it was intimat to the brethrein that be ane act in the last generall assemblie, it is statute and ordeinit that na sessioun of na particular kirk, na presbyteriis, nor synnodall assembleis mak actis [*two thirds of the line blank*] that ar nocht grundit on actis alreddy made or to be made in the generall assembly, at the lest not put in executioun quhill thay be first presentit to the generall assembly and thair ratefeit and approvit, and thairfor the haill brethrein is admonesit to obey the said act.

Punesing off excommunicantis: The samin day it was intimat to the brethrein that the kingis majestie hes promesit to the kirk to puneis all excommunicat personis civillie according to the lawis (thair particular naimis beand gevin up) and thairfor it is ordeinit be the generall assemblie that ilk presbytery gif up the naimis of all excommunicat personis within thair boundis, for the quhilk caus it is ordeinit that ilk minister gif up the naimis of all excommunicantis that he knawis to the presbytery to the effect foirsaid.

Kirkis in Strathern adjonit: The samin day it was intimat to the brethrein that be act of the last generall assemblie thair is iiij parroche kirkis in Strathern adjonit to this presbytery, viz., Muthill, Strwen, Stragayth and Tillechettill.

William Stirling: The quhilk day the brethrein, being advysit with the accusationis layit againis William Stirling, reder, and his answeris made thairto, undirstandis him to be penitent for his offencis as ane wretein subscryvit with his hand at lynthe beris. Thairfor the brethrein ordanis the said William Stirling to mak publict repentence on Sonday the xij of this instant in the parroche kirk off Kincardin in the tyme of sermond at the plaice appointit for penitenttis for his offencis and sclandering of the kirk thairby in the said parrochun, and that Michaell Lermonthe, minister, ressave the same repentence, and als ordanis the said William to mak publict repentence in the parroche kirk of Kippen on ane Sonday betuix and the xxiiij day of *Junij* nixt for his offencis and sclandering of the kirk thairby in the said parrochun, and that Patrik Gillaspie, minister, pas to the said kirk and ressave his repentence. The brethrein, inrespect of his penitencie, continewis the said William Stirling in reidein in the kirk, marein of personis and ministratioun of baptisme to the nixt generall assemblie.

Breking of the Sabbothe day : The brethrein, undirstandand that on Sonday last thair was ane drum strukin in the brugh of Stirling be ane certane of servand men and boyis, and May playis usit quhairby the Sabbothe day was prophainit and the kirk sclanderit, thairfor the brethrein ordanis the minister of Stirling to command the bailleis of the toun in name of the kirk to tak ordur with the saidis personis, prophanairis of the Sabboth day and puneis thame in exampill of utheris and nocht to suffir the lyk in tymis cuming undir the paine of the censuris of the kirk to be execute againis thame.

Patrik Layng : The quhilk day the brethrein undirstandand that forsamekill as anent certane accusatiounis layit againis Patrik Layng, of the quhilkis the said Patrik denyit the maist part quhilkis was assignit probatione as actis maid thairupone beris of the det the xix day of Merche last bypast, nochttheless the said Patrik sensyne, oft and dyvers tymis, hes promesit to produce in wret befoir the brethrein his confessioun of the haill trewthe of the heddis quhairof he was accusit and lykwys of all uthiris quhairof he thinkis him self worthie to be accusit and insafar as it salbe fund that he hes offendit againis the actis of the kirk submittis him self to the brethreinis will thairanent, quhilk as yit the said Patrik hes nocht done, thairfor the brethrein ordanis and commandis the said Patrik Layng (beand personallie present) to produce in wret befoir the brethrein on the xxj day of May instant his confessioun of the trewthe of his saidis accusatiounis and utheris befoir specefeit undir the paine of disobedience.

Adulteraris in Tullicultrie: The quhilk day Robert Mentayth, minister at the kirk of Alvayth, reportit to the brethrein that he hade lauchfullie admonesit sindrie tymis William Wat and Jonet Dugy, incesteus adulteraris, in Tullicultrie to obey and satisfie the kirk for thair proud contemp againis the samin as his said admonitionis put in wret at mair lynthe beris, and that according to the commone ordur tane be the kirk and the brether command gevin to him thairanent, and as yit na obedience is offirit be thame, and thairfor inquyrit gif he sall pronunce the sentence of excommunicatioun againis thame conform to the decreit pronuncit be the brether thairanent. The brethrein commandis and ordanis him to pronunce the sentence againis the saidis personis according to thair decreit in all pointis inrespect of thair malicius and obstinat disobedience.

Adulteraris in Clakmannan: The brethir undirstanding that forsameikill as upone the xvij day of Aprill, the yeir of God im vc lxxxij yeiris James Tailyour, Jonet Aickein, Johnne Seath and Jonet Wallace, adulteraris, within the parrochun of Clakmannan was decernit be thame to be excommunicat for thair contemp and disobedience to the voice of the kirk, as at mair lynthe is conteinit in thair said decreit of the det foirsaid, nochtwithstanding the brethrein understanding na executioun to have follwit as yit on thair said decreit, thairfor commandis and ordanis Patrik Layng, minister at Clakmannan, to admoneis the saidis personis and ilk ane of thame publictlie in pulpet four sindrie Sondayis according to the commone ordur to obey the voice of the kirk undir the paine of the sentence of excommunicatioun to be pronuncit againis thame, and the said Patrik to report the forme of his admonitiounis in wret to be considderit by the brethrein on the iiij day of *Junij* nixt.

Chrystis woll: The brethrein undirstandand ane gret abuse usit be the rascall sort of pepill that passis in pilgrimage to Chrystis woll and usis gret idolatrie or superstitioun thairat expres againis Godis law and becaus the kingis majestie with avys of his thre estaittis of parliament hes statut be act of parliament certane puneismentis alsweill corporall painis as pecuniall sowmis of mony to be execute againis sic personis, and for executioun of the quhilkis againis personis passand to the said woll, the brethrein undirstandis my lord of Doun, stewart of Mentayth, hes commissioun gevin to him to that effect, nochttheles seing puneisment is nocht execute

L

conform to the said act, thairfor the brethir ordanis and gevis commissioun to Mr Andro Yung, Mr William Stirling and Michaell Lermonthe to pas to my lord of Doun to treat with him for executioun of puneisment againis the personis passaris thairto according to the said act and his commissioun.

At Striviling the xiiij day of May, 1583

Presentes: Mr Williame Stirling, moderatour, James Andirsone, Mr Andro Grahame, Mr Andro Yung, Alexander Fargy, Robert Mentyathe, Patrik Gillaspie, Mr Arthur Futhie, Michaell Lermonthe and Andro Forester, ministeris; Mr James Pont, Umphra Cunynghame and Robert Alexander, elderis; and Mr Alexander Iule, ane brothur of exerceis.

Chrystis woll: The brethrein ordanis and gevis commissioun to the brether indwellaris in Dunblane or ony thrie of thame to pas to Chrystill [*sic*] woll this nixt Setterday at evin, accumpanyit with sic personis as thai may have to espy quhat personis cumis to the said woll and report the naimis of sic personis as thai may gait to the brethrein.

Robert Mentayth, minister at Alvayth, producit his buik of disceplein to be veseit be the brethrein.

Robert Fogo decernit to be excommunicat: The quhilk day ane summondis beand producit lauchfullie execute and indorsit upone Robert Fogo in Doun chairgeing him to have compeirit the said day to heir and se him self decernit to be excommunicat for his contemp and disobedience as at mair lynthe is conteinit in the summondis producit thairupone, quhilk Robert being oft tymis callit compeirit nocht, and the brethrein having diligentlie wyit and deiplie considderit his gret obstinacie and manifest contemp of the lauchfull chairgis of the kirk ordanis and decernis the said Robert Fogo to be excommunicat and cuttit off fra the societie of Chrystis kirk and to be delyverit into the handis of the devill for destructioun of his flesche that his saull may be saif in the day of the Lord Jesus, and commandis Michaell Lermonthe, minister at Kilmadok, to pronunce the sentence of excommunicatioun againis him conform to this decreit, lauchfull admonitiounis to be gevin be the said Michell passand befoir.

Mairtein Sawer: Anent the tryell gif Mairtein Sawer, parrochinnar in Alvayth, be excommunicat or nocht, seeing the minister that is allegit to have pronuncit the sentence is departit furth of this lyf, thairfor ordanis Michaell Lermonthe, scryb to the bischop of Dunblane, visitur of the said kirk and kepar of the buik of actis made the tymis of the said bischopis visitatioun to vesie ovir the same buik, and gif he find ony actis thairin makand mentioun of the said Mairteinis excommunicatioun that he extract thame and produce thame befoir the brethir, and als ordanis Robert Mentayth to tak diligent tryell thairanent amangis the elderis and deacunis of his awin kirk of Alvayth, and quhat he findis thairby to report the samin to the brethir.

William Harvy: The quhilk day ane summondis beand producit lauchfullie execute and indorsit upone William Harvy in Both-kenner, chairgeing him to compeir the said day to answer at the instance of the kirk for adultrie committit be him, as at mair lynthe is conteinit in the summondis producit thairupone, compeirit the said William Harvy and confessis that he was mareit withe [*blank*] quha hes nocht anneirit [*recte*, adheirit] to him the speace of xx yeir past and mair, and als that it is four yeir and mair sen he saw hir last and confessis he hes begottin twa bairnis by his said wyf with Marione Yung, the ane befoir he saw hir last, and the uthir sensyne, and that he is credablie informit that his wyf was departit furth of this lyf befoir he gat the last bairne, and thairfor allegis his last fault is bot fornicatioun. The brethrein, being advysit with the said Williamis confessioun, findis thai can nocht decern gif the last fault be adultrie or nocht quhill thay have sufficient tryell quhethir his wyf was thane alyve or nocht or quhen scho deit, and thairfor ordanis the said William with all possablle diligence to act cautioun in the commissaris buikis of Striviling that he sall satisfie the kirk for the saidis offencis as he salbe commandit, and separat the said Marione Yung fra him with diligence and nocht ressave hir againe in hous with him under the paine of xx libis.

At Striviling the xxj day of May, 1583

Presentes: James Andirsone, Mr Andro Yung, Robert Mentayth, Mr Andro Grahame, Mr Alexander Chisholme, Patrik Gillaspie,

Michaell Lermonthe and Alexander Fargy, ministeris; Mr James Pont, Umphra Cunynghame, elderis; and Mr Alexander Iule, brothur off exerceis.

The quhilk day Mr Alexander Chisholme producit his buik of disceplein to be veseit and considderit be the bretherin.

Robert Fogo: The quhilk day compeirit Robert Fogo in Doun (beand of befoir decernit to be excommunicat for disobedience) and offerit him self in the will of the kirk thairfoir, and the said Robert, beand accusit be the moderatour of certane offencis done be him in his offeice as eftir follwis, answerit thairto as heireftir is mentionat. First, being accusit for mareing of personis and ministratioun of the sacrament of baptisme without lauchfull admissioun, the said Robert ansorit that he was admittit be Mr Johnne Row, commissionar in tha parttis for the tyme, be word to bapteis bairnis lauchfullie gottin, quhilk Alexander Fargy, minister, testefeit, and lykwys allegit that he was sensyne admittit be Mr Andro Grahame, visitur, to bapteis bairnis lauchfullie gottin be word, quhilk the said Mr Andro denyit, and being accusit gif he hade ony admissioun to ministrat bapteim [*sic*] in wret, answerit that he hade nane bot ane testimoniall of his admissioun be Mr Johnne Row, quhilk he producit, and eftir the samin beand red was fund be the brethrein to contein na admission of the said Robert bot onelie to reid. Secundlie, being accusit for ane sellar of the sacrament of baptisme, in taking of silvir thairfoir, and for mareing, the said Mr Robert denyit the samin *simpliciter*. Thridlie, being accusit for baptezein of ane bairn gottin in adultrie last be William Murray, he nocht satisfeand the kirk thairfoir, the said Robert denyit the samin *simpliciter*. Fourtlie, being accusit for baptezein of ane bairne gottin in fornicatioun be William Gilroy on Merjorie Drummond, parrochinnar in Logy, the kirk nocht be[and] satisfeit for the said fault, the said Robert grantis the samin and submittis him self in the will of the brethrein thairfoir. The brethrein continewis thair jugementis anent his disobedience and accusatiounis layit to him to the iiij day of *Junij* nixt, the said Robert warnit thairto *apud acta*.

Johnne Wod, Johnne Brown: The quhilk day ane summondis beand producit lauchfullie execute and indorsit upone Johnne Wod and Johnne Broun, schulmaisteris at the kirkis of Muthill and Strogayth, chairgeing thame to compeir the said day to answer at the instance of

the kirk for playing of clark playis on the Sabboth day thairby
abusing the samin for ministratioun of baptisme and mariage without lauchfull admissioun as at mair lynthe is conteinit in the said
summondis, compeirit the said Johnne Wod and being accusit be
the moderatour for abusing of the Sabboth day in playing of clark
playis thairon, the said Johnne confessit the same and is penitent
thairfoir and offeris him self in the will of the kirk thairfoir, quha is
ordeinit to mak publict repentence thairfoir in the kirk of Muthill
and confes his fault in presens of the congregatioun immediatelie
eftir the sermond and ordanis the brethrein of Dunblane to try his
habilitie for teiching of ane schulle, and thaireftir to report it to the
brethrein. The said Johnne Broun, being oft tymis callit, compeirit
nocht. Thairfor ordanis him to be summond of new to the effect
foirsaid undir the paine of excommunicatioun.

Excommunicantis in Alvayth: The quhilk day, Robert Mentayth,
minister at Alvayth, reportit to the brethir that he, at thair command,
hade pronuncit the sentence of excommunicatioun lauchfullie
according to the ordur againis William Watt and Jonet Dugy,
incesteus adulteraris, quha as yit schawis na signis of repentence. The
brethrein ordanis him to produce the nixt sessioun the forme of the
sentence pronuncit and of the admonitionis he gave befoir in wret
that the brethrein may advys thairwith.

Sawer and Aitkein pronuncit excommunicat: The samin day, Robert
Mentayth, minister, reportit that forsamekill as in the last sessioun
he was ordeinit to tak diligent tryell of the elderis and deacunis of
the kirk of Alvayth anent Mairtein Sawer, allegit to be excommunicat, according to the quhilk command the said Robert hes
upone the xix day of May last bypast examinat the elderis of the said
kirk of the ordur of pronunciatioun of the sentence of excommunicatioun againis Mairtein Sawer, *alias* Ayckein, and Bessie Gibsone,
adulteraris, quha hes deponit in ane publict sessioun conveinit all in
ane voice that the said Mairtein and Bessie was denuncit excommunicat be Alexander Drysdell, reder for the tyme, for thair said
offence and malicius, obstinat disobedience to the voice of the kirk
the speace of ten yeiris syne or thairby, quhilkis was delatit and gevin
up to the bischop of Dunblane, visitur, in his visitatioun, and also
deponit that the laird of Cars, barroun of the barrony of Alvayth,
made actis in his court that na mane sould hant nor cum in his

cumpany under the paine of unlawis usit and warnit. The samin day Michaell Lermonthe beand requyrit to declair quhat actis he hes fund in the buik of visitatioun concerning the excommunicatioun of Mairtein Sawer, the said Michaell declairit that he hade fund ane act quhair the said Mairtein was gevin up as excommunicat to the bischop of Dunblane, visitur for the tyme, off the quhilk act the tennour follwis:

The visitatioun of the kirk of Dulicultrie [sic] made at the samin upone Twisday the xxiij day of July, 1577

Mairtein Aikein with Bessie Gibsone, adulteraris, being bayth excommunicat for the said offence and yit continewing without amendiment contempteusly, quhairfor the bischop, with advis of the assembly present, expreslie inhibittis that na persone or personis within the said parrochun, and speciallie Johnne Watt and Jonet Alexander onnawayis ressave the saidis personis within thair housis or ony manir of way accumpany with thame in eatting, drinking or communicatioun unto sic tyme thai submit thame selffis to the kirk for thair former offencis and this to be publesit be the reder to the haill parrochinnaris that thai pretend na ignorance thairof in tyme cuming.

At Striviling the xxviij day of May, 1583

Presentes: Mr William Stirling, James Andirsone, Mr Andro Grahame, Mr Arthur Futhie, Mr Andro Yung, Robert Mentayth, Patrik Gillaspie, Michaell Lermonthe, Mr Adame Merschell, Alexander Fargy, Johnne Row, ministeris; Mr James Pont, Robert Alexander, elderis; and Mr Alexander Iule, ane brothur of exerceis.

Chrystis woll: The quhilk day the brethrein undirstanding that ane gret numbir of pepill hes resortit and resorttis in pilgramage to Chrystis well using thairat superstitioun and idolatrie expres agains Godis law and the actis of parliament, thairfore and for remade quhairof the brethrein ordanis summondis to be direct chairgeing sic of the saidis personis quhais namis salbe gevin in wret to the clark to compeir befoir the brethrein to answer thairfoir to the effect ordur may be tane with thame that hes bein thair to the glorie of God and executioun of the kingis majesteis lawis and in example of utheris to do the lyk.

The samin day Robert Mentayth, minister at Tullicultrie, producit befoir the brethrein in wret the forme of the admonitionis
gevin be him publictlie to William Wat and Jonet Dugy for thair
obedience unto the kirk togethir with the forme of the sentence of
excommunicatioun pronuncit be him againis thame inrespect of
thair contumax as the samin at mair lynthe beris, quhairof the
tennour follwis.

Adulteraris in Tullicultrie pronuncit excommunicat: Upone Sonday
the vij day of Aprill the yeir of God im vc lxxxiij yeiris, I, Robert
Mentayth, minister of the Word of God at the kirk of Tullicultrie,
past at the command of the presbytery of Striviling to the said
parroche kirk of Tullicultrie, and thair immediatlie eftir the
sermond publictlie admonesit William Watt and Jonet Dugy,
delaitit as incestius adulteraris dwelland within the parrochun of the
said kirk, to submit thame selffis to the disceplein of the kirk for thair
contumacie and malicius disobedience this lang tyme past undir the
paine of excommunicatioun, and that as for the first admonitioun
befoir the sentence conforme to the ordur, quhilk I did in presens of
the haill pepill conveinit to heir Godis Word for the tyme. [*Signed*]
Robert Menteht, minister of the evangell.

Upone Sonday the xxviij day of Aprill the yeir of God foirsaid,
I, Robert Mentayth, minister of the Word of God, past at the
command of the said presbytery to the said parroch kirk and thair
immediatlie eftir the sermond publictlie admonesit the saidis
William Wat and Jonet Dugy, as said is, undir the paine of excommunicatioun, and that as for the secund admonitioun befoir the
sentence, conforme to the ordur, quhilk I did in presens of the haill
pepill conveinit to heir Godis Word for the tyme. [*Signed*] Robert
Menteht, minister of the evangell.

Upone Sonday the fyft day of May the yeir of God foirsaid, I,
Robert Mentaythe, minister, at command of the said presbytery past
to the parroche kirk of Tullicultrie foirsaid and thair immediatlie
eftir the sermond publictlie admonesit the said William Wat and
Jonet Dugy, as said is, undir the paine of excommunicatioun, and
that as for the thrid and last admonitioun befoir the prononceing of
the sentence, conforme to the ordur, quhilk I did in presens of the
haill pepill conveinit to hier Godis Word for the tyme.

Watt and Dugy pronuncit excommunicat: Upone Sonday the xix day of May the yeir of God foirsaid, I, Robert Mentayth, minister, at command of the said presbytery past to the said parroche kirk of Tullicultrie and thair immediatlie eftir the sermond inquyrit the elderis of the said kirk, beand present for the tyme, gif ony of the saidis personis haid offerit to ony of thame be thame selffis or be ony uthir in thair namis obedience unto the kirk, quha answerit to me negateivlie, and als inquyrit gif the saidis personis or ony in thair namis wald promeis obedience thairof presentlie to the kirk, quha promesit nane, and thairfoir I, the said minister, pronuncit the saidis personis excommunicat and ilk ane of thame according to the ordur and decreit of the brethrein of the presbytery of Striviling in all pointis, quhilk I did in presens of the haill pepill conveinit to heir Godis Word for the tyme, in witnes of the quhilkis, I have subscryvit thir admonitionis and sentence of excommunicatioun with my awin hand as follwis. [Signed] Robert Menteht, minister of the evangell.

Johnne Broun: The quhilk day thair was ane summondis producit befoir us dewlie execute and indorsit upone Johnne Broun, scholmaistir at Stragaithe, chairgeing him to compeir befoir us the said day to answer at the instance of the kirk, as at mair lynthe is conteinit in the said summondis, compeirit the said Johnne Broun personallie, and being accusit for disobeying ane admonitioun gevin to him be Mr Alexander Chisholme, minister, in prophaning of the Sabboth day in playing of clerk playis thairon, withdrawing thairby sindrie of the pepill fra the preiching eftir the said admonitioun was gevin to him, the said Johnne denyit the samin, bot confessit gif ony play was playit on the Sabboth day it was playit be the bairnis by his avys. Secundlie, beand accusit for abusing the sacrament of baptisme and mariage in ministring the same without lauchfull admissioun to that functioun, the said Johnne denyit *simpliciter* the ministering ather of mariage or baptisme. The brethrein being advysit with his answeris ordanis and decernis him to produce the register of the clark play (playit be his bairnis as he allegis) befoir the brethrein on the xj day of *Junij* nixt to be sein and considerit be thame, and to heir and se farther tryell tane anent his accusatiounis under the paine of disobedience, the said Johnne warnit thairto *apud acta*.

Disobedients in Dunblane: The quhilk day thair was ane summondis producit befoir us dewlie execute and indorsit upone George Dugall at brig end of Dunblane, Thomas Quhyttat, servand to Thomas

Alexander, Thomas Drummond and Margaret Drummond in Corskapill eftir chairgeing thame to compeir befoir the brethrein the said day to answer at the instance of the kirk for disobedience to the voice of the sessioun of thair awin elderschip and sessioun of the kirk of Dunblane, as at mair lynthe is conteinit in the said summondis, compeirit all the saidis personis except Thomas Quhyttat and grantit thair offence and submitit thame selffis in the will of the kirk thairfoir, and thairfor was ordeinit be the brethrein to pas hame and obey the voice of the said sessioun and nawayis be disobedient thairunto in tymis cuming undir the paine of the censuris of the kirk to be execute againis thame with all rigour. The said Thomas Quhytet being oft tymis callit compeirit nocht. Thairfor the brethrein ordanis him to be summond of new to the effect foirsaid undir the paine of excommunicatioun.

Nicoll Fargus contra *Jonet Wrycht*: The quhilk day thair was ane summondis producit befoir us dewlie execute and indorsit upone Jonet Wricht, dochter to Henrie Wricht in Forest, chairgeing hir to answer at the instance of Nicoll Fargus, parrochinnar in Clakmannan, and to schawe and declair befoir the brethrein ane ressonablle caus quhy scho will nocht compleit mariage with the said Nicoll according to ane matremoniall contract made betuix thame, as at mair lynthe is conteinit in the said summondis, the said Jonet beand oft tymis callit compeirit nocht. Thairfor the brethrein ordanis the said Jonet to be summond of new to the effect foirsaid undir the paine of excommunicatioun.

At Striviling the iiij day of *Junij*, 1583

Presentes: Mr William Stirling, James Andirsone, Patrik Gillaspie, Mr Andro Yung, Mr Alexander Chisholme, Michaell Lermonthe, Mr Adame Merschell, Alexander Fargy and Patrik Layng, ministeris; Alexander Balvaird, Andro Kirk and William Stirling, rederis; Mr Alexander Iule, ane brothur of exerceis; Robert Alexander and Umphra Cunynghame, elderis.

Robert Fogo: In the terme assignit to the brethrein to advys with the accusationis layit againis Robert Fogo in Doun, the said Robert compeirand personallie, he was accusit be the moderatour gif he baptezit the bairne gottin first in adultrie be William Murray now in Strathern on [blank] (the kirk nocht beand satisfeit thairfoir), the said Robert Fogo confessit the same. The brethrein, being advysit with the accusatiounis layit againis him and his answeris made thairto, findis the said Robert Fogo to have abusit the sacrament of baptisme and mariage in ministratioun of thame without ony lauchfull admissioun thairto in wret as aucht to have bein, and lykwys findis him to have baptezit bairnis, ane gottin in adultrie and ane uthir in fornicatioun (the kirk nocht beand satisfeit be thair parentis), againis the actis of the kirk, and thairfor dischairgis the said Robert Fogo *simpliciter* that he tak nocht upone hand at ony tyme fra thisfurthe nather to ministrat baptisme nor mariage to na personis undir the paine of the censuris of the kirk to be execute againis him with all rigour, and als ordanis the said Robert to compeir befoir the brethrein the xxv day of *Junij* instant in the parroche kirk of Striviling to gif ane tryell of his reiding as he salbe desyrit and to heir and se tryell tane of his lyf and conversatioun undir the paine of deprivatioun of him fra reiding in the kirk.

Commissionaris to Muthill: In the terme assignit to Mr Andro Yung, Mr William Stirling and Michaell Lermonthe, commissionaris appointit to pas and vesie the kirk of Muthill as ane act made thairupone on the ix day of Aprill last bypast at mair lynthe beris, and that quhat thay fand be thir said visitatioun to report the samin to the brethrein this day, the saidis commissionaris beand personallie present was requyrit to declair to the brethrein thair report, as thay war commandit. The saidis commissionaris answerit that the tyme thai passit to the said kirk thair was nocht ane sufficient numbir of the parrochun conveinit, and thairfor continewit thair visitatioun quhill ane greter numbir of the parrochun mycht be gottin conveinit to that effect. The brethrein continewis the saidis personis commissionaris as was of befoir to the [blank] day of [blank] and ordanis thame to report to the brethrein the said day quhat thai find be thair said visitatioun.

Thomas Quhyt, adulterar: The quhilk day thair was ane summondis producit befoir us lauchfullie execute and indorsit upone Thomas Quhyt in Kildeis chairgeing him to have compeirit the said day to heir and se him self decernit to be excommunicat for his contemp and disobedience, as at mair lynthe is conteinit thairin, compeirit the said Thomas personallie and grantis his disobediencis, for the quhilk he submittis him self in the will of the brethrein, and being accusit be the moderatour for adultrie with Agnes Gentill, inrespect he is mareit with Jonet Drummond quha is yit alyve, the said Thomas confessis him mareit with the said Jonet and grantis carnall copulatioun with the said Agnes by his wyf, and thairfor is fund be the brethrein to have committit adultrie, for the quhilk he is ordeinit to pas to the nixt synnodall assemblie of this province to be haldin in Edinbrugh the first day of October nixttocum, thair to ressave injunctionis to be injonit to him for his said offence and obey thame undir the paine of disobedience, and lykwys is admonesit to abstein fra the said Agnes in carnall dell in all tymis cuming undir the paine of excommunicatioun.

Nicoll Fargus contra *Jonet Wrycht*: The quhilk day ane summondis beand producit lauchfullie execut and indorsit upone Jonet Wrycht, dochter to Henrie Wricht in Forest, chairgeing hir to compeir befoir the brethrein the said day to answer at the instance of Nycoll Fargus in Brachteburn within the parrochun of Clakmannan, to schaw and declair ane ressonablle caus quhy scho will nocht compleit mariage according to ane matrimoniall contract made betuix the said Henrie Wrycht and hir, on that ane part, and the said Nycoll, on that uthir part, as at mair lynthe is conteinit in the said summondis producit thairupone, baithe the saidis parteis compeirand personallie, and the said Jonet Wricht, beand requyrit to declair ane ressonablle caus quhy sche wald nocht compleit mariage with the said Nycoll, could declair nane bot continewit still obstinat in refuis of the same, and farther beand requyrit be the moderatour to declair gif scho was contractit in mariage with consent of hir parentis to the said Nycoll, scho and hir fathir, also being present, confessit bayth the same and that thair banis war proclamit thre sindrie Sondayis according to the ordur. With the quhilkis, the brethrein being advysit findis the said Jonet Wricht inconstant in passing fra the promeis of mariage quhilk scho haid made, as said is, and lykwys the said Henrie, hir fathir, in approving hir passing thairfra againis his awin formar consent to the said promeis, and thairfor inrespect of the said Jonettis malicius refuis decernis the said Nycoll Fargus fre to marie in the Lord nochtwithstanding of the formar contract, and for the said Jonet and Henreis inconstancie decernis the said Jonet to mak publict repentence in the parroche kirk of Clakmannan the nixt Sonday, viz., the ix of this instant, in the plaice appointit for penitentis in tyme of sermond according to the ordur, undir paine of disobedience, and the said Henrie, hir fathir, inrespect of his refuis to compleit the said mariage nochtwithstanding of his formar consent, being hir fathir, decernis him to pay x libis. usuall mony of this realme, to be applyit to the decoratioun of thair parroche kirk of Clakmannan, according to ane act of the generall assemblie made thairanent, and farther inhibitis and forbiddis the minister of Clakmannan and all uthir ministeris or rederis havand functioun within the kirk that nane of thame minister ony benefeit of the kirk to the said Henrie nor his said dochter ay and quhill the saidis Henrie and Jonet satisfie our said decreit in all pointis alsweill civillie as spirituallie, as thay or ony ane of thame will answer thairfoir to the kirk.

Adulteraris in Clakmannan: The quhilk day Patrik Layng being desyrit be the moderatour to declair quhow oft he haid admonesit the personis dwelland within the parrochun of Clakmannan that ar decernit to be excommunicat to submit thame selffis to the disceplein of the kirk for thair contumacie, and lykwys being desyrit to produce the forme of his admonitionis in wret as he was ordeinit, the said Patrik ansorit that he hade admonesit thame lauchfullie on twa sindrie Sondayis and as tuiching the forme of his admonitiounis confessit he hes nocht as yit put thame in wret in perfyt forme but he sall do it and produce thame befoir the brethir on the xviij day of *Junij* instant. The brethrein ordanis him to gif the saidis personis the thrid admonitioun befoir the sentence on Sonday nixt and to produce the forme of his haill admonitionis according to his promeis.

Patrik Layng: The samin day Patrik Layng beand desyrit to produce his answeris to the accusatiounis layit againis him according to the brethreinis ordinance made on the vij of May last bypast, compeirit the said Patrik and producit his answeris in wret as thai bair in thame selffis, with the quhilkis the brethrein tuik to advys to the xviij day of *Junij* instant the said Patrik warnit thairto *apud acta*.

Patrik Layng: The brethrein undirstandand Patrik Layng to have ressavit summondis for chairgeing of Margaret Bruce to compeir befoir the brethrein to answer at the instance of the kirk for adultrie allegit committit be hir with Robert Bruce of Clakmannan, quhilk summondis he hes sindrie tymis neglectit in the executioun, thairfor the moderatour, in name of the brethrein, chairgis the said Patrik to execute the said summondis on the said Margaret and to produce the samin deulie execut and indorsit upone the xviij day of this instant undir the paine of *simpliciter* deprivatioun of him fra the offeice of the ministrie, and that conforme to ane generall ordinance made thairanent the xij day of Merche last.

Anent the proclamatioun of Johnne Aissone and Violat Rind: The quhilk day it was proponit to the brethrein be James Andirsone, minister, that quhair ane man callit Johnne Aisson, born in Craiginforth within the parrochun of S. Ninianis kirk, quha hes dwelt ane lang tyme sensyne in the brugh of Striviling and now is ane traffiquer be sie and hes na certane dwelling plaice, quhilk Johnne is contractit in mariage with Violat Rind, ane parrochinnar in Perthe, quhais bannis ar proclamit, or to be proclamit, in the parroche kirk of Perthe, for the said Violattis part, and that the said Johnne desyris that his bannis be proclamit in Striviling, for his part, and thairfor inrespect of the premisis the said minister inquyrit gif his bannis salbe proclamit in Striviling, as he desyris, or nocht. The brethrein ordanis his bannis to be proclamit in the kirkis of Striviling and S. Niniane, lauchfullie according to the ordur, and the ministeris thairof to report to the minister of Perthe thair testemoniallis testefeand the trewthe.

Anent repentence of Johnne Aissone: Secundlie, the said minister of Striviling declairit that the saidis Johnne Aissone and Violat Rind hes gottin ane bairne in fornicatioun in the plaice of Kilmaronock, for the quhilk as yit the kirk is nocht satisfeit and (as the said minister informit) the said Johnne dar nocht pas to the kirk of Kilmaronock to satisfie the samin for his said fault without gret dainger of his lyf, and trew it is that the said Violat was lichter of the said bairne in Striviling quhair scho remainit the speace of sex oulkis or thairby, and thairfor *queritur* quhair the said Johnne sould mak repentence in respect of the premisis. The brethrein ordanis him to mak publict repentence in the parroche kirk of Striviling, according to the ordur.

Johnne Kemp: Thridlie, the said minister declairit that he is informit that Johnne Kemp, allegit reder at Lecrop, hes baptezit the said bairne gottin be the saidis personis without ony admissioun and that abusitlie in ane prophane hous in the Latein langage. For tryell of the quhilkis, the brethrein ordanis him to be summond to the nixt sessioun to answer thairfor and sic uthir thingis that salbe layit unto his chairge undir the paine of disobedience.

Chrystis woll: The quhilk day thair was ane summondis producit dewlie execute and indorsit upone Margaret Wrycht in Cambus, Johnne Kidstoun thair and Thomas Patersone in Blak Grainge chairgeing thame to compeir befoir the brethrein the said day to answer at the instance of the kirk for passing in pilgrimage to Chrystis woll and using of superstitioun and idolatrie thairat undir the paine of disobedience, quhilkis being oft tymis callit compeirit nocht, thairfor the brethrein ordanis thame to be summond of new to the effect foirsaid under the paine of excommunicatioun.

William Wingyett: The quhilk day ane summondis beand producit lauchfullie execute and indorsit upone William Wingyet and Jonet Johnesone chairgeing thame to compeir the said day to heir and se thame selffis decernit to be excommunicat for thair contemp and wilfull insisting in the vyce of fornicatioun without amendiment, as at mair lynthe is conteinit in the said summondis producit thairupone, compeirit the said William personallie and promesis to obey the censuris of the kirk and to abstein in all tymis cuming fra the said Jonet or ellis marie hir. The brethrein decernis and ordanis the said William Wingyet to act cautioun in the commissaris buikis of Striviling betuix and the xviij day of *Junij* instant that he sall obey and satisfie the injunctiounis of the kirk for his said offence and to abstein fra the woman with all possablle diligence or ellis compleit mariage with hir under the paine of xx libis. [excommunication, *deleted*] and this cautioun to be actit, as said is, under the paine of excommunicatioun.

Robert Leckie: The quhilk day ane summondis beand producit lauchfullie execute and indorsit upone Robert Leckie of Kepderrocht chairgeing him to have compeirit the said day to answer at the instance of the kirk for disobedience to the voice of the sessioun of his awin parroche kirk of S. Niniane [Clakmannan, *deleted*] and to heir and se him self decernit to have committit adultrie with Jonet Mairtein, yunger, and to underly the censuris of the kirk alswell for his disobedience to the voice of the said sessioun as for his said adultrie allegit committit be him under the paine of disobedience, quhilk Robert being oft tymis callit compeirit nocht, thairfor the brethrein ordanis him to be summond of new to the effect foirsaid under the paine of excommunicatioun.

Mr Andro Graham: The same day the brethrein, upone ressonablle considerationis, grantis lycence to Mr Andro Grahame to pas to his fathir for performing of sic ressonablle bissines as he hes ado, provyding he appoint to the moderatour betuix and the xviij day of this instant ane peremptour of day of his returne within ane moneth or thairby.

At Striviling the xj day of *Junij*, 1583

Presentes: Mr William Stirling, James Andirsone, Patrik Gillaspie, Mr Andro Yung, Robert Mentayth, Alexander Fargy, Mr Alexander Chisholme, Mr Arthur Futhie, ministeris; Johnne Erskein of Dun, Alexander Forester of Garden, Umphra Cunynghame, Robert Alexander, elderis; and Mr Alexander Iule, ane brothur of exerceis.

McKie, Stewart: The quhilk day Alexander Fargy, minister at Logy, reportit to the brethir that he hade admonesit James McKie and Jane Stewart, adulteraris, thre sindrie Sondayis lauchfullie according to the ordur to submit thame selffis to the disciplein of the kirk for thair contumacie and malicius disobedience to the voice thairof undir the paine of excommunicatioun and as yit seis na obedience offirit. Thairfor the brethrein ordanis the said Alexander Fargy to proceid and pronunce the sentence of excommunicatioun againis thame lauchfullie according to the ordur gif thai continue still obstinat.

Johnne Broun: The quhilk day being assignit to Johnne Broun, scholmaistir at Stragayth, to produce the register of ane clark play playit be his bairnis (as he allegis), compeirit the said Johnne Broun and producit the register of the said play. For veseing of the quhilk buik, the brethrein appointis the brethrein in Striviling to vesie the same and to report thair jugementis thairof to the brethrein on the ij day of July nixt, the said Johnne warnit thairto and to answer to uthir accusatiounis *apud acta* undir the paine of disobedience.

Johnne Broun: The samin day the brethrein appointis to the said Johnne Broun this thesis, viz., it is lesum to play clark playis on the

Sabboth day or nocht, and quhethir gif it be lesum or nocht to mak clark playis on ony part of the scripture, quhilk thesis the said Johnne is ordeinit to put in Latein, and to use sic proballle argumentis as he can for preving of bayth the partis of the said thesis and to produce the samin in wret befoir the brethrein on the ij day of July nixt undir the paine of disobedience.

Disobedientis at Chrystis woll: The quhilk day ane summondis beand producit lauchfullie execute and indorsit upone Jonet Tailyour, spous to Robert Cowane in Touch, Marione Watsone thair, Marjorie Fargussone thair, Margaret Downy in Polmais, Jonet Mayne dwelland undir Johnne Downy in Mossyd, chairgeing thame to have compeirit the said day to answer at the instance of the kirk for passing in pilgramage to Chrystis woll and using of superstitioun and idolatrie thairat expres againis Goddis law, undir the paine of disobedience, quhilkis personis being oft tymis callit compeirit nocht, thairfor the brethrein ordanis the saidis personis to be summond of new to the effect foirsaid undir the paine of excommunicatioun.

Johnne Wilsone: The quhilk day compeirit Johnne Wilsone in Polmais, quha being accusit be the moderatour for haulding of Agnes Mentayth quhomewith he committit fornicatioun in hous with him, as yit, quhom he was ordeinit be the brethrein to have separat fra him ane lang tyme sensyne, the said Johnne answerit that he had lang syne dischairgit the said Agnes his hous, quha, as yit, hes nocht obeyit his command. The brethrein ordanis the said Johnne Wilsone to remove the said Agnes furthe of his and nocht to ressave hir thairin at na tyme thaireftir with all possablle diligence and that he cum nocht in hir cumpany in na plaice that may gif ony suspitioun off hurdum under the paine of excommunicatioun, with certificatioun and he failze ordanis Patrik Gillaspie, minister, to pronunce the sentence of excommunicatioun againis him according to the ordur.

Johnne Kemp: The quhilk day ane summondis beand producit lauchfullie execute and indorsit upone Johnne Kempe, allegit reder at the kirk of Lecrop, chairgeing him to have compeirit the said day to answer at the instance of the kirk for ministratioun off baptisme without admissioun and abusing of the sacrament thairof in ministratioun of the same in ane prophane hous in ane uncouthe and strainge langage as at mair lynthe is conteinit in the summondis producit thairupone, compeirit the said Johnne Kemp personallie and being desyrit be the moderatour to declair gif he baptezit ane bairne gottin in fornicatioun be Johnne Aissone, sone to James Aissone in Craginforth, on Violat Rind, now in Perthe (quhilkis parentis haid nocht satisfeit the kirk for the said fornicatioun), the said Johnne Kemp confessit the baptezein of the same bairne. Farder the said Johne being desyrit to declair in quhat plaice he baptezit the same, in quhat langage, and the remanent of the circumstancis thairof, the said Johnne confessit he baptezit the said bairne in Alexander Wilsonis hous in Knokhill in the Latein langage on the first Sonday of Lenterun betuix ix and x houris in the morning in presens of the said Alexander Wilson, Jonet Ewein, his spous, Merjorie Robertsone in Castell hill and James Aissone, brothur to the fathir of the said bairne. The said bairne was callit James Aissone and denyit that he ressavit ony thing thairfoir. Secundlie, the said Johnne Kemp being desyrit be the moderatour to declair gif he baptezit ane bairne gottin be William Murray in adultrie last by his wyf, quha haid nocht satisfeit the kirk thairfoir, and the circumstancis thairof, as said is, the said Johnne Kemp confessit the baptezein of the said bairne in Nicoll Andersonis hous, *alias* Nycoll Millar in the Keir, in the Latein langage, the said Nycoll beand present, and denyit he ressavit ony thing thairfoir.

Deprivatioun off Johnne Kemp: The brethrein, having diligentlie considderit the accusatiounis layit againis the said Johnne Kemp and his answeris made thairto, and being ryplie advysit thairwith, findis the said Johnne Kemp ane prophaner of the sacrament off baptisme in ministring the samin in prophaine housis in ane uncouthe and strainge langage expres againis Godis word, and findis the said Johnne nocht lauchfullie admittit to ministrat baptisme in the kirk of God and thairfor thocht the said Johnne Kemp worthie to be deposit and deposis him *simpliciter* fra reding in the kirk of God and all functioun thairof and exerceis of ony part of the ministrie thairof at all tymis frat[h]isfurth, and ordanis thir his offencis confessit be him to be delaitit to the kingis majestie for puneisment of the same, and gif the bairne salbe haldin as lauchfullie baptezit or nocht and tuiching the said Johnne Kempis repentence, the brethrein continewis thair jugementis thairin quhill thai be farder advysit, quhilk

M

deprivatioun of the said Johnne Kemp is presentlie intimat to him be the moderatour that he pretend na ignorance thairof.

Chrystis woll, Thomas Patersone: The quhilk day ane summondis beand producit lauchfullie execute and indorsit upone Margaret Wrycht in Cambus, Jonet Kidstoun thair, and Thomas Patersone in Blak Grainge, chairgeing thame to have compeirit the said day to answer at the instance of the kirk for passing in pilgrimage to Chrystis woll and using of superstitioun and idolatrie thairat expres againis Godis law under the paine of excommunicatioun, compeirit the said Thomas Patersone and being accusit be the moderator for his passing to the said woll and desyrit him to declair quhat was the occasioun of his thair ganging and quhat he usit and did quhen he was thair, the said Thomas confessit he past to the said woll to gait his haill becaus he is seik lyk as he hes bein this lang tyme and that he past sone gaittis about the woll and sat doun on his kneis and prayit, and drank of the woll and cust waltir on his hed and wosche his hed and breist and tuke ane peice of the breist of his sark about ane bus besyd the woll and left it thair, and als confessis that Jonet Kidston, Hellein Scott, Margaret Bwey in Cambus and Robert Andirsone was at the said woll with him, and submittis him self in the will of the kirk for his offence. The brethir continewis thair jugementis heirin quhill thai be farther advysit.

Disobedientis: The said Margaret Wrycht and Jonet Kidstoun being oft tymis callit compeirit nocht. Thairfor the brethrein findis thame contumax and ordanis thame to be excommunicat for thair contumacie with certificatioun and thai failze the brethrein will proceid and decern thame to be excommunicat, as said is.

Thomas Quhytet: The quhilk day ane summondis beand producit lauchfullie execute and indorsit upone Thomas Quhytet, servand to Thomas Alexander, chairgeing him to have compeirit the said day to answer at the instance of the kirk for disobedience to the voice of the sessioun and elderschip of his awin kirk of Dunblane and to underly disceplein thairfoir undir the paine of excommunicatioun, quhilk Thomas being oft tymis callit compeirit nocht, thairfor the brethren findis the said Thomas contumax, and thairfor ordanis him to be summond to heir and se him self decernit to be excommunicat for his contumacie, with certificatioun and he failzie the brethrein will proceid and decern him to be excommunicat, as said is.

Disobedientis at Chrystis woll: The quhilk day ane summondis beand producit lauchfullie execute and indorsit upone Jonet Porter, spous to James McCalpie in Bohaldie, and Hellein Dow in Lyttill Coig, chairgeing thame to have compeirit the said day to answer at the instance of the kirk for passing in pilgrimage to Chrystis woll and using of superstitioun and idolatrie thairat againis the law of God undir the paine of disobedience, quhilk personis, being oft tymis callit, compeirit nocht, thairfor the brethrein ordanis thame to be summond of new to the effect foirsaid undir the paine of excommunicatioun.

Buik of disciplein of Alvayth veseit: The samin day the buik of disceplein of the parrochun of Alvayth was veseit and admittit for the present and delyverit againe to Robert Mentayth, minister thairof, and praysis his diligence, bot findis that the particular sessioun of the said parrochun hes mellit with civill thingis, namelie, anent trublance, castein of stouppis and capitall crymis as stelling of yowis and peis, and thairfor ordanis the minister nocht to suffir na thingis to be trettit in the said sessioun in tymis cuming bot ecclesiasticall causis and also admonesis the said Robert to register in ane buik all bairnis baptezit be him, mariagis compleit be him and personis bureit within his parrochun.

The brethrein, understandand Mr Arthur Futhie to have sum ressonablle bissines ado furth of thir partis, thairfor grantis him lycence to be absent the speace of ane moneth.

At Striviling the xviij day of *Junij*, 1583

Presentes: Mr William Stirling, James Andirsone, Patrik Gillaspie, Patrik Layng, Mr Andro Yung, Michaell Lermonthe, Alexander Fargy, ministeris; Umphra Cunynghame, Mr James Pont, Robert Alexander, elderis; and Mr Alexander Iule, ane brothur off exerceis.

Patrik Layng: In the terme assignit to Patrik Layng to produce the first of his admonitionis gevin be him to the personis within the parrochun of Clakmannan, quha ar dicernit to be excommunicat for disobedience to the kirk, and lykwys to produce ane summondis dewlie execute and indorsit on Margaret Bruce according to actis made thairanent, compeirit the said Patrik and confessit he hes admonesit the saidis personis decernit to be excommunicat thre sindrie Sondayis according to the ordur, and findis na obedience in nane of thame as yit, bot he hes nocht put the saidis admonitionis in wret in perfyt forme as yit, bot he sall do the samin sason as he can gudlie, and as tuiching the executioun of the said summondis on Margaret Bruce allegit he was manasit and bostet be Robert Bruce of Clakmannan with mony injurius wordis, quhilk he promesit to performe in deid incaice he execute the said summondis. The brethrein, yit as of befoir, commandis and chairgis the said Patrik Layng to produce befoir the brethrein on the ij day of July nixtocum the forme of his said admonitionis in wret, the said summondis dewlie execute and indorsit, and his buik of disceplein to be sein and considderit be the brethrein undir the paine of deprivatioun with certificatioun and he failze in ony of thame he salbe deprivit *simpliciter.*

Patrik Layng: In the terme assignit to the brethrein to advys with the answeris producit be Patrik Layng to the accusatiounis layit againis him, the said Patrik compeirand personallie, the brethrein, having red the saidis answeris, findis the said Patrik to have wretten in the beginning thairof ane answer to the first hed of his accusatioun (as appeiris be the beginning of the secund answer), quhilk answer the said Patrik hes ryvin away (as he presentlie confessis), quhilk appeiris to the brethrein to be varie suspicius, and thairfor commandis him to produce the samin first answer ryvin away, as said is, befoir the brethrein on the secund day of July nixt under hiest paine and chairge that may follw be the censuris of the kirk.

Parrochinneris of Kippen, Chrystis woll: *Agnes Grahame, Margaret Bauchok, Jonet Harvie, Ewffame Mureson, William Kay*: The quhilk day ane summondis beand producit lauchfullie execute and indorsit upon Agnes Grahame, spous to Robert Lockart in Arnepriour, Margaret Bauchok in Arnenanwall, Jonet Harvy, spous to Thomas Michell in Arnebeg, Margaret Wrycht, spous to Robert Harvy in Arnebeg, Elezabeth Galbrayth, spous to Johnne Campbell in Arngibbon, Cristane Clark, spous to [John] McHenrie in Boclyvie, Elezaboth Levenox, spous to Johnne McAndro in Boclyvie, Agnes Blair, spous to Johnne Dow in the garran of Boclyvie, Ewffame Moreson, dochtir to umquhill Johnne Moresone *alias* Chapman at the kirk of Kippen, Jonet Gairdner, spous to Patrik McIlhois in

Scheirgartane, Johnne Grahame, sone to Robert Henriesone in the Port, William Kay in Bruigh and Johnne Leckie in Balegan, chairgeing thame to have compeirit the said day to answer at the instance of the kirk for passing in pilgramage to Chrystis woll and using of superstitioun and idolatrie thairat againis the law of God ilk persone under the paine of disobedience, compeirit the said Agnes Grahame personallie and confessit scho passit to the said woll and quhen scho come thair scho past round about it and cust the waltir of it ovir hir schulduris, and confessit that Margaret Bauchok was with hir, and Jonet Wrycht, spous to Johnne Harvy in Kippen. The said Margaret Bauchok compeirand personallie, confessit scho past to the said woll with the said Agnes Grahame and that scho past round about the woll bot drank nocht of it. The said Jonet Harvie compeirit personallie and confessit scho past to the said woll becaus scho was seik in hir hairt and in hir hed and lipnit that the woll sould have helpit hir seikness, and confessit that scho past about the woll and cust the waltir ovir hir schuldur and drank of it and left ane peice suwde behind hir and prayit Chrystis woll to help hir. The said Ewffame Moresone compeirit personallie and confessit lyk the said Jonet Harveis confessioun in all thingis except that scho prayit nocht to Chrystis woll to help hir. The said William Kay compeirit personallie and confessit he passit to Chrystis woll for ane bairne of his awin, callit Johnne Kay, that was seik and that he tuik with him ane apprun string of the bairne and that he past about the woll and prayit to Chrystis Sonday to help his bairne and brocht hame the walter of the said woll and gaif to the bairne to drink and left the bairnis apprun string at the woll behind him and confessis that Hobbie Clark, *alias* Robert Clark, ane common begger, that usis maist in Fintrie, was thair at the said woll. The remanent of the saidis personis being oft tymis callit compeirit nocht. Thairfor the brethrein ordanis thame to be summond of new to the effect forisaid undir the paine of excommunicatioun.

Chrystis woll, Hellein Scott, Margaret Bwey: The quhilk day ane summondis beand producit lauchfullie execute and indorsit upone Hellein Scott, Margaret Bwey in Cambus, and Robert Andirsone chairgeing thame to have compeirit the said day to answer at the instance of the kirk for passing in pilgramage to Chrystis woll and using of superstitioun and idolatrie thairat expres againis Godis law under the paine of disobedience, compeirit the said Hellein Scott and confessit scho past to Chrystis woll for seiknes at hir hairt and ane sairnes that was in his arme, and that scho past about the woll and prayit to Chrystis Sonday and drank of the walter thairof and layd it on hir hed and hir arme and thaireftir left ane peice of hir leace behind hir. Compeirit the said Margaret Bwey and confessit scho past to the said woll becaus scho hade the miegroun in hir hed and farther confessit lyk the said Hellein Scott in all thingis except that scho left behind hir ane peice of threid and confessit that Robert Andirsone foirsaid was present thair, quha being oft tymis callit compeirit nocht. Thairfor the brethrein ordanis him to be summond of new to the effect foirsaid undir the paine of excommunicatioun.

Margaret Wrycht, acquyt; *Jonet Kidstoun*: The quhilk day ane summondis beand producit lauchfullie execut and indorsit upone Margaret Wrycht in Cambus and Jonet Kidstoun thair chairgeing thame to have compeirit the said day to heir and se thame selffis decernit to be excommunicat for thair contemp and disobedience compeirit bayth the saidis personis and grantit thair offence and disobedience to the kirk and offirit thame selffis in the will of the brethrein thairfoir. Als, the said Margaret Wrycht being accusit for passing in pilgramage to Chrystis woll, the said Margaret denyit the samin *simpliciter*, and becaus the samin could nocht be varefeit the said Margaret was acquyt thairof. The said Jonet Kidstoun, being accusit for passing in pilgramage to the said woll, confessit scho past thair to get help for ane sairnes in hir syd and confessis scho past about the woll and prayit to Chrystis Sonday and drank of the woll and wische hir syd with the walter thairof and left behind hir ane sowein threid.

Chrystis woll, Marione Fargusson, Jonet Tailyour, denyit: The samin day compeirit Marione Fargussone in Touch and Jonet Tailyour, spous to Robert Cowane in Touch, quha was chairgit to have compeirit the xj day of this instant to have answerit at the instance of the kirk for passing in pilgramage to Chrystis woll and using of superstitioun and idolatrie thairat, the saidis Marione and Jonet denyit *simpliciter* that thay passit to the said woll nor was nocht myndit thairto bot allegit that sindrie personis that was thair beand apprehendit and desyrit to declair thair namis fenzeit thair awin namis and gaif up the namis of uther personis that was nocht thair, quhilk allegeance was understand to the brethrein to be of varitie in sum, and thairfor the brether acquyttis the saidis Marione Fargussone and Jonet Tailyour of the said pilgramage.

Robert Leckie: The quhilk day ane summonids beand producit lauchfullie execut and indorsit upone Robert Leckie of Kepderroch, chairgeing to have compeirit the said day to answer at the instance of the kirk for disobedience to the voice of the elderschip of his awin parroche kirk of S. Niniane and to heir and see him self decernit to have committit adultrie with Jonet Mairtein, yunger, and to underly the censuris of the kirk, alsweill for his disobedience to the voice of the said elderschip as for the said adultrie allegit committit be him undir the paine of excommunicatioun, quhilk Robert being oft tymis callit compeirit nocht, and thairfor was fund be the brethrein contumax and ordeinit to be summond to heir and se him self decernit to be excommunicat for his contumacie and malicius disobedience with certificatioun and he failze the brethrein will proceid and decern him to be excommunicat, as said is.

At Striviling the xxv day of *Junij*, 1583

Presentes: Mr William Stirling, Mr Alexander Chisholme, Robert Mentaythe, Patrik Gillaspie, Michaell Lermonthe, Mr Adame Merschell and Alexander Fargy, ministeris; Umphra Cunynghame, Robert Alexander, Alexander Patersone, notar, elderis; and Mr Alexander Iule, ane brothur of exerceis.

Niniane Aickein, adulterar: The quhilk day compeirit Niniane Aikein, adulterar with Hellein Hendersone, and being accusit be the moderatour quhy he past nocht to the last synnodall assemblie haldin in Edinburgh, as he was warnit be Andro Forester, now his minister, the said Niniane ansorit he was nocht warnit be his said minister to that effect, bot promesit in tymis cuming to obey all that the kirk will command him. The brethrein with consent of the said Niniane ordanis him to compeir befoir the brethrein on Twysday befoir none immediatlie preceding the fest of Michalmes, viz., on the xxiiij day of September nixt to ressave directionis and admonitiounis, thame to be gevin to him under the paine of excommunicatioun, quhilk ordinance the said Niniane promesis to obey.

McKie, Stewart: The quhilk day, Alexander Fargy, minister at Logy, being inquyrit gif he hade pronuncit the sentence of excommunicatioun againis James McKie and Jane Stewart, adulteraris, as he was ordeinit or nocht, the said Alexander Fargy ansorit that he hade pronuncit the sentence of excommunicatioun againis the saidis personis according to the brethreinis ordinance in all pointis. The brethrein ordanis the said Alexander to produce in wret in perfyt forme the sentence pronuncit be him with the forme of the admonitionis gevin be him of befoir on the ix day of July nixt that farder ordur may be tane thairanent.

William Wingyet: The brethrein undirstandand that forsamekill as upone the iiij day of *Junij* instant William Wingyet was decernit and ordeinit to act cautioun in the commissaris buikis of Striviling betuix and the xviij day of *Junij* instant that he sall obey and satisfie the injunctionis of the kirk for his offence of fornicatioun and to abstein fra the woman with all possablle diligence or ellis compleit mariage without dely undir the paine of xx libis., and this cautioun to be actit, as said is, under the paine of excommunicatioun, as at mair lynth is conteinit in the said act of the det foirsaid, nochttheles the brethrein understandand be report of the said commissar that the said William hes nocht as yit actit cautioun, as said is, and thairfor is jugit to have incurrit the sentence of excommunicatioun to be pronuncit againis him becaus the said xviij day of *Junij* is alreddy bypast, and is ordeinit be the brethrein to be summond to heir and se him selff decernit to be excommunicat for his said failze and disobedience with certificatioun and he failze, the brethrein will proceid and decern him to be excommunicat, as said is, and als that Jonet Johneston, fornicatrix with the said William Wingyet, be lykwys summond to heir and se farther proces led againis hir in the said mater undir the paine of disobedience.

Johnne Wod: It beand reportit be the brethrein of Dunblane and in speciall be Mr Andro Yung on the xviij day of this instant that he hade gevin to Johnne Wod, scholmaister at Muthill, lang sensyne ane thesis, as it bure in the selff, quhairupoun he was commandit to make declamatioun and to report the samin againe to the brethrein of Dunblane, quhairbe thai mycht have haid tryell of his habilitie to teiche ane schulle that thai mycht report the samin to the brethrein according to thair ordinance made on the xxj day of May last bypast, quhilk delcamatiounis the said Johnne Wod hes nevir reportit to the brethrein of Dunblane as yit, and thairfor the scryb at command of the brethrein wret ane misseive in name of the brethir desyrand him to compeir the said day and produce before the haill brethrein his declamatioun on the thesis ressavit be him, fra the said Mr Andro Yung, as the scryb testefeit at mair lynthe, and for satisfeing of the desyr of the quhilk misseive, Mr Alexander Chisholme producit for ane excuis of his noncomperance ane epistill in Latein, as it beris in the selff, quhilk epistill was committit to be veseit and examinat be Maisteris James Pont and Alexander Iule, and thay to report thair jugementis thairof to the brethrein on the ix day of July nixt.

Thomas Quhytet decernit to be excommunicat: The quhilk day thair was ane summondis producit dewlie execute and indorsit upone Thomas Quhytet, servand to Thomas Alexander, chairgeing him to have compeirit the said day to heir and se him self decernit to be excommunicat for his contumacie and malicius disobedience, as at mair lynthe is conteinit in the said summondis, the said Thomas being oft tymis callit compeirit nocht, and the brethrein, having diligentlie wyit and advysit the said Thomas contumacitie in manifest contemp of the chairgis of the kirk, ordanis and decernis the said Thomas Quhytet to be excommunicat and cuttit aff fra the societie of Chrystis kirk and to be delyverit in the handis of the devill for destructioun of his flesche that his saull may be saif in the day of the Lord Jesus, and commandis and ordanis Mr Andro Yung, minister to the said Thomas, to proceid in admonitionis againis the said Thomas Quhyt[et] for calling of him to obedience according to the ordur and incaise of nonobedience (as God forbid) to proceid to pronunce the sentence of excommunicatioun againis him.

Chrystis woll, Jonet Porter: The quhilk day ane summondis beand producit lauchfullie execute and indorsit upone Jonet Porter, spous to James McCalpie in Bahaldie, and Hellein Dow in Litill Coig chairgeing thame to compeir the said day to answer at the instance of the kirk for passing in pilgrimage to Chrystis woll and using of superstitioun and idolatrie thairat expres againis Godis Word undir the paine of excommunicatioun, compeirit the said Jonet Porter quha, being accusit for passing in pilgramage, as said is, confessit that scho past to the said woll becaus scho was seik, and confessis scho drank of it and that scho past about the said woll and sat doun on hir kneis and prayit to Chrystis Sonday and Chrystis woll to help hir befoir scho drank of it and denyis all uther ceremoneis. The said Hellein Dow being oft tymis callit compeirit nocht. Thairfor the brethrein findis her contumax and thairfor ordanis hir to be summond to heir and se hir self decernit to be excommunicat for his contumacitie and malicius disobedience with certificatioun and scho failze the brethrein will proceid and decern hir to be excommunicat, as said is.

Margaret Downy, Jonet Allane: The quhilk day ane summondis beand producit deulie execute and indorsit upone Marione Watsone in Touch, Margaret Downy in Polmais, Jonet Mayne, dwelland undir Johnne Downy in Mossyd, chairgeing thame to have compeirit befoir us the said day to answer at the instance of the kirk for passing in pilgramage to Chrystis woll and using of superstitioun and idolatrie thairat expres againis Godis Word undir the paine of excommunicatioun, compeirit the said Margaret Downy and confessis scho past furth of hir awin hous myndit to have past to the said woll and wald have past thair war nocht ane certane halbert men met thame ane lytill or thai come to the woll and struik them away, and confessis the occasioun quhairfor scho was myndit to have past thair was becaus of seiknes scho hade and belevit to have bein the better throw hir passing thair. Compeirit Jonet Allane, spous to Richard Nycoll in Carse, and confessit conforme to the said Margaret Downy in all pointis. With the quhilkis confessionis, the brethir, being ryplie advysit, findis the saidis personis nocht to have compleit thair pilgramage nor committit na idolatrie at the said woll as utheris did. Thairfoir thai ar bayth ordeinit to mak public repentence in the publict plaice appointit for penitentis in thair parroche kirk of Sanct Ninniane on Sonday nixt, viz., the last day of this instant in tyme of sermond undir the paine of disobedience. The saidis Marione Watsone and Jonet Mayne, being oft tymis callit, compeirit nocht. Thairfor the brethrein findis thame contumax and ordanis thame to be summond to heir and se thame selffis decernit to be excommunicat for thair contumacitie and malicius disobedience, with certificatioun and thai failze the brethrein will decern thame to be excommunicat, as said is.

At Striviling the ij day of July, 1583

Presentes: Mr William Stirling, Patrik Gillaspie, Mr Alexander Chisholme, Michaell Lermonthe, Alexander Fargy, Robert Mentayth, Patrik Layng, ministeris; Mr James Pont, Robert Alexander, Umphra Cunynghame, elderis; Mr Alexander Iule, ane brothur of exerceis; Alexander Balvaird, William Stirling, rederis.

Robert Fogo: The quhilk day the brethrein undirstanding that forsamekill as upone the iiij day of *Junij* last bypast Robert Fogo in Doun was decernit and ordeinit to have compeirit befoir thame on the xxv day of *Junij* last to have gevin ane tryell of his habilitie for reding in the kirk as he sould have bein requyrit and to have hard and sein tryell tane of his lyf and conversatioun undir the pane of deprivatioun of him *simpliciter* fra all reiding in the kirk, as at mair lynthe is conteinit in the said ordinance, nochttheles the said Robert compeirit nocht the xxv day, as said is, and thairfor inrespect of his disobedience deservis *simpliciter* deprivatioun according to the formar ordinance. Thairfor the brethrein ordanis the said Robert to be summond to heir and se him self decernit to be deprivit *simpliciter* fra reding in the kirk of God and all functioun thairin as unmeit to beir offeice thairin, with certificatioun and he failze the brethrein will proceid and decern him to be deprivit *simpliciter*, as said is.

Johnne Brounis play: In the terme assignit to the brethrein of Striviling appointit to vesie the register of the clark play playit be the bairnis of Johnne Broun, scholmaister at Stragayth, to report thair jugementis anent the same, the said brethrein reportit thai hade fund oft tymis thairin mekill baning and swering, sum badrie and filthie baning, the said Johnne Broun beand present quha denyit nocht the sam.

Johnne Broun: In the terme assignit to Johnne Broun to produce declamatiounis on the thesis ressavit be him fra the brethir, compeirit the said Johnne and producit declamatiounis on the said thesis in prois and vers, as they beir in thame selffis, with the quhilkis the brethir tuik to advys.

Johnne Wilsone: The quhilk day compeirit Johnne Wilsone in Polmais and declairit that he hade satisfeit the injunctionis injonit to him be the brethren as ane relaps fornicatioun [*recte*, fornicatour], quhilk Patrik Gillaspie, his minister, testefeit to be of trewthe, and thairfor desyrit his bannis to be proclamit with Agnes Mentayth, with quhome he hade committit the said fornicatioun, quhairwith the brethrein, being advysit and understanding that albeit the said Johnne hade committit adultrie yit he was nocht divorcit thairfoir, and thairfor inrespect of the departing of his wyf, undirstandis him to be fre, quhairfor ordanis the said Patrik Gillaspie, his minister, to proclame his bannis with the said Agnes lauchfullie, according to the ordur, and gif na lauchfull impediment be opponit in the contrar to compleit mariage betuix thame.

Patrik Layng: The quhilk day being assignit to Patrik Layng to produce ane summondis dewlie execute and indorsit on Margaret Bruce, his buik of disceplein to be veseit be the brethrein, the answer made to his first accusatioun, quhilk the brethrein hes fund to be rivin away fra the beginning of his answeris gevin in befoir thame, and also his admonitiounis in perfyt forme made be him againis the disobedientis of Clakmannan, conforme to the brethreinis ordinance made on the xviij day of *Junij* last bypast, compeirit the said Patrik and, being desyrit be the moderatour to produce as is abone specefeit, ansorit he hade na thing to produce, except the admonitiounis usit be him againis the disobedientis, quhilk was nocht fund formall, eftir that thai war considderit be the brethir. Farder, the said Patrik being accusit for taking of ix s. for compleiting of mariage in the kirk of Clakmannan on Sonday last betuix David Lindsay and Jonet Donaldsone, the said Patrik denyit the samin *simpliciter*. The answeris of the said Patrik Layng with the said accusatioun and utheris accusatiounis gevin in againis him of befoir being considderit be the brethrein, thay find the said Patrik fengzeit in his speikin, sayand now that he hes nocht ane buik of disceplein quhilk befoir he confessit to have hade, negligent in his offeice and disobedient to the voice of the kirk in nocht executing of the said summondis being oft tymis commandit, and to appeir to be varie sclanderus in his offeice in selling of the sacramentis and utheris benefeittis of the kirk. Thairfor the brethrein suspendis the said Patrik fra all functioun in the kirk ay and quhill he produce the said summondis dewlie execute and indorsit on Margaret Bruce, with certificatioun gif he use ony functioun in the kirk in the mentyme he salbe deprivit for evir. Quhilk ordinance beand made be the brethrein, the said Patrik producit ane wreting in manir of appellatioun fra the jugement of the brethir unto the generall assemblie, as it beris in the self.

Communeris with ane excommunicatt in Dunblane: The quhilk day ane summondis beand producit lauchfullie execute and indorsit upone Andro Broun in Dunblane, Johnne Lamb in Bahaldie and William Dawsone, officer, chairgeing thame to have compeirit the said day to answer at the instance of the kirk for speiking and haulding purpois with Sir William Drummond, ane man excommunicat, as at mair lynthe is conteinit in the said summondis producit thairin, compeirit the said William Dawsone and denyit *simpliciter* that he spak ony thing to the said Sir William, in respect quhairof the brethrein gevis commission to the particular sessioun of Dunblane to examine certane witnessis for probatioun of the said mater, and thai to report againe the samin to the sessioun the ix of July instant. The said is Andro Broun and Johnne Lamb being oft tymis callit and compeirit nocht, thairfor the brethrein ordanis thame to be summond of new, to the effect foirsaid, undir the paine of excommunicatioun.

William Wingyet decernit to be excommunicat: The quhilk day ane summondis beand producit lauchfullie execute and indorsit upone William Winyet chairgeing him to have compeirit the said day to heir and se him self decernit to be excommunicat for his contumacitie and malicius disobedience, as at mair lynthe is conteinit in the said summondis, the said William being oft tymis callit compeirit nocht. Thairfor the brethir, having diligentlie wyit and advysit the said Williamis contumacitie, ordanis and decernis him to be excommunicat and cuttit aff fra the societie of Christis kirk and to be delyverit in to the handis of the devill for destructioun of his flesche that his saull may be saif in the day of the Lord Jesus, and commandis and ordanis Patrik Gillespie, minister to the said William, to proceid in admonitionis againis him lauchfullie according to the ordur for calling of him to obedience, and incaice of nonobedience (as God forbid) to proceid and pronunce the sentence of excommunicatioun againis him.

Johnne Murehed, disobedient: The quhilk day ane summondis beand producit lauchfullie execute and indorsit upone Johnne Murehed, yunger, smyth, chairgeing him to have compeirit befoir

the brethrein the said day to answer at the instance of the kirk for
disobedience to the voice of the elderschip of his awin parroche
kirk of S. Niniane and to heir and se him self decernit to have
committit fornicatioun and to undirly the censuris of the kirk, as
at mair lynthe is conteinit in the said summondis, the said Johnne
being oft tymis callit compeirit nocht. Thairfor the brethrein
ordanis to summond him of new *litteratorie* to the effect foirsaid
undir the paine of excommunicatioun.

Chrystis woll, Jonet Mayne, Jonet Gray: The samin day compeirit
Jonet Mayne, dwelland undir Johnne Downy in Mossyd, and confessit scho past the maist part of the gait to Chrystis woll and haid
past thair, war nocht scho was stayit be men, hopand thairby to
have bein mendit of hir diseas. Lykwys compeirit Jonet Gray and
confessit conforme to the said Jonet Mayne in all pointis, for the
quhilk the said Jonet Mayne and Jonet Gray ar ordeinit be the
brethrein to mak publict repentence on Sonday nixt in tyme of
sermond in thair parroche kirk of Sanct Niniane in the plaice
appointit for penitentis undir the paine of disobedience.

At Striviling the ix day of July, 1583

Presentes: Mr William Stirling, James Andirsone, Mr Johnne
Campbell, bischop of Iyllis, Patrik Gillaspie, Mr Alexander
Chisholme, Alexander Fargy, Mr Andro Yung, Robert Mentayth,
Michaell Lermonthe, ministeris; Andro Kirk, William Stirling,
rederis; Mr Alexander Iule, ane brothur of exerceis.

Patrik Layng: The brethrein, considering the gret sclandir that
daylie mair and mair incressis of Patrik Layng bayth as concerning
his behaviour in his offeice and in lyf and conversatioun to the end
the samin may be ather removit (he beand fund innocent) or
thane he worthelie deprivit, he beand fund nocent, hes thocht gud
and ordanis probatioun of witnes to be laid againis the said Patrik
for preving of the accusationis gevin in againis him of befoir and
utheris to be gevin in and thairfor ordanis the said Patrik to be
summond to that effect *litteratorie*.

Advysment of Johnne Brounis declamatiounis: The brethrein
undirstanding that the declamatiounis and vers made be Johnne
Broun on the thasis ressavit be him as yit is nocht advysit, thairfor

the brethrein ordanis and gevis commissioun to the brethrein to vesie the same and to report thair jugementis thairon to the haill brethrein the vj day of August nixt.

William Dawsone: The quhilk day being assignit to the minister of Dunblane [to] report the depositionis of certane witnessis on that accusatioun layit againis William Dawsone, viz., for speiking and haulding purpois with Sir William Drummond, ane excommunicat man, etc., the said minister reportit that he could find na thing be tryell bot that the said William Dawsone stude be syd the said excommunicat bot spak na thing to him. The brethrein ordanis the said minister to admoneis the said William Dawsone nocht to use the lyk in tymis cuming undir the paine of the censuris of the kirk to be execute againis him.

Johnne Muirhed satisfeit: The samin day Patrik Gillaspie, minister at S. Ninianis kirk, reportit to the brethrein that Johnne Muirhed, yungar, quha was chairgit to have compeirit befoir the brethrein the last sessioun for disobedience to the elderschip of the said kirk hes this last Sonday submittit him self to the disceplein of the kirk befoir the said elderschip and hes enterit in the plaice of repentence this last Sonday.

William Wingyet: The quhilk day Patrik Gillaspie being inquyrit be the moderatour gif he hade admonesit William Wingyet on Sonday last as for the first admonitioun to obey the ordinance of the kirk under the paine of excommunicatioun, as he was commandit in the last sessioun, the said Patrik reportit that sensyne, the said William is contractit in mariage with Jonet Johneson, quhomwith he committit the offence of fornicatioun, and hes promesit to compleit mariage with diligence. The brethrein ordanis the said Williamis repentence to be metigat gif he compleit mariage according to his promeis.

Communioun at Kippen: Anent ane complent proponit be ane elder of the kirk of Kippen schawand that it is ane lang tyme sen thai hade the communioun ministrat in thair kirk and, becaus thai hade nocht ane minister to ministrat the same, desyrit the brethrein to appoint sum of the brethir to ministrat the same thair and the parrochun sall caus be furneist all thingis neciser thairto, the brethrein ordanis Mr Alexander Chisholme to ministrat the communioun in the said kirk sasone as he may guidlie, provyding that

ane part of the kirk be made waltirticht and repairit utherwayis
that the samin may be done reverentlie as it aucht to be.

Mr Johnne Campbell: The quhilk day compeirit Mr Johnne
Campbell, bischop of Iyllis, and desyrit the brethrein to tak farther
tryell of him of the hedis conteinit in the act of the generall assemblie
becaus thair was sindrie of the Iyllis present in this toun with my
lord of Argyll. The quhilk desyr being considderit be the brethrein,
it was thocht gude and ordeinit, nochtwithstanding of ane peremptur day assignit to produce the bretheris jugementis, yat my Lord
McLane and utheris that was present with him quha hade knawlege
of the said Mr Johnis diligence in doctrine and in lyf sould be
summond to the nixt sessioun for farther probatioun of tha thingis
conteinit in the act of the generall assemblie foirsaid and siclyk
ordanis James Andirsone and Patrik Gillaspie to speik my lord of
Argyll, the laird off Ardkinlayis and utheris befoir specefeit anent
the said accusatiounis and to request thame that thai wald obey the
summondis quhen thai sould be chairgit thairto, the said Mr
Johnne warnit to the xvj day of July instant to heir and se the saidis
witnessis ressavit, sworne and admittit *apud acta*.

Ben fyris: The brethrein undirstandand ane grit abuse and superstitioun usit be sindrie and dyvers personis within the boundis of
this presbytery in setting furthe of ben fyris midsomer evin last,
expres againis Godis Word and the lawis of the realme, thairfor ilk
minister within the boundis of this presbytery is commandit to
warne befoir thair awin sessioun all personis within thair awin
parrochun setteris furth of the saidis ben fyris and eftir just tryell
and convictioun to report thair namis to the presbytery.

McKie and Stewart: The quhilk day being appointit to Alexander
Fargy to produce in wret the forme of the sentence of excommunicatioun pronuncit be him againis James McKie and Jane
Stewart with the admonitionis gevin be him of befoir, compeirit
the said Alexander Fargy and producit in wret the forme of the
said sentence of excommunicatioun with the admonitionis gevin be
him as it beris in the self. The brethrein appointis and gevis commissioun to the brethrein in Striviling to vesie the said forme
producit be the said Alexander and report thair jugementis thairof
on the day xxiij day of July instant.

Johnne Adame: The same day compeirit Johnne Adame in

Kippen, quha being accusit be the moderatour for blasphemus speiking at the mercat croce of Striviling tending to the allwance of pilgramagis to Chrystis woll, the said Johnne confessit that he spak at the said croce of Striviling that gif he wist to gait his haill at Chrystis woll he wald pas thair quha wald quha wald [sic] nocht. For the quhilk caus the brethrein ordanis the said Johnne to mak publict repentence in the kirk of Striviling at the plaice appointit for penitentis on Sonday the xxj day of July instant undir the paine of disobedience.

At Striviling the xvj day of July, 1583

Presentes: Mr William Stirling, James Andirsone, Alexander Fargy, Mr Andro Yung, Mr Adame Merschell, Mr Arthur Futhie, Patrik Gillaspie, Mr Alexander Chisholme, Michaell Lermonthe, Johnne Duncansone, ministeris; Mr Johnne Campbell, bischop of Iyllis; Mr Duncane Nevein, William Stirling, rederis; Umphra Cunynghame, elder; Mr Alexander Iule, ane brothur of exerceis.

Anent Mr Robert Montgumrie: The brethrein undirstandand that Mr Robert Montgumrie hes bein travelland schort syne in sum parttis of Mentayth besyd Kilbryd, albeit he be excommunicat, and thairfor the brethrein desyris Michaell Lermonthe, minister, to try with quhat personis he hes bein with in tha partis and quahir he lugit and quhat [sic] conferit and spak with him, and ordanis him to report thair namis the nixt sessioun.

Excommunicantis in Dunblane: The brethir ordanis and gevis commissioun to the brethrein in Striviling to vesie the process of excommunicatioun deducit againis excommunciantis in Dunblane and to report thair jugementis thairof to the haill brethrein the nixt sessioun.

William Stirling: The quhilk day, James Andirsone, minister at Striviling, producit befoir the brethrein ane misseive wreting send to him be Mr Patrik Walkinschaw, minister at the kirk off Drimmen berand in effect that quhair William Stirling, allegit minister at Kippen, hade committit als grit offencis as evir he did befoir sen his confirence with the said James Andirsone as heireftir particularlie is mentionat, and thaireftir desyrit the brether to tak tryell thairintill, as at mair lynthe is conteinit in the samin of the dett the xij day of

N

Junij instant, beressone quhairof the moderatour accusit the said William Stirling (beand personallie present) gif he is this instant moneth baptezit ane bairne at the kirk of the Port of Inchemahome gottin be Johnne McVenatar in the parrochun of Drimmen in adulterie by his wyf on Jonet Drummond (the kirk nocht beand satisfeit), the said William denyit *simpliciter* the baptezing of the said bairne. Secundlie, beressone of the said wreting, the moderatour accusit the said William gif he on the [*blank*] day of the samin moneth baptezit ane uther bairne at the said kirk of Port gottin be ane sarly Buchannane in adultrie on Jonet Nicilwreid, spous to the said Johnne McVenatar, nather of the parentis beand present nor the kirk satisfeit, nathir yit ony promeis cravit for satisfeing of the kirk for the said offence. The said William denyit the haill accusatioun *simpliciter*. For farther tryell of the quhilkis, the brethir ordanis the said Mr Patrik Walkinschaw to be desyrit to send heir the extract of the depositionis of certane witnessis ressavit and examinat be him in the said mater with the circumstancis thairof to the effect the brethir may tak farther ordur thairanent for purging the kirk of sic sclandir.

Andro Broun: The quhilk day ane summondis beand producit lauchfullie execute and indorsit upone Andro Broun in Dunblane chairgeing him to have compeirit the said day to answer at the instance of the kirk for speiking and haulding purpois with William Drummond, ane mane excommunicat and cuttit of from the societie of the faithfull publictlie at the mercat croce of Dunblane on Sonday the xxiij day of *Junij* last at xij houris at none expres againis Godis Word, and to underly the disceplein of the kirk thairfoir undir the paine of excommunicatioun, quhilk Andro being oft tymis callit compeirit nocht. Thairfor the brethrein ordanis him to be summond *litteratorie* to heir and se him self decernit to be excommunicat for his contumacie and malicius disobedience with certificatioun and he failze we will proceid and decern him to be excommunicat, as said is, according to Godis Word.

Mr Johnne Campbell: The quhilk day ane summondis beand producit lauchfullie execut and indorsit upone Lachlane McLane of Duart, Johnne Dow McLane, fathir brothur to the said Lachlane, Johnne Dow Campbell and Johnne Auchinros, servandis to the said

Lachlane, chairgeing thame to compeir the said day to beir lell and suithfast witnessing anent the diligence of Mr Johnne Campbell, bischop of Iyllis, in doctrein and disceplein within the hielandis, and speciallie within the said Lauchlanis boundis, anent his lyf and conversatioun and dilapidatioun of the patrimony of the kirk and sic uthir thingis as thai salbe inquyrit of, insafar is thai knaw or salbe speirit at thame, ilk persone undir the paine of disobedience, the said Mr Johnne Campbell being personallie present, compeirit all the saidis witnessis, quha was ressavit, sworne and admittit and examinat thairupone, as the depositionis beris.

Mr Johnne Campbell: The samin day James Andirsone and Patrik Gillaspie, appointit in the last sessioun to speik my lord off Argyll, the laird of Arkinglas and utheris befoir specefeit anent the premisis and to request thame to obey the summondis, reportit to the brethrein that thai hade spokin my lord of Argyll and the said laird of Arkinlayis according to thair commissioun, quha ansorit that my lord was to ryd this day in the morning and the said laird of Ardkinglas and thairfor could nocht be present in tyme of sessioun, and thairfor thai desyrit the said noblle lord and laird to declair to thame the trewthe insafar as thai knew anent Mr Johnne Campbellis diligence in doctrein and disceplein, his lyf and conversatioun and dilapidatioun of the patrimony of the kirk, quha deponit according to thair report to be made and wretin with the depositionis of the remanent witnessis foirsaid.

Mr Johnne Campbell: The brethrein, undirstanding that the brethir of the presbytery off Glasgw hes bettir knawlege of the trewthe of the said Mr Johnnis procedingis anent sic thingis as ar mentionat in the act of the generall assemblie nor we have, thairfor thinkis gude and ordanis that adverteisment be made to thame anent the tryell of the said Mr Johnne desyrand thame to take sic tryell as thai may guidlie of the said Mr Johnnis procedingis anent the heddis conteinit in the act of the generall assemblie and quhat thai find thairby to report the same againe to the brethir betuix and the first Twysday efter S. Lowrence day, viz., the xiij day of August nixt, the said Mr Johnne warnit thairto *apud acta*.

Chrystis woll, Hellein Galbrayth, Elezabeth Levenox, Agnes Blair: The quhilk day ane summondis beand producit dewlie execute and indorsit upone Margaret Wricht, spous to Robert Harvy in Arnbeg,

Hellein Galbrayth, spous to Johnne Campbell in Arnegibbon, Cristane Clark, spous to Johnne McHenrie in Boclyvie, Elezabeth Levenox, spous to Johnne McAndro in Boclyvie, Agnes Blair, spous to Johnne Dow in the Garrane of Boclyvie, Jonet Gairdner, spous to Patrik McIlhois in Scheirgartane, and Johnne Lecky in Balegorte, chairgeing thame to have compeirit the said day to answer at the instance of the kirk for passing in pilgramage to Chrystis woll and using of superstitioun and idolatrie thairat againis the law of God, ilk persone undir the paine of excommunicatioun, compeirit personallie the said Hellein Galbrayth and confessit that scho past ane lairge part of the gait to Chrystis woll, mynding to have past thairto to have gottin hir haill war nocht scho was stoppit be the way, for the quhilk intent and purpos the brethrein ordanis the said Hellein to mak publict repentence in hir awin parroche kirk of Kippen on Sonday nixt in tyme of preiching or prayeris. Compeirit the said Elezabeth Levenox and grantit scho past to Chrystis woll becaus hir foirbearis past thair and becaus scho hade ane sair leg, and confessit that scho belevit the woll sould have helpit it, and confessis scho past ainis about the woll and that scho drank of it. Compeirit the said Agnes Blair personallie and confessis scho past to the said woll to gait health to ane scharg bairne, quhilk scho hade, and belevit that be the waschein of the bairne with the waltir of the said woll he sould ather dee or leive, and confessis that scho past ainis about the woll. The remanent of the saidis personis being oft tymis callit compeirit nocht. Thairfor the brether findis thame and ilk ane of thame contumax, and thairfor ordanis thame to be summond to heir and se thame selffis decernit to be excommunicat for thair contumacie and malicius disobedience to the voice of the kirk, with certificatioun and thai failze we will proceid and decerne thame and ilk ane of thame excommunicat for the caus foirsaid according to Godis Word.

Chrystis woll, Marione Gilfillan, Jonet Mairtein, Marjorie Galbrayth: The quhilk day ane summondis beand producit lauchfullie execute and indorsit upone Jonet Neicklay, spous to Neillen [Allane, *deleted*] Gilfillane, Marione Nekla in Boclyvie, Marione Gilfillane, spous to Duncane Provand, Duncane Watsone, Jonet Mairtein in Garden, Margaret Neill thair, Margaret Leckie, spous to Donald Ure, Margaret Galbrayth, spous to Waltir McAlaster, and the said

Walter McAlaster, and Marjorie Galbraith, spous to Umphra
Levenox, chairgeing thame to have compeirit the said day to
answer at the instance of the kirk for passing in pilgramage to
Chrystis woll and using of superstitioun and idolatrie thairat expres
againis Godis Word, ilk persone undir the paine of disobedience,
compeirit personallie the said Marione Gilfillane and confessit sho
past to Chrystis woll becaus scho haid ane sair leg to gait remade
thairat to it, and confessis scho drank of it and wische hir leg with
the waltir thairof and past ainis about the woll, belevand alwayis
scho sould have bein the better of thir hir doingis. Compeirit
personallie the said Jonett Mairtein and grantis scho past in pilgramage to Chrystis woll, and thairby belevit to have bein lichter of
hir bairne scho was with, and past ainis about the woll and wische
hir feit and handis with the waltir thairof, denyis scho drank of it
and that scho left ony thing behind hir thairat. Compeirit the said
Marjorie Galbrayth and confessit scho past to the said woll becaus
scho haid ane sair ee and belevit to have gottin help thairto be the
said woll and confessit scho wische hir ee and hir forrat with the
waltir thairof. The remanent of the saidis personis being oft tymis
callit compeirit nocht. Thairfor the brethrein ordanis thame to be
summond of new to the effect foirsaid undir paine of excommunicatioun.

    Robert Lecky: The quhilk day compeirit Robert Lecky of
Kepderroch, spous to [*blank*], and grantis him to have committit
adultrie with Jonet Mairtein, yunger, by his wyf, for quhilk he
submittis him self in the will of the brethir. The brethrein ordanis
and commandis him to pas to ye nixt provinciall assemblie of this
province to be haldin in Edinburgh the first Twysday of October,
viz., the first day thairof, thair to ressave his injunctionis for his
said offence of adultrie and to obey thame undir the paine of
excommunicatioun. Attour, commandis and ordanis the said
Robert Lecky to act caution in the commissaris buikis of Striviling
with all diligence that he sall obey and satisfie the said ordinance in
all pointis undir the paine of xl libis., to be payit be the said cautioner
incaice of disobedience with certificatioun and the said Robert
failze in acting off cautioun, as said is, the brethir will ordaine
Patrik Gillaspie, his minister, to proceid in admonitiounis againis
him according to the ordur, and incaice of disobedience (as God

forbid) to proceid to the sentence of excommunicatioun againis him according to our decreit pronuncit thairupone in all pointis, as the samin of the dett the [*blank*].

At Striviling the xxiij day of July, 1583

Presentes: James Andirsone, Patrik Gillaspie, Mr Andro Yung, Mr Arthur Futhie, Robert Mentayth, Michaell Lermonthe, Alexander Fargy, ministeris; Mr Alexander Iule, ane brothur of exerceis; Mr Duncane Nevein, Alexander Balvaird, rederis; and Robert Alexander, elder.

James Castellaw: The quhilk day compeirit personallie James Castellaw and Margaret Bavarage in quhais presens James Andirsone, minister at Striviling, declairit to the brethrein that thai war conveinit befoir the particular sessioun of the said kirk on the xviij day of this instant and was accusit severallie for ressaving of Mr Robert Montgumrie in thair hous, being excommunicat, on the xv day of this instant quhair he remainit, as was allegit, to the xvij day thairof at eftir none. To the quhilk, the said James Castellaw ansorit that he was him self furth of this toun the mest part of all the said tyme and that he knew nocht nor wist nocht that the said Mr Robert was thair the said tyme, nather yit saw him nocht the said tyme, bot confessit that his wyf grantit be him that the said Mr Robertis wyf hade tane ane chalmir fra hir ij or iij dayis befoir the said Mr Robertis allegit cuming in his hous and keipit the key thairof with hir self at all tymis and gif the said Mr Robert was in that chalmir or nocht the said speace, the said James Castellaw knew nocht bot verraly he nevir kennit, met nor drink to gang furth of his hous to that chalmir nor na servand of his, for the said Mr Robertis wyf evir dynit and supit in his hall with sic cumpany as was thairin as his wyf schew him. To the quhilk answer the said Margaret Bavarage in hir answer aggreit in all. Farther, the said James was inquyrit gif he at ony tyme sen the said Mr Robert was excommunicat lugit in his hous in Glasgw, the said James confessit he lugit in his hous sensyn bot his arrand thair was to crave silvir fra the said Mr Robertis wyf and, as the said James allegit, at his thair being nather was the said Mr Robert nor yit his wyf thair in thair hous bot was furth of the toun. Quhilkis answeris the said minister declairit that the brethrein of the said particular sessioun remittit to the jugementis of the brethrein of this presbytery. The said James Castellaw and his wyf, being now presentlie desyrit to declair the trewthe of the saidis accusatiounis, ansorit baithe conforme to the said ministeris report in all thingis without ony discrepance. The brethrein, being ryplie advysit efter long ressoning, findis the said James to have committit ane gret fault in luging in the said Mr Robertis hous, being excommunicat, and thairby gaif ane gret sclandir to this kirk and the kirk of Glasgw, and thairfor ordanis and decernis him to stand up in the plaice quhair he sittis in the kirk of Striviling quhen the minister callis upone him immediatlie eftir the sermond befoir none and thair publictlie confes he lugit in the said Mr Robertis hous, being excommunicat, and the occasioun that movit him thairto, in the quhilk doing to confes he hes offendit the kirk and sclanderit the same thairby and that on the nixt Sonday that he happinis to be in this toun of Striviling undir the paine of disobedience. And anent the said Mr Robertis allegit being in the said James hous the tyme foirsaid, the moderatour, in name of the brethir, admonesis the said James Castellaw and Margaret Baverage, his spous, nocht to set na chalmir nor gif na key of nane to the said Mr Robertis wyf at na tyme fra this furth, except that the said James serce the samin chalmir daylie gif the said Mr Robert Montgumrie cum thair or nocht, quhome gif he find that he with all diligence thaireftir mak intimatioun of him to sum of the brethir of the ministrie in this toun, with certificatioun and he failze or, in his absence, his wyf that he and his wyf salbe haldin ressavaris and menteinaris of the said Mr Robert being excommunicat and sall sustein disceplein thairfoir.

Thomas Quhytett: The quhilk day compeirit Thomas Quhytet, servand to Thomas Alexander, in the parrochun of Dunblane, (being decernit to be excommunicat for disobedience) and confessit he hade offendit the kirk in his lang disobedience, quhilk he confessit to be onlie of simplle ignorance without knawlege of his dewatty and thairfor offirit him self in the will of the kirk. The brethir ordanis the said Thomas to compeir befoir the particular sessioun of the kirk of Dunblane on the xxvj day of this instant and to obey as he salbe commandit be thame undir the pain of excommunicatioun.

Excommunicantis in Dunblane: The brethrein in Striviling, havand commissioun to vesie certan procesis deducit againis excommunicantis in Dunblane, reportit to the brethrein that thai hade veseit the proces of excommunicatioun deducit againis Andro Blakwod in Dunblane, Sir William Blakwod thair, Sir Williame Drummond thair, Elezabeth Carnwethe and Agnes Cowall thair, and hes fund the samin proces ordurlie led and sufficient and thairfor the haill brethir ordanis the said proces to be delyverit to Mr Andro Yung, minister of Dunblane, that he may present the same to the kingis minister that lettres may be rasit thairon according to the ordur.

Mr Robert Montgumrie: The brethrein, undirstandand that Mr Robert Montgumrie lugit and was ressavit in the plaice of Kilbryd all nycht on the xiij day of July at evin instant, the lady beand thair, and that he was in Archibald Edmestonis hous in the gait syd and ressavit and interteneit thair, thairfor ordanis Dame Marie Duglas, comptas of Mentayth, and maistres of the said plaice, and the said Archibald Edmestoun to be summond *litteratorie* to answer at the instance of the kirk for the caus foirsaid and to underly the disceplein of the kirk thairfoir under the paine off disobedience.

Patrik Layng: The quhilk day ane summondis beand producit dewlie execute and indorsit upone David Lindsay, James Donaldsone, Johnne Archebauld and David Bruce of Grein chairgeing thame to have compeirit the said day to beir lell and suithfast witnessing anent the accusationis gevin in againis Patrik Layng and utheris to be gevin in againis him, safar as thai knaw and salbe speirit at thame, ilk persone undir the paine of disobedience, and als chairgeand the said Patrik Layng to compeir the said day and plaice to heir and se the saidis witnessis ressavit, sworne and admittit as at mair lynthe is conteinit in the said summondis, the said Patrik Layng compeirand personallie. The saidis witnessis, being oft tymis callit, compeirit nocht. Thairfoir the brethrein ordanis the saidis witnessis to be summond of new *litteratorie* to compeir the penult day of this instant to the effect foirsaid undir the paine of excommunicatioun, the said Patrik warnit thairto *apud acta*.

Robert Andirsone: The quhilk day ane summondis beand producit lauchfullie execute and indorsit upone Robert Andirsone in Tullibody chairgeing him to have compeirit the said day to answer at the instance of the kirk for passing in pilgramage to Chrystis

woll and using of superstitioun and idolatrie thairat expres againis
Godis law undir the paine of excommunicatioun, quhilk Robert
being oft tymis callit compeirit nocht, thairfor the brethrein ordanis
the said Robert Andirsone to be summond *litteratorie* to heir and se
him self decernit to be excommunicat for his contumacie and
malicius disobedience, with certificatioun and he failze the brethrein
will proceid and decern him to be excommunicat, as said is.

Anent tryell of bischopis: The samin day it was reportit to the
brethir be Patrik Gillaspie that, be act of the last generall assemblie,
this presbytery was ordeinit to proceid in tryell and disceplein
againis the bischoppis of Dunblane and Yllis according to thair
commissioun gevin to thame of befoir.

McKie and Stewart excommunicat: The brethrein in Striviling,
havand commissioun to vesie the admonitionis and sentence of
excommunicatioun gevin and pronuncit be Alexander Fargy,
minister of Logy, againis James McKie and Jane Stewart, reportit
to the remanent brethir that thay fand that the said Alexander hade
proceidit ordurlie and the samin put in sufficient forme, quhilk
was approvit be the brethir quhairof the tennour follwis.

James McKie and Jane Stewart pronuncit excommunicat: Upone
Sonday the xix day of May the yeir of God im vc lxxxiij yeiris, I,
Alexander Fargy, minister of Godis Word at the kirk of Logie,
past to the said parroche kirk, at command of ane ordinance of the
presbytery of Striviling, chairgeand ilk minister within the boundis
of the said presbytery to proceid with the censuris of the kirk
againis all adulteraris disobedient within the same boundis that hes
nocht past to the last synnodall assemblie haldin in Edinburgh the
secund day of Aprill last bypast to have ressavit thair injunctionis
as thai war ordeinit, as at mair lynthe is conteinit in the said
ordinance of the dett the ix day of Aprill last bypast, and becaus
James McKie and Jane Stewart, adulteraris and inhabitaris within the
said parrochun of Logie, was ordeinit and promesit to pas to the said
last synnodall assemblie to the effect foirsaid and hes failzeit bayth
thairintill, thairfor I, at command of the said ordinance, immediatelie
eftir the sermond publictlie admonesit the saidis James McKie and
Jane Stewart, adulteraris and inhabitaris within the said parrochun,
to submit thame selffis to the disceplein of the kirk for thair contumacie and oft disobedience dyvers and sindrie tymis undir the

paine of excommunicatioun, and lykwys I admonesit sum of the elderis in speciall to speik and exhort the saidis personis to submit thame selffis to the disceplein of the kirk undir the said paine and that as for the first admonitioun befoir the sentence conforme to the ordur, quhilk I did in presens of the haill pepill to heir Godis Word for the tyme. [*Signed*] Alexander Fargy, minister of Logy, with my hand.

McKie and Stewart, excommunicat: Upone Sonday the xxvj day of May, the yeir of God foirsaid I, Alexander Fargy, minister of the Word of God, past to the said parroche kirk and thair made intimatioun publictlie eftir the sermond that I, accompaneit with Johnne Grahame in Atheray, Andro Henrisone in Lochtburne and Johnne Duncansone in Logy, elderis of the said kirk, past to the personall presens of the said James McKie and Jane Stewart, quhair we privellie and most gentlie exhortit thame to submit thame selffis to the disceplein of the kirk, as said is, and fand na obedience, quhilk the saidis elderis testefeit in presens of the congregatioun, and thairfoir I, according to the ordinance of the brethrein of the said presbytery, publictlie admonesit the saidis personis, as said is, undir the paine of excommunicatioun and that as for the secund admonitioun befoir the sentence conforme to the ordur, quhilk I did in presens of the haill pepill convenit to heir Godis Word for the tyme. [*Signed*] Alexander Fargy, minister of Logie with my hand.

Upone Sonday the secund day of *Junij* the yeir of God foirsaid I, Alexander Fargy, minister of the Word of God, eftir that the foirsaidis elderis and I hade reportit to the brethir of our particular sessioun our privie admonitiounis gevin to the saidis personis togethir with thair obstinacie, I, according to the ordinance of the brethir of the said presbytery, past to the said parroche kirk of Logy and thair inquirit the haill elderis of the said kirk, beand present for the tyme, gif the saidis personis or ony of thame hade offirit, be thame selffis or ony uthir in thair namis, obedience unto the kirk, quha ansorit negativelie and thairfoir, immediatlie eftir the sermond, I publictly admonesit the said James McKie and Jane Stewart, as said is, undir the paine of excommunicatioun, and thaireftir prayeris beand made be me with exhortatioun to all the congregatioun to pray for thame and that as for the thrid and last admonitioun befoir the pronuncein of the sentence conform to the ordur, quhilk I did in presens of the haill pepill conveinit to heir Godis Word for the tyme. [*Signed*] Alexander Fargy, minister of Logy, with my hand.

Upone Sonday the xvj day of *Junij* the yeir of God foirsaid, I, Alexander Fargy, minister at the said kirk, past to the said parroche kirk and thair made intimatioun publictlie to the haill congregatioun eftir the sermond that I, accumpaneit with the elderis befoir-mentionat, past to the personall presens of the said James McKie and Jane Stewart sen our last privie admonitiounis gevin to thame of befoir and admonesit thame privallie of new and maist ernistlie exhortit thame to submit thame selffis to the disceplein of the kirk, as said is, and fand na obedience quhilk the saidis elderis thane testefeit to be of trewthe, and lykwys I thane inquyrit the saidis elderis and the remanent eldaris thair present for the tyme gif the saidis personis, or ony of thame, hade offerit obedience to the kirk be thame selffis or ony utheris in thair naimis, quha ansorit nega-tivelie, and als inquyrit gif the saidis personis, or ony utheris in thair naimis, wald thane promeis obedience to the kirk, and trew it is nane compeirit to that effect, and thairfor I, the said minister at command of the brethrein of the said presbytery, denuncit thame and ather of thame excommunicat for thair cryme and contemp foirsaid and delyverit thame ovir in the handis of Sathan to the destructioun of the flesche that the spirit may be saif in the day of the Lord Jesus, according to the Word of God and ordinance of the brethrein of the presbytery foirsaid in all pointis. Quhilk I did in presens of the haill pepill conveinit to heir Godis Word for the tyme, and immediatlie thaireftir I admonesit the said congregatioun and everie ane of thame to abhor the foirsaidis personis, excom-municat as hethinis and publicanis, and to have na kynd of societie with thame lest thai be partakeris of thair sinnis and of the curs of the samin, and this I admonesit thame to be war of, under the paine of the censuris of the kirk to be usit againis sic as hade ony kynd of familiaritie with thame unto the tyme thai war absolvit fra the said sentence and restorit againe to the societie of the kirk. In witnes of the quhilkis, I, the said minister, hes subscryvit thir my admonitionis and sentence of excommunicatioun pronuncit be me, as said is, with my awin hand as follwis. [*Signed*] Alexander Fargy, minister of Logy, with my hand. [*In margin*: 21 July 1590, Mr Johnne Davidsone receavit James McKie to the societie of the kirk, at command of the presbyterie of Dunblane, quhilk he reported to thame on the 16 of August 1592, as ane act of the said presbyterie beris.]

At Striviling the penult day of July, 1583

Presentes: Mr William Stirling, James Andirsone, Mr Alexander Chisholme, Mr Arthur Futhie, Patrik Gillaspie, Alexander Fargy, Andro Forester, ministeris; Mr Alexander Iule, ane brothur of exerceis; Adame, commendatar of Cambuskynneth, Alexander Forester of Garden, Duncane Narne, Mr James Pont, Alexander Patersone, and Robert Alexander, elderis.

William Michell: The quhilk day compeirit William Michell in Coustrie and desyrit the brethrein to gif command to sum minister to bapteis ane bairne of his gottin on Jonet Crystesone, his wyf (as he allegis). The brethrein undirstanding that, as yit, it lyis undiscussit gif the said Jonet may be his lauchfull wyf or nocht, inrespect of adultrie committit be hir of befoir by Andro Wilsone, hir lauchfull husband, for the quhilk he obteinit ane decreit of seapratioun fra hir. Thairfor the brethir ordanis the said William to act caution for him in the buikis of the commissar of Dunblane that he sall separate him self fra the said Jonet Crystesone with all diligence and remane fra hir ay and quhill sentence be pronunceit gif scho may be his lauchfull wyf or nocht undir the paine of xl libis., quhilk beand done the brethir ordanis his bairne to be baptezit.

James Castellaw: The quhilk day it was declairit to the brethrein be James Andirsone, minister at Striviling, that forsamekill as upone the xxiij day of July instant James Castellaw was decernit and ordeinit be the brethir to mak repentence in the kirk of Striviling in the plaice quhair he sittis on the nixt Sonday that the said James sould happin to be in this toun, for his luging in Mr Robert Montgumreis hous, being excommunicat, and trew it is that the said James was in this toun on Sonday last and albeit he was warnit be William Stevinsone, officer, to cum to the kirk the said Sonday and obey the said ordinance, nochttheles the said James Castellaw disobeyit, thairfor the said minister desyrit the brethrein to advys quhat thai thocht gude to be done thairanent. The brethrein ordanis the said James Castellaw to be summond *litteratorie* to mak repentence according to the formar ordinance upon Sonday nixt, viz., the iiij day of August nixt tocum or ellis compeir befoir the brethrein on the vj of August nixt and schaw ane ressonabill caus of his absence on Sonday last, viz., the xxviij day of July instant, undir the paine of disobedience.

Patrik Layng: The quhilk day ane summondis beand producit deulie execute and indorsit upone David Lindsay, James Donaldsone, Johnne Archebauld and David Bruce of Grein, chairgeing thame to compeir the said day to beir lell and suithfast witnessing anent the accusatiounis gevin in againis Patrik Layng and utheris to be gevin againis him safar as thai knaw or salbe speirit at thame ilk persone undir the paine of excommunicatioun, the said Patrik Layng beand personallie present, compeirit the saidis David Lindsay, James Donaldsone and Johnne Archebauld quha was ressavit, sworne and admittit and examinat as thair depositionis beris.

Patrik Layng: The samin day the said Patrik Layng beand accusit gif he hade exercisit ony functioun in the ministrie sen he was suspendit, the said Patrik ansorit and confessit he hes continewallie sensyne teichit, baptezit and mareit personis, as of befoir inrespect of his appellatioun. Farder, the said Patrik being desyrit, yit as off befoir, to declair the trewthe gif he tuik ony silvir for making of mariagis, the said Patrik confessit he takis na thing for making of mariagis bot sum tymis the brydell lawein and sum tymis the half of the brydell lawein. Farder, being desyrit, yit as of befoir, to declair the trewthe gif he takis ony silvir for baptezein of bairnis or nocht, the said Patrik denyis *simpliciter* that he takis silvir for baptezein of bairnis ather gottin in adultrie, fornicatioun or lauchfull. The brethir ordanis utheris witnessis to be summond *litteratorie* to the vj day of August for farther tryell of the said mater, the said Patrik warnit thairto *apud acta*.

Johnne Crystesone, adulterar in Strogayth: The quhilk day compeirit Johnne Crystesone, parrochinnar in Stragayth, spous to Jonet Allane, and grantis him to have gottin ane bairne in adultrie by his wyf on Jonet Mwll, for the quhilk caus the said Johnne is ordeinit to pas to the nixt provinciall assemblie of this province to be holden

in Edinburgh the first day of October nixt thair to ressave injunctionis to be injonit to him for his said offence and to obey the same
undir the paine of excommunicatioun.

Elezabeth Mwlle, adultrix in Strogayth: The samin day compeirit
Elezabethe Mwlle and grantis hir to have borne ane bairn gottin
with hir in adultrie be James Grahame in Bardrellis, husband to
[*blank*], and confessit that Sir David Murie, at the command of
Mr Johnne Hommill, baptezit the said bairne in Ochtirardur kirk
half ane yeir syne or thairby, hir self beand present, for the quhilk
the said Elezabeth is ordeinit to pas to the nixt provinciall assemblie
of this province to be haldin in Edinburgh the first day of October
nixt, thair to ressave injunctionis to be injoint to hir for the said
adultrie and to obey the same undir the paine of excommunicatioun.

Christane Jarvie: The quhilk day, it was schawin to the brethir be
Patrik Gillaspie, minister at S. Ninianis kirk, that quhair Cristane
Jarvie in Polmais, ane of the parrochinnaris of the said kirk, beand
excommunicat, offiris obedience to the kirk and desyris to be
ressavit againe amangis the societie of the faithfull. The brethir
gevis commissioun and libertie to Patrik Gillaspie and Alexander
Patersone, notar, or ony of thame to confer with the said
Cristane and mak hir ane bill as scho desyris to gif in to the
brethirein.

Adultrix in S. Ninianis parrochun: The samin day compeirit
Agnes Moderall, spous to Johnne Hall in Drusaill, and confessit
scho was lauchfullie mareit with hir said husband bot allegis that
albeit hir said husband lay dyvers tymis with hir yit he hade nevir
carnall dell with hir and now confessis scho is with bairne gottin on
hir be William Campbell dwelland at the mure miln, and being
accusit be the moderatour gif scho plengyet to ony persone that hir
husband hade nocht carnall dell with hir befoir hir carnall copulatioun with the said William Campbell, the said Agnes grantis scho
confessit nocht befoir the said tyme. The brethir findis the said
Agnes to have committit adultrie with the said William Campbell
by hir husband and thairfor ordanis hir to pas to the nixt provinciall
assemblie of the province to be haldin in Edinburgh the first day of
October nixt thair to ressave injunctionis to be injoint to hir for the
said adultrie and to obey the same undir the paine of excommunicatioun.

At Striviling the vj day of August, 1583

Presentes: Mr William Stirling, James Andersone, Patrik Gillaspie, Mr Arthur Futhie, Robert Mentayth, Michaell Lermonthe, Alexander Fargy, Mr Alexander Chisholme, ministeris; William Stirling, Alexander Balvaird, rederis; Mr James Pont, elder; and Mr Alexander Iule, ane brothur of exerceis.

Robert Andirsone: The quhilk day compeirit Robert Andirsone in Tullibody and grantis him to have bein disobedient to the chairgis of the kirk bot allegis he did the samin of ignorance, for the quhilk he offeris him in the will of the kirk, and als confessis that he at command of Bessie Hendirsone, his mother, tuik his gait in name of his mothir in pilgramage to Chrystis woll for ane diseas scho had in hir leggis and body thru the quhilk scho mycht nocht travell and denyis that he drank of the walter thairof nor yit did ony thing thairat, bot allegit that quhowsone he saw the said woll he belevit weill thair was na help to his mothur to be gottin thair and thairfor returnit hame againe nocht doing na thing thairat. The brethir being advysit with the said Robertis confessioun findis him self and his mothur to have bein deliberat in mynd to have committit idolatrie and superstitioun at the said woll, for the quhilk and his pilgrammage takein, the brethir ordanis him and his said mothur to mak publict repentence in thair parroche kirk of Tullibody according to the ordur on the nixt Sonday that Alexander Fargy sall requyr thame thairto undir the paine of disobedience.

The quhilk day all the brethrein within this presbytery ar inhibit to ministrat baptisme fra this furth aff the Sonday in landwart and aff the sermond day in brugh ay and quhill the brethrein be certifeit of actis of the generall assemblie made thairanent.

James Castellaw: The quhilk day ane summondis beand producit deulie execute and indorsit chairgeing James Castellaw to compeir the said day to declair ane ressonablle caus of his absence and nocht obeying of our ordinance on the xxviij day of July last as at mair lynthe is conteinit in the said summondis, compeirit the said James personallie and schew to the brethir ane caus of his absence the said day quhilk was fund be the brethir ressonablee. Farder, the said James promesis to mak repentence in the plaice quhair he sittis within the kirk of Striviling for luging in Mr Robert Montgumreis hous being excommunicat on Sonday immediatlie preceiding the fest of Michalmes, viz., the xxij day of September and satisfie the brethreinis ordinance in all pointis made on the xxiiij day of July last or sonner on ane Sonday that it sall happin the said James to adverteis the minister or reder of Striviling on the nycht befoir, quhilk promeis the said James is ordeinit to keip under the paine of disobedience.

Patrik Layng: The samin day compeirit Patrik Gillaspie and producit ane summondis deulie execute and indorsit on James Smyth in Elphinstoun, chairgeing him to compeir the said day to beir lell and suithfast witnessing anent certane accusatiounis layit againis Patrik Layng insafar as he knawis or salbe speirit at him under the paine of disobedience. The said Patrik Layng beand personallie present, compeirit the said James Smyth quha was ressavit, sworne and admittit and examinat as his depositioun beris. Eftir quhais admissioun the said Patrik departit fra the sessioun and beand chairgit to remaine to answer at the instance of Patrik Gillaspie, his accusar, under the paine of [*blank*] maist contemptuouslie disobeyit the said chairge and past his way.

The samin day, the brethrein undirstandand be Patrik Layngis awin confessioun that he hes contravenit thair suspensioun in teiching, mareing, ministratioun of baptisme continuallie sen he was suspendit as of befoir, thairfor the brethrein commandis and ordanis Robert Mentayth, minister at Alvayth, to pas to the parroche kirk of Clakmannan on Sonday nixt the xj day of August, and thair publictlie to mak intimatioun to the parrochinnaris of the said kirk of Clakmannan of the suspending of the said Patrik Layng fra all functioun in the kirk, and that he command and chairge the saidis parrochinnaris in name of the eternall God and his kirk that thay na manir of way acknawlege the said Patrik fra this furthe as ane man havand ony offeice or auctoritie in the ministrie nor crave ony benefeit of the kirk fra him ay and quhill he be lauchfullie restorit againe to his offeice under the paine of the censuris of the kirk to be execute againis thame and ilk ane of thame that dois in the contrar.

The quhilk day the brethrein ordanis Patrik Layng to be summond *litteratorie* to compeir befoir the provinciall assemblie of the presbytereis of Edinbrugh, Dalkayth, Striviling and Linlythquow to be haldin in Edinburgh the first day of October nixt to heir and se the jugementis of the brethrein of the said assemblie pronuncit anent the suspensioun of the said Patrik Layng fra all functioun in the kirk and his contravening of the same, his takin of silver oft and dyvirs tymis for compleiting of mariagis and his disobedience to this presbytery in passing fra the sessioun thairof the maist disobedientlie eftir he was chairgit to remane and to heir and se thair auctoritie interponit to the brethreinis proceidingis thairintill undir the paine of excommunicatioun, with certificatioun and he failze the brethir of the said assemblie will proceid againis him according to the Word of God and disciplein of the kirk, havand the warrand thairof thairin.

Johnne Broun: The quhilk day being assignit to the brethrein in Striviling to report thair jugementis to the remanent brethrein of the presbytery thairof on the declamatiounis and vers producit be Johnne Broun on the thesis gevin to him, reportit that thai jugit be the said productionis and privie confirence hade be the maistir of the grammir scholl of Striviling with the said Johnne that he was instructit ressonablle weill in the grundis of the Latein grammir and was ablle to teiche and proffeit the youthe thairin and that he was (as appeirit to thame) of gude inclinatioun and abilitie to proffeit him self and of a gude will daylie mair and mair to incres in the knawlege of his professioun. The said Johnne Broun compeirand personallie, the haill brethir present eftir deliberat advysment admittis him to teiche Latein grammir at the kirk of Strogayth quhair he is presentlie or in ony uthir plaice quhair he may proffeit the kirk of God in teiching of the youthe.

At Striviling the xiij day of August, 1583

Presentes: Mr William Stirling, James Andirsone, Patrik Gillaspie, Mr Andro Yung, Robert Mentayth, Mr Adame Merschell and Mr Johnne Campbell, ministeris; William Stirling, reder; Mr James Pontt, elder; and Mr Alexander Iule, ane brothur of exerceis.

Patrik Layng: The quhilk day Robert Mentayth, minister of Alvayth, beand inquyrit be the moderatour gif he hade made intimatioun at the kirk of Clakmannan of Patrik Layngis suspentioun according to ane ordinance made in the last sessioun or nocht, the said Robert ansorit that he, upone Sonday the xj day of August

o

instant, past to the parroche kirk of Clakmannan and thair publictlie
to the auditour convenit for the tyme made dew intimatioun to
the parrochinnaris thair that Patrik Layng, thair minister, was
lauchfullie suspendit fra all functioun of the kirk be the brethrein
of the presbytery of Striviling and that he chairgit all and sindrie
the parrochinnaris of the said kirk in name of the eternall God and
his kirk that thai na manir of way acknawlege the said Patrik fra
that furth as ane man havand ony offeice or auctoritie in the ministrie
nor yit crave ony benefeit of the kirk fra him ay and quhill he be
lauchfullie restorit againe to his offeice undir the paine of the censuris
of the kirk to be execute againis thame and ilk ane of thame that
dois in the contrar, and becaus the laird of Clakmannan, principall
man in the toun thairof, was absent furth of the kirk thairfor he thaireftir past to the personall presens of the said David Bruce of Grein
and Gilbert Coustoun, elderis in the said parrochun, and made intimatioun to thame of the suspentioun of the said Patrik Layng as is
abone wrettin in all pointis, and this he did befoir thir witnes David
Mentayth, servand to my lord of Mar, Alexander Hamiltoun,
Johnne Hendirsone and Thomas Coustoun.

Mr Johnne Campbell: The quhilk day beand assignit to the
brethrein to pronunce thair jugementis anent the accusatiounis layit
againis Mr Johnne Campbell, bischop of the Iyllis, and als appointit
to the brethrein of the presbytery of Glasgw to report to the brethrein heir quhat thay find be tryell tane be thame (according to the
brethreinis desyr) of the said Mr Johnnis procedingis in thair partis
anent the heddis conteinit in the act of the generall assemblie.
Quhilk report of the presbytery of Glasgw is nocht as yit cumit,
thairfor the brethrein ordanis the scryb to wret to Glasgw of new and
to desyr the brethrein thair to send thair report anent the premisis
heir againe the xx day of this instant to the quhilk day the brethrein
continewis the pronuncein of thair jugementis anent the accusatiounis layit againis the said Mr Johnne, he warnit thairto *apud acta*.

At Striviling the xx day of August, 1583

Presentes: Mr William Striviling, James Andirsone, Patrik
Gillaspie, Michaell Lermonthe, Mr Alexander Chisholme, Alexander Fargy, Mr Andro Yung, Mr Johnne Campbell, ministeris;

Mr James Pont, Robert Alexander, elderis; William Stirling; Mr Alexander Iule, ane brothur of exerceis; Mr Johnne Broun.

Mr Johnne Campbell: The quhilk day thair was producit be ane barer direct fra the presbytery of Glasgw ane testificatioun concerning the lyf and conversatioun of Mr Johnne Campbell, bischop of Iyllis, quhairof the tennour follwis: xvj *Augusti*, 1583. The quhilk day the moderatour and presbytery of Glasgw eftir the reding of this your godlie request fyndis no thing at all in lyf and conversatioun of the bischop of the Ylis in this our cuntrie bot honestie lykwys as your writt proporttis. Subscryvit, as follwis at the command of the said brethrein. *Sic subscribitur* Wylie, *scriba dictorum moderatoris et presbyterii Glasguensis sua manu.*

Mr Johnne Campbellis absolvitur: The quhilk day being assignit be the brethrein of the elderschip foirsaid to pronunce thair decreit and declaratour anent the tryell of Mr Johnne Campbell, bischop of Yllis, tuiching his doctrein, ministratioun of the sacramentis, negligence of preiching and disceplein, hanting and frequenting the cumpanie of excommunicat personis, waisting of the patrimony of the kirk, setting of takis againis the actis of the kirk, geving collatiounis of beneficis againis the tennour of the same actis and finallie for geving sclandir ony wayis in lyf and conversatioun, conform to ane act of the generall assemblie of the det the xiij day of October, *anno* etc., lxxxij yeiris, the said Mr Johnne beand personallie present, the foirsaidis brethrein being assemblit, eftir publict edickis beand lauchfullie execute chairgeand all and sindrie that wald object or oppone againis the said Mr Johnne tuiching the premisis to have compeirit at ane certane day bypast to that effect and eftir depositionis of dyvers famus witnes togethir with the report of the elderschip of Glasgw anent the foirsaidis, and being ryplie advysit thairwith absolvit and absolvis the said Mr Johnne fra all and sindrie pointis and artickillis conteinit in the foirsaid act of the generall assemblie and decernis him quyt thairfra, excep the disjunctioun and separatioun of the abbacie of Ycolumkill fra the bischoprik of the Yllis laitlie procurit be the said Mr Johnne as als ane confirmatioun gevin be him to the Erll of Argyll of the landis of Skirkennyth quhilkis befoir was sett in fefi be Mr Johnne Carswall, his predicessur, as he allegis, and continewis the decisioun of the samin to the nixt generall assemblie of the kirk to be haldin in

Edinbrugh the x day of October nixt to be declairit gif the said separatioun and confirmatioun or ony ane of thame be delapidatioun of the patrimony of the kirk or nocht. Becaus dyvers dyettis beand observit in taking of the said tryell of the said Mr Johnne, it was onnawayis varefeit nor provin to the said elderschip that he was culpablle of ony of the artickillis conteinit in the said act of the generall assemblie alwayis suspendand the declaratioun of the twa pointis befoir exceptit to the said generall assemblie, conform to the jugement of the synnodall assemblie of the said elderschip, and to that effect the said brethrein hes warnit and chairgit the said Mr Johnne to compeir befoir the generall assemblie to be haldin, day and plaice foirsaid, to heir and sie diclaratur gevin anent the twa pointis abonespecefeit.

Countas off Montayth: The quhilk day ane summondis beand producit deulie execute and indorsit upone Marie, Comptas of Menteyth, chairgeing hir to compeir the said day to answer at the instance of the kirk for speiking with Mr Robert Montgumrie, beand excommunicat, interteneing him in hir hous, eating and drinking with him, compeirit the said Comptas of Mentayth and confessis Mr Robert Montgumrie was in hir hous bot allegis scho knew nocht that the said Mr Robert was excommunicat and that his wyf come to hir plaice befoir him self and assurit hir that the said Mr Robert was aggreit with the kingis grace and the kirk in all thingis excep ane quhilk wald be lykwys aggreit, quhilk ex-communicatioun gif sche hade knawin affermit that he sould nocht have cumit in na plaice quhair scho was and Michaell Lermonthe, thene minister at Kilbryd kirk, being askit be the moderatour gif he intemeit the excommunicatioun of the said Mr Robert Mont-gumrie in the said Comptas parroche kirk of Kilbryd or nocht answerit negativelie. Inrespect of the quhilk nonintimatioun and misknawlege hade be the said Comptas of the said excommuni-catioun, the moderatour in name of the brethir onlie admonesit the said Comptas nocht to commone with the said Mr Robert nor interteine him na manir of way frathisfruth, quhill he be absolvit fra the said sentence of excommunicatioun undir the paine of the censuris of the kirk to be execute againis hir maist scherplie gif scho do in the contrar, quhilk admonitioun the said Comptas promisit to obey.

Laird of Tirinteran [sic]: The quhilk [day], forsamekill as the brethrein understandis that the communioun was ministrat in the kirk of Kippen on Sonday the xviij day of August and that the parrochinnaris thairof was examinat of befoir and as thai ar informit that Alexander Levingstoun of Tintirane, Margaret Grahame, his dochter in law, Alexander Frissall, Cristane Wod and Issobell Forester, servandis to the said Alexander, and parrochinnaris of Kippen, presentit nocht thame selffis to the examinatioun nor yit to the communioun and sacrament of the Lordis Supper the tyme of the ministratioun thairof the said day, thairfore the brethrein ordanis to summond the saidis personis *litteratorie* to compeir befoir the brethrein to answer at the instance of the kirk for the caus foirsaid and to underly disciplein thairfoir ilk persone undir the paine of disobedience.

Mr Andro Grahame: The quhilk day the brethrein undirstanding that upone the xvj day of Aprill last bypast Mr Andro Grahame, bischop of Dunblane, was decernit and ordeinit be thame to have producit befoir the brethir of the generall assemblie on the xxv day of the said moneth of Aprill ane auctentick register of the haill fewis and takis sett be him of the fruictis of the said bischoprik sen his entires thairto to be sein and considderit be the brethrein of the said assemblie and in speciall the fewis and takis sett to my lord Grahame, the Maister of Mar and Maister of Levingstoun, and trew it is thair was na thing done in the said assemblie thairanent bot ordeinit the brethrein of this presbytery to proceid in tryell and disceplein againis the said Mr Andro according to the commissioun gevin to thame of befoir, thairfor the brethrein ordanis the said Mr Andro to be summond *litteratorie* to compeir befoir thame to heir and se the said mater proceid quhair it left, viz., to produce befoir thame ane auctentik register of the haill fewis and takis sett be him of the fruictis of the said bischoprik sen his enteres thairto and in speciall the fewis and takis particularlie befoir expremit to be sein and considderit be thame and to heir and se thair jugementis pronuncit anent the same, undir the paine of disobedience.

Issobell Grahame, allegit adultrix: The samin day compeirit Cristane McInturnur, quha allegis hir mareit on Finlay McVoreist in the kirk of Drimmen be Sir Neill Mentayth, reder at the said kirk for the tyme, and for verefeing quhairof scho producit the said

rederis testimoniall subscryvit with his hand and allegit farther that
hir said husband lyis in adultrie with Issobell Grahame, dwelland
with the laird Dormond within the parrochun of Port and dochter
to umquhill Thomas Grahame, and thairfor desyrit the brethrein
to tak ordur with the said adultrie committit, as said is. The brethrein ordanis the said Issobell Grahame to be summond *litteratorie* to
heir and se hir self decernit to have committit the said adultrie and
to undirly the disceplein of the kirk thairfoir undir the paine of
disobedience.

At Striviling the xxvij day of August, 1583

Presentes: Mr William Stirling, James Andirsone, Patrik Gillaspie,
Mr Andro Yung, Mr Arthur Futhie, Mr Alexander Chisholme,
Robert Mentayth, Michaell Lermonthe, ministeris; Mr James Pont,
Duncane Narne, elderis; and Mr Alexander Iule, ane brothir of
exerceis.

James Blakwod: The quhilk day ane summondis beand producit
deulie execute and indorsit upone James Blakwod and William
Thomesone in Dunblane chairgeing thame to compeir the said day
to answer at the instance of the kirk for speiking, eatting and
drinking with Sir William Blakwod and Sir William Drummond,
personis being excommunicat, as at mair lynthe is conteinit in the
said summondis, compeirit the said James Blakwod personallie,
quha being accusit for eatting and drinking with Sir William
Blakwod, beand excommunicat, ansorit that he nathir eat, drank
nor commonit with him in his awin hous nor in na uther hous
excep in the housis of my lord Graham and the laird of Tullibairdin
or in sic uthir plaicis quhair he mycht nocht eschew his cumpany,
and tuiching the said Sir Williamis viveris and uthir necisaris neciser
to him in Dunblane, the said James confessis he send thame furth
of his awin hous to the said Sir Williamis chalmir and thaireftir the
said James producit ane answer in wret, as it beris in the self. The
brethrein tuik to advys with the said answer producit to the secund
Tuysday eftir the nixt generall assemblie and grantis lycence to the
said James to send the said Sir Williamis neciseris to his awin chalmir
allanirlie and him self to confer with him to the said day allanirlie
sum tymis for calling of him fra that damnablle idolatrie, in the

quhilk he is, to the trew licht of Chrystis evangell, and that
the said James report the said day quhat he proffeittis the
said Sir William be his confirence and that he compeir the said
day to heir the brethreinis jugementis pronuncit on his answer
producit.

William Thomeson: Compeirit the said William Thomesone and
being accusit for commoning, eatting and drinking with Sir
William Drummond, beand excommunicat, the said William denyit
the haill accusatioun *simpliciter* bot confessis he sendis the said Sir
William Drummondis neciseris to his awin chalmir to him bot
gangis nocht to him himself, quhilk the brethir gevis lycence to the
said William to do in tymis cuming, provyding he nather eat, drink
nor commone with him.

Andro Broun: The samin day compeirit Andro Broun in Dunblane
and confessis that he was passand to faiche ane elnwand and be
accident met with Sir William Drummond, excommunicat, and
spak to him, for the quhilk the said Andro is ordinit to stand up
in his awin sett in the kirk of Dunblane quhair he sittis quhen the
minister callis his name and grant he sclanderit the kirk in speiking
to the said Sir William and offendit thairin on the nixt Sonday in
tyme of sermond and is admonesit nocht to do the lyk in tymis
cuming.

The quhilk day compeirit Andro Crumbie in Dachirlie, parrochinnar of Muthill, and confessis carnall copulatioun with Margaret
Stalkar and that the said Margaret confessit to him that scho was
mareit with Andro Dune and thaireftir was lauchfullie partit fra
him in Sanctandrus. The brethir ordanis Mr Alexander Chisholm
to try gif the said allegit separatioun be in veritie or nocht and
quhat he findis thairby to report to the brethrein on the [*blank*]
day of [*blank*] to the effect the brethir may juge gif the said Andro
Crumbie hes committit adultrie or fornicatioun with the said
Margaret Stalkar.

James Hudsone, adulterar: The quhilk day ane summondis beand
producit lauchfullie execute and indorsit upone James Hudsone,
adulterar in Alvayth, chairgeing him to compeir the said day to
answer at the instance of the kirk for his disobedience in nocht
passing to the last synnodall assemblie of this province, nather yit
the uther synnodall assemblie proceiding the samin, to have ressavit

his injunctionis for adultrie committit be him with Issobell Fargy, as at mair lynthe is conteinit in the said summondis, compeirit the said James and grantis his disobedience thruch misknawlege of the dayis quhen the said assembleis was haldin be his foryetfulnes [*sic*], for the quhilk he submittis him self in the will of the kirk. The brethrein commandis and ordanis him to pas and compeir befoir the nixt provinciall assemblie of this province to be haldin in Edinburgh the first day of October nixt thair to ressave the injunctionis to be injonit to him for his said adultrie and to obey thame undir the paine of excommunicatioun. [*In margin*: On the xxviij of Januar 1583, compeirit James Hudson withinwrittin and confessit that he past to the synnodall assemblie heir specefeit and satisfeit this ordinance in all pointis, quhilk Robert Mentayth, his minister, testefeit in all pointis, and thairfor the brethir is contentit with him and consentis that ane act actit in the commissaris buik of Striviling of caution for him be deleit.]

Tintirrane: The quhilk day ane summondis beand producit deulie execute and indorsit upone Alexander Levingstoun of Tintirane, Margaret Grahame, his dochtir in law, Alexander Frissall, Cristan Wod and Issobell Forester, servandis to the said Alexander, chairgeing thame to compeir the said day to answer at the instance of the kirk for nocht presenting thame selffis to the examinatioun amangis the rest of the parrochinnaris of Kippen befoir the ministratioun of the communioun in the kirk thairof and for nocht presenting thame selffis to the communioun, the sacrament of the Lordis Supper, ministrat in the said kirk on Sonday the xviij day of August instant, thairby contemnand the same and to underly disceplein thairfoir ilk persone undir the paine of disobedience, quhilkis personis being oft tymis callit compeirit nocht, thairfor the brethrein ordanis thame to be summond of new to the effect foirsaid undir the paine of excommunicatioun.

At Striviling the iij day of September, 1583

Presentes: James Andirsone, Patrik Gillaspie, Mr Alexander Chisholme, Alexander Fargy, Robert Mentayth, Mr Andro Yung, Mr Adame Merschell, ministeris; and Mr Alexander Iule, ane brothur of exerceis.

Mr Andro Grahame: The quhilk day ane summondis beand producit deulie execute and indorsit upone Mr Andro Grahame, bischop of Dunblane, chairgeing him to have compeirit the said day to heir and se the brethrein proceid quhair thay left anent the tryell of him according to the act of the generall assemblie, viz., to produce befoir thame the said day ane auctentik register of the haill fewis and takis sett be him of the fruictis of the said bischoprik sen his enteres thairto and in speciall the fewis and takis set to my lord Grahame, the Maister of Mar and the Maister of Levingstoun to be sein and considderit be thame and to heir and se thair jugementis pronuncit anent the same undir the paine of disobedience, quhilk Mr Andro being oft tymis callit compeirit nocht, thairfor the brethrein ordanis the said Mr Andro to be summond of new *litteratorie* to the effect foirsaid undir the paine of excommunicatioun, with certificatioun and he compeir nocht the brethrein will proceid according to Goddis Word and the disceplein of the kirk.

Prophanaris of the Sabbothe, Johnne Drummond, Patrik Wilsone: The quhilk day, it was meinit to the brethrein be Mr Alexander Chisholme, minister at Muthill, that upone Sonday the first of this instant he beand instantlie passand in the kirk of Muthill to mak the sermond, Johnne Drummond *alias* Denmark, and Patrik Wilsone drawis swordis in the kirkyaird and thairby makis trubill amangis the haill congregatioun, prophanis the Sabboth day thru the quhilk the maist part of the said congregatioun war withdrawin and hauldin fra the sermond to the grit hinderance of Godis glorie and evill exampill to utheris to do the lyk. The brethrein ordanis the saidis personis to be summond *litteratorie* to answer at the instance of the kirk for the caus foirsaid and to undirly disciplein thairfoir, ilk persone under the paine of disobedience.

Patrik Layng: The quhilk day Patrik Layng being desyrit to declair gif he hes baptezit ony bairnis gottin in adultrie or fornicatioun (the kirk nocht beand satisfeit with thair parentis) sen he was last accusit or nocht, and in speciall gif he baptezit Margaret Bruce bairne gottin on hir in adultrie, as is allegit, be Robert Bruce of Clakmannan, the said Patrik confessis he baptezis bairnis lauchfullie gottin and teichis as he usit of befoir, inrespect of his appellatioun fra the brethreinis jugementis, bot denyis *simpliciter* the baptezein of ony bairnis unlauchfullie gottin sen the tyme foirsaid.

Robert Fogo: The quhilk day compeirit Robert Fogo in Doun, reder at the kirk of Kilmadok, and offirit him self to be tryit in his reding and of his lyf and conversatioun as he was ordeinit on the iiij day of *Junij* last bypast, the moderatour in name of the brethir askit the said Robert quhy he compeirit nocht on the xxv day of the said moneth of *Junij* as he was thane ordeinit to have gevin ane tryell of his redein and to have hard and sein tryell of his lyf and conversatioun. The said Robert ansorit that sen the said iij day of *Junij* he mycht nocht cum in this toun ontrublit be warding or uthirwayis for certane mony addettit be ane man in Mentayth for quhome he became cautioner to ane man in this toun quhill now that he hes aggreit with the man quhom to the silvir was awand, quhilk nocht onlie wald have bein trubill to him bot also sclanderus to the kirk he berand offeice in the same, quhilk excuse allegit be the said Robert was knawin be sum of the brethir present to be trew and thairfor the brethrein dispensis with the said Robertis absence the said day and warnis him *apud acta* to compeir on the x day of September instant to gif ane tryell of his reding and to heir and se tryell tane of his lyf and conversatioun, undir the paine of deprivatioun.

At Striviling the x day of September, 1583

Presentes: Mr William Stirling, James Andirsone, Patrik Gillaspie, Mr Andro Yung, Mr Arthur Futhie, Alexander Fargy, Robert Mentayth, Michaell Lermonthe, ministeris; William Stirling, Robert Fogo, rederis; Alexander Forester of Garden, elder, and William Norwall, elder; Mr Alexander Iule, ane brothur of exerceis.

Robert Fogo deprivit simpliciter: The quhilk day being assignit to Robert Fogo, reder at the kirk of Kilmadok, to compeir and gif ane tryell of his reiding and to heir and se tryell tane of his lyf and conversatioun, compeirit the said Robert personallie to quhom was cassin up ane chaptur in the New Testament and commandit to reid the same and eftir reiding of ane portioun thairof thair was gevin to him twa prayeris in the psalme buik to reid. Eftir reiding of the quhilkis, the brethrein being ryplie advysit findis the said Robert Fogo can nocht proffeit the kirk of God be his reiding becaus he reidis nocht distinctlie, keipis na point in his reiding nor undirstandis nocht quhat he reidis, for the quhilk caus, and for ministratioun of the sacrament of baptisme and mariage without lauchfull admissioun thairto, as his confessioun thairanent on the xxj day of May last at lynthe beris and the brethreinis jugement thairon pronuncit on the iiij day of *Junij* last, and for baptezein of bairnis, ane gottin in adultrie and uthir in fornicatioun (the kirk nocht beand satisfeit with thair parenttis) againis the actis of the generall assemblie. Thairfor the haill brethrein jugit the said Robert Fogo worthie to be deposit and deposis him *simpliciter* fra reiding in the kirk of God and all functioun thairin and exerceis of ony part of the ministrie thairof at all tymis fra thisfurthe, quhilk depositioun is presentlie intimat to the said Robert, beand personallie present.

Concerning adulteraris: The brethrein ordanis to summond the haill adulteraris convict within the boundis of this presbytery that hes nocht as yit endit thair haill injunctionis to compeir befoir the provinciall assemblie of the presbyteriis of Edinburgh, Dalkayth, Striviling and Linlythquow to be haldin in Edinburgh the first day of October nixt, thair to ressave thair injunctionis and sum of thame to end thair injunctionis in linning clathis as the copy of the summondis sall declair unto thame.

At Striviling the xvij day of September, 1583

Presentes: Mr William Stirling, James Andirsone, Johnne Duncanson, Alexander Fargy, Patrik Gillaspie, Mr Alexander Chisholme, Mr Andro Yung, Mr Arthur Futhie and Michaell Lermonthe, ministeris; Alexander Forester of Garden, Umphra Cunynghame, Mr James Pont and Mr Alexander Iule, ane brothur of exerceis.

The quhilk day Patrik Gillaspie and Alexander Fargy producit thair buikis of disceplein to be veseit be the brethrein.

Margaret Gib, adultrix: The samin day compeirit Margaret Gib in Stirling and grantis hir mareit on Alexander Gibsone thair and confessis hir to have borne ane bairne gottin on hir in adultrie be umquhill Alexander Johnesone, messinger, as scho allegis, for the quhilk the brethrein ordanis hir to pas to the nixt provinciall assemblie of this province to be haldin in Edinburgh the first day

of October nixt, thair to ressave injunctionis to be injonit to hir
for the said adultrie and to obey thame undir the paine of excommunicatioun, and becaus it is allegit the said fathir of hir bairne
be fengzeit and nocht of veretie, thairfor the brethrein ordanis the
minister and sessioun of the kirk of Striviling to try befoir thame
quha is the richt fathir thairof that thaireftir ordur may be tane with
him (gif he be alyve) as effeiris. Attour, the brethrein ordanis and
commandis the minister of Striviling to bapteis hir said bairne, scho
findand cautioun of befoir to obey and satisfie the kirk for hir said
offence in all thingis undir the paine of x merkis mony.

At Striviling the xxiiij day of September, 1583

Presentes: Mr William Stirling, James Andirsone, Patrik Gillaspie,
Michaell Lermonthe, Robert Mentayth, Alexander Fargy, Mr
Andro Yung, Thomas Swintoun, Mr Adame Merschell, Mr James
Pont, elder; Mr. Alexander Iule, ane brothur of exerceis.

Johnne Clark, a man slayer: The quhilk day compeirit Johnne
Clark in Waster Corscaplie within the parrochun of Dunblane and
grantis him on ane suddentie be negligence to have slaine Williame
Robertsone thair on the xxv day of August, for the quhilk he is
sorie fra his hairt and hes obteinit remissione fra the kingis majestie
and hes satisfeit the partie thairfoir. The brethrein ordanis the said
Johnne to compeir befoir the nixt provinciall assemblie of this
province to be haldin in Edinburgh the first day of October nixt
thair to ressave injunctionis to be injonit to him for the said slauchtir
and to obey thame undir the paine of excommunicatioun.

Mr Andro Grahame: The quhilk day Mr Andro Grahame, bischop
of Dunblane, beand summond, the moderator producit ane wretein
of his direct to the brethrein berand his excuis of the noncomperance
this day, quhairof the tennour follwis.

God blis you all with his Holie Spirit thruch Jesus Christ our only
Mediatour.

Brethrein, I ressavit your godlie ordinance chairgein me to be
thair at you in Striviling the xxiiij of this instant to produce the
auctentik copeis of the fewis and takis sett sen my intromissioun.
First, as to the day appointit to me seing that yistirday I ressavit
your command, it lyis nocht in my habilitie to keip the same bayth

inrespect of the far distance of the plaice, and alswa that of accident my hors ar presentlie absent frome me besyd Dunnotar. As to the uther point concerning the productioun, I have promesit alreddie befoir your wisdomes to do the samin and sall, Godwilling, satisfie you thairintill gif that ye think expedient to grant me sufficient tyme quhairby I may recovir the copeis out of the handis of thame that hes thame presentlie, quhilk I dout nocht to performe betuix and the xx day of October nixt, swa that as I have hethirtillis reverencit the kirkis ordinancis, I wald alwayis now in this caice wis you to juge of me cheritablie: for God is my witnes quhow sair againis my will I was careit away ather to prejuge the patrimony of the kirk or to molest ony persone in thair roumis. The pruif heirof is manifest in that I regairdit nocht to incur the indignatioun of my cheif be productioun of ane oblegatioun befoir the lordis quhairby the present possessuris can nocht be trublit for thair lyftymes. Yit in this I purge nocht my self, and meikil les in ony uther pairt of my calling: bot grantis me the first of thame that ar sclanderus or negligent alwayis I do submit my self with modestie to your jugementis gif that ony wayis thair hes bein fund in my walking befoir you ather stuburnnes, arrogancie, craft or curiositie as sindrie utheris of this odius name hes declairit thame selffis (quhilk I lament) to the grit disquyetnes of Christis kirk, flattering of the cheif men of this cuntrie, exaltatioun of thame selffis above thair dewatie. Swa hoping that your wisdomes will pondir diligentlie and prudentlie with your selffis this caice of myne as it standis, I lippen that rather of your dewtiful cheritie ye will minister unto me that is cassin doun justlie by sindrie visitatiounis of the Lord occasioun of confort nor mater of infame and reproche quhilk salbe mair grevous a grit deall to my conscience nor the los of quhatsumevir uther warldlie benefeit appertening to the body. Swa recommendis you all unto the saiffgaird of the Lord Jesus, that mercifull juge of his elect and penitent, bot feirfull to the reprobat and thame that can nocht repent. Off Morphy the xxj of September, 1583. I purpois with Goddis graice to be in Dunblane this nixt Fryday or Setterday at the farthest. *Sic subscribitur*, your wisdomes loving and maist obedient in the Lord Jesus, Andro Grahame, minister att Dunblane.

The brethrein, inrespect of the said wreting producit, continewis the pronuncein of thair jugementis in the said Mr Andro Grahamis mater to the viij day of October nixttocum.

At Striviling the viij day of October, 1583

Presentes: Mr William Striviling, James Andirsone, Patrik Gillaspie, Michaell Lermonthe, Mr Andro Yung, Mr Arthur Futhie, Alexander Fargie, ministeris; Mr Duncane Nevein, Alexander Balvaird, rederis; Mr James Pont and Umphra Cunynghame, elderis.

Mr Andro Grahame: The quhilk day the brethrein, being advysit with the proces deducit befoir thame againis Mr Andro Grahame, bischop of Dunblane, concerning his tryell of certane heddis conteinit in ane act of the generall assemblie of the dett the xiij day of October *anno* etc., lxxxij yeiris as the samin beris in the self, findis the said Mr Andro giltie in thir heddis follwing, that is to say, of negligence in doctrein and disceplein, waisting of the patrimony of the kirk, setting of takis againis the actis of the kirk, and as to the rest of the heddis conteinit in the said act, findis the said Mr Andro innocent, and swa inrespect of the heddis quhairof he is fund giltie, findis him to have incurit the puneisment conteinit in the actis of the generall assemblie made thairanent, and thairfor ordanis our brethir, commissionaris to the generale assemblie, to advys with the said assemblie and to crave thair jugementis quhat finell sentence salbe pronuncit againis him and ordanis the said Mr Andro to be summond to compeir befoir us in the kirk of Striviling the iij day of December nixtocum to heir and se the said sentence pronuncit againis him, with certificatioun that quhiddir he compeir or nocht the samin wilbe pronuncit againis him according to the proces deducit.

Robert Veiche: The samin day the moderatour producit befoir the brethrein ane summondis dewlie execute and indorsit gevin at thair command chairgeing Robert Veiche, sumtyme gwarden of the Gray freiris in Striviling, to have compeirit befoir the synnodall assemblie of the elderschippis of Edinburgh, Striviling, Linlythquow and Dalkayth haldin in Edinburgh the first day of October instant befoir none to have gevin ane confessioun of his fayth and religioun as lykwys to have ressavit disciplein for his formar abusis as the brethrein of the said assemblie sould have injonit to him undir the paine of excommunicatioun, as at mair lynthe is conteinit in the said summondis and executioun, lyk as alsua the said moderatour intimat to the brethrein ane act of the said assemblie made anent the said freir, Robert Veiche, inrespect of his noncomperance, berand in effect that the brethrein thairof hes continewit the pronuncein of the sentence till the nixt generall assemblie and willit the cautioner to produce him thair and ordeinit the cautioner to be summond to that effect. Inrespect of the quhilk ordinance, the brethrein ordanis Michaell Rynd, gouldsmyth in Striviling, cautioner for the said Robert Veiche, to be summond to compeir him self and entir the said freir Robert Veiche and produce him befoir the generall assemblie to be haldin in Edinburgh on the thrid day thairof, viz., the xij day of October instant, to gif ane confessioun of his faithe and religioun as lykwys to ressave disceplein for his formar abusis and disobedience, as the brethir of the said assemblie sall injone to him, to heir and se thair sentence pronuncit thairanent undir the paine of disobedience, with certificatioun and the said Michaell failzie in entering of the said freir Robert Veiche the said day, as said is, the brethrein of the said assemblie will decern the censuris of the kirk to be execute againis him with all rigour.

Persone of Cultir: The quhilk day compeirit Archebauld Levingstoun, persone of Cultir, and declairit that becaus he was lauchfullie provydit to the parsonage of Cultir, he acknawlegit him self to be bund thairby of his dewatie to serve in the cuir of the ministrie at the kirk thairof and to the effect he may entir in the said cuir with the bettir ordur desyris the brethrein of this presbytery to gif him thair testemoniall of his lyf and conversatioun direct to the presbytery of Lainrig, in the quhilk boundis the said kirk of Cultir is, that thaireftir he may be lauchfullie admittit thairto be the said presbytery of Lainrig. Quhilk desyr beand hard be the brethrein and eftir diligent inquisitioun beand tane among thame all conveinit, thair was na thing fund in his lyf and conversatioun bot honestie and thairfor ordanit his said desyr to be grantit.

At Striviling the xxij day of October, 1583

Presentes: Mr William Stirling, James Andirsone, Patrik Gillaspie,

Michaell Lermonthe, Mr Alexander Chisholme, Mr Arthur Futhie, Mr Andro Yung, Mr Neill Campbell, Robert Mentayth, Alexander Fargy, ministeris; Alexander Forester of Garden, elder; Mr Alexander Iule, ane brothur of exerceis; Mr Duncan Nevein, William Stirling and Alexander Balvaird, rederis.

Moderator: The quhilk day Patrik Gillaspie, minister at Sanct Ninianis kirk, be voit of the haill brethrein was chosin moderatour in this presbytery to the nixt provinciall assemblie.

The quhilk day the moderatour foirsaid made intimatioun to the haill brethrein that thair was ane publict fast appointit be the last generall assemblie to be observit publictlie be the haill kirk of Scotland upone the secund and thrid Sondayis of December nixt and thairfor desyrit everie ane of the brethrein to mak dew intimatioun unto thair parrochinnaris of the same and to exhort thame to observe the same according to the ordur.

Item, the said moderatour made intimatioun lykwys that the nixt generall assemblie is to be haldin in the toun of Sanctandrus on the xxiiij day of Aprill excep be parliament or uthir occasiounis the samin be prevenit be adverteisment of the brethir of Edinburgh.

The quhilk day the moderator reportit that ane summondis beand producit befoir the generall assemblie lauchfullie execute and indorsit upone the xij day of October instant chairgeing Michaell Rynd, gouldsmyth in Striviling, to produce befoir thame the said day freir Robert Veiche, sumtyme gwarden of the Gray freiris in Striviling, as cautioner for him as the samin in the self at mair lynthe beris, quhilk summondis togethir with the haill proces deducit befoir us and the synnodall assemblie of this province beand sein and considderit be the said assemblie, the said assemblie hes ordeinit that the said freir Robert Veiche sould be summarlie excommunicat be the brethrein of the presbytery of Striviling according to the certificatioun conteinit in the summondis producit on him befoir the said provinciall assemblie becaus of his non-comperiance and disobedience thair. Quhilk ordinance of the generall assemblie beand considderit be the brethrein, thay have ordeinit James Andirson, minister at Striviling, to pronunce the sentence of excommunicatioun againis him and to begin the admonitionis preceding the samin on Sonday nixt the xxvij of

October instant and thaireftir to proceid summarlie according to the ordur and to report the samin to the nixt sessioun.

Mr Alexander Chisholme: The quhilk day Mr Alexander Chisholme, minister at Muthill, exponit and declairit to the brethrein that Archibald Ogilvie of Lawtoun, his fathir in law, was departit furth of this lyf and thairfor his aigit mothur hade desyrit him to dwell in hous with hir famelie and do the part of ane faythfull and obedient sone to hir, quhilk of his dewatty he could nocht gudelie refuse, yit becaus hir dwelling hous is mair neir to Perthe nor this brugh desyris lycence of the brethrein that he may resort and keip exerceis with the brethrein of the presbytery of Perthe in tymis cuming inrespect of his maist neir dwelling thairto, as said is. The brethrein, being advysit with the said Mr Alexander desyr, grantis lycence to him to resort to the exerceis of the presbytery of Perthe only quhill the nixt provinciall assemblie of this province, provyding alwayis that him self and his flock be in the mentyme subject to the disceplein of this presbytery.

Auldy: The quhilk day compeirit Patrik Crichtoun of Strathurd and producit befoir the brethrein in name of Elezabeth Crichtoun, lady Auldy, ane bill gevin in to the last generall assemblie of the kirk with ane ordinance of the samin on the bak thairof desyrand the brethrein of this presbytery to call befoir thame the laird of Auldy, husband to the said Elezabeth, and to admoneis him to do his dewatty to ane man chyld quhairof his said spous was delyvir in the moneth of *Junij* last and in speciall to caus bapteis him as becumis ane Christiane man to do to his awin chyld or ellis to schaw ane ressonablle caus quhy, as at mair lynth is conteinit in the said bill. With the quhilk, the brethrein being advysit findis that the said laird of Auldy dwellis presentlie within the boundis of this presbytery and siclyk ar [is, *deleted*] willein to obey the said ordinance, thairfor ordanis the said laird of Auldy, callit Andro Merser [of] Miclour, to be summond *litteratorie* to compeir befoir thame to heir and se him self decernit to present the said mane chyld to be baptezit as his awin lauchfull sone or ellis to allege ane ressonabill caus quhy the samin sould nocht be done undir the paine of disobedience.

James Blacwod: The quhilk day being assignit to James Blacwod, brothir to Sir William Blacwod, excommunicat, to report quhat he

P

hes proffeitit the said William be his confirence with him sen the xxvij day of August last bypast and als to heir and se the jugementis of the brethrein pronuncit on ane answer in wret producit be the said James Blacwod, compeirit the said James Blacwod personalie quha being desyrit to report quhat he hes proffeit the said William Blacwod be his confirence with him ansorit that he hade nevir confirence with him sensyne excep ainis or twys becaus he hes bein almest continuallie sensyne furth of Dunblane in landwart. Nochttheles gif it sall plais the brethrein to grant farther lycence to him to confer with his brethur and furneis him his necisaris, as of befoir, he sall do according to his powar to convert him fra the damnabill idolatrie of papistrie to the cleir lycht of the evangell. The brethrein grantis lycence to the said James Blacwod, as of befoir, to send the said Williamis neciseris to his awin chalmir allanirlie and him self with ane or twa of the elderschip of Dunblane conjunctlie to confer with him to the nixt provinciall assemblie of this province, viz., the vij of Aprill nixt to the effect foirsaid and this for answer to the wret producit be the said James Blacwod befoir specefeit and als ordanis the said James Blacwod to report to the brethrein on the xiiij day of the said moneth of Aprill quhat he proffeitis the said William be his confirence undir the paine of disobedience.

At Striviling the xxix day of October, 1583

Presentes: Patrik Gillaspie, Mr William Stirling, Alexander Fargie, Mr Arthur Futhie, Mr Andro Yung, Mr Adame Merschell, Robert Mentayth, Michaell Lermonthe, ministeris; Mr Alexander Iule, ane brothur of exerceis.

The quhilk day the moderatour askit James Andirsone gif he hade admonesit freir Robert Veiche, as he was ordeinit in the last sessioun. The said James ansorit that upone Sonday last he hade gevin him the first admonitioun befoir the sentence according to the ordur and he fand na obedience offirit be him nor nane in his name. The brethrein ordanis him to proceid and gif the secund admonitioun according to the ordur on Sonday nixt and report the samin on the v day of November nixt.

Patrik Layng: The quhilk day Patrik Layng being desyrit, yit as of befoir, to declair the trewthe gif he takis silvir for mariagis and baptisme ministrein, the said Patrik ansorit and confessit that he takis silvir for the ministratioun baithe of mariagis and baptisme and grantis he baptezit ane bairne in Airthe gottin in adultrie quhairof the parentis hade nocht satisfeit the kirk. The brethrein continewis thair jugementis heirin and anent his uthir accusatiounis quhill thai be farther advysit.

Auldy: The quhilk day ane summondis beand producit dewlie execute and indorsit upone Andro Merser of Micklour chairgeing him to have compeirit the said day to heir and se him self decernit to have presentit his sone gottin on Elezabeth Crichtoun, his spous, to be baptezit as his awin lauchfull sone or ellis to have allegit ane ressonablle caus quhy the samin sould nocht be done under the paine of disobedience, quhilk Andro Merser being oft tymis callit compeirit nocht except James Blakwod, reder, quha compeirit and in his name proponit ane excuis of his absence quhilk was admittit for this day onelie, nochttheles the brethrein ordanis the said Andro to be summond *litteratorie* to the effect foirsaid undir the paine of disobedience.

Archibald Smyth, adulterar in Striviling: The quhilk day ane summondis beand producit lauchfullie execute and indorsit upone Archibald Smyth, yunger, in Striviling, chairgeing him to have compeirit befoir the brethrein the said day to heir and se him self decernit to be excommunicat for his disobedience in nocht compeirin befoir the last synnodall assemblie of this province haldin in Edinburgh the first day of October instant to have ressavit injunctionis to have bein injonit to him for adultrie committit be him with Margaret Gib, as he was lauchfullie chairgit be the sessioun of the kirk of Striviling undir the said paine of excommunicatioun, compeirit the said Archibald personallie and grantis the said adultrie, as said is, and allegit that his noncomperance befoir the said assemblie was nocht of na contemp nor disobedience that he meinit to the kirk bot onelie inrespect of ane sinister informatioun he gat assurand him that his comperance befoir the synnodall assemblie was nocht neidfull the said day, nochttheles the said Archibald confessit his disobedience and offirit him self in the brethreinis will thairfoir. The brethrein dispensis with the said Archibald disobedience, inrespect his said allegence was understand to sum of thame to be trew, and ordeinit him with all diligence to act cautioun in the commissaris buikis of Striviling that he sall compeir in Edinburgh befoir the provinciall assemblie of this province thair to be hauldin on the first Twysday of Aprill nixt to ressave injunctionis to be injonit to him for adultrie with Margaret Gib, spous to Alexander Gibsone, and to obey thame undir the paine of xl libis.

Adulterar in Logy: The quhilk day compeirit Robert Hendirsone, parrochinnar in Logy, husband to Elezabeth Hendirsone, and grantis him to have gottin ane bairne in adultrie with Margaret [Agnes, *deleted*] Smyth, now in Keir, and grantis the said fault was made in his awin hous within the said parrochun of Logy and offiris obedience to the kirk for his said fault and thairfor desyris that Alexander Fargy, his minister, be commandit to bapteis his said bairne. The brethrein ordanis the said Robert to compeir befoir the nixt provinciall assemblie of this province in Edinburgh, the first Twysday of Aprill nixt, viz., the [*blank*] day of the samin, thair to ressave injunctionis to be injonit to him for his said adultrie and to obey the samin and that he with all diligence act cautioun in the commissaris buikis of Striviling for him that he sall obey thair said ordinance in all pointis undir the paine of xx libis., quhilk cautioun being actit, as said is, the brethrein ordanis Alexander Fargy to bapteis his said bairne.

Kinnimmond in Clakmannan parrochun: The quhilk day compeirit Hellein Kinnimmond and grantis hir to have bein mareit on Johnne Blak quha departit fra hir to Flandiris to the weris, thre yeir syne or thairby, and as scho is credablie informit allegis him ded thair ane yeir or mair syne, and sen his deces the said Hellein grantis that James Schaw, apperand of Sauchie, hes gottin ane bairn with hir in fornicatioun quhairof scho is delyvir schort syne, for the quhilk fault the said Hellein offiris to satisfie the kirk and thairfor desyris command to Alexander Fargy to bapteis hir bairne. The brethrein, being advysit with the said Hellein confessioun, findis na sufficient testimony of the deathe of hir said husband befoir hir carnall copulatioun with the said James and thairfor can nocht presentlie decern gif hir said fault be adultrie or fornicatioun. Nochttheles thai ordein that sufficient cautioun be actit in the commissaris buikis of Striviling for the said James and Hellein that thai and ilk ane of thame under the paine of fourty pundis money sall satisfie the kirk as thai salbe commandit at quhat tyme thai be requyrit thairto, quhilk cautioun be actit as said is, ordanis Alexander Fargy to bapteis hir bairne.

At Striviling the fyft day of November, 1583

Presentes: Patrik Gillaspie, James Andirsone, Mr William Stirling, Mr Andro Yung, Alexander Fargy, ministeris; Mr Alexander Iule; Mr James Pont, elder; Umphra Cunynghame, elder; William Stalkar, baillie in Stirling.

Freir Veiche: The quhilk day the moderatour askit James Andirson, minister at Striviling, gif he hade gevin the secund admonitioun to freir Robert Veiche as he was ordeinit in the last sessioun. The said James ansorit that he hade don the samin on Sonday last and fand na obedience offirit be him nor na uthir in his name. The brethrein ordanis him to proceid and gif the thrid admonitioun according to the ordur on Sonday and report the samin on the xij of this instant.

Auldy: The quhilk day ane summondis beand producit deulie execute and indorsit upone Andro Merser of Meiklour chairgeing him to have compeirit befoir us the said day to have hard and sein him self decernit to have presentit his sone gottin on Elezabeth Crichtoun, his spous, to be baptezit as his awin lauchfull sone or ellis to have allegit ane ressonabill [caus] quhy the samin sould nocht be done undir the paine of disobedience, quhilk being oft tymis callit compeirit nocht, thairfoir the brethrein, undirstandand the ordinance of the generall assemblie gevand chairge to thame to summond the said Andro to the effect foirsaid besyd thair awin powar ovir him dwelland within the boundis of the said presbytery, findis he is twys ordurlie summond and hes disobeyit and thairfor findis him contumax, for the quhilk caus the brethrein ordanis him to be summond of new *litteratorie* to the effect foirsaid undir the paine of excommunicatioun.

Jarvie, excommunicat: The quhilk day compeirit Cristane Jarvie dwelland in S. Ninianis parrochun lauchfullie excommunicat for disobedience to the kirk conjonit with adultrie committit be hir with Johnne Knox in Carnock and offirit to satisfie the kirk and thairfor desyrit to be absolvit fra the sentence of excommunicatioun. The brethrein ordanis the said Cristane with all diligence to act cautioun in the commissaris buikis of Striviling that scho sall compeir befoir the nixt provinciall assemblie of this province to be haldin in Edinburgh the first Twysday of Aprill nixt, thair to ressave injunctionis to be injonit to hir for hir disobedience conjonit with the cryme of adultrie undir the paine off xx lib.

At Striviling the xij day of November, 1583

Presentes: Mr William Stirling, Alexander Fargy, Michaell Lermonthe and Thomas Duncansone, ministeris; Mr Duncan Nevein, William Stirling, Alexander Balvaird, rederis; Umphra Cunynghame, Robert Alexander, elderis; and Mr Alexander Iule, ane brothur of exerceis. [*No minutes.*]

At Striviling the xix day of November, 1583

Presentes: Michaell Lermonthe, minister; Mr Duncane Nevein, reder; Umphra Cunynghame, elder; and Mr Alexander Iule, ane brothur of exerceis.

Auldy: The quhilk day compeirit Patrik Crichtoun of Strathurd, procurator for Elezabeth Crichtoun, lady Auldy, and producit ane procuratorie subscryvit be the said Elezabeth, as it beris in the self, with ane summondis deulie execute and indorsit upone Andro Merser of Meiclour chairgeing him to have compeirit befoir us the said day to have hard and sein him self decernit to have presentit his sone gottin on Elezabeth Crichtoun, his spous, to be baptezit as his awin lauchfull sone or ellis to have allegit ane ressonablle caus quhy the samin sould nocht be done under the paine of excommunicatioun. Compeirit Robert Hobrun in Stirling, in name of the said Andro Merser, havand his command and powar to that effect be ane misseive wreting and producit the said Andro Merseris answer to the said summondis in wret, as it beris in the self. The brethrein continewis farther proceidein in the said mater to the xxvj day of November instant and ordanis the defender to be summond to compeir the said [day] personallie to heir and se farder proces deducit in the said mater undir the paine of excommunicatioun.

At Striviling the xxvj day of November, 1583

Presentes: Patrik Gillaspie, James Andirsone, Mr William Stirling, Mr Arthur Futhie, Michaell Lermonthe, Alexander Fargy, Mr Andro Yung; Mr Duncane Nevein, reder; Umphra Cunynghame, elder.

Auldy: The quhilk day compeirit Elezabeth Crichtoun, lady Auldy, and producit ane summondis deulie execute and indorsit upone Andro Merser of Auldy, hir husband, chairgeing him to have compeirit personallie the said day to heir and sie farder proces deducit befoir the brethrein anent the refusall of the said Andro to bapteis his allegit bairne quhairof his said spous was lichter undir paine of excommunicatioun. Quhilk Andro being oft tymis callit compeirit nocht personallie, as he was lauchfullie warnit, and thairfor was fund be the brethrein contumax and is ordeinit to be summond *litteratorie* to compeir befoir us personallie to heir and se him self decernit to be excommunicat for his contemp and malicius disobedience, with certificatioun and he failze we will proceid and decern him to be excommunicat, as said is, according to the Word of God and disceplein of the kirk havand the warand thairof thairin.

The samin day, James Andirsone was askit be the moderatour gif he hade gevin Robert Veiche the 3 admonitioun, quha answerit he hade gevin the 3 and 4 admonitioun and hard na obedience offirit. The brethrein ordanis him to pronunce the sentence of excommunicatioun againis him on Sonday nixt and report the samin the nixt sessioun.

At Striviling the iiij day of December, 1583
Presentes: Patrik Gillaspie, James Andirsone, Johnne Duncansone, Andro Yung, Mr Arthur Futhie, Alexander Fargy, Robert Mentayth, Johnne Row, ministeris; Umphra Cunynghame, elder, and [*blank*] kirk reder.

Mr Andro Grahame: The quhilk day Mr William Stirling and James Andirsone, commissionaris to the last generall assemblie, was desyrit to report to the jugement of the said assemblie tuiching our finall sentence to be producit againis Mr Andro Grahame, conforme to ane ordinance made of befoir and commissioun gevin to thame to that effect, quha ansorit that the said mater beand proponit be thame to the haill assemblie was refarrit to the privie confirence of the moderatour of the said assemblie and his assessuris and albeit thai cravit that mater to be rassonit dyvers tymis and to have the said assembleis jugement thairin, yit thruch uthir mony weghtie materis that was in handlein the samin was past ovir without ony answer, quhairwith the brethrein being advysit thinkis gude that the said mater be continewit, as of befoir, to the nixt generall assemblie.

The quhilk day ane summondis beand producit deulie execute and indorsit upone Andro Merser of Nicklour [sic] chairgeing him to have compeirit the said day to have hard and sein him self decernit to be excommunicat for his contemp and disobedience as at mair lynthe is conteinit in the said summondis, compeirit the said Andro Merser and Elezabeth Crichtoun, his spous, baithe personallie. The said Andro was first accusit be the moderatour for his disobedience to the kirk and was desyrit to declair quhat was the caus thairof, the said Andro answerit that he hade declairit to sum of the brethrein ane excuis for his absence besyd ane wreting anent the same that he wret to the haill brethrein in the last sessioun, bot seing his excuis was nocht fund ressonablle he presentlie offiris him self in the will of the kirk for his said disobedience.

Auldy: The samin day the said Andro Merser of Nicklour [sic] being inquyrit be the moderatour of this presbytery to declair quhy he will nocht bapteis the mane chyld quhairof Elezabeth Crichtoun, his spous, was delyvir of in the monethe of *Junij* last bypast, the said Andro answerit and confessit the said mane chyld to be his and promesit to desyr Mr Adam Mairschell, minister of his parroche kirk, to bapteis the samin in his name within twenty dayis nixt heireftir and sall do thairanent as becumis of his dewatie, and to that effect sall send for his said bairne on Monunday or Twysday nixt and bring him to his plaice of Auldy or ellis sall ressave his said bairne fra quhome it sall plais the said Elezabeth Crichtoun to send him, with quhilk promeis the brether fundis rassonablle, and thairfor ordanis the samin to be done as said is. [*In margin*: On the 17 of December it was reportit be the lairdis misseive wreting producit be Robert Hobrun that he hade satisfeit this ordinance in all pointis.]

Freir Robert Veiche: The quhilk day James Andirsone, minister at
Striviling, was inquyrit be the moderatour gif he hade pronuncit
the sentence of excommunicatioun againis freir Robert Veiche as
he was ordeinit or nocht, the said James ansorit that according to
the brethreinis ordinance and inrespect na obedience was offirit be
the said freir nor na uthir in his name, he hade pronuncit the sentence
of excommunicatioun againis him on Sonday last according to
the ordur, quhilk sentence and admonitionis gevin to him of befoir
at command of the brethrein the said James hes producit, quhilk
beand red and considderit be the brethrein thay have fund that the
said James hes proceidit ordurlie againis the said freir Robert Veiche,
according to the brethreinis ordinancis, and the said admonitionis
and sentence put in dew and convenient forme quhairof the
tennour follwis.

1. *Admonitioun*: Upone Sonday the xxvij day of October instant
anno im vc lxxxiij yeiris, I, James Andirsone, minister of Godis
Word at Striviling, at command of ane ordinance of the presbytery
of the said brugh in the parroche kirk of the samin immediatlie
eftir sermond publictlie admonesit freir Robert Veiche, sumtyme
gwardein of the Gray freiris of Striviling, to randir obedience to
the reformit kirk of Christ within this realme, to gif ane confessioun
of his faithe and religioun publictlie according to his promeis made
befoir the brethrein of the said presbytery of Striviling, to recant
his papisticall erruris, quhilk he hes menteinit in tymis past, according to his said promeis, to submit him self to the disciplein of the
said kirk and to undirly the samin disceplein for dissaving of the
pepill and abusing of the sacramentis, undir the paine of excommunicatioun, and this as for the first admonitioun befoir the
sentence conforme to the ordur, quhilk I did in presens of the haill
pepill conveinit to heir Godis Word for the tyme. James Andirsoun,
minister foirsaid.

2. *Admonitioun*: Upone Sonday the iij day of November the yeir
of God im vc lxxxiij yeiris, I, James Andirsone, minister of Godis
Word at Striviling, at command of ane ordinance of the presbytery
of the said brugh within the parroche kirk of the samin immediatlie
eftir sermond publictlie admonesit freir Robert Veiche, sumtyme
gwarden in the Gray freiris of Striviling, to randir obedience to the
reformit kirk of Christ within this realme, to gif ane confessioun of

his faithe and religioun publictlie according to his promeis made befoir the brethrein of the said presbytery of Striviling, to recant his papisticall erruris quhilk he hes menteinit in tymis past according to his said promeis, to submit him self to the disceplein of the said kirk and to underly the samin disceplein for dissaving of the pepill and abusing of the sacramentis undir the paine of excommunicatioun and this, as for the secund admonitioun befoir the sentence, conforme to the ordur quhilk I did in presens of the haill pepill conveinit to heir Godis Word for the tyme. James Andersoun, minister off the evangell at Striviling.

3. *Admonitioun*: Upone Sonday the x day of November the yeir of God im vc lxxxiij yeiris, I, James Andersone, minister at Striviling, at command of ane ordinance of the presbytery of the said brugh in the parroche kirk of the samin immediatlie eftir sermond publictlie admonesit freir Robert Veiche, sumtyme gwarden of the Gray freiris in Stirling, to randir obedience to the reformit kirk of Christ within this realme, to gif ane confessioun of his fayth and religioun publictlie according to his promeis made befoir the brethrein of the said presbytery, to recant his papisticall erruris quhilk he hes menteinit in tymis past according to his said promeis, to submit him self to the disceplein of the said kirk and to undirly the samin disceplein for dissaving of the pepill and abusing of the sacramentis undir the paine of excommunicatioun, and this as for the admonitioun befoir the sentence conforme to the ordur, and thaireftir I made prayeris for his conversioun and exhortit all the congregatioun to pray for him, quhilk I did in presens of the haill pepill conveinit to heir Godis Word for the tyme. James Andersoun, minister off the evangell at Striviling.

4. *Admonitioun*: Upone Sonday the xxiiij day of November the yeir of God foirsaid, I, James Andirsone, minister of Godis Word at Striviling in the parroche kirk thairof, immediatlie eftir sermond publictlie admonesit freir Robert Veiche, sumtym gwarden of the Gray freiris in Striviling, to randir obedience to the reformit kirk of Christ within this realme, to gif ane confessioun of his fayth and religioun publictlie according to his promeis made befoir the brethrein of the presbytery of the said brugh, to recant his papisticall erruris quhilk he hes menteinit in tymis past according to his said promeis, to submit him self to the disceplein of the kirk and to

undirly the samin disceplein for dissaving of the pepill and abusing
of the sacramentis undir the pain of excommunicatioun, and this
as for the fourt admonitioun befoir the pronuncein of the sentence
of excommunicatioun to the effect the said freir sould have na
occasioun to allege ovir summar proceiding againis him nor
sufficient admonitiounis gevin befoir the pronuncein of the sentence
and immediatlie thaireftir I made solem prayer for his conversioun
and exhortit all the congregatioun to pray for him, quhilk I did
in presens of the haill pepill conveinit to heir Godis Word for the
tyme. James Anderson, minister off the evangell at Striviling.

Upone Sonday the first day of December the yeir of God foirsaid,
I, James Andersone, minister of Godis Word at Striviling, at
command of the brethrein of the presbytery of the said brugh in
the parroche kirk of the samin immediatlie eftir sermond inquyrit
the elderis and deacunis of the said kirk beand present for the tyme
thane to declair gif freir Robert Veiche, be him self or utheris in
his name, hade offirit to ony of thame to obey the ordinance of the
kirk and admonitiounis gevin to him thairanent in name of the
kirk quha keipit all sylence and als inquyrit publictlie gif the said
freir Robert Veiche, or ony in his name, wald thane compeir and
promeis obedience to the kirk and trew it is nane compeirit to that
effect and thairfor for his proud contemp and malicius disobedience
to the voice of the kirk (besyd his formar offencis), I, the said
minister, at command of the brethrein of the said presbytery,
pronuncit the sentence of excommunicatioun againis the said freir
Robert Veiche, conform to the ordur, and denuncit him excommunicat and delyverit him ovir into the handis off Sathane to the
destructioun of the flesche that the saull may be saif in the day of
the Lord Jesus according to the Word of God, ordinance of the
generall kirk and brethrein of the presbytery foirsaid in all pointis,
quhilk I did in presens of the haill pepill conveinit to heir Godis
Word for the tyme, and immediatlie thaireftir I admonesit all the
faythfull and in speciall the said congregatioun and everie ane of
thame to abhor the said freir Robert Veiche, excommunicat as ane
hathin and publicane, and to have na kynd of societie with him
lest thai be partakeris of his sinnis and of the curs of the same, and
this I admonesit thame to bewar of, undir the paine of the censuris
of the kirk to be execute againis sic as sould haif ony kynd of

familiaritie with him, unto the tyme he be absolvit fra the said
sentence and restorit againe to the societie of the kirk. In witnes of
the quhilkis, I, the said minister, hes subscryvit thir my admonitiounis and sentence off excommunicatioun with my awin hand as
follwis. James Andersone, minister off the evangell at Striviling.

At Striviling the [*blank*]

Upone the x day of December the brethrein of the presbytery
of Striviling conveinit nocht inrespect of the exerceis of the generall
fast.

At Striviling the xvij day of December, 1583

Presentes: Mr William Stirling, James Andirsone, Michaell
Lermonthe, Mr Andro Yung, Mr Alexander Chisholme, Alexander
Fargy, ministeris; Duncane Nevein, reder; Robert Alexander and
Umphra Cunynghame, elderis.

Generall fast: The quhilk day the moderator inquyrit gif the fast
was deulie observit within the boundis of this presbytery and gif
doctrein was teichit be the brethrein according to the ordur. It was
ansorit be the haill ministeris present that the fast was deulie keipit
within thair boundis (as thay undirstude) and doctrein was teichit
be ilk ane of thame respective to thair awin flockis according to
the ordur.

Robert Mentayth: The samin day, it was intimat to the brethrein
that it was allegit that Robert Mentayth, minister at Alvayth,
abusit the tyme of the said generall fast on the Sondayis and oulk
dayis appointit be the generall kirk to be keipit at the lest in allwing
of brydellis, bankettis at bairnis having with playing on pyppis and
uther instrumentis thairat etc., to the grit sclandir of the kirk and
contemp of the ordinance of the generall assemblie, for the quhilkis
causis the said Robertis ordeinit to be summond to answer at the
instance of the kirk for the said abuse and sic uther thingis as he
salbe accusit of and to underly disceplein thairfoir undir the paine
of disobedience.

The brethrein thinkis gude and ordeinis Alexander Fargy,
minister at Logy, to teiche in his kirk the Actis of the Apostillis.

At Striviling the xxiiij day of December, 1583

Presentes: Patrik Gillaspie, James Andirsone, Mr Andro Yung, Michaell Lermonthe, Alexander Fargy, Robert Mentayth, Mr Neill Campbell, ministeris; Mr Alexander Iulle, Mr Andro Murdo, brethir of exerceis; and Umphra Cunynghame, elder.

Robert Mentayth: The quhilk day ane summondis beand producit deulie execute and indorsit upone Robert Mentayth chairgeing him to compeir the said day to answer at the instance of the kirk for abusing and prophaning the tyme of the generall humiliatioun and fast as the samin at lynthe beris, compeirit the said Robert personallie quha being [accusit] be the moderatur of the offencis follwing, first for making of ane mariage in the kirk of Alvayth on the first Sonday of the fast, viz., the secund Sonday of December expres againis ane act of the generall assemblie, quhilk mareit personis was accumpaneit with ane pyper playand with thame to the kirk. The said Robert grantit the making of the said mariage on the said day at viij houris in the morning and that ane pyper playit with thame, as said is, to the kirk.

Secundlie, being accusit for making of ane mariage betuix twa personis parrochinnaris in Clakmannan in the said parroche kirk of Alvayth without lycence of the presbytery and that on the nixt Twysday follwing the first Sonday of the fast, the said Robert grantit the making of the said mariage on the said day at ix houris befoir none as said is.

Thridlie, being accusit for allwing of ane bankat in Johnne Duncansonis hous at the wod syd on the said day and being present him self thairat, the said Robert confessit that the said bankat was in the said Johnnis hous the said day and that he him self drank thairat in ane quyet hous.

Fourtlie, being accusit for baptezein of the bairnis gottin within the parrochun of Clakmannan lauchfullie at the said kirk of Alvayth on the said Twysday expres againis ane act of the generall assemblie and allwing of banquettis to be in thair parentis housis the said day. The said Robert confessit the baptezein of the saidis bairnis the said day bot denyit that he knew ony banquettis to be in thair parentis housis the said day and that he expreslie forbaid the same.

The brethrein being advysit with the saidis accusationis and answeris made thairto findis the said Robert giltie of thame all and findis him to have brokin sindrie acts of the generall assemblie speciallie in making of mariagis within the tyme of the generall fast, in mareing of uther parrochinnaris nor his awin without lycence, in baptezein of bairnis and making of mariagis in landwart aff ane Sonday and in allwing of ane banket in Johnne Duncansonis hous in tyme of the fast in that, that he was present him self thairat, for the quhilkis sclanderus offencis the brethrein decernis the said Robert to pay in penalty fourty schillingis on the last of this instant to be convertit at the sicht and discretioun of the brethrein of this presbytery and thaireftir to make publict repentence in his awin parroche kirk of Alvayth on Sonday the ix day of Fabruar nixt undir the paine of disobedience, and ordanis Mr William Stirling, minister at Abirfull, to pas to the said parroche kirk the said day and ressave his repentence with certificatioun to the said Robert that gif the lyk of ony of the saidis faultis be fund in him againe he salbe perpetuallie deprivit frome all functioun in the kirk. [*In margin*: The penaltie within writtin payit, 28 January 1583 and repentence made. J, Duncansone.]

Anent pyperis at mariagis: The quhilk day the brethrein undirstanding ane grit abuse and superstitioun usit be sindrie personis that cumis to parroche kirkis to be mareit in causing pyperis and fidlayeris play befoir thame to the kirk and fra the kirk, to the grit dishonour of God, for avoiding of the quhilk abbuse, it is statute and ordeinit be the haill brethrein that na minister within the boundis of this presbytery marie ony personis that ar acompaneit to the kirk with playing on pyppis or ony uthir instrumentis on that day that thai ar swa accumpaneit bot sall suffir thame to depart hame on that day unmareit and swa to do thaireftir quhill thay cum to the kirk reverentlie as becumis thame without ony playing, certifiand ilk minister or reder that dois in the contrar in tymis cuming sall suffir the disceplein of the kirk thairfoir according to his demereittis.

At Striviling the last day of December, 1583

Presentes: Patrik Gillaspie, James Andirsone, Mr William Stirling, Mr Andro Grahame, Mr Andro Yung, Mr Arthur Futhie, Michaell

Lermonthe, Mr Neill Campbell, Robert Mentayth, ministeris; Mr Alexander Iule, ane brothur of exerceis. [*No minutes.*]

At Striviling the vij day of Januar, 1583

Presentes: Patrik Gillaspie, James Andirsone, Alexander Fargy, Michaell Lermonthe, Mr Johnne Campbell, bischop of Iyllis, Mr Alexander Chisholme, Mr Andro Grahame, Mr Andro Yung, Robert Mentayth, ministeris; Alexander Forester of Garden, Umphra Cunynghame, commissar of Striviling, and Alexander Patersone, merchant, elderis.

Johnne Crystesone, adulterar: The quhilk day compeirit Johnne Crystesone, parrochinnar in Stragayth, adulterar with Jonet Mwll by Jonet Allane, his spous, as he confessit on the penult day of July last and promesit obedience to the kirk for his said offence, and thairfor desyrit ane command to Mr Alexander Chisholm, his minister, to bapteis his bairne gottin on the said Jonet Mwlle, as said is. With the quhilk, the brethrein being advysit ordeinis the said Johnne to compeir befoir the nixt provinciall assemblie of this province to be haldin in Edinburgh the first Twysday of Aprill nixt, viz., the vij day of the samin moneth, thair to ressave injunctionis injonit to him for his said offence and to obey thame undir the paine of excommunicatioun and that he with all possablle diligence act cautioun ather in the buikis of the commissar of Striviling or Dunblane that he sall obey and satisfie the said ordinance in all pointis undir the paine of fourty pundis mony, quhilk cautioun beand actit, as said is, ordanis the said Mr Alexander Chisholme to bapteis his said bairne.

George Edmestoun, adulterar: The quhilk day compeirit George Edmestoun and confessit him to have committit adultrie with Mathie Grahame, spous to Donald McAdame, parrochinnar of Abirfoull, for the quhilk he offiris him self in the will of the kirk and confessit that the said fault was committit in the parrochun of Kilmadok and thairfor desyris command to Michaell Lermonthe, his minister, to bapteis his bairne gottin as said is. With the quhilk the brethrein being advysit, ordeinis the said George to compeir befoir the nixt provinciall assemblie of this province to be hauldin in Edinburgh the first Twysday of Aprill nixt, viz., the vij day of the samin moneth, thair to ressave injunctionis to be injonit to him for his said offence and to obey thame undir the paine of excommunicatioun and that he with all possablle diligence act cautioun in the commissaris buikis of Dunblane that he sall obey and satisfie the said ordinance in all pointis undir the paine of fourty pundis mony, quhilk beand done ordanis his said bairne to be baptezit.

Margaret Smyth, adultrix: The quhilk day compeirit Margaret Smyth in Keir, within the parrochun of Dunblane, and grantis hir to have committit adultrie with Robert Hendersone, parrochinnar of Logy, husband to Elezabeth Hendersone, and grantis the said fault was committit in his hous within the parrochun of Logy, for the quhilk scho offiris hir self in the will of the kirk. The brethrein ordanis and commandis the said Margaret to compeir befoir the nixt provinciall assemblie of this province to be haldin in Edinburgh the first Twisday of Aprill nixt, viz., the vij day of the samin moneth, thair to ressave injunctionis to be injonit to hir for hir said adultrie and to obey thame undir the paine of excommunication.

At Striviling xiij day of Januar, 1583

Presentes: Patrik Gillaspie, moderatour, James Andirsone, Mr Andro Yung, Mr William Stirling, Mr Arthur Futhie, Alexander Fargy, Johnne Duncanson, Mr Andro Grahame, ministeris; Mr Duncane Nevein, reder; Mr Johnne Broun.

Mr Andro Grahame: The quhilk day the moderator, in name of the kirk, desyrit Mr Andro Grahame to declair gif he sett ony of the bischoprik of Dunblane in few or be tak to ony persone sen he was last tryit thairanent or nocht. The said Mr Andro answerit he hade sett nane thairof in few nor tak nor utherwayis to ony persone farther nor he hade gevin up in wret to the brethrein of the said presbytery of befoir, and siclyk the said Mr Andro beand myndfull nocht to hurt the kirk nor his successur be setting of ony mair of his said leving bot foirseing the utilitie and proffeit of the samin hes interdytit him self and be thir presentis interdyttit him fra setting of the said bischoprik or ony part thairof in tymis cuming in few or tak and fra making of facturis or takismen thairto without the advys and consent of the brethrein of the said presbytery, quhilk the said Mr Andro be the tennour heirof promessis to observe and keip firmlie and suirlie undir the paine of perjure, defamatioun, and perpetuall deprivatioun. In witnes heirof, I have subscryvit thir presentis with my hand, day, yeir, plaice foirsaid. Androu, B. Domblan.

The quhilk day, Patrik Gillaspie, minister at Sanct Ninianis kirk, exponit and declairit to the brethrein that Thomas Murdo, husband to Doratie Buchannan, is allegit adulterar with [*blank*] Waltir, for the quhilk he, as ane parrochinnar of the said kirk, hes bein oft and dyvers warnit to have compeirit befoir the particular sessioun of the said parroche kirk to have hard tryell tane thairanent, quha will nocht obey thair citatioun without he be compellit. Thairfor the brethrein ordanis the said Thomas to be summond *litteratorie* to compeir, befoir the brethrein to answer for the said disobedience and to heir and se him self decernit to have committit adultrie with [*blank*] undir the paine of disobedience.

At Striviling the xxij day of Januar, 1583

Presentes: Patrik Gillaspie, James Andirsone, Mr William Stirling, Robert Mentayth, Mr Andro Yung, Alexander Fargy, Michaell Lermonthe, Mr Andro Grahame, ministeris; Mr James Pont, Robert Alexander, Umphra Cunynghame, elderis; Mr Alexander Iull, ane brothur of exerceis.

Jonet Baxter, adultrix: The quhilk day compeirit Jonet Baxter, parrochinnar of Kilmadok, and grantis hir to have borne ane bairne gottin on hir in adultrie be Alexander Edmestoun, parrochinnar siclyk of Kilmadok, husband to Jonet Norie. For the quhilk offence the said Jonet offiris to obey the kirk and thairfor desyris ane command to Michaell Lermonthe, hir minister, to bapteis hir said bairne. The brethrein ordanis and commandis the said Jonet to compeir befoir the nixt provinciall assemblie of this province to be haldin in Edinburgh the first Twysday of Aprill nixt, viz., the vij day of the samin thair to ressave injunctionis to be injonit to hir for hir said adultrie and to obey thame undir the paine of excommunicatioun, and that scho with all diligence act cautioun in the commissaris buikis of Striviling that scho sall obey the said ordinance

Q

in all pointis undir the paine of xl lib., and ordanis the said Alexander to be summond *litteratorie* for the said adultrie undir the paine of disobedience, quhilkis beand done ordanis the said Michaell to bapteis the said bairne.

At Striviling the xxviij day of Januar, 1583

Presentes: Patrik Gillaspie, James Andirsone, Alexander Fargy, Mr Neill Campbell, Robert Mentayth, Mr Adam Merschall, ministeris; William Stirling, reder; Umphra Cunynghame, elder; Mr Andro Murdo, ane brothur of exerceis.

Laird of Tulliallun: The quhilk day ane summondis beand producit deulie execute and indorsit upone James Blacatur of Tulli-alloun, allegit adulterar with Margaret Murray, chairgeing him to have compeirit befoir us the said day to heir and se him self decernit to have committit adultrie with the said Margaret, as at mair lynth is conteinit in the said summondis, compeirit the said James personallie, quha being accusit be the moderatour for adultrie with the said Margaret Murray, inrespect he haldis hous with the said Margaret and hes carnall copulatioun with hir as his wyf albeit the kirk undirstandis him to have bein lauchfullie mareit with Ellesone Bruce, quha as yit levis in this lyf (as is belevit), the said James ansorit and denyis adultrie with the said Margaret becaus that he upone the xix day of Aprill the yeir of God im vc lxxxj yeiris was lauchfullie devorcit be the commissaris of Edinburgh fra the said Ellesone Bruce thane his spous, for adultrie committit be him with Elezabeth Hozok *alias* Quene, with libertie thairin to the said Ellesone to marie in the Lord, quhilk allegence the said James varefeit be the extract of the said commissaris decreit subscryvit be thair clark, quhilk he producit befoir the brethrein and was fund be thame aggreablle to the said allegeance in all pointtis. And farder the said James allegit that upone the x day of August the yeir of God foirsaid he was lauchfullie mareit in the parroche kirk of Tullialloun with the said Margaret Murray be Alexander Mwre, minister, eftir he was lauchfullie proclamit with hir, and for varefeing of the quhilk he producit the said ministeris testimoniall of the dett foirsaid, subscryvit with his awin hand, as appeirit, and thairfor inrespect of his said mariage with the said Margaret Murray allegit he hes committit na adultrie with hir bot confessis adultrie with the said Elezabeth Hozok befoir his said devorcement, for the quhilk he offiris him self to obey the kirk as he salbe commandit. And being accusit be the moderatour to declair gif he hade carnall dell at ony tyme with the said Margaret befoir he was partit fra the said Ellesone Bruce, the said James denyit the samin *simpliciter*. Farder, the said James being desyrit to declair gif the said Alexander Mwre, minister, was musellit or ony wayis disgysit the tyme he mareit him with the said Margaret Murray and quhat pepill was in the kirk the tyme of his mariage and gif the day of his mariage was on ane Sonday or nocht, the said James answerit that the said minister was na manir of way disgysit on his faice nor utherwayis the tyme of the said mariage bot was honestlie claid in blak as becumis ane minister and that thair was ane lairge numbir of honest personis of the parrochun, men and wemen, in the kirk the tyme of the said mariage. And as for the day, he answerit that he remembrat nocht gif it was on ane Sonday or nocht. Als, the said James being requyrit gif he wald preive his last answer be famus witnes, viz., the apparell of the minister that he haid on the tyme of the mariage, the numbir of the pepill that was present thairat, and gif the day of his mariage was on ane Sonday or nocht, the said James offirit to do the samin. And for productioun of his witnessis to the effect foirsaid, the brethrein assignis to him the iiij day of Fabruar instant. The brethrein being advysit with the pretendit mariage made betuix the said James and Margaret continewis thair jugementis thairin quhill thay be advysit with the brethrein of the nixt provinciall assemblie of this province to be haldin in Edinburgh the first Twysday of Aprill nixt, viz., the vij day of the samin moneth, and warnis the said James *apud acta* to compeir befoir the said assemblie, day and plaice foirsaid, to heir and se the jugementis of the said assemblie pronuncit anent the said mariage quhethir gif it be lauchfull or nocht, and that he siclyk ressave injunctionis fra the said assemblie for the said adultrie committit be him with the said Elezabeth Hozok, *alias* Quene, as salbe injonit to him and to obey thame undir the paine of excommunicatioun.

Margaret Bruce: The quhilk day ane summondis beand producit deulie execute and indorsit upone Margaret Bruce chairgeing hir to have compeirit befoir us the said day to haif answerit at the instance

of the kirk and to have hard and sein hir self decernit to have committit adultrie with Robert Bruce of Clakmannan and to undirly
the disceplein of the kirk thairfoir undir the paine of excommunicatioun, quhilk Margaret being oft tymis callit compeirit nocht, and
thairfor was fund contumax, quhairfor ordanis the said Margaret to
be summond *litteratorie* to heir and se hir self decernit to be excommunicat for hir contemp and malicius disobedience with certificatioun and scho failze to compeir and randir obedience to the voice
of the kirk we will proceid and decern hir to be excommunicat, as
said is, according to the Word of God and disceplein of the kirk
havand warand thairof thairin.

Robert Bruce of Clakmannan: The quhilk day ane summondis
beand producit befoir us dewlie execute and indorsit upone Robert
Bruce of Clakmannan chairgeing him to have compeirit befoir us
the said day to heir and se him self decernit to have committit
adultrie by his lauchfull wyf with Margaret Bruce and thairfor to
undirly disceplein of the kirk undir the paine off disobedience,
quhilk Robert being oft tymis callit compeirit nocht and thairfor
the brethrein ordanis the said Robert to be summond of new
litteratorie to the effect foirsaid undir the paine of excommunicatioun.

Robert Millar, adulterar and ane incesteus man: The quhilk day
compeirit Robert Millar, husband to Marjorie Murray in the
parrochun of Fossoway, and grantis him to have committit adultrie
with Margaret Murray, brothur dochter to his said spous, for the
quhilk he submittis him self in the will of the kirk and thairfor
desyris his bairne gottin in adultrie on the said Margaret to be
baptezit. The brethrein findis the said Robert to have committit
adultrie and incest with the said Margaret Murray inrespect of his
awin confessioun and thairfor ordanis and commandis the said
Robert to compeir befoir the nixt provinciall assemblie of this
province to be haldin in Edinburgh, the first Twysday of Aprill
nixt, viz., the [*blank*] day of the samin moneth, thair to ressave
injunctionis to be injonit to him for his adultrie and incest, to obey
thame undir the paine of excommunicatioun and that he with all
diligence act cautioun in the buikis of the commissar of Striviling
that he sall obey the said ordinance in all pointis undir the
paine of xl libis., quhilk beand done, as said is, his said bairne to be
baptezit.

At Striviling the iiij day of Fabruar, 1583

Presentes: Patrik Gillaspie, James Andirsone, Johnne Duncanson, Mr Andro Graham, Michaell Lermonthe, Mr Alexander Chisholme, Mr Andro Yung, Mr William Stirling, Alexander Fargy, Mr Arthur Futhie, Robert Mentayth, ministeris; Umphra Cunnynghame, Robert Alexander, elderis; Mr Alexander Iull, Mr Andro Murdo, brethir of exerceis.

James Blacatur, Tulliallun: In the terme assignit to James Blacatur of Tullialloun to produce witnessis to preve the mariage of the said James on Margaret Murray, now his allegit spous, and gif the minister that ministrat the samin was musellit or nocht, the tyme of the ministratioun thairof, and quhat numbir of pepill was in the kirk the tyme of the ministratioun thairof, and gif the day of his mariage was on ane Sonday or nocht, compeirit the witnessis follwing, parrochinnaris of Tullialloun, viz., Johnne Meffane, elder in Tullialloun, Henrie Bennet thair, Johnne Jamesone thair, Johnne Thomesone, elder thair, Johnne Thomesone, yunger thair, and James Jamesone thair, quha being ressavit, sworne and admittit was examinat, as thair depositionis beris. The brethrein being advysit with the depositionis of the saidis witnessis findis that the said James Blacatur of Tullialloun was mareit in the parroche kirk thairof on the said Margaret on Sanct Lowrence day, viz., the x day of August twa yeiris bypast on ane oulk day be ane honest lyk man cled lyk ane minister with ane taffety hatt quhais name thai knew nocht, undisguysit on faice or utherwayis in presens of the saidis witnessis quha was requyrit be the said James Blacatur to cum to the said kirk the said day and with sum utheris with thame in the kirk the tyme thairof, and thairfor findis the said James allegence concerning his said mariage deulie varefeit.

Freir Veiche: The brethrein thinkis gude and ordeinis the haill ministeris within the boundis of this presbytery to mak dew intimatioun, as effeiris, in thair parroche kirkis that freir Robert Veiche is excommunicat lauchfullie in the parroche kirk of this brugh be James Andirsone, minister thairat, at our command on the first day of December last bypast and that thai notefie the causis thairof conteinit in the proces deducit againis him and siclyk ordeinis the moderatour and scryb to mak adverteisment in name of this sessioun

to all the presbyteriis within this realme of the said excommunicatioun and the causis thairof, desyrand thame to caus intimatioun
thairof to be made, as effeiris, in everie ane of thair parroche kirkis
as thai and everie ane of thame will answer to the generall assemblie
of the kirk.

Yung Fintrie excommunicat: The quhilk day compeirit Johnne
Duncanson, minister to the kingis majestie, and declairit to the
brethrein that he was commandit be the brethrein of the presbytery
of Edinburgh to mak intimatioun to this presbytery lyk as he
presentlie makis intimatioun that David Grahame, apperand of
Fintrie, was excommunicat in the parroche kirk of Dundie be
William Cristeson, minister thairof, on the xv day of December
last bypast for his feirfull apostacie fra the trew religioun of Jesus
Christ professit in Scotland to papistrie and superstitioun, and for
his abyding thairat, as at mair lynthe is conteinit in the proces
deducit thairanent againis him, and desyrit the brethrein of this
presbytery to caus intimatioun to be made within thair boundis as
effeiris. According to the quhilk desyr, the haill brethrein within
the boundis of this presbytery ar ordeinit to mak dew intimatioun
in ilk ane of thair parroche kirkis respective of the said excommunicatioun and causis thairof, certifiand all personis that conferris or
interteneis him ony manir of way that the censuris of the kirk salbe
execute againis thame with all vigour.

William Lochart: The quhilk day ane summondis beand producit
deulie execute and indorsit upone William Lockart, tailyour,
chairgeing him to have compeirit befoir this sessioun the said day
to heir and se the jugementis of the brethrein thairof pronuncit
anent the thingis concerning religioun, quhairof he was tryit
befoir the particular sessioun of the kirk of Striviling, and to
undirly disceplein according to his demereittis undir the paine
of disobedience, quhilk William being oft tymes callit compeirit
nocht. Thairfor the brethrein ordanis the said William to be
summond *litteratorie* to the effect foirsaid undir the paine of excommunicatioun.

At Striviling the xj day of Februar, 1583

Presentes: Patrik Gillaspie, James Andirson, Mr William Stirling,

Mr Andro Yung, Alexander Fargy, Mr Alexander Chisholme and Robert Mentayth, ministeris; Robert Alexander, elder; Maisteris Alexander Iull, Andro Murdo, brethir of exerceis; and William Stirling, reder.

William Stirling: The quhilk day compeirit William Stirling, reder, quha being accusit be the moderator for mareing of Jonet Hay, adultrix, with Thomas Thomson, husband to [*blank*] on Andro Smart in Kippen, the kirk nocht beand satisfeit be the said Jonet for hir adultrie. The said William Stirling confessit he mareit the saidis personis bot allegis the said Jonet satisfeit the kirk according to Mr Andro Grahamis ordinance, beand commissionar for the tyme, and confessis that scho compeirit nevir befoir the synnodall assemblie for the said caus. Secundlie, the said William being accusit for baptezein of ane bairne gottin in fornicatioun be Gilbert Graham, servand to David, commendatar of Dryburgh, in Striviling on Agnes Allane (the parentis quhairof having nocht satisfeit the kirk) thairfoir, the said William confessit the baptezein of the said bairne bot allegit that the said Gilbert hade fund cautioun to him that he and the woman sould satisfie the kirk of Striviling for the said offence. Thridlie, the said William being accusit for mareing of Johnne Duthie in Boquhen and Jonet Maclun, parrochinnaris of Sanct Ninianis kirk, in the kirk of Kippen without testimoniall of the lauchfull proclamatioun of thair bannis in the said parroche kirk, the said William grantit the said mariage, as said is, bot allegit that the said Johnne Duthie promesit to delyvir him the said testimoniall subscryvit on the same day eftir none that thai war mareit on. Fourtlie, the said William being accusit for mareing of Johnne McNair in Abirfoull and Margaret Campbell in Port within the kirk of the Port within the tyme of the last generall fast, viz., on the Twysday efter the first Sonday of the fast expres againis the actis of the generall assemblie, the said William confessit the samin bot allegit he did it thruch ignorance. The brethrein continewis thair jugementis on the premisis quhill thay tak farther tryell of the said William Stirling.

Thomas Murdo allegit adulterar: The quhilk day ane summondis beand producit deulie execute and indorsit upone Thomas Murdo, husband to Doratie Buchannan, allegit adulterar with Euffame Waltir, chairgeing him to compeir the said day to answer at the instance of the kirk for disobedience to the voice of the sessioun of his awin parroche kirk of Sanct Ninianis kirk and to undirly disciplein thairfor and to heir and se him self decernit to have committit adultrie with the said Euffame Waltir undir the paine of disobedience, compeirit the said Thomas Murdo personallie and grantis him to have gottin ane bairne on the said Euffame Waltir in Touchadame, within the parrochun of Sanct Niniane, in fornicatioun bot denyis adultrie with hir becaus (as he allegit) his said umquhill spous callit Dorathrie Buchannan past fra him fyve yeir syne or thairby and that he is trewlie informit that scho is departit furth of this lyf in Ingland lang befoir he hade ony carnall copulatioun with the said Euffame, and offiris to preive the samin be sufficient testimoniall, and thairfor denyis adultrie but offiris him self to obey the kirk, as effeiris, for fornicatioun with the said Euffame, inrespect quhairof the said Thomas desyrit the brethrein to gif command to Patrik Gillaspie, his minister, to bapteis his bairne gottin on the said Euffame. The brethrein, being advysit with the said Thomas allegence, findis that presentlie thay can nocht decern gif the said fault be adultrie or fornicatioun and thairfor assignis to the said Thomas the last Twisday of Merche, viz., the last day of the samin moneth, to preive his said allegence be sufficient testimoniall, he warnit thairto *apud acta* undir the paine of disciplein and ordeinis the said Thomas to caus cautioun be actit with diligence in the buikis of the commissar of Striviling for him self and the said Euffame that thay sall bayth obey and satisfie the kirk as thay salbe commandit eftir tryell be tane of the said offence under the paine of xl libis., quhilk beand done ordanis the bairne to be baptezit.

William Lockart: The quhilk day ane summondis beand producit deulie execute and indorsit upone William Lochart, tailyour, chairgeing him to compeir the said day to heir and se the jugementis of the brethrein pronuncit anent tha thingis concerning religioun quhairof he was tryit befor the particular sessioun of the kirk of Striviling and to underly disceplein according to his demereittis undir the paine of excommunicatioun, compeirit the said William Lockart personallie, and eftir that the brethrein haid hard and considderit the tryell tane of him be the sessioun of the kirk of Striviling thruch intimatioun of the actis thairof, thay ordeinit the minister of Striviling and Mr Alexander Iulle, maistir of the grammir schull thairof, to confer with the said William privellie anent the cheiff heddis of religioun and quhat thai find in him be thair privie confirence that thai report it the nixt sessioun on the xviij of this instant, and the said William warnit thairto *apud acta* undir the paine of excommunicatioun.

At Striviling the xviij day of Fabruar, 1583

Presentes: Patrik Gillaspie, James Andirson, Alexander Fargy, Mr Alexander Chisholme, Mr Andro Yung, Mr Andro Grahame, Michaell Lermonthe, ministeris; Mr James Pont, elder, William Norwall, elder; Maisteris Alexander Iull and Andro Murdo, brethir of exerceis.

William Lockart: The quhilk day, James Andirsone and Mr Alexander Iull, beand desyrit be the moderator to report thair jugementis quhat thai fand of William Lockart be thair privie confirence hade with him, reportit that he willinglie aggreit with all heddis of the trew religioun of Jesus Christ professit in Scotland and (as appeirit to thame) he was nocht obstinat and that the wordis that he had spokin in menteinance of the mes was mair of ignorance nor uthirwayis. The said William beand callit, compeirit personallie quha was ordeinit to subscryve the confessioun of the fayth subscryvit be the kingis majestie, and thaireftir on Sonday nixt befoir none immediatlie eftir sermond that he rys on his feit in the kirk of Striviling quhen he is callit be the minister thairof and thair confes that he hes offendit God in geving of his corporall presens to the mes in France and in speiking in this toun in menteinance thairof, and that he publictlie dam the samin and all papistrie in generall and in speciall according to the said confessioun of fayth and declair that he willinglie fra his hairt imbressis the trew religioun professit in Scotland.

Exerceis beginnis at ix houris: The brethrein ordanis the exerceis to begin fra thisfurth at ix houris in the morning and the bell to ring in dew tym thairto.

John Burges; crippill woman: The quhilk day ane summondis beand producit direct be the presbytery of Dunbartane deulie execute and indorsit upone Johnne Burges, dwelland with Agnes

Fargusone within the parrochun of Balfrone, chairgeing him to compeir befoir this presbytery the said day, compeirit the said Johnne Burges and Jonet Hardy in Gargunnok personallie and the said Jonet maid hir complent befoir the brethrein on the said Johnne as follwis, viz., that he haid gottin ane mane chyld on hir in fornicatioun quhairof scho was lichter on the xij day of December quhilk he refusit to acknawlege as his awin bairne and to caus bapteis the samin. According to the quhilk complent, the moderatour examinat the said Johnne at lynthe quha confessit that he hade carnall copulatioun with the said Jonet dyvers tymis bot denyit the said bairne to be his inrespect it come nocht to his reckning, nochttheles in his answeris he was fund to fengze and could nocht allege na uthir speciall mane to the said Jonet, and sindrie honest men hir nychtburis being inquyrit gif thai hard ony uthir man bruittit with hir quha ansorit nane, and thairfor inrespect of the premisis the brethrein findis the said bairne to be his, and ordanis him to do thairfor as becumis him and als ordanis the said Johnne and Jonet to satisfie the kirk of Sanct Niniane for the said fornicatioun, confurm to the ordur and that thai compeir to that effect befoir the particular sessioun of the said kirk the nixt Sonday, viz., the xxiij day of Fabruar instant undir the paine of excommunicatioun.

Mr William Moresone: The quhilk day it was proponit to the brethrein that ane sclandir is rissin in this toun thruch Mr William Moresone, allegeand that he sould have spokin sclanderuslie againis the trew religioun of Jesus Christ professit in Scotland to the grit hinderance of Godis glorie and disconfort of the faithfull, viz., on the xij day of this instant, inrespect quhairof the brethrein ordanis the said Mr William to be summond *litteratorie* to answer to sic thingis as salbe layit unto his chairge undir the paine of disobedience.

At Striviling the xxv day of Fabruar, 1583

Presentes: Patrik Gillaspie, James Andirsone, Mr Arthur Futhie, Mr Andro Grahame, Mr Andro Yung, Michaell Lermonthe, Robert Mentayth, Alexander Fargy, ministeris; Mr Duncan Nevein, William Stirling, rederis; Maisteris Alexander Iull and Andro Murdo, brether of exerceis.

Tirinterane: The quhilk day ane summondis beand producit deulie execute and indorsit upone Alexander Levingstoun of Terinterane, Margaret Grahame his dochter in law, Alexander Frissell, Cristane Wod and Issobell Forester, servandis to the said Alexander, chairgeing thame to have compeirit the said day to answer at the instance of the kirk for nocht presenting thame selffis to the examinatioun with the rest of the parrochinnaris of Kippen befoir the communioun according to the ordur of the kirk, and for absenting thame selffis fra the communioun the tyme of the ministratioun thairof in thair said parroche kirk of Kippen and to have undirlyne disceplein thairfoir ilk persone undir the paine of excommunicatioun, quhilkis personis being oft tymis callit compeirit nocht and thairfor is fund contumax, quhairfor the brethrein ordanis the saidis personis and ilk ane of thame to be summond *litteratorie* to heir and se thame selffis and ilk ane of thame decernit to be excommunicat for thair contemp and malicius disobedience to the weill of the kirk, with certificatioun and thai or ony of thame failze to compeir and randir obedience to the voice of the kirk, as said is, we will proceid and decern thame to be excommunicat according to the Word of God and disceplein of the kirk havand the warrand thairof thairin.

Mr William Moresone: The quhilk day ane summondis beand producit deulie execute and indorsit upone Mr William Moresone chairgeing him to have compeirit befoir the brethrein the said day to answer to sic thingis as salbe layit unto his chairge undir the paine of disobedience, compeirit Mr Alexander Iull and in the said Mr Williamis name producit ane misseive wreting of his direct to the brethrein berand ane excuis of his noncomperance this day and ane promeis that he sould compeir the nixt sessioun day, viz., the iij day of Merche nixt tocum and obey the said summondis, quhilk excuis the brethrein findis rassonablle and continewis farther proceiding againis him to the said iij day of Merche nixt tocum.

Margaret Murray, adultrix and ane incestuus woman: The samin day compeirit Margaret Murray in the parrochun of Fossowy and grantis hir to have committit adultrie with Robert Millar thair, husband to Marjorie Murray, hir fathir sistir, quhilk is fund be the brethrein to be incest and adultrie, and thairfor the brethrein ordanis hir to compeir befoir the nixt provinciall assemblie of this province to be haldin in Edinburgh the first Twisday of Aprill, viz., the vij day of the samin moneth, thair to ressave injunctionis to be injonit to hir for hir said adultrie and incest and to obey thame undir the paine of excommunicatioun.

At Striviling the iij day of Mairche, 1583

Presentes: Patrik Gillaspie, James Andirsone, Johnne Duncansone, Alexander Fargy, Mr Andro Yung, Mr Andro Grahame, Mr Alexander Chisholme, Mr William Stirling, Michaell Lermonthe, ministeris; Alexander Forester of Garden, Robert Alexander, elderis; Mr Duncane Nevein, reder at Dunblane.

Intimatioun of the excommunicantis in Dunblane: The quhilk day the brethrein understanding the lang speace sen Sir William Blackwod, Sir William Drummond and Andro Blakwod war excommunicat in the parroche kirk of Dunblane be the minister thairof for the tyme for nonrecantatioun of the papisticall religioun according to the proces deducit againis thame and incaice the commone pepill pretend ignorance thairof or suspect thame to be ressavit againe to the kirk sensyne, thairfor it is thocht gude and ordeinit that ilk minister within the boundis of this presbytery mak new intimatioun in thair parroche kirkis of the excommunicatioun of the saidis personis, and that thai swa remaine yit unabsolvit be the kirk, and thairfor to command all personis to hauld thame as hathinis and publicanis and to have na kynd of societie with nane of thame undir the paine of the sensuris of the kirk to be execute againis everie ane that dois in the contrar.

Anent setting of ministeris stipendis: The quhilk day it is statute and ordeinit be the haill brethrein that thai, nor nane of thame, sall sett in tak or assedatioun thair beneficis or stependis or ony part thairof nor mak ony facturis thairunto without the advys and consent of the sessioun of this presbytery, quhilk thai promeis faythfullie to observe and keip undir the paine of perjurie, defamatioun and perpetuall deprivatioun. In witnes thairof, thai have subscryvit thir presentis with thair handis as follwis, day, yeir, plaice foirsaid. [*A space follows for signatures but none is entered.*]

At Striviling the x day of Merche, 1583

Presentes: Patrik Gillaspy, James Andirsone, Mr Andro Grahame, Mr William Stirling, Mr Andro Yung, Michaell Lermonthe, Johnne Duncanson, Alexander Fargy, Robert Mentayth, ministeris; Mr James Pont, Duncane Narne, elderis; and William Stirling, reder.

Adulteraris: The quhilk day the brethrein ordanis the haill adulteraris within the boundis of this presbytery convict thairin that as yit hes nocht fullalie satisfeit the kirk thairfoir to be summond to compeir befoir the nixt provinciall assemblie of this province to be hauldin in Edinburgh in the est kirk thairof on the vij day of Aprill nixt to ressave disceplein for the said fault, ilk persone undir the paine of excommunicatioun with certificatioun and thai or ony of thame failze the kirk will proceid summarlie and decern the sentence of excommunicatioun to be pronuncit againis thame.

James Chisholmis anent yung Fintrie: The quhilk day the brethrein undirstanding that David Graham, apperand of Fintrie, is lauchfullie excommunicat for sic causis as ar conteinit in the proces deducit againis him and that sen syne he is ressavit and interteneit in James Chisholmis hous in Dunblane and remanit thair ane haill nycht (as is allegit), thairfor the brethrein ordanis and gevis commissioun to Maister Andro Yung, minister at Dunblane, Mr Andro Grahame, Mr William Stirling and Michaell Lermonthe, or ony thre, twa or ane of thame, to caus summond the said James Chisholme of Cromlickis and James Chisholme, yunger, his sone, to compeir befoir the nixt sessioun of the particular elderschip off Dunblane, and thair in presens of the elderis and deacunis of the said kirk to be conveinit for the tyme to try and examin the saidis James Chisholmis, elder and yunger, anent the allegit ressaving and interteneing of the said excommunicat mane in the said hous and the causis thairof and quhat thai fund thairby to report againe the same to the brethrein on the xvij day of Merche instant.

Montrois anent yung Fintrie: The quhilk day the brethrein undirstanding that David Graham, apperand of Fintrie, Sir William Blackwod in Dunblane, James McKie, smyth in Abrevane, Jane Stewart thair, and Johnne Graham, burges of Edinburgh, ar lauchfullie excommunicat for sic causis as ar particularlie expremit in the procesis respective deducit againis thame and becaus thai ar

athir freindis, tennentis or servandis to ane noblle and potent lord
Johnne, Erlle of Montrois, Lord Graham, etc., and thairthrw may
have occasioun to resort to his lordschippis plaice and cumpany
and ar bruittit alreddy to have resortit thairto, thairfor ordanis our
brothur Mr Andro Grahame to pas to the said noblle and potent
lord and to admoneis him that he onnawayis ressave ony of the
saidis personis in his plaice nor cumpany, nathir suffir nane of
thame to be ressavit be ony of his domestickis in the samin, for gif
it cum to our knawlege that his lordschip dois in the contrarie,
quhilk we luik nocht for, we can nocht of our dewatie bot pres his
lordschip with disceplein thairfoir, and ordanis the said Mr Andro
to report againe to the brethrein his diligence in obeying this our
ordinance on the xvij day of Merche instant.

William McKayis, adulterar in Drimmen: The quhilk day compeirit William McKayis dwelland in the parrochun of Dunblane,
spous to [*blank*], and grantis him to have committit adultrie with
Euffame Donaldsone within the parrochun of Drimmen and offiris
him self to obey the kirk thairfoir. The brethrein findis the said fault
committit outwith the boundis of this province in the boundis of
the provinciall assemblie of Glasgw and thairfor ordanis the said
William to compeir befoir the nixt provinciall of that province to
be hauldin in the cietie thairof on the [*blank*] day of [*blank*], thair
to ressave disceplein for his said adultrie and to obey the same undir
the paine of excommunicatioun.

Terinterane and his famelie: The quhilk day ane summondis beand
producit deulie execute and indorsit upone Alexander Levingstone
of Terinterane, Margaret Graham his dochtir in law, Alexander
Frissall, Cristane Wod and Issobell Forester, servandis to the said
Alexander, chairgeing thame to have compeirit the said day to heir
and se thame selffis decernit to be excommunicat and malicius
disobedience to the voice of the kirk, as at mair lynthe is conteinit
in the said summondis producit thairupone, compeirit all the saidis
personis personallie (except Margaret Grahame) and grantis that
thair disobedience in nocht obeying the summondis of the kirk
was upone ignorance and na contemp, for the quhilk thai offir
thame selffis in the will of the kirk, and being all accusit for nocht
presenting thame selffis to the sacrament of the Lordis Supper
ministrat in thair parroche kirk of Kippen on the [*blank*] day of

[*blank*] and for nocht presenting thame selffis to the examinatioun of befoir, according to the rest of the parrochinnaris, ansorit ilk ane respective for thair awin parttis and schew ane excuis of thair absens baith frome the ane and the uthir, quhilk excuisis was admittit be the brethir and fund ressonablle for this present allanirlie. Nochttheles, the moderatour, at command of the brethrein, admonesit all the saidis personis that thai be nawayis absent fra the said sacrament quhen it is ministrat in thair awin parroche kirk in tymis cuming and that thai keip ordur the tyme of the examinatioun as ye rest of the parrochun dois undir the paine of the censuris of the kirk to be execute againis ilk ane of thame that dois in the contrar.

At Striviling the xvij day of Mairche, 1583

Presentes: Patrik Gillaspie, James Andirsone, Mr Alexander Chisholme, Mr Arthur Futhie, Alexander Fargy, Mr Andro Grahame, Mr Andro Yung, ministeris; Umphra Cunynghame, elder; Mr Alexander Iulle and Mr Duncane Nevein, brethir of exerceis.

Chisholmis anent Fintrie, excommunicat: The quhilk day the moderatour, in name of the haill brethrein present, inquyrit the brethrein of the ministrie in Dunblane to report quhat thai hade done anent the tryell of James Chisholme of Cromlikis and James Chisholme, his sone, tuiching the ressaving and interteneing of David Grahame, apperand of Fintrie, excommunicat, in the said James Chisholme elderis hous in Dunblane, according to the commissioun gevin to thame in the last sessioun, ansorit that on thair sessioun day in Dunblane bayth the saidis James Chisholmis was absent furth of the toun and thairfor thai hade done na thing thairanent as yit. The brethrein ordanis thame, as of befoir, to examin the saidis James Chisholmis anent the premisis conform to the formar commissione gevin to thame, on thair nixt sessioun day and quhat thai find thairby to report the same on the xxiiij day of this instant.

Montrois anent yung Fintrie: The samin day Mr Andro Grahame being inquyrit be the moderatour to report gif he hade admonesit Johnne, Erlle of Montrois, lord Grahame, etc., anent David Grahame, apperand of Fintrie, and uthir excommunicattis conteinit in the commissioun gevin to him conforme thairto or nocht, the said Mr Andro ansorit that he was occupyit utherwayis sen the said commissioun was gevin him quhairthrw he hade done na thing thairintill. The brethrein ordanis the said Mr Andro to obey and satisfie his commissioun as he was ordeinit and to report againe to the brethrein his diligence in obeying the samin on the xxiiij day of this instant.

Stewart, adultrix in Airthe: The quhilk day compeirit Margaret Stewart, dwelland in the parrochun of Airthe and grantis hir to have committit adultrie with James Smyth thair, thane spous to [*blank*], for the quhilk scho offiris to obey the kirk. The brethrein ordanis hir to compeir befoir the nixt provinciall assemblie of this province to be haldin in Edinburgh the vij day of Aprill nixt, thair to ressave injunctionis to be [givin] hir for hir said adultrie undir the paine of excommunicatioun, with certificatioun and scho failze the kirk will proceid summarlie and decern hir to be excommunicatt.

At Striviling the xxiiij day of Mairche, 1583

Presentes: Patrik Gillaspie, James Andirsone, Mr Andro Yung, Michaell Lermonthe, Robert Mentayth, Alexander Fargy, ministeris; Mr James Pont, Umphra Cunynghame, elderis; Mr Alexander Iull, ane brothur of exerceis; and William Stirling, reder.

Chisholmis anent yung Fintrie: The quhilk day Mr Andro Yung, minister at Dunblane, beand requyrit be the moderatour to report quhat he hes done in trying of James Chisholme of Cromlickis and James Chisholme, his sone, anent the ressaving and interteneing of David Grahame, apperand of Fintrie, excommunicat, in thair hous of Dunblane according to the commissione gevin to him and utheris of the ministrie in Dunblane thairanent, the said Mr Andro answerit that the said James Chisholmis, elder and yunger, was convenit befoir the sessioun in Dunblane, and the said James Chisholme elder, beand examinat quhy he ressavit the said excommunicat mane in his hous, answerit that he come suddenlie in his hous unknawn to him quhill he was thairin. Secundlie, being examinat quhy he suffirit the said excommunicat man to remane all nycht in his hous and keip familiar cumpany with utheris thairin answerit that he did the samin thruch solistatioun and request of the auld lady Tullibairdin, callit [*blank*] Grahame. Thridlie, being examinat anent the said excommunicat mane tareing in his hous quhill the morne at none or thairby, answerit that he was desyrit be the auld laird of Fintrie to travell with him for persuading him to imbres the religioun professit be the kingis grace and his estaitis quhilk he did indeid quhairthrw he was movit to suffir him to remane in his hous langer nor he wald have done uthirwayis, and siclyk the said James Chisholme, yunger, being examinat quhy he keipit cumpany with the said excommunicat mane and commonit with him, answerit that he undirstude that ony mane furth of the kingis hous mycht speik with him quhill the nixt generall assemblie becaus the sentence of excommunicatioun was summarlie pronuncit agaìnis him (as he allegit), quhilk sentence (as he undirstude) was to be reducit be the nixt generall assemblie.

Montrois anent yung Fintrie: And farther the said Mr Andro Yung producit ane misseive wreting subscryvit be Mr Andro Grahame, direct to the brethrein berand ane excuis of his absence and his report anent his travelling with Johnne, Erlle of Montrois, lord Grahame, etc., according to his commissioun tuiching David Grahame, apperand of Fintrie, and utheris excommunicattis bruittit to be ressavit be him, quhais answer was that he nevir ressavit the said yung Fintrie to mentein him in ony point of papistrie or oppinioun repugnant to our religioun professit presentlie within this realme bot evir seikand be all meinis possablle to draw him to the menteinance of the samin. Farther, quhair he was desyrit that he sould nocht ressave him in his plaice in ony tymis cuming, ansorit that quhensoevir it plaisit the brethrein of the presbytery to direct unto him the minister of Stirling, accumpaneit with ane barrun, or Johnne Duncansone, with ane barrun, his lordschip sould nocht faill to send ane ressonablle and direct answer anent the hanting and ressaving of sic a persone as is disobedient unto the kirk. With the quhilkis reporttis, the brethrein being advysit findis that the said Erlle of Montrois, James Chisholme of Cromlickis and James Chisholme, his sone, hes ressavit in thair housis and cumpaneis the said David Grahame, apperand of Fintrie, sen he was excommunicat without the knawlege of the kirk or lycence obteinit

R

thairunto and als findis the excusis allegit be thame all of na effect
and swa mereittis the disceplein of the kirk, bot becaus the day of
the provinciall assemblie of this province approchis neir, the
brethrein countinewis farther proceiding in the said mater quhill
thai be advysit with the brethrein of the said assemblie, and as
tuiching the uthir excommunicattis conteinit in the said Mr Andro
Grahamis commissioun findis nathing reportit in the said wreting
anent thame and thairfor the brethrein continewis the samin to the
said Mr Andro Grahamis awin presens.

Jonet Wilsone, fornicatrix: The quhilk day compeirit Jonet Wilsone
and grantis hir to have borne sex bairnis in fornicatioun to the men
eftir specefeit, for nane of the quhilkis scho hes satisfeit the kirk as
scho confessis, ane thairof gottin on hir xiiij yeiris syne or thairby
in fornicatioun be Henrie Stirling of Airdocht in the plaice of Keir,
twa thairof gottin on hir thair be Johnne Stirling *alias* Johnne Bute,
twa thairof gottin on hir in fornicatioun be Mr James Chisholm,
aircheden of Dunblane, ane of the samin gottin four yeir syne or
thairby, and ane uthir of thame sensyne in the parrochun of Strogayth, and the sext bairne gottin on hir be William Quhytburn
alias William Cuik, servand to the Errle of Arrall [*recte*, Erroll], in
the parrochun of Strogayth and baptezit in the kirk of Fowllis be
William Scott. The said first bairne that scho boire was baptezit
in Dunblane be Mr Robert Montgumrie, minister thairof for the
tyme, the secund in Dunblane be Robert Mentayth, thane minister
thairof, the thrid in Dunblane be Mr Andro Young, thane minister
thairof, and the last bairne gottin be the archiden baptezit be the
said William Scott in the kirk of Fowllis fyve quarteris of ane yeir
syne the uthir bairne, scho allegit, deit unbaptezit. The brethrein
being advysit with the said Jonettis confessioun findis hir to have
sclandirit the kirk varie lairgelie be hir lang continuance in huirdum
with foir sindrie men and siclyk disobedient to the kirk of Dunblane
as hir self hes confessit, and thairfor ordanis hir to mak publict
repentence in secclayth in the parroche kirk of Dunblane thre
sindrie Sondayis and to begin the nixt Sonday and swa furth ilk
Sonday quhill the saidis thre Sondayis be compleit, and immediatlie
thaireftir to mak publict repentence in the parroche kirk of Muthill,
beand the kirk nixt adjacent to the said kirk of Strogayth quhairin
thair is ane minister, uthir thre Sondayis, twa thairof in hir awin

clathis and the thrid in secclayth, undir the paine of excommunicatioun with certificatioun and scho failze in compleiting of the
said Sondayis, as said is, the brethrein will proceid summarlie and
decern hir to be excommunicat. [*In margin*: xiiijo *Aprilis* 1584, Mr
Andro Yung, minister of Dunblane, reportit that Jonet Wilson hes
made repentence in the kirk of Dunblane, conform to this act
withinwrittin in all pointis. J. Duncansone.]

At Striviling the last day of Mairche, 1583

Presentes: Patrik Gillaspie, James Andirsone, Mr Alexander
Chisholme, Mr Arthur Futhie, Michaell Lermonthe, Mr Andro
Yung, Alexander Fargy, Mr Neill Campbell, William Scott,
ministeris; Maisteris Alexander Iull, Andro Murdo, brethir of
exerceis; Umphra Cunynghame, elder; and William Stirling, reder.

Thomas Murdo, allegit adulterar: In the terme assignit to Thomas
Murdo, allegit husband to Dorathie Buchannan, to preive be
sufficient testimoniall that the said Dorathie, his spous, is departit
furth of this lyf in Ingland lang befoir he hade ony carnall copulatioun with Euffame Waltir, quha being oft tymis callit compeirit
nocht and thairfor the brethrein findis him to have succumbit in
probatioun of the said allegeance and ordanis him to be summond
to heir and se him self decernit to have committit adultrie with the
said Euffame and to underly disceplein thairfoir, nochtwithstanding
of the said allegeance becaus he is succumbit in preiving of the
samin or ellis to allege ane ressonablle caus quhy the samin sould
nocht be done, with certificatioun and he failze the brethrein will
decerne, as said is, and ordane him to undirly the disceplein of the
kirk thairfoir as effeiris.

Issobell Finlay, adultrix in Airthe: The quhilk day compeirit
Issobell Finlay in Airthe, spous to Andro Yung, and grantis hir to
have committit adultrie with William Murray, cuik to the Maister
of Elphingstoun, and offiris hir self in the will of the kirk thairfoir.
The brethrein ordanis hir to compeir befoir the nixt provinciall of
this province to be haldin in Edinburgh in the est kirk thairof
on the vij day of Aprill nixt thair to ressave injunctionis to be
injonit to hir for hir said adultrie undir the paine of excommunicatioun, with certificatioun and scho failze the brethrein

will proceid summarlie and decern hir to be excommunicat, as said is.

Margaret Moir: The quhilk day ane summondis beand producit dewlie execute and indorsit upone Margaret Moir, parrochinnar of Kilmadok, chairgeing hir to compeir the said day to heir and se tryell tane anent the fathir of ane bairne, quhairof the said Margaret is lichter, and to underly disciplein according to hir demereittis under the paine of disobedience, and als chairgeand James Dog, Walter Dog, sonnis to Alexander Dog, and Cristane Gourlay, maidwyf, to have compeirit the said day to beir lell and suithfast witnessing in the said mater insafar as thai knaw or salbe speirit at thame, ilk persone under the paine of disobedience, compeirit the said Margaret Moir personallie and grantis hir lichter of ane [*blank*] or thairby and, being requyrit to declair quha is the fathir thairof, denyit that scho knew ony fathir thairto and that scho wist nocht quhen it was gottin, and being scherplie admonesit to declair gif scho hade evir carnall dell with ony mane ansurit negativelie, excep that Johnne McIlhois in the Strath of Mentayth hade ainis carnall dell with hir againis hir will in the harvest feild at the letter lady day in harvest, viz., the viij day of September last or thairby, bot denyit *simpliciter* that he was the father of hir bairne becaus he hade nevir carnall dell with hir at na uther tyme quhilk scho knew. The said James Dog, Walter Dog and Cristane Gourlay, witnessis, being oft tymis callit compeirit nocht. Thairfor the brethrein ordanis thame to be summond *litteratorie* to the effect foirsaid under the paine of excommunicatioun and continewis farther examinatioun of the said Margaret Moir quhill the brethrein tak farther tryell thairanent utherwayis.

Upone the vij day of Aprill 1584, the brethrein was in Edinburgh at the provinciall assemblie of this province and thairfor thair was na exerceis nor sessioun in Stirling the said day.

At Striviling the xiiij day of Aprill, 1584

Presentes: Patrik Gillaspie, James Andirsone, Mr Arthur Futhie, Alexander Fargy, Mr William Stirling, Mr Andro Yung, Mr Andro Grahame, Michaell Lermonthe, Mr Adame Merschell, ministeris;

Mr James Pont, elder; Maisteris Alexander [*recte*, Andro] Murdo and Alexander Iull, brethir of exerceis.

Placis of the synnodall assemblie: The quhilk day the moderatour made intimatioun that the nixt provinciall assemblie of this province is to be haldin, Godwilling, on the first Twisday of October nixt in Dalkayth, the second provinciall assemblie in Linlythquow on the first Twisday of Aprill nixt, the thrid provinciall in [*sic*] assemblie on the first Twisday of October 1585 in Stirling, and the fourt assemblie to be hauldin in Hadintoun the first Twisday of Aprill *anno* 1585, excep the samin be chengit thruch occasionis to fall out heireftir.

Mr Andro Grahamis excuis for his absence fra the synnodall: The quhilk day the moderatour made intimatioun to Mr Andro Grahame that he was decernit be the last provinciall assemblie to pay iij libis., in penaltie for his absence thairfra, as for the secund fault siclyk xxx s. for his penaltie for his absence fra the provinciall assemblie of this province haldin in Edinburgh the first day of October last for his first fault, quhilk penalteis respective the moderatour desyrit the said Mr Andro Grahame to pay and delyvir presentlie according to the ordinance of the said assemblie. The said Mr Andro answerit and allegit for excuis of his absence fra the last provinciall assemblie, to wit, that he was undir the dainger of horning at the tyme quhen he sould have past to the last provinciall assemblie be chargis of letters for payment of his part of the contributioun to the lordis of sessioun, and for obeying of the quhilk chairge he past to Fyf to have gottin silvir to pay the samin and thocht to have past ovir the walter thaireftir to Edinburgh and keipit the said assemblie. Nochttheles, he gat na silvir thair bot was constrainit (to saif him self fra the horne) to returne and pas ane uthir way to gait silvir for obedience of the kingis letters. Secundlie, allegit that he was diligent in repairing the kirk off Dunblane quhair his hors (on the quhilk he rydis) was ledane stennis thairto, inrespect of the quhilkis the said Mr Andro allegit that he could nocht be present at the last provinciall assemblie. The brethrein ordanis the saidis excusis to be proponit to the nixt provinciall assemblie, and the said Mr Andro betuix and the nixt sessioune day to consigne in the handis of James Duncansone, clark, iiij lib. x s. as for his penaltie the first and secund tyme thair

to remaine quhill the said excusis be discussit and the samin to be
payit to collectar of sic penalteis gif the saidis excusis be repellit,
and gif thai be admittit the said Mr Andro to have the said soume
redelyverit to him againe.

Disobedient adulteraris: The quhilk day the brethrein, undirstandand sindrie adulteraris within the boundis of this presbytery
that hes disobeyit the summondis thairof in nocht compeiring befoir
the provinciall assemblie of this province in Edinburgh the vij day
of Aprill instant as thai war lauchfullie summond, thairfor ordanis
thame, ilk ane of thame as thai ar merkit disobedient in the said
summondis, to be summond of new to compeir befoir this presbytery to heir and se thame selffis decernit to be excommunicat for
thair contemp and malicious disobedience to the voice off the kirk
conjonit with thair said fault of adultrie or ellis to allege ane ressonablle [*sic*] quhy, with certificatioun and thai failze the brethrein
will proceid and decern thame to be excommunicat, as said is,
according to the Word of God and disceplein off the kirk havand
the warrand thairof thairin.

Disobedientis in Dunblane parrochun: The samin day ane summondis beand producit deulie execute and indorsit upone Jonet
Forfar and Margaret Hynd in Wolcoig chairgeing thame to have
compeirit the said day to answer at the instance of the kirk for
disobedience to the voice of the sessioun of thair awin parroche
kirk of Dunblane and to underly disceplein thairfoir, ilk persone
undir the paine of disobedience, quhilk personis being oft tymis
callit compeirit nocht, thairfor the brethrein ordanis the saidis
personis to be summond *de novo* to the effect foirsaid, under the
paine of excommunicatioun.

Haigy and Sandiris, fornicatouris: The quhilk day compeirit
William Haigy in Tullibody and grantis fornicatioun withe Issobell
Sandiris thair, for the quhilk he offiris him self in will of the kirk
and offiris vj s. viij d. for ane penaltie thairfoir, and thairfor desyris
his bairne gottin, as said is, to be baptezit. The brethrein ordanis
the said William and Issobell to mak publict repentence for thair
said fault, quhilk beand done ordanis Alexander Fargy to bapteis
thair said bairne.

Burne and Allane, fornicatouris: The quhilk day compeirit Walter
Burne and grantis him to have committit fornicatioun with

Catherein Allane in Clakmannan, for the quhilk he offiris wilinglie in penaltie for the said fault vj s. viij d. and to satisfie the kirk and thairfor desyris his bairne to be baptezit. The brethrein ordanis the said Walter and Catherein to mak publict repentence for thair said fault in Clakmannan, quhilk beand done ordanis Alexander Fargy to bapteis thair bairne.

At Striviling the v day of May, 1584

Presentes: Patrik Gillaspie, James Andirsone, Mr Arthur Futhie, [Mr Andro Yung, Michaell Lermonthe, *deleted*], Alexander Fargy, ministeris; Maisteris Alexander Iull, Andro Murdo, brethir of exerceis; Johnne Duncansone, minister; Mr Alexander Chisholme, Robert Mentayth, ministeris; and Mr James Pont, elder.

Moderatour chosin: The quhilk day Mr Arthur Futhie, minister at Airthe, be voit of the haill brethrein present was chosin moderatour in this presbytery to the nixt provinciall assemblie.

Patrik Layng: The samin day compeirit Patrik Layng and desyrit that the faultis fund in him concerning his offeice may be advysit with be the brether and inrespect of the lang suspentioun of him fra his offeice desyris that he may be restorit againe to the executioun of his offeice and promesis nevir to fall in the lyk of ony of the foirsaidis faultis in tymis cuming. The brethrein ordanis the said Patrik to mak publict repentence in the parroche kirk of Clakmannan quhair he committit the said faultis on Sonday the xvij day of May instant quhill thai be farther advysit and that Robert Mentayth, minister of Alvayth, ressave the same.

At Striviling the xij day of May, 1584

Presentes: Mr Arthur Futhie, James Andirsone, Patrik Gillaspie, Mr Andro Yung, Michaell Lermonthe, Alexander Fargy, ministeris; Maisteris Alexander Iulle, Andro Murdo, brethir of exerceis.

Mr Andro Grahame: The quhilk day, the moderatour inquyrit the brethrein of Dunblane to declair quhair Mr Andro Grahame was, seing he hes bein absent fra this sessioun the last day thairof and this, quha answerit that as thai undirstude he was departit to the Mernis. Secundlie, being inquyrit quhen he teichit last in

Dunblane, ansorit that he teichit nocht thair sen his last cuming to
Dunblane, viz., sen the moneth of December last. The brethrein
continewis farther proceiding in the said mater quhill thai be
farther advysit.

Isosbell Merser in Dunblane: The quhilk day compeirit Issobell
Merser in Dunblane and grantis hir delyvir of ane maidin bairne
ix oulkis syne or thairby gottin on hir in fornicatioun (as scho
allegis) be William McWillie, servand to the lady Rickartoun.
Nochttheles the said Issobell confessis that the said William denyis
the said bairne to be his and will nocht grant the samin without
he be compellit. The said Issobell beand askit be the moderatour
to declair quhw oft the said William hade carnall dell with hir,
quha ansorit that he hade carnall dell with her twa sindrie tymis
within aucht dayis, to uthir at midsomer last. The brethrein, at the
desyr of the said Issobell, ordanis the said William to be summond
litteratorie to answer at the said Issobellis instance to heir and se
tryell tane in the said mater undir the paine of disobedience.

At Striviling the xix day of May, 1584

Presentes: Mr Arthur Fethie, Patrik Gillaspie, James Andirsone,
Mr Andro Yung, Robert Mentayth, Michaell Lermonthe, Alex-
ander Fargy, ministeris; Mr Andro Murdo, brothur of exerceis,
Alexander Balvaird, reder.

Patrik Layng: The quhilk day compeirit Patrik Layng and
declairit to the brether that upone Sonday the xvij day of this
instant he hade made publict repentence in the parroche kirk of
Clakmannan for the faultis committit be him to Robert Mentayth,
minister of Alvayth, quha was appointit be the brethrein to ressave
the same according to the brethreinis ordinance made thairanent on
the fift day of May instant in all pointtis, quhilk declaratioun the
said Robert Mentayth testefeit to be of varetie and thairfor the said
Patrik desyrit the brethrein to relax him fra the suspending of him
fra his offeice in the ministrie and to readmit him thairto. The
brethrein relaxis the said Patrik fra the said suspentioun and to the
effect that thai may have perfyt tryell of the said Patrik in ministratioun of the sacramenttis and teiching of the Word of God
appointis unto him ane text concerning baptisme, viz., in the

xxviij chaptur of the evangelist Mathow, beginnand at the 16 vers of the samin unto the end, to be teichit be him in the kirk of Striviling on the xxvj day of May instant at viij houris befoir none.

Robert Mentayth, for absence fra the synnodall: The quhilk day the moderatour made intimatioun to Robert Mentayth that he was decernit be the last provinciall assemblie to pay iij libis., mony in penaltie for the secund fault in being absent fra the said assemblie, quhilk penaltie the moderatour desyrit him to pay presentlie according to the ordinance of the said assemblie. The said Robert answerit that the tyme of the said assemblie he was seik and thairfor mycht nocht be thair. The brethrein ordeinit the said Robert to consigne in thair clarkis handis the said penaltie, thair to remain quhill the said excuis be proponit in the nixt provinciall assemblie becaus this sessioun is nocht juge thairto, and gif the said excuis be nocht admittit be the said assemblie the said penaltie to be payit be the moderator, uthirwayis the said Robert Mentayth to have the said penaltie redelyverit againe to him self.

James Blacwod: The quhilk day compeirit James Blackwod, brothur to Sir William Blackwod, excommunicat, quha beand desyrit be the moderator to report quhat he had profetit his said brothur be confirence with him sen the xxij day of October last bypast according to his lycence thane grantit to him to that effect. The said James ansorit that he hade nevir confirence with his said brothur at na tyme sen the said day. Nochttheles he allegit he hade sindrie bissines to do with him concerning wrettis that was in his handis neciser to sindrie personis in the cuntrie, quhilk behovit of necessitie to be sein. Thairfor the said James desyrit lycence to pas to his said brothur anent the said wrettis quhen necessitie cravit and als to confer with him quhen tyme best servit, quhairbe he may be perswadit to renunce that damnablle religioun of papistrie and imbrece the trew lycht of the evangell. The brethrein, yit as of befoir, grantis lycence to the said James to pas with ane minister and ane elder conjunctlie to the presens of the said excommunicat, at sic tymis as thai thocht meit to confer with him anent the religioun, and quhen the said James hes to do with him in civill effairis that he pas to him his allane provyding that he mak adverteisment of befoir to ane of the ministeris in Dunblane, and that the said James send the said excommunicat manis necesaris to him to his awin chalmir allanirlie. And this lycence to indure to the sex day of October nixt allanirlie, and the nixt Twysday thaireftir the said James to report to this sessioun quhat he proffeittis the said Sir William Blackwod be his confirence with him.

[*Hiatus in the register with the proscription of presbyteries by act of parliament in May 1584. Two blank folios follow.*]

At Sterling the xxj day of *Junij* the yeir of God jm vc lxxxvj yeiris

Presentes: James Andirsone, commissionar, Patrik Gillaspie, Mr Arthur Fethie, Alexander Fargy, ministeris; Mr Alexander Iull, ane brothur of exerceis.

Bischopp off Abirdein: The quhilk day ane summondis direct be the last generall assemblie of the kirk, beand producit dewlie execute and indorsit upone Mr David Cunynghame, bischop of Abirdein, chairgein him to compeir the said day befoir us the brethrein of the presbytery of Sterling and the brethrein of the presbytery of Glasgw, to answer to the sclandiris conteinit thairin, speciallie concerning the abuse of his bodie with ane woman callit Elezabeth Suthirland (as is allegit), berand also commissione to the brethrein of the saidis presbyteriis to try the said sclandir or adultrie committit with hir or ony uther persone, as at mair lynth is conteinit in the said summondis. And we, the brethrein of the presbytery of Sterling, lukand for the comperance of the brethrein of the said presbytery of Glasgw to have conjonit with us in this assemblie to have tane tryell of the said Mr David concerning the sclandir abone writtin, according to the commissione foirsaid, nochttheles thai nor nane of thame compeirit, bot send the wretingis follwing, with ane burges man, quhilkis war producit, viz., ane misseive wreting berand in effect that thai war advertesit be an letter of the said Mr Davidis that he was nocht ablle to keip this day bot that he wald keip the xxj day of the nixt moneth and thairfor desyrit that the said mater sould be continewit etc., and siclyk thair was producit ane summondis direct fra the said presbytery of Glasgw dewlie execute and indorsit upone the said Elezabeth Suthirland, dochtir to William Suthirland, messinger, chairgeing hir to compeir this day to answer concerning the sclandir abone writtin, as at mair lynthe is conteinit thairin. Attour, thair was producit ane extract of proces deducit befoir the sessione of the kirk of Glasgw concerning the said adultrie allegit committit be the said Mr David with the said Elezabeth Sutherland undir the subscriptione of Mr Johnne Allansone, scrib to the said sessioun, as it beris in the self. The saidis Mr David and Elezabeth Sutherland, being oft tymes callit, compeirit nocht, bot Cathrein Wallace, spous to the said Mr David, compeirit and producit ane wret misseive wretein of hir husbandis direct to the brether of the saidis presbyteriis berand in effect that he was havallie trublit with seiknes, nochtwithstanding quhairof he hade travellit with grit painis to Falkland quhairfra the said wreting is direct, quhair he was contramandit to cum farther inrespect of present circumstancis and conventione at Edinburgh, quhairupone his majestie desyrit to wret to the brethir foirsaid to crave thair ovirsycht for the present and that it wald plais thame inrespect of his former honestie and lait purgatiounis in the said mater of sclandir ather to refar the samin to the nixt assemblie generall, or ellis to ane new dyet quhen he mycht mair assuritlie travell, as the samin of the deat at Falkland the xx day of *Junij*, 1586 at mair lynthe beris. The brethrein of the presbytery of Sterling, havein sein the haill wrettis producit and being advysit with the said commissione, findis thame selffis nocht jugis competent to the sclandir abone writtin this day berassone of the absence of the brethrein of the presbytery off Glasgw, quha ar conjonit with the brethrein of this presbytery conjunctlie to be jugis in this mater and na uthirwayis, as the said commissione beris expreslie, and swa we, the brethrein present, nocht beand jugis competent, could nocht proceid nor continew the said mater nather yit ordane the saidis proceis to be summond of new and thairfoir lavis aff farther proceidein in the said mater quhill the brethrein of the kirk be farther advysit thairto.

At Sterling the xxviij day of *Junij*, 1586

Presentes: James Andirsone, commissionar, Patrik Gillaspie, Mr Arthur Fethie, Alexander Fargy, ministeris; and Mr Alexander Iull, ane brother of exerceis.

Mr James Cokburne: The quhilk day the brethrein, undirstanding that Mr James Cokbrun is provydit to the personage and vicarage of the kirk of Muckert, quhilkis ar benefecis of cure, and yit mackis nocht residence and serveice at the kirk thairof as becumis, as is allegit, thairfoir ordanis the said Mr James Cokbrun to be summond *litteratorie* to compeir befoir the brethrein to mak declaratioun and informatione to thame of the forme and manir of his admissione to the saidis beneficis and to that effect to bring with him and produce his presentatione thairunto, his collatione thairupone, gif he ony hes, with all uthir richtis and documentis that he hes concerning the said mater to be sein and considderit be thame undir the paine of disobedience.

At Sterling the fyft day of July, 1586

Presentes: Patrik Gillaspie, Mr Arthur Futhie, Alexander Fargy, ministeris; and Mr Alexander Iull, ane brother of exerceis.

Mr James Cokburn: The quhilk day ane summondis beand producit upone Mr James Cokburn dewlie execute and indorsit chairgeing him to compeir the said day to mak declaratione to the brethrein of the forme and manir of his provisione and admissione to the personage and vicarage of the kirk of Muckert and to that effect to bring with him and produce his presentatione thairunto, his collatione thairupone gif he ony hes, with all uthir rychtis and documentis that he hes concerning the said mater to be sein and considderit be the brethrein under the paine of disobedience, quhilk Mr James being oft tymis callit compeirit nocht. Thairfor the brethir ordanis the said Mr James to be summond of new to the effect foirsaid undir the paine of excommunicatione.

At Sterling the xix day of July, 1586

Presentes: James Andirsone, Patrik Gillaspie, Mr Arthur Fethie, Andro Forester, Robert Mentayth, Alexander Fargy, ministeris; Mr Alexander Iull and Mr Henrie Layng, brethir of exerceis.

Concerning baptisme: The brethrein undirstanding that mony personis presentis nocht thair bairnis to be baptesit on the nixt sermond day eftir thair birthe, as aucht to be, bot deleyis and continewis the same ane lang speace thaireftir on sum warldlie respectis, quhairthrw sindrie bairnis departis this lyf without the said sacrament in default of the parentis that will nocht present thair bairnis and crave the samin quhen it is offirit ilk sermond day, as lykwys eftir the parentis hes deleyit the craving of the sacrament in dew tyme, as said is, sum of thair bairnis thruch seiknes being at the departing furth of this lyf, the parentis quhairof urgis the minister with inoportune sute to bapteis thair bairnis in tymis nocht convenient for ministratione of the samin, for remade quhairof, it is ordeinit be the haill brethrein that all personis within the boundis of this presbytery, namelie, mareit personis present thair bairnis to baptisme on the nixt sermond day immediatlie eftir the birthe thairof, and that na persone urge ane minister to bapteis ony bairne aff ane sermond day nor at ane uthir tyme, bot the speciall tyme appointit for ministratioun of the samin, and ordanis ilk minister to mak intimatione of this ordinance publickie to thair congregatione on ane Sonday immediatlie eftir the sermond that nane pretend ignorance of the samin.

Approbatioun off certane actis made of befoir concerning polecie: The quhilk day the brethrein undirstanding that thair is certan gude actis made in this presbytery concerning polecie and gude ordur to be observit be the ministrie within the boundis thairof, quhilkis ar becumit in oblivione inrespect of the lang speace sen thay war made, thairfor the brethrein present having revesit the samin actis and being advysit thairwith hes approvit and allwit the actis follwing respective and haill effect thairof, viz., in the first, ane act made on the xxix day of August 1581 berand that na minister ministrat mariage within brugh aff ane sermond day and in landwart aff ane Sonday in tyme of preichein, and that na minister marie personis quhairof nane of thame is his parrochinnaris albeit thay bring testimoniallis without lycence of the presbytery. Item, ane act made on the ix day of Januar 1581 contenand penalteis to be payit be the brethrein that faillis to mak and ad in the exerceis quhen it fallis thame in the cathalog. Item, ane act made on the xvj day of Januar 1581 contenand ane penaltie to be payit be ilk brother that repairis nocht to be exerceis ilk day appointit to the making thairof. Item, ane act made on the vj day of Fabruar 1581 commanding that ilk minister declair to the brethrein quhat text thai teiche and quhat commentaris thai follw. Item, ane act made on the xij day of Merche 1582 commanding ilk minister to caus to execute all summondis direct from the presbytery on ony of his parrochinnaris and report the samin deulie execute and indorsit. Item, ane act made the samin day forbidding all ministeris to ministrat baptisme, mariage nor exame nane of his congregatioun nor use na uthir chairge on the Twysday that may withhauld thame frome the exerceis undir the paine of suspentione and that the communione be nocht ministrat on that day callit peace day of auld nor yit within the speace of Lenterun. Item, ane act made on the xxvj day of Merche 1583 commanding ilk minister to register all mariagis, baptezein of bairnis, personis that deis within the parrochun and almws collectit to the pure with the distributione thairof, as lykwys to produce thair buikis of disceplein with the register of the foirsaidis befoir the presbytery twys ilk yeir to be veseit and redelyverit againe to the minister producer thairof. Item, ane act made on the ix day of Aprill 1583 making intimatioun of ane ordinance of the synnodall assemblie dischairgeing haulding of mercattis on Sondayis, and that ilk minister proceid with the sensuris of the kirk againis the contravenaris thairof beand his awin parrochinnaris. Item, ane act made on the vij day of May, 1583 contenand intimatioun of ane act of the generall assemblie forbidding the making of ony statuttis in ecclesiasticall assembleis bot sic as ar grundit on the actis of the generall assemblie. Item, ane act made on the xxiiij day of December 1583 forbiddand all ministeris within the boundis of this presbytery to marie ony personis that ar accompaneit to the kirk with pyperis or fidleris, etc., on that day that thay ar swa accumpaneit bot to suffir thame pas hame unmareit, undir the paine of disceplein to be execute againis the minister that dois utherwayis. And the brethrein in this assemblie commandis and ordanis that the saidis actis abone specefeit be keipit and observit in all pointis within the boundis of this presbytery, according as thai bear in thame selffis respective, undir the painis conteinit in thame to be execute on the contravenaris thairof.

At Sterling the secund day of August, 1586

Presentes: James Andirsone, Patrik Gillaspie, Robert Mentayth,

Mr Arthur Fethie, Alexander Fargy, Mr Andro Yung, ministeris;
Mr Alexander Iull, Mr Henrie Layng, brethir of exerceis.

Crawfurd contra *Cunynghame*: The quhilk day compeirit Robert
Crawfurd at the milne of Innerallone within the parrochun of
Lecrop, quha in the name of Margaret Crawfurde, his dochtir,
producit ane summondis dewlie execute and indorsit upone Thomas
Cunynghame, spous to the said Margaret in the law, within the
said parrochun, chargeing him to compeir the said day to heir and
sie him self decernit and ordeinit to desyr the sacrament of baptisme
to ane mane chyld, quhairof the said Margaret is delyvir in the
moneth of November last gottin on hir be the said Thomas hir
husband, as scho allegis, or ellis to schaw ane ressonablle caus quhy
the samin sould nocht be done undir the paine of disobedience.
Compeirit the said Thomas Cunynghame and allegit he wald nocht
desyr the said bairne to be baptesit becaus it was nocht his. The
brethrein, being advysit with the said answer, ordanis him ather to
intent actione of devorcement befoir the juge ordinar againis his
said spous for gaitting of the said bairne in adultrie and thairby
to pruif hir ane hure, or ellis acknawlege and confes the said bairne
to be his awin and to do thairfoir as apperteinis, to the quhilk he
was desyrit be the moderatour to gif his answer quhilk of the twa
he wald do. The said Thomas desyrit that he mycht have rassonablle
tyme to advys with his answer. The brethrein assignis to him the
ix day of August instant to gif his answer to the heddis foirsaidis,
he warnit thairto *apud acta*, and ordanis the said Margaret Crawfurd
to be summond *litteratorie*.

At Sterling the ix day of August, 1586

Presentes: James Andirsone, commissionar; Patrik Gillaspie,
Alexander Fargy, ministeris; Mr William Moresone, Mr
William Patone, Mr Alexander Iull, brethir of exerceis. [*No
minutes.*]

At Sterling the xxiij day of August, 1586

Presentes: James Andirsone, commissionar; Mr Andro Yung,
Alexander Fargy, ministeris; Mr Alexander Iull, Patrik Layng,

William Sterling, William Moresone, Mr Henrie Layng, Mr William Patone, brethir of exerceis.

William Sterling: For the bettir tryell of Williame Sterling gif he be meit and abill in literatur and conversatione to bruik offeice as ane pastur in the kirk for ministratione of the Word and sacramentis, the brethrein appointis him to teiche prevatlie on the xij chaptur of Mathowis evangell, beginning at the 38 vers thairof on the vj day of September nixt, according to the desyr of the kingis majesteis letter.

Margaret Crawfurd contra *hir husband*: The quhilk day ane summondis beand producit dewlie execute and indorsit upone Margaret Crawfurd and Thomas Cunynghame, hir spous, chairgeing thame to compeir the said day to heir and sie that mater concerning the baptezein of the bairne quhairof the said Margaret is delyvir proceid quhair it lest, viz., to heir and sie the said Thomas declaratione concerning the heddis quhairon he tuke to advys conteinit in the last act, compeirit the said Thomas Cunynghame and allegit that his said spous be hir ayth wald nocht afferm that the said man chyld quhairof scho was delyvir was gottin be him, and that scho hade carnall deill with na uthir man bot him, quhilkis gif scho will afferm be hir grit ayth the said Thomas promesis to accep the said bairne as his awin, present the samin to the sacrament of baptisme and do thairfoir as apperteinis ane father to do to his child, and gif scho confes uthirwayis, the said Thomas protestit that he may be decernit fre thairof, and the said Margaret Crawfurd siclyk compeirand personallie gaif hir aithe and desyrit ane day to be assignit to hir to advys with hir depositione. The brethir assignis to hir the penult day of this instant moneth to depone, parteis warnit *apud acta*.

Fornicaturis, Levingstone, Richie: The quhilk day compeirit Johnne Levingstone, brother to Gabriell Levingstone of Tirrintirrane, and grantis him to have committit fornicatione relaps with Jonet Richie in Tirintirrane and continewit lang in cumpany with hir to the grit offence of God and sclandir of his kirk, for the quhilk he confessis him self to be sorrie and repentis, and for avoyding of the quhilk in tymis cuming the said Johnne with consent of the said Gabriell, his brother, promesis to compleit mariage with the said Jonet, lauchfullie as effeiris, in feace of hallie kirk betuix and the fyft day of October nixt and promesis with all diligence to act cautione in the commissaris buikis of Sterling that he sall compleit mariage, as said is, betuix and the said day undir the paine of fourtie poundis mony to be tane up in name of the brethrein of this presbytery and convertit *ad pios usus* quha sall receive his cautionar thairof quhow oft neid beis. Inrespect of the quhilk, the brethrein ordanis (eftir the said cautione be actit, as said is) that the said Johnne Levingstone sall mak publict repentence in his awin parroche kirk thre soverall Sondayis and thaireftir his bairne to be baptezit, with certificatioun gif the mariage be nocht compleit betuix and the said day the said repentence salbe hauldin as na repentence bot thaireftir sall satisfie in repentence as ane adulterar and his said cautionar to undirly the penaltie foirsaid.

Sinclaris: Compeirit Ewmond and Herculus Sinclaris, sonnis to Mr Alexander Sinclar in Denny within the parrochun of Falkirk, quha in the name of thair said fathir exponit and declairit to the brethrein that it was of veritie that of auld in tyme of papistrie, the said Mr Alexander was mareit on Hellesone Hairstennis in ane hous privallie be ane preist in presens of certane witnessis, quhilk woman contenwallie sensyne hes remanit with him and hes borne to him the said Ewmond and Herculus, and the said Mr Alexander havand rycht and titill to sindrie thingis that will succeid to his narrest and lauchfull air eftir his deceis and that the witnessis present at the completing of the said mariage ar now all departit furth of this lyf, and thairfor thair is nane levand presentlie to preive the samin, and swa eftir the said Mr Alexander deceis, we, his lauchfull bairnis gottin on his said wyf, may be defraudit of our lauchfull rycht alleging us to be bot bastardis for the caus foirsaid, and thairfoir for detecting of the trewthe to the glorie of God and removing of all occasione of sclandir furth of the cuntrie (gif ony be), allegeand thame nocht to be mareit and swa lyis in hurdome, maist earnestlie desyris the brethrein to gif command to Andro Forester, thair minister of Falkirk, to accept and ressave the confessionis of the said Mr Alexander and Hellesone Hairstennis concerning the trewthe and manir of thair said mariage publictlie in thair parroche kirk on ane Sonday in the tym of the conventione on the congregatione to heir the Word and thay gevand full consent, as is requisit, that the said minister solemnizat the band of matremony of new betuix thame according to the ordur reformit. The brethrein,

S

being advysit with the said petitione, ordanis the said Andro Forester to do as is requyrit in all, he proclamand ane promeis made betuix the said Mr Alexander and Hellesone Hairstenis of befoir lauchfullie according to the ordur and na impediment being opponit in the contrar.

At Sterling the penult day of August, 1586

Presentes: James Andirsone, Patrik Gillaspie, Mr Arthur Fethie, Robert Mentayth, Mr Adame Merschell, Mr Alexander Wallace, Andro Forester, Mr William Sterling and William Sterling, ministeris; Mr Alexander Iull, Mr Henrie Layng, Mr William Moresone and Mr Williame Patoun, brethir of exerceis.

Margaret Crawfurd contra *hir husband*: In the terme assignit to Margaret Crawfurd, the spous off Thomas Cunynghame, to depone gif hir bairne quhairof scho was last delyvir be hir husbandis or nocht, as at mair lynthe is conteinit in the last act made thairanent, compeirit the said Margaret and hir husband personallie, quhilk Margaret deponit be hir grit aythe that hir said bairne, quhairof scho was last delyvir, was gottin on hir be hir said husband and na uther mane and that scho hade carnell deill with na uthir mane bot him inrespect of the quhilk depositione and of the said Thomas promeis conteinit in the last act, the brethrein ordanis him to present the samin bairne to baptism and to desyr the samin to be baptisit as his awin bairne and farther to do thairfoir as apperteinis ane fathir to do his chyld.

At Sterling the vj day of Semptember [*sic*], 1586

Presentes: James Andirsone, Mr Arthur Fethie, ministeris; Mr Robert Bruce, Mr Alexander Iull, Mr William Moresone, brethir of exerceis; and Johnne Schaw of Bruigh.

William Sterlingis tryell: The quhilk day being appointit to William Sterling to gif ane tryell of his doctrein on the text appointit to him privallie, the said William in presens of the brethrein foirsaid teichit on the said text, viz., on the xij chaptur of Mathowis evangell, beginnand at the 38 vers thairof inclusive to the 41 vers of the samin exclusive, quhais doctrein being hard and the brethreinis jugementis thairon cravit, the samin w[a]s fund sound sound [*sic*] aggreing with the annalegie of fayth. Yit for farther tryell of his habilitie to continew in the ministrie, the brethrein admittis and ordanis him to teiche publictlie in the exerceis, quhen he salbe commandit, and presentlie dischairgis him frome usein of all farther functione in the kirk bot onlie to reid in his awin kirk allanirlie ay and quhill he be admittit of new to farther [functione].

At Sterling the xxvij day of September, 1586

Presentes: James Andirsone, Patrik Gillaspie, Andro Forester, Robert Mentayth, Alexander Fargy, ministeris; Mr Alexander Iull, Mr William Moresone and Mr William Patoun, brethrein of exerceis.

Mr Henrie Layng: The quhilk day compeirit Duncane Narne of Lokishill quha, for him self and in name of the particular sessione of the kirk of S. Niniane, exponit and declairit to the brethrein the grit seiknes and infirmitie that thair minister, Patrik Gillaspie, was subject unto quhairthrw he was inablle to use and exerceis his offeice in thair kirk as becumis, quhilk the said Patrik confessit to be of trewthe and thairfor the said Patrik Gillaspie, minister foirsaid, and Duncan Nairne, in name of the said sessioun, nominat and presentit Mr Henrie Layng, ane yung man of honest report newlie returnit frome the schollis, quhome thay desyr the brethrein to try in literatur and conversatione, quha being fund meit and ablle to the effect undirwrittin desyris that he be admittit pastour and coadjutor with the said Patrik Gillaspie at thair said kirk during the said Patrikis lyftyme. Quhilk desyr being hard be the brethrein and jugit rassonablle and thay according to the said desyr willing to tak tryell first of his doctrein and being advysit with his doctrein teichit alreddie in thair presens in form of exerceis findis the samin sound and proffitablle and ar satisfeit with him concerning that point of tryell and for farther tryell of him concerning his forme of doctrein in pulpet withe applicationis as effeiris. The brethrein ordanis and appointis him to teiche on the xx chaptur of Mathowis evangell, beginnand at the 18 vers inclusive, and to tak furth according to his awin jugement and that in the kirk of Sterling on Thurisday the vj day of October nixt, beand ane ordinar preiching day in the said toun.

At Sterling the vj day of October, 1586

Presentes: James Andirsone, commissionar; Mr Arthur Fethie, Patrik Gillaspie, Mr William Sterling, Mr Andro Yung, his assessuris; Andro Forester, Alexander Fargy, Mr Alexander Wallace, Mr Alexander Chisholme and William Drummond, ministeris; and Mr Alexander Iull, ane brothur of exerceis.

Tryell off Mr Henrie Layng: The quhilk day Mr Henrie Layng having teichit publictlie in the pulpet of Sterling in presens of the said brethrein and congregatione of the said brugh on the 20 chaptur of Mathowis evangell, beginning at the 28 vers thairof inclusive to the 30 vers of the samin exclusive, according as he was ordeinit be the presbytery for tryell of his forme of publict doctrein with applicationis as effeiris, the brethreinis jugementis being cravit thairon, he was fund sound in doctrein and appeirit to have gude giftis abill to proffeit in the kirk, and the brethrein is satisfeit with him concerning the said point of tryell and remittis him to be farther tryit on the commone placis and grundis of religione and pointis thairto, the x day of November nixt.

At Sterling the xj day of October, 1586

Presentes: Patrik Gillaspie, Alexander Fargy, ministeris; Mr Alexander Iull, Mr Henrie Layng and Mr William Moresone, brethir of exerceis. [*No minutes.*]

At Sterling the xviij day of October, 1586

Presentes: James Andirsone, Patrik Gillaspie, Mr Arthur Fethie, Andro Forester, Alexander Fargy, Johnne Duncansone, William Drumond, ministeris; Mr Alexander Iull, Mr Henrie Layng, Mr William Moreson, brethir of exerceis.

Triall off Mr Adame Mairschell: The quhilk day Mr Adame Mairschell having teichit on the ordinar text of the exerceis, viz., on the fyft chaptur to the Hebrwis at the beginning to the 5 vers thairof exclusive, on the quhilk the brethrein jugementis being cravit according to the ordur, the samin doctrein was fund to be aggreabill with the annalegie of fayth bot nocht sufficient in ex-positione of the said text as becumis, nather yit hes he attenit to

the purpois and mening of the apostill thairintill and thairfor concerning this point of his tryell in exerceis, the brethrein jugis him nocht
meit to continew a minister in the kirk, yit for farther knawlege of
the said Mr Adame in his doctrein the brethrein ordanis him to teiche
privallie on the first chaptur of Markis evangell beginning at the
4 vers and to tak swa meikill as he plasis, and that in form of publick
doctrein withe applica[tio]nis as apperteinis, and this to be done
on the first day of November nixt in presens of the brethrein.

At Sterling the xxv day of October, 1586

Presentes: James Andirsone, Patrik Gillaspie, Alexander Fargy,
Robert Mentayth, ministeris; Mr Alexander Iull, Mr Henrie Layng,
Mr William Moresone, brethir of exerceis.

Patrik Layng: According to ane act of the last synnodall assemblie
of this province commanding the brethrein of this presbytery to
try and examin Patrik Layng and utheris in this presbytery concerning thair doctrein and conversatione, the brethrein ordanis the
said Patrik to teiche prevallie on the fyft chaptur of the epistill to
the Romanis at the beginning thairof in forme off exerceis on the
viij day of November nixt, quhairbe the brethrein may undirstand
gif he be proffitablle in the kirk and worthie to continue as ane
pastor thairin or nocht.

At Sterling the first day of November, 1586

Presentes: James Andirsone, Mr Arthur Fethie, Andro Forester,
Mr Alexander Wallace, Mr Adame Merschell, ministeris; and Mr
Alexander Iull, ane brother of exerceis.

Tryell off Mr Adame Merschell: The quhilk day being appointit
to Mr Adame Merschell to gif ane tryell privallie on his forme of
publict doctrein with applicationis on the text appointit to him,
the said Mr Adame in presens of the brethrein foirsaid teichit on
the said text, viz., on the first chaptur of S. Mark evangell, beginning
at the 4 vers inclusive to the 7 vers of the samin exclusive, quhais
doctrein bein hard and the brethrein jugementis thairon cravit, the
samin was fund sound aggreing with the annalegie of fayth bot
insafar as thay hard of the said Mr Adame as yit concerning his

doctrein speciallie this point of tryell, the brethrein juges him nocht meit to continew as minister in the kirk. Nochttheles, for farther knawlege of his habilitie, he is ordeinit to teiche privallie in forme of exerceis on the xj chaptur of S. Mathowis evangell beginning at the 27 vers thairof inclusive to the end of the chaptur, upone the x day of November instant.

Tryell off Mr William Patone: The quhilk day, at the ernest sute of Mr William Patone to be tryit in publict doctrein to the effect he may have the brethreinis jugementis gif thay find apperance in him that he may be abill to be ane pastour in the kirk that he may the bettir addres him self thairunto, the brethrein findis the said Mr Williamis sute rassonablle and having hard him alreddy sindrie tymis in exerceis ordanis him to teiche publictlie in the pulpet of Sterling on the xvij day of November nixt upone the x chaptur of S. Mathowis evangell, beginning at the 15 vers thairof and to apply thairupone, as effeiris.

At Sterling the viij day of November, 1586

Presentes: James Andirsone, Johnne Duncansone, Robert Mentayth, Alexander Fargy, ministeris; Mr Alexander Iull, Mr Henrie Layng, Mr William Moresone and William Sterling, brethir of exerceis.

Tryell off Patrik Layng: The quhilk day being appointit to Patrik Layng to gif tryell of his doctrein in forme of exerceis privallie on the text appointit to him, the said Patrik in presens of the brethrein foirsaid teichit privallie on the said text., viz., on the fyft chaptur of the epistill to the Romanis at the beginning, quhais doctrein being hard and the brethreinis jugementis thairon cravit, the samin was fund to be sound doctrine, inrespect quhairof the brethrein admittis the said Patrik to teiche in the publict exerceis on the ordinar text thairof quhen he salbe commandit as for ane farther tryell of his habilitie to continew a pastur in the kirk.

At Sterling the x day of November, 1586

Presentes: James Andirsone, Mr Andro Yung, ministeris; and Mr Alexander Iull, ane brother of exerceis.

The quhilk day being appointit to Mr Henrie Layng to gif ane tryell of his knawlege in the commone placis and grundis of religione, compeirit the said Mr Henrie and being examinat thairupon at lynthe was fund to have gude and rassonablle knawlege thairin, quhairanent the brethrein was satisfeit with him concerning that point of tryell. Nochttheles, inrespect of the few numbir present of the brethrein, thai continew his admissione to the xvij day of November instant.

At Sterling the xv day of November, 1586

Presentes: James Andirsone, Johnne Duncansone, Andro Forester, Alexander Fargy, Robert Mentayth, ministeris; Mr Alexander Iull and Mr William Moresone, brethrein of exerceis.; and Mr Henrie Layng. [*No minutes.*]

At Sterling the xvij of November [1586]

Presentes: James Andirsone, Johnne Duncansone, Mr Andro Yung, Patrik Gillaspie, Alexander Fargy, Mr Alexander Wallace, ministeris; Mr Alexander Iull and Mr William Moresone, brethrein of exerceis.

Tryell of Mr William Patone: The quhilk day being appointit to Mr William Patone to teiche publicklie on the text appointit to him, the said Mr William having teichit thairon, viz., on the x chaptur of S. Mathowis evangell beginning at the 15 vers thairof publictlie, as said is, with applicationis, his doctrine was fund be the brethrein sound, and thairby appeirit to thame that he salbe ane proffitabill instrument in the kirk, nochttheles continewis him, quhill the brethrein tak fatrher tryell as apperteinis as occasione sall offir.

Admissione of Mr Henrie Layng: The quhilk day being assignit be the brethrein to pronunce thair jugementis anent the admissione of Mr Henrie Layng coadjutor with Patrik Gillaspie, the said Mr Henrie being personallie present, and the brethrein advysit with the tryell tane of his habilitie to entir in the ministrie anent his teichein bayth in forme of exerceis and publict doctrein also concerning his qualificatione and knawlege of the commone placis and grundis of religione, as particular actis made of befoir at lynthe beris, and heiring na thing of his lyf and conversatione bot honestie findis him qualefeit and meit in the offeice eftir specefeit, sound in doctrein and as appeiris to have gude giftis abill to proffeit in the kirk, and thairfore upone the declaratione made be the said Patrik Gillaspie, minister at S. Ninianis kirk, of the infirmitie in his persone thruch seiknes and grit disais knawin to the brethrein quhairthrw he is inabillit to do his awin offeice at his said kirk as becumis, quhairby he and the particular sessione of his kirk ar movit to sute the said Mr Henrie Layng to be admittit coadjutor with him (he being fund qualefeit and meit), the brethrein hes admittit and admittis the said Mr Henrie Layng pastour and minister of the Word of God and sacramentis as coadjutor with the said Patrik Gillaspie during his lyftyme to the said kirk of S. Niniane, and eftir the said Patrikis deceis to continew as the brethrein of the said presbytery and parrochinnaris sall juge the said Mr Henrie meit and abill to sustein and exerceis the burdein and chairge as only minister to the said parrochun, and the brethrein ordanis James Andirsone, minister at Sterling, commissionar, to notefie thir presentis to the parrochinnaris of the said kirk on Sonday nixt immediatlie eftir the sermond and to desyr declaratione of thair consent to the said Mr Henreis admissione, as said is, quha consentand thairto that he plaice him minister coadjutor with the said Patrik thairat, as said is, according to the ordur.

At Sterling the xxij day of November, 1586

Presentes: James Andirsone, Mr Arthur Fethie, Patrik Gillaspie, Robert Mentayth, Alexander Fargy, Mr Henrie Layng, ministeris; and Mr Alexander Iull, ane brother of exerceis. [*No minutes.*]

At Sterling the xx day of December, 1586

Presentes: James Andirsone, commissionar; Andro Forester, Robert Mentayth, Alexander Fargy, Mr Henrie Layng, ministeris; Mr Alexander Iull, Mr William Moresone, brethir of exerceis.

The brethrein undirstanding that thair is ane gentilman dwelland within the brugh of Sterling, callit Waltir Buchannan, brother to Johnne Buchannan of Arnepriour, newlie returnit with ane Flemis woman, allegit to be his wyf, furth of cuntreis quhair papistrie is publictlie professit and authoresit be sword and fyr, speciallie the cuntreis of Spaine and Flanderis and hes dwelt in the said brugh the speace of [blank] oulkis or thairby, quha, nor yit his wyf, hes at na tyme repairit to preiching nor prayeris in the kirk thairof sen thair cuming to the said toun, inrespect of the quhilkis, the brethrein ordanis the said Waltir Buchannan to be summond *litteratorie* to gif and declair ane confessione and declaratione of his fayth and religione undir the paine of disobedience to the voice of the kirk.

At Sterling the xxvij day of December, 1586

Presentes: James Andirsone, Mr Arthur Fethie, Andro Forester, Alexander Fargy, Mr Henrie Layng, ministeris; Mr Alexander Iull, and Mr William Moresone, brethir of exerceis.

Walter Buchannane: The quhilk day ane summondis beand producit deulie execute and indorsit upone Waltir Buchannan, brother to Johnne Buchannan of Arnepriour, chairgeing him to compeir the said day to gif ane confessione and declaratione of his fayth and religione undir the paine of disobedience, the said Waltir being oft tymis callit compeirit nocht. Nochttheles, compeirit Alexander Saittone of Gargunnok, brother in law to the said Walter, quha ernestlie desyrit that the brethrein sould continew farther proceidein agaínis the said Walter to the thrid day of Januar nixt and in the mentyme the said Alexander promesit to confer with him. The brethir according to the saidis Alexander desyr, being ane godlie mane and weill reportit of, continewis the said mater to the thrid day of the said moneth of Januar and ordanis the said Alexander to confer with the said Walter and sic uthir off the brethrein, as the said Alexander sall requyr, and that the said Alexander report quhat he findis in him on the said iij day of Januar nixt.

At Sterling the iij day of Januar, 1586

Presentes: James Andirsone, Johnne Duncansone, Patrik Gillaspie, Mr Henrie Layng, Mr Arthur Fethie, Alexander Fargy, Robert Mentayth, ministeris; Mr Alexander Iull and Mr William Moresone, brethrein of exerceis.

Waltir Buchannan: In the term assignit to Alexander Saittone of

Gargunnok to report quhat he fand in confirrence hade with Waltir Buchannan, compeirit the said Alexander and declairit that he hade conferrit withe the said Waltir bot hade nocht gottin answer as yit worthie to be reportit, nochttheles desyrit the brethrein continew all farther proceiding, as of befoir, to the x day of Januar instant and promesis to caus James Andirsone, minister at Sterling, confer with the said Walter betuix and the said day, quha may try his religione and do as thay sall think meit. The brethrein grantis to the said Alexanderis desyr and ordanis the said James Andirsone to do according thairto and quhat he findis in the said Waltir Buchannan eftir confirrence hade with him that he report the samin to the brethrein the x day of Januar instant.

At Sterling the x day of Januar, 1586

Presentes: James Andirsone, Patrik Gillaspie, Andro Forester, Alexander Fargy, Mr Alexander Wallace, ministeris; Mr Alexander Iull, Mr William Moresone, Mr William Patoun, brethrein of exerceis.

Waltir Buchannane: In the terme appointit to James Andirsone, minister, to report quhat he hade fund in conference hade with Waltir Buchannan, the said James Andirsone reportit that he hade conferrit with the said Waltir, quha schew him warldlie excuis that he could nocht subscryve to our religione presentlie nor yit publictlie profes the samin, to wit, becaus the samin will be the tinsall of his wyffis heritage and leving, quhilk scho hade in Flandiris, and thairfor quhill he hade tane sum ordur thairanent he could nawayis imbraice our religione. To the quhilk, the said James ansorit (as he reportit) that the brethrein (as he belevit) wald nocht admit the samin for ony rassonablle excuis for sindrie rassonis conteinit in the Word of God, quhilk he declairit to him in particular, and thairfor in the name of God admonesit him to obey his maistir, Jesus Christ, and randir obedience to the trewthe, of quhome thane he could gait na direct answer; and thairfor James Andirsone delyvirit in the handis of Alexander Saittone, his brother in law, quha contenwis oft tymis in cumpanie with the said Waltir, the confessione of fayth and to schow to the said Waltir and caus him advys thairwith that thaireftir be the bettir advysment he may gif answer to the brethrein. And siclyk compeirit Robert Buchannan of Lany and testefeit the said report to be of varetie bot allegit that the said Waltir hade bot varie laitlie sein the said confessione of fayth and thairfor was nocht weill advysit thairwith, as yit, and thairfor desyris that farther proceiding agains the said Waltir may be continewit to the xvij day of this instant moneth that he may in the mentyme advys the bettir. The brethrein willing rather to win the said Waltir thane to los him grantis continewatioun to the said xvij day of this moneth and exhortis the said Robert to caus the said Waltir confer with sum of the brethrein on thais thingis quhairof he douttis and that he compeir the said day and gif his answer to the brethrein.

Johnne Harrwar, incesteus: The quhilk day compeirit Johnne Harrwar, in Brydiswallis in Forrest within the parrochun of Clakmannan, and confessis him to have committit huredum in gaittein of ane bairne with Jonet Maistirtoun, brother dochtir to Elezabeth Patok, with quhome siclyk he confessis he gat ane uthir bairne in fornicatioun. Inrespect of the quhilk confessione, the brethrein findis that the said Johnne hes committit incest with the said Jonet Maistirtoun, being sib to the said Elezabeth Patok, with quhome he hade siclyk carnell deill of befoir within the degreis defendit be the Word of God, and eftir the moderatour hade schawin to the said Johnne the grevusnes of his offence, he declairit signis of repentence and desyrit his minister to be commandit to bapteis his bairne gottin in incest as said is. The brethrein ordanis the said Johnne Harrwar to act cautione in the buikis of the commissar of Sterling that he sall compeir befoir the nixt synnodall assemblie of this province to be haldin in Dunblane the first Twysday of Aprill nixt, thair to ressave injunctionis to be injonit to him for the said incest and that he sall obey the samin undir the paine of xl libis. And thaireftir, the said Jonet Maistirton compeiris siclyk and schawis signis of repentence and causit act cautione in manir foirsaid. The brethrein ordanis that thaireftir the minister of Clakmannan bapteis the said bairne gottin in incest, as said is.

At Sterling the xvij day of Januar, 1586

Presentes: Alexander Fargy, Robert Mentayth, Mr Arthur Fethie,

Mr Alexander Wallace, Mr Henrie Layng, ministeris; Mr Alexander Iull, Mr Richard Wrycht, brether of exerceis.

Waltir Buchannan: In the terme assignit to Waltir Buchannan to gif answer of his fayth and religione upone his advysment hade with the confessione of fayth, the said Waltir being oft tymis callit compeirit nocht. Nochttheles, compeirit Alexander Saittone of Gargunnok, quha, in the name of the said Waltir, desyrit that farther proceiding againis the said Waltir mycht be continewit to the xxiiij day of this instant moneth of Januar that in the mentyme he may be farther resolvit with the said confessione of fayth. Quhilk desyr the brethrein grantit, and ordanit the said Walter to compeir personallie befoir thame the said xxiiij day of this instant moneth and gif his awin answer heirupone.

Jonet Maistirtoun, incestuus: The quhilk day compeirit Jonet Maistirtoun in Larbart furde within the parrochun of Clakmannan and grantis hir to have committit huredum with Johnne Harrwar, and confessis that scho knawis the said Johnne Harrwar to have gottin ane bairne of befoir in fornicatioun with Elezabeth Patok, hir fathir sister. Inrespect of the quhilk confessione, the brethrein jugis the said Jonet to have committit incest with the said Johnne and thairfor the weghtines of hir offence being declairit, the said Jonet wald schaw na signis of repentence, and thairfor the brethrein continewis farther proceidein with hir quhill thai be farther advysit.

At Sterling the xxiiij day of Januar, 1586

Presentes: Patrik Gillaspie, Alexander Fargy, Andro Forester, Mr Alexander Wallace, Mr Henrie Layng, ministeris; Mr William Patoun, Mr Alexander Iull, Patrik Layng and Mr William Moresone, brethir of exerceis.

Waltir Buchannan: In the terme assignit to Walter Buchannan to compeir and gif ane confessione and declaratioun of his fayth and religioun, compeirit the said Waltir Buchannan and allegit as yit that he was nocht resolvit with the confessione of fayth to gif answer quhethir he wald subscryve the samin or nocht, and allegit farther that he was boun schortlie out of the cuntrie and thairfor desyrit the brethrein as yit to continew farther proceidin againis him ane gude rassonablle speace, in the quhilk tyme he sould ather remove him self aff the countrie or ellis compeir againe befoir the brethrein on the day to be appointit be thame and gif answer quhethir he will subscryve the confessione of fayth subscryvit be the kingis majestie or nocht. The brethrein, willing to remove all occasione of sudden proceiding againis the said Waltir, quhilk utherwayis perchance he wald allege, continewis, yit as of befoir, all proceiden againis him the speace of ane moneth, ordening him in the mentyme to desyr confirrence with sum of the brethir and advys with the said confessione of fayth, frequent the kirk in tyme of serveice, speciallie in tyme of preichein, and that he compeir befoir the brethrein againe on the xxj day of Fabruar nixt and gif ane direct answer gif he will embras our religione and subscryve the said confessione of fayth or ellis that he, betuix and the said xxj day of Fabruar, remove him self and his wyf furth of the cuntrie, according to the act of parliament made thairanent.

At Sterling the last day of Januar, 1586

Presentes: Mr Henrie Layng, minister; Mr Alexander Iull, Mr William Patoun and Mr William Moresone, brethir of exerceis. [*No minutes.*]

At Sterling the vij day of Fabruar, 1586

Presentes: Andro Forester, Robert Mentayth, Mr Henrie Layng, ministeris; Mr Alexander Iull and Mr William Moresone, brethir of exerceis. [*No minutes.*]

At Sterling the xiiij day of Fabruar, 1586

Presentes: Johnne Duncansone, Mr Arthur Fethie, Robert Mentayth, Mr Henrie Layng, ministeris; Mr Alexander Iull, Mr William Moresone and Mr Richerd Wrycht, brethir of exerceis. [*No minutes.*]

At Sterling the xxj day of Fabruar, 1586

Presentes: Mr Henrie Layng, Mr Andro Murdo, ministeris; Mr

Alexander Iull, Mr William Moresone and Mr Richard Wrycht, brethir of exerceis.

Waltir Buchannan: In the terme assignit to Waltir Buchannan, brother to Johnne Buchannan of Arnepriour, to compeir and gif ane confessione of his fayth and religione as he was ordeinit on the xxiiij day of Januar last bypast, the said Waltir being oft tymis callit compeirit nocht. The brethir continewis farther proceidein againis him to ane mair full sessione.

Duncane and Trumbill: The quhilk day compeirit Johnne Duncan, sone of umquhill Brys Duncan in Boquhen, within the parrochun of S. Niniane, and Marione Trumbill, dochtir to umquhill Robert Trumbill in Gargunnok, within the samin parrochun, and producit ane bill of complent on Mr Henrie Layng, thair minister, berand in effect that thay compeirit befoir the said Mr Henrie and confessit mutuall promeis of mariage was made betuix thame and thairfor desyrit him to proclame the samin according to the ordur that mariage mycht be solemnizat betuix thame, quha promesit to do the samin lyk as he did ainis and sensyne hes stayit. Quhilk Mr Henrie, being askit be the moderatour quhy he wald nocht proceid, ansorit that eftir he hade ainis proclamit the saidis personis Alexander Saittone of Gargunnok, heritur of the land quhairon the said Marione Trumbillis fathir dwelt, compeirit and allegit that he was left, be hir fathir, tutur and administratour to his bairnis and ovirman to his executouris to se that his movablle gudis war usit and imployit according to his lettir will and testament, quhilk offecis he hade tane on him and done according to the said umquhill Robertis lettir will, and farther allegit that the said Marione Trumbill hade made the said promeis of mariage to the said Johnne by his advys and consent, beand left tutour and administratour to hir, as lykwys by the consent of Alexander Trumbill in Flukhennis, hir brother, and all uthir hir friendis to hir grit hurt, having ane rassonabill portione of gair left to hir be hir father and weill imployit for hir weill to this present to marie the said Johnne, beand ane mane that hes na gair and als hes spendit all that he hade. Inrespect of the quhilk allegeance, the said Mr Henrie ansorit that he had stayit in farther proceiding in the said mater quhill the brethrein hade discussit the said allegeance. Compeirit the said Alexander Saittone and Alexander Trumbil land affermit the said

Mr Henreis report concerning thair said oppositione to be of varetie in all, and of new allegit the samin in presens of the brethrein. The said Marione Trumbill ansorit and allegit that scho was nocht bund to abyd be ony of hir freindis consent in the said mater becaus scho was of perfyt aige, viz., of xx yeir or thairby and thairfor was fre to marie the said Johnne nochtwithstanding of the said allegance, and also the said Marione and Johnne confessit that thay hade carnall copulatione togethir, for the quhilk eftir the moderatour hade thratnit the jugementis of God thay appeirit to be penitent for thair said offence and offirit thame selffis in the will of the kirk thairfor, and desyrit the brethrein to repell the said allegeance made be the saidis Alexander Saittone and Alexander Trumbill inrespect of hir answer thairto, and to command the said Mr Henrie Layng to proceid in proclamatioun of thair bannis according to the ordur and thaireftir to thair mariage. The brethrein continewis the pronunsein of thair jugementis on the saidis allegeance to the vij day of Merche nixt, bayth the saidis parteis warnit thairto *apud acta*.

At Sterling the vij day of Mairche, 1586

Presentes: Alexander Fargy, Robert Mentayth, Mr Henrie Layng, ministeris; Mr Alexander Iull, Mr William Moresone and Mr Richard Wrycht, brethir of exerceis.

Waltir Buchannane: The brethrein undirstanding that Waltir Buchannan, brother to Johnne Buchannan of Arnepriour, obteinit of the brethrein ane lang day to advys with the confessione of fayth betuix and the quhilk he was ordeinit ather to remove him self and his wyf af the cuntrie or ellis to compeir on the day appointit to him, viz., on the xxj day of Fabruar last bypast to gif direct answer of his fayth and religione, quha compeirit nocht the said day nather yit is removit aff the cuntrie, thairfor the brethrein ordanis him to be summond *litteratorie* to the effect foirsaid undir the paine of disobedience.

At Sterling the xiiij day of Merche, 1586

Presentes: Johnne Duncansone, Mr Alexander Wallace, Mr Henrie

Layng, ministeris; Alexander Fargy, minister; Mr Alexander Iull, Mr William Muresone and Mr Richard Wrycht, brethir of exerceis.

Waltir Buchannan: The quhilk day ane summondis beand producit dewlie execute and indorsit upone Waltir Buchannan, brother to Johnne Buchannan of Arnepriour, chairgein him to compeir the said day to gif his answer gif he will subscryve the confessione of fayth subscryvit be the kingis majestie and his houshald and profes the religione thairin conteinit or nocht undir the paine of disobedience, quhilk Waltir being oft tymis callit compeirit nocht. Thairfor the brethrein ordanis him to be summond of new to the effect foirsaid undir the paine of excommunicatione.

Jonet Maistirtoun, incesteus: The quhilk day compeirit Jonet Maistirtoun in Larbert furd within the parrochun of Clakmannan and grantis hir to have offendit God in committing incest with Johnne Harrwar, as at mair lynthe is conteinit in ane uthir act made at Sterling the xvij day of Januar last bypast, for the quhilk the said Jonet schew signes of repentence and offirit to obey the kirk as thai wald command, and desyrit ane command to be gevin to Mr Alexander Wallace, minister of the said parrochun, to bapteis the bairne gottin on hir be the said Johnne in incest, as said is. The brethrein ordanis the said Jonet to act caution in the commissaris buikis of Sterling that scho sall compeir befoir the nixt synnodall assemblie to be hauldin in Dunblane the first Twysday of Aprill nixt, thair to ressave injunctionis to be injonit to hir for hir said offence and to obey the samin undir the paine of xl libis., quhilk beand done the brethrein ordanis the said Mr Alexander Wallace to bapteis hir said bairne.

At Sterling the xxj day of Mairche, 1586

Presentes: James Andirsone, Mr Henrie Layng, ministeris; Mr Alexander Iull and Mr William Moresone, brethir of exerceis.

Waltir Buchannan: The quhilk day ane summondis beand dewlie execute and indorsit upone Waltir Buchannan, brother to Johnne Buchannan of Arnepriour, chairgein him to compeir the said day to gif his answer gif he will subscryve the confessione of fayth subscryvit be the kingis majestie and his houshald and profes the

religion thairin conteinit or nocht undir the paine of excommunicatioun, compeirit the said Waltir Buchannan and allegit that as
he was nocht resolvit with the confessione of fayth and thairfor
desyrit langer tyme to be assignit to him to advys with the samin.
The brethrein, yit as of befoir, at his awin desyr continewis farther
proceidein againis him to the iiij day of Aprill nixt, and in the
mentyme ordanis him to advys with the confessione of fayth, confer
with sum brethrein anent ony thing quhairof he douttis, frequent
sermondis, and warnis him *apud acta* to compeir in the cathedrall
kirk of Dunblane befoir the synnodall assemblie of this province
to be haldin thairin the said iiij day of Aprill, and thair to gif ane
confession of his fayth and religione, with certificatioun and he
failze the said assemblie will proceid according to the Word of
God, actis of our soverane lordis parliamentis and actis of the
generall assemblie of the kirk.

At Sterling the xxviij day of Merche, 1587

Presentes: James Andirsone, Mr Arthur Fethie, Robert Mentayth,
Andro Forester, Alexander Fargy, Mr Henrie Layng, Mr Alexander
Wallace, ministeris; Mr Alexander Iull and Mr William Patone,
brethrein of exerceis.

*Impediment allegit againis mariage to be made betuix Johnne Duncan
and Marione Trumbill*: The quhilk day ane summondis of walkning
being producit dewlie execute and indorsit upone Alexander
Saittone of Gargunnok and Alexander Trumbill in Flukhennis
chairgein thame to compeir the said day to heir and sie that mater
concerning the impediment allegit be thame for staying of mariage
to be compleit betuix Johnne Duncan in Boquhen and Marione
Trumbill, sister to the said Alexander Trumbill, walknit and
proceid quhair it lest, viz., to heir and se the brethreinis jugementis
producit in the samin, the said Alexander Trumbill and Johnne
Duncane compeirit personallie and the said Alexander Saittone
being oft tymis callit compeirit nocht. The said Alexander Trumbill
was requyrit be the moderatour gif he hade ony farther to say
befoir the pronunsein of the brethreinis jugementis on the allegeance
alreddie made. He ansorit he hade nane. The brethrein, being
advysit with the haill allegeancis made *hinc inde*, findis na thing

T

relivant as yit allegit be the said Alexander Saittone nor Alexander Trumbill to stay the said mariage inrespect of Godis Word and answer made to the said allegeance, and thairfor ordanis Mr Henrie Layng, thair minister, to proceid in proclamatioun of the said promeis of mariage according to the ordur, and gif na farther impediment be opponit in the contrar that he solemnizat mariage betuix thame as apperteinis. Bot befoir the compleiting of the samin, the brethrein ordanis the said Johnne Duncan and Marione Trumbill to mak publict repentence in thair parroche kirk of S. Niniane for the fornicatione committit be thame on ane Sonday in tyme of sermond as the particular sessione of the said kirk sall appoint, and als that thai pay ane penaltie for satisfactione of the act of parliament made anent fornicatioun as thair particular sessione sall think meit, quhilkis beand done, that the said Mr Henrie proceid in mariage, as said is, gif na farther impediment be opponit in the contrar.

Robertsone contra *Richie*: The quhilk day ane summondis beand producit dewlie execute and indorsit upone Margaret Richie, dochtir to Thomas Richie, undir the castell wall of Sterling, chairgeing hir to compeir the said day to answer at the instance of Marjorie Robertsone in castell hill to ane complent gevin in be hir againis the said Margaret, compeirit the said Marjorie and producit the said summondis with ane bill of sclandir berand in effect that the said Margaret upone the vij day of Merche instant sclandirit hir and Hellein Aissone, hir oy, in thir wordis, sayand to the said Marjoreis self that scho hade tane thair cowis mylk fra thame and thane instantlie askit the samin fra hir agane for Godis saik. On the quhilk wordis the said Margaret Richie being examinat, scho confest scho said the samin, according to the bill in all, and desyrit ane day to be assignit to hir that scho may gif answer gif scho will tak upone hand to preive that the said Marjorie hes tane away the milk fra hir saydis cow be wichcraft or nocht. The brethir assignis to the said Margaret to gif hir answer on the xviij day of Aprill nixt, bayth the parteis warnit *apud acta*, and the said Marjorie Robertsone past fra the persute of the remanent sclandir conteinit in the said bill on hir oy, Hellein Aissone.

Mr William Patone: The quhilk day compeirit Mr William Patone, ane brothir of this exerceis, quha exponit to the brethrein that forsamekill as this lairge tyme past he hade exercesit with the brethrein and teichit publict doctrein, as he was appointit, hoiping to have bein placit ane pastour at sum kirk vacand within the boundis of this presbytery (gif the brethrein eftir tryell sould have fund him meit thairfoir) and now seing he can persave the par- rochinnaris of na kirk suttand him that hes ony rassonablle stipend appointit to gif ane pastour, thairfor he desyris the brethrein to gif him thair testimoniall of his habilitie to entir in the ministrie insafar as thay have hard direct to Mr Andro Clayhillis, minister at Jedward, and Mr John Knox, minister at Mewrus, and utheris brethrein in thais boundis. The brethrein, having hard the said Mr Williamis desyr and being advysit with the tryell of his doctrein alreddie tane, ordanis the commissionar and scrib to direct ane testimoniall to the personis foirsaidis in thair namis, testefeand thair tryell of him privatlie and publictlie in forme of exerceis sindrie tymis, as also in forme of publict doctrein publicklie, quhairof thai hade gude lyking and hopis he salbe ane proffitabill instrument in the kirk and knawis na thing in his lyf and conversatione bot gude and honestie.

Upone the nixt day of exerceis the iiij day of Aprill, 1587 the synnodall assemblie of this province was haldin in Dunblane, quhair the brethrein of this exerceis was present.

At Sterling the xj day of Aprill, 1587

Presentes: James Andirsone, Johnne Duncansone, Mr Henrie Layng, Alexander Fargy, ministeris; Mr Alexander Iull and Mr William Muresone, brethir of exerceis.

The said day James Andirsone propheceithe and Alexander Fargy addit thairto in the secund plaice, as thai war ordeinit.

Waltir Buchannan: The quhilk day ane summondis producit dewlie execute and indorsit upon Waltir Buchannan, brother to Johnne Buchannan of Arnepriour, chairgeing him to compeir the said day to gif ane confessione and declaratioun of his fayth and religioun and to subscryve the confessione of fayth subscryvit be the kingis majestie and his houshald undir the paine of excom- municatione, quhilk Waltir being oft tymis callit compeirit nocht, bot Mr Henrie Layng, minister at S. Ninianis kirk, producit ane misseive wreting send to him be Alexander Saittone of Gargunnok subscryvit be the said Walter and him (as appeiris) berand in effect that he behovit to keip ane tryst appointit at Kippen this day for addressein of materis neidfull to be schortlie handlit for staying of grit inconveniencis amangis freindis, and thairfor excusand his absence fra this assemblie this day and promesand to be present in our nixt assemblie personallie and answer to sic thingis as he salbe demandit of, as at mair lynthe is conteinit in the samin of the deat at Sterling, the x day of Aprill 1587. Quhilk wreting being red and considderit, the brethrein continewis farther proceidein againis the said Waltir to thair nixt assemblie, viz., the xviij day of Aprill instant in the samin forme and effect as the samin mater standis presentlie, with certificatione gif the said Waltir compeir nocht the said day, according to his said promeis, the brethrein will proceid thane as now, viz., to ordein the said Waltir to be summond of new *litteratorie* to heir and se him self decernit to be excommunicat as ane papeist, refusar to profes our religione, aggreing with the Word of God, and for disobedience to the kirk.

Adulteraris, Murdochsone, Waltir: Compeirit Thomas Murdoch-sone, within the parrochun of S. Niniane, and Euffame Waltir in Canglour, within the samin parrochun, and grantis thame to have committit adultrie togethir, the said Thomas beand mareit on Dorathie Buchannan, quha is yit alyve, and the said Thomas allegit that he mycht nocht compeir befoir the last synnodall assemblie hauldin in Dunblane, being swa neir to Mentayth, quhair the men of Mentayth hantis oft tymis berassone of the dedlie fed that remanis betuix the Grahamis in Mentayth and him as ane freind to the laird of Lecky, and thairfor desyrit that his absence fra the said synnodall assemblie sould nocht be hauldin disobedience, and quhatsoevir the brethrein wald injone for the said offence, the said Thomas and Euffame promesit to obey the samin. The brethrein dispensis with the absence of the said Thomas and Euffame fra the synnodall assemblie inrespect of the said deidlie feud knawin to be of varetie and ordanis thame and everie ane of thame to mak publict repentence in thair paroche kirk of S. Niniane ilk Sonday in thair awin clathis quhill the nixt synnodall assemblie to be hauldin in Sterling the first Twysday of October nixt, on the quhilk day the said Thomas and Euffame sall compeir befoir the samin assemblie in linning clathis and ressave sic farther injunctionis as thane salbe injonit to thame respective undir the paine of disobedience.

At Sterling the xviij day of Aprill, 1587

Presentes: James Andirsone, Mr Arthur Fethie, Andro Forester, Robert Mentayth, Alexander Fargy, Mr Henrie Layng, ministeris; Mr Alexander Iull and Mr William Moresone, brethrein of exerceis.

The quhilk day Alexander Fargy propheceithe and Robert Mentayth addit thairto in the secund plaice, as thai war ordeinit.

Waltir Buchannan: In the terme appointit to Waltir Buchannan, brother to Johnne Buchannan of Arnepriour, be him self in his awin misseive wreting producit the last sessione to compeir in this assemblie to answer to sic thingis as he salbe demandit of, the said Waltir being oft tymis callit compeirit nocht. Thairfor the brethrein ordanis the said Waltir to be summond *litteratorie* to heir and sie him self decernit to be excommunicat as ane papeist, refusar to profes our religione, aggreing with the Word of God, and to subscryve the confessione thairof subscryvit be the kingis majestie and his houshauld, and for disobedience to the kirk, with certificatioun and he failze the brethrein will proceid and decern, as said is, according to the Word of God.

Robertsone contra *Richie*: In the terme assignit to Margaret Richie, dochtir to Thomas Richie, to gif answer gif scho will tak upone hand to preive that Marjorie Robertsone hes tane away the milk fra hir fatheris cow be wichcraft or nocht, bayth the parteis comperand personallie, the said Margaret allegit that scho was nocht fullie advysit as yit with hir answer and thairfor desyris ane langer day to be assignit to hir to gif hir answer that in the mentyme scho may the bettir advys thairwithe. The brethrein yit as of befoir continewis the said mater, and ordanis the said Margaret Richie ather to tak upone hand to preive hir said allegeance on the said Marjorie to be of varetie on the xxv day of Aprill nixt or ellis the brethrein will decern the said Margaret ane idolater and ane sclanderer and to undirly sic disceplein thairfoir as thane salbe appointit, bayth the parteis warnit thairto *apud acta*.

Concerning tryell of Patrik Layng, William Sterling, Mr Adam Merschell, Richard Fleming: The brethrein undirstanding that be act of the last synnodall assemblie thay war ordeinit to proceid in tryell with Patrik Layng, William Sterling, Mr Adame Mairschell and Richard Fleming allegit ministeris, to try gif thay or ony of thame be abill and qualefeit to continew as pastoris and ministeris in the kirk, as at mair lynthe is conteinit in the said act, thairfor the brethrein ordanis all the saidis personis to be summond *litteratorie* to heir and sie farther tryell tane of thame and everie ane of thame concerning thair habilitie to bruik offeice as ministeris in the kirk, according to the said ordinance, undir the paine of disobedience.

Hendirsone, Forester: The quhilk day ane summondis beand producit dewlie execute and indorsit upone Johnne Hendirsone, yunger, baxter in Sterling, Hellein Forester, dochtir to umquhill George Forester in Schiphaucht, and Hellein Donaldsone, hir mother, chairgeing thame and Johnne Hendersone, elder, thair cautionar, to compeir the said day to gif answer quhy mariage is nocht desyrit to be solemnizit betuix the said Johnne Henderson, yunger, and Hellein Forester according to thair promeis made thairanent with consent of the said Hellein Donaldson, mother to the said Hellein Forester, in presens of James Duncansone, reder at Sterling, and to heir tryell tane thairanent, compeirit the said Johnne Hendirsone, yunger, and allegit the caus of nocht desyring of the said mariage to be compleit was nocht in him bot in the said Hellein Forester and hir mother quha, and the said Johnne Hendirsone, elder, being oft tymis callit, compeirit nocht. Thairfor the brethrein ordanis the saidis personis disobedient to be summond of new to the xxv day of this instant moneth to the effect foirsaid undir the paine off excommunicatioun, the said Johnne Hendersone, yunger, warnit thairto *apud acta*.

At Sterling the xxv day of Aprill, 1587

Presentes: James Andirsone, Andro Forester, Mr Henrie Layng, Robert Mentayth, ministeris; Mr Alexander Iull, ane brother of exerceis.

Robert Mentayth propheceithe and James Andirsone addithe thairto in the plaice ordinar of Mr Alexander Wallace, quha was nocht advertesit to keip the samin and thairfor it is jugit that he may nocht justlie be accusit for neglecting of the secund plaice.

Hendirsone, Forester: The quhilk day ane summondis beand producit dewlie execute and indorsit upone Hellein Forester, dochtir to umquhill George Forester in Schiphaucht, Hellein Donaldsone, hir mother, chairgeing thame and Johnne Hendirsone, elder, baxter, to compeir the said day to gif answer quhy mariage is nocht desyrit to be solemnizit betuix Johnne Hendirsone, yunger, baxter in Sterling, and the said Hellein Forester according to ane promeis made thairanent be thame with consent of hir said mother etc., undir the paine of excommunicatioun, compeirit the said Johnne Henderson, yunger, as he quha was warnit to this day *apud acta* in the last sessione and offirit to abyd tryell in the said mater. Compeirit siclyk the said Johnne Hendirsone, elder, and confessit that he become cautionar for performance of the said mariage be bayth the saidis parteis and offirit to undirly the brethrein jugementis thairanent. The saidis Hellein Forester and Hellein Donaldsone, being oft tymis callit, compeirit nocht. Thairfoir the brethrein ordanis the saidis personis disobedientis to be summond to the secund day of May nixt to heir and se thame selffis decernit to be excommunicat for thair contemp and disobedience to the kirk with certificatioun and thai failze the brethrein will proceid and decern, as said is, according to Godis Word, etc., the saidis Hendirsonis warnit thairto *apud acta*.

Robertsone contra *Richie*: In the terme assignit to Margaret Richie, dochtir to Thomas Richie, undir the castell wall of Sterling to gif answer gif scho will tak upone hand to prove that Marjorie Robertsone hes tane away the milk fra hir fatheris cow be wichcraft or nocht, bayth the parteis compeirand personallie, the said Margaret Richie refusit to prove hir said allegeance and thairfor refarrit hir self in the will of the brethrein for hir said wordis. The brethrein, being advysit with the said Margarettis confessione of the wordis abone specefeit and of hir confessione that scho askit the said milk againe fra the said Marjorie for Godis saik, findis the said Margaret to have committit idolatrie in seiking fra ane creatur, viz., the said Marjorie Robertsone, quhilk scho aucht onlie to have socht fra the Creator and findis hir also ane sclanderer of the said Marjorie in calling hir ane wiche, in effect, quhilk scho could nawayis preive to be of varetie, and thairfor the brethrein ordanis the said Margaret for hir said idolatrie to ask God forgevenes for the same and the congregatioun of Sterling, quhome scho hes sclandirit thairby, publictlie in the kirk of Sterling upone Sonday nixt immediatlie eftir the sermond and that scho than instantlie ask the said Marjorie forgevenes for sclandiring of hir innocentlie and confes that in swa doing scho offendit hir and now to grant scho knawis na thing to hir bot ane honest woman. [*In margin* : Satisfeit in all. J. Duncansone.]

Waltir Buchannan : The quhilk day ane summondis beand producit dewlie execute and indorsit upone Waltir Buchannan, brother to Johnne Buchannan of Arnepriour, chairgeing him to compeir the said day to heir and sie him self decernit to be excommunicat as ane papeist, refusar to profes our religione, aggreing with the Word of God, and to subscryve the confessione thairof, subscryvit be the kingis majestie and his houshald, and for disobedience to the kirk, as at mair lynthe is conteinit in the said summondis, the said Walter being oft tymis callit compeirit nocht, and the brethrein, being advysit with the indorsatione of the said summondis, findis thairby the said Waltir to be summond at his dwelling hous in Kippen, and the brethrein beand incertane gif the said Waltir dwellis in Kippen or nocht, thairfor thai think gude to continew the pronunsein of the decreit of excommunicatioun quhill he be summond of new, and ordanis that he be summond *litteratorie* in the samin forme and effect according to the summondis producit this day.

At Sterling the secund day of May, 1587

Presentes : James Andirsone, Patrik Gillaspie, Robert Mentayth, Mr Henrie Layng, Mr Alexander Wallace, Mr Adame Merschall, ministeris; Mr Alexander Iull and Mr William Moresone, brethir of exerceis.

Mr Alexander Wallace propheceithe, and the secund plaice vaikithe in absence of Mr Arthur Fethie quha sould have occupyit the samin.

Tryell off William Sterling : The quhilk day ane summondis beand producit dewlie execute and indorsit upone Patrik Layng, William Sterling, Mr Adam Merschell and Richard Fleming chairgeing thame to compeir the said day to heir and sie farther triall tane of thame and everie ane of thame concerning thair habilitie to bruik offeice in the ministrie, as effeiris, according to the ordinance of the last synnodall assemblie of this province made thairanent, compeirit William Sterling and allegit that he is alreddie examinat in his habilitie schort syne and as yit hes nocht gottin declaratur of the brethrenis jugementis thairupone and thairfore desyrit the brethreinis jugementis gevin alreddy upone his former tryell to be veseit and the extract thairof gevin unto him. The brethrein thinkis gude that thair jugementis gevin on the said tryell tane be revesit, and appointis the xvj day of May instant to pronunce thair declaratur thairupone, the said William warnit thairto *apud acta*.

Mr Adame Merschell: Compeirit Mr Adame Mairschell and offiris him self to tryell. The brethrein, undirstanding that as yit he hes nocht teichit on the last text that was appointit to him on the first day of November last bypast, thairfor ordanis him to teiche on ony Tuisday he plasis betuix and the xxiiij day of *Junij* nixt on the samin text, viz., the xj chaptur of S. Mathowis evangell, beginning at the 27 vers thairof to the end, and that privallie in forme of exerceis.

Richard Fleming: The said Richard Fleming being oft tymis callit compeirit nocht, bot for excuis of his absence thair was ane wreting producit subscryvit be the said Richard, as appeirit, berand in effect that he doth nather ryd nor gang berassone of infirmitie and seiknes and that he may nocht resort to our presbytery becaus he is nocht ablle of body nor yit hes expensis to travell with, beseiking thairfor the brethrein to suffir him remane with the presbytery of Linlythquow quhair he was befoir, as at mair lynth is conteinit in the said wreting. Inrespect of the quhilk wretein, the brethrein acceptis the samin as for lauchfull excuse for his absence this day and continewis farther tryell of the trewthe thairof to Andro Foresteris presens, quha dwellis nixt to him.

Patrik Layng: The said Patrik Layng being oft tymis callit compeirit nocht. Thairfor the brethrein ordanis the said Patrik to be summond of new to the effect foirsaid *litteratorie* undir the paine of excommunicatioun.

Cristane Jarvy, adultrix: The quhilk day Patrik Gillaspie, minister at S. Ninianis kirk, declairit to the brethrein that forsamekill as Cristane Jarvy, parrochinnar of the said kirk, was excommunicat for disobedience to the kirk conjonit with adultrie committit be hir with Johnne Knox in the said parrochun, and now be hir bill gevin in to the particular sessione of the said kirk declairit hir self penitent for the saidis offencis and offirit hir self in the will of the kirk thairfoir and desyrit to be absolvit fra the said sentence and ressavit againe in the bosum of the kirk, and thairfor the said minister, in name of his particular sessione, desyrit the brethreinis jugementis quhat answer thay sould gif to the said bill. The brethrein ordanis the said minister and sessione to try the said Cristanis repentence gif it be fenzeit or nocht according to the ordur usit be the kirk in sic materis, quhilk repentence beand fund unfenzeit that the said minister absolve hir fra the said excommunicatioun, according to the ordur, and thaireftir to compell hir compeir befoir the presbytery to ressave farther injunctionis to be injonit to hir for hir saidis offencis, according to the ordur.

Hendirsone contra *Forester*: The quhilk day ane summondis beand producit be Johnne Hendirsone, yunger, dewlie execute and indorsit upone Hellein Forester, dochtir to umquhill George Forester in Schiphaught and Hellein Donaldsone, hir mother, chairgein thame to compeir the said day to heir and sie thame selffis decernit to be excommunicat for thair contemp and disobedience to the kirk, as at mair lynthe is conteinit in the said summondis, compeirit the said Hellein Forester and Hellein Donaldsone, hir mother, quha being accusit for thair disobedience being twa severall tymis of befoir lauchfullie summond and wald nocht compeir, thay answerit the occasione thairof was be ignorance and knew nocht that thai aucht to compeir befoir ony assemblie bot the particular assemblie of thair awin parroche kirk. Nochttheles, thay offir thame selffis in the will of the kirk thairfoir. Inrespect quhairof, the brethrein continewis all farther proceidein for the said disobedience againis thame quhill thay be farther advysit. Farther, the said Hellein Forester and hir mother being examinat upone the caus quhairfor thay war first summond, to wit, quhy thay desyr nocht mariage to be solemnizit betuix the said Johnne Hendirsone, yunger, baxter, and the said Hellein Forester, according to ane mutuall promeis made thairanent be thame with consent of thair parentis in presens of the reder of Sterling, it was ansorit be all the saidis personis that they confessit the samin promeis of mariage was made withe consent, as said is. And the said Hellein Donaldsone allegit the stay thairof was only in hir that mycht nocht be lasarit nor could nocht gait thingis necisar for hir dochteris mariage nor banquet as yit. And the said Hellein and hir said dochter being desyrit to appoint ane uther day for completing of the samin with consent of the said Johnne as yit ansorit that presentlie thay was nocht resolvit thairwith and thairfor desyrit ane day to be assignit to thame that in the men tyme scho may advys quhat day thai will appoint. The brethrein assignis to thame to gif answer on the xvj day of May instant, baithe the parteis warnit thairto *apud acta*.

Buikis off disceplein, etc., to be producit: The quhilk day it is ordeinit that ilk minister and reder, ministratouris of baptisme and mariage within the boundis of this presbytery, produce thair buikis of disceplein with the register of all mariagis thai solemnizat, bairnis that they bapteis, the almus collectit for the pure at thair kirk duris with the rollis of the distributione thairof and the namis of the personis that deis within the parrochun on the nixt Twysday eftir midsomer nixt befoir the brethrein to be sein and considderit be thame and thaireftir to be redelyverit to the producear.

At Sterling the ix day of May, 1587

Presentes: James Andirsone, Andro Forester, Mr Henrie Layng, ministeris; Mr Alexander Iull, Mr Richard Wrycht, Mr Johnne Broun, Mr William Moresone and Patrik Layng, brethir of exerceis.

The making of the exerceis was neglectit this day in absence of Mr Arthur Fethie quha sould have made the same. And Andro Forester was present quha was appointit to ad in the secund plaice, reddie to keip the samin plaice gif the first plaice hade bein keipit.

Patrik Layng: The quhilk day ane summondis beand producit dewlie execute and indorsit upone Patrik Layng chairgeing him to compeir the said day to heir and se farther tryell tane of him concerning his habilitie to bruik offeice in the ministrie, as effeiris, according to the ordinance of the last synnodall assemblie of this province made thairanent undir the paine of excommunicatione, compeirit the said Patrik and offirit him self to tryell, quha, to that effect, is ordeinit to teiche in the publict exerceis and, in speciall, to teiche on the ordinar text of the exerceis in the secund plaice on the xxiij day of May instant, and that he be present at the exerceis on the xvj day of May instant quhair he may undirstand at quhat plaice the text beginnis quhairon he sould teiche on the said xxiij day of May.

Richerd Fleming: The quhilk day the moderatour, in name of the brethrein, declairit to Andro Forester, minister dwelland nixt to Richard Fleming, that at the command of the last synnodall assemblie he was summond to the secund day of May instant to heir and sie farther tryell tane of him concerning his habilitie to continew in the ministrie, quha compeirit nocht the said day bot send ane wreting, testefeand grit inhabilitie in his persone thruch seiknes and laik of mony to be his expensis quhairfor he desyrit the brethrein to excuse him for his absence, and thairfor the said Andro Forester is requyrit to declair the trewthe concerning his saidis excusis gif thay be of trewthe or nocht. The said Andro ansorit that he knew perfytlie be sycht of his persone and uthirwayis the said excuse to be of trewthe, bayth in seiknes in his person and scairsnes of silvir to be his expensis. Inrespect of the quhilk, the brethrein continewis farther tryell of him quhill thai be farther advysit and that the said Richard be mair abill to travell.

At Sterling the xvj day of May, 1587

Presentes: James Andirsone, Andro Forester, Patrik Layng, ministeris; William Sterling, Mr Richard Wrycht, Mr Alexander Iull and Mr William Moresone, brethir of exerceis.

The quhilk day Andro Forester propheceithe, as he was ordeinit, and the secund plaice vacand thruch the absence of Mr Arthur Fethie, quha sould have occupyit the samin, James Andirsone voluntarilie occupyithe the samin.

Hendirsone contra *Forester*: In the terme assignit to Hellein Donaldsone and Hellein Forester, hir dochtir, in Schiphaucht to gif answer quhat peremptur day thai will appoint for compleiting of mariage betuix Johnne Hendirsone, yunger, baxter in Sterling, and the said Hellein Forester, compeirit the said Johnne Hendirsone and Johnne Hendirsone, his father, and the said Hellein Donaldsone and hir dochtir, being oft tymis callit, compeirit nocht. Thairfor the brethrein ordanis the saidis personis disobedient to be summond be thair summondis to compeir befoir the particular sessione of the kirk of Sterling lyk as the saidis Johnne Hendirsonis, elder and yunger, ar summond *apud acta* to compeir befoir the samin sessione on the xviij day of this instant, and thair with ane consent to appoint ane peremptur day for completing of the said mariage with certificatioun, as effeiris, and to caus the samin promeis of mariage be lauchfullie proclamit in hir parroche kirk of S. Niniane, lyk as the samin is alreddy done in the said Johnnis parroche kirk of Sterling.

William Sterling: In the terme assignit be the brethrein to gif thair declaratur on thair jugementis gevin on the tryell alreddie tane of William Sterlingis doctrein, the said William comperand personallie, the brether findis be the actis made anent his formar tryell that his doctrein is sound aggreing with the annalagie of fayth bot nocht sufficient nather in expositione nor in edificatione as is requisit to be ane pastour burdenit with the weghtie offeice of ane minister in the kirk of God. Nochttheles, for avoyding of all occasione of sudden proceidein with the said William, the brethir thinkis gude that, as yit, he be farther tryit in manir follwing, to wit, first, in forme of exerceis privallie, secundlie, in forme of publict doctrein with applicationis privallie, thridlie, to answer to questionis on the commone placis and grundis of religione, and last to be tryit in lyf and conversatione according to the ordur, quhilk tryell being tane, the brethrein to pronunce thair jugementis thairon, as apperteinis. Farther, the said William Sterling being accusit for ministratione of the sacrament of baptisme, sen he was dischairgit be the brethrein fra exercesein and usein of all farther functione in the kirk excep onlie to reid, and in speciall for baptezein of ane bairne gottin in fornicatioun be William Fargy on [*blank*] within the parrochun of S. Niniane, the kirk nocht beand satisfeit, and without testemoniall of the minister of the parrochun quhair the samin was borne, the said William confessit the ministratione of the sacrament of baptisme to sindrie bairnis and in speciall the said William Fargyis bairne, bot allegis that the said William Fargy fand cautione to him of befoir that he sould satisfie the kirk for his said fornicatione. Nochttheles, he confessis in doing of the samin he hes offendit, for the quhilk he offiris him self in the will of the brethrein of this presbytery. The brethrein continewis thair jugementis in the saidis offencis quhill thai be farther advysit, and in the mentyme ordanis the said William Fargy to be summond *litteratorie* to compeir befoir this presbytery to answer and undirly disceplein for the said fornicatioun, and to answer farther, as he salbe requyrit, undir the paine of disobedience.

Waltir Buchannan: The quhilk day ane summondis beand producit dewlie execute and indorsit upone Waltir Buchannan, brother to Johnne Buchannan of Arnepriour, chairgeing him to compeir the said day to heir and se him self decernit to be excommunicat as ane papeist, refusar to profes the religione, authoresit be the kingis majestie and his thre esteattis of this realm, aggreing with the Word of God, and to subscryve the confession thairof, subscryvit be his majestie and his houshauld, and for disobedience to the kirk quha, being oft tymis callit, compeirit nocht. Nochttheles, the brethrein considdering the weghtines of the sentence of excommunicatioun gif thai proceid this day, as justlie thay may, and inrespect of the absence of sum discreit brethrein, thay continew the pronuncein of thair decreit off excommunicatioun to the penult day of July instant, and ordanis the said Waltir to be summond thairto in the samin forme and effect as he was summond to this day.

Concerning absens off rederis fra the synnodall: The brethrein undirstanding that forsamekill as be act of the last synnodall assemblie Robert Mentayth, yunger, reder at Alvayth, Symone Pattone, reder at Glendoven, Johnne Hammiltoun, reder at Bothkenner, and Alexander Cuthbert, reder at Falkirk, ar convict everie ane of thame in ane certane penalty for thair absence fra the said last synnodall assemblie and the moderatour of the presbytery ordeinit to caus uplift the samin and to be answerabill thairfoir to the nixt synnodall, as at mair lynthe is conteinit in the ordinance made thairupone, thairfor the brethrein ordanis the saidis rederis to be summond *litteratorie* to produce and delyvir thair penalteis respective, quhilk thay and everie ane of thame ar decernit respective to pay be the said ordinance for thair absence fra the said assemblie, undir the paine of disobedience.

Absens of Patrik Layng fra the synnodall: The quhilk day Patrik Layng, beand requyrit to produce his penaltie quhairin he was convict be act of the last synnodall assemblie haldin at Sterling for his absence thairfra on the secund day thairof, ansorit that he mycht nocht tarie the said day for laik of expensis. Nochttheles, he refarris him self in the will of the nixt synnodall assemblie thairfoir, to the quhilk tyme the brethrein continewis the uplifting of his penaltie.

Thomas Potraill, adulterar and incestuus: Compeirit Thomas Potraill in Ester Greinyairdis within the parrochun of S. Niniane and confessis him self to have committit adultrie with Marione Stein, sister to Jonet Stein, presentlie his wyf, and is with bairne to him, for the quhilk he offeris him self in the will of the kirk. The brethrein findis that the said Thomas hes committit adultrie and incest with the said Marjorie and thairfor is ordeinit to compeir befoir the nixt synnodall assemblie of this province to be hauldin in Sterling the first Twsday of October, thair to ressave injunctionis to be injonit to him for his said offence and to obey the samin undir the paine of disobedience.

At Sterling the xxiij day of May, 1587

Presentes: James Andirsone, Mr Arthur Fethie, Robert Mentayth, Alexander Fargy, Mr Henrie Layng, ministeris; Mr Alexander Iull and Mr William Moresone, brethir of exerceis.

Tryell of Patrik Layng: Mr Richard Wrycht propheceithe on the x chaptur to the Hebrewis beginnand at the 19 vers thairof inclusive to the 24 vers of the samin exclusive, and Patrik Layng addithe thairto in the secund plaice, according as he was ordeinit for ane part of the tryell of his doctrein. The brethrein continewis thair jugementis on the said Patrikis doctrein quhill thay heir him teiche the vj day of *Junij* nixt in the first plaice on the ordinar text of the exerceis and thane to juge on baithe.

Mr Arthur Fethie: Mr Arthur Fethie, being accusit for his absence fra the exerceis thir mony dayis past and for neglecting of teiching in the secund plaice thairof as he was ordeinit, ansorit that he was nocht advertesit to keip the secund plaice nather of the tymis that he was absent nather personallie nor be word nor wret that he ressavit, bot confessit that he was in Angus sen he was last present doand sum necissar bissines, quhilk the brethrein tryit and admittit the samin for lauchfull excuse of his absence.

We, the brethrein of the presbytery of Sterling undirsubscrivand, undirstanding the travellis and painis susteinit be our brother James Duncansone in wrettein in our sessionis and assembleis and doing thairin the offeice of ane clark as appertenis sen Witsonday in *anno* etc., four scoir, sex yeiris without ony recompance or gratitude

provydit to him thairfoir as yit, for remade quhairof we, the said
brethrein, with ane consent aggreis and voluntarlie promesis for
the present necessitie to content to pay to him ten pundis mony of
feall thairfoir yeirlie at twa termis in the yeir, Witsonday and
Mertimes, be equall portionis ay and quhill we obtein to him ane
better feall thairfoir uthirwayis, the first yeiris paymentt thairof to
begin at the feast of Witsonday in this instant yeir of God im vc
lxxxvij yeiris. Quhilk soume we, and everie ane of us respective,
voluntarlie oblesis us to pay to the said James at the termis foirsaidis,
during the said speace according as it is devydit and particularlie
indorsit in ane uthir tickat subscryvit also with our handis respective.
In witnes quhairof, we have subscryvit thir presentis with our
handis in this our assemblie haldin at Sterling, day [and] yeir foirsaid.
[*Blank space for signatures follows.*]

   Cristane Jarvie, adultrix: Compeirit Cristane Jarvie in Carnok and
confessis hir to have committit adultrie with Johnne Knox in
Auchinbowie, mareit, for the quhilk (as scho confessis) scho
compeirit befoir the synnodall assemblie of this province and
ressavit injunctionis injonit to hir for the samin, quhilk injunctionis
scho wald nocht obey, and thairfoir was excommunicat fra the
societie of the kirk, bot thruch the mercie of God scho hes repentit
[of, *deleted*] hir disobedience and unfenzitlie confessit hir said offence
of adultrie and hes offirit hir self in the will of the kirk thairfoir. In
respect quhairof, and eftir dew tryell tane of hir said repentence
be the particular sessione of hir parroche kirk of S. Niniane, thay
be advys of this presbytery hes absolvit hir fra the sentence of
excommunicatioun, at quhais command the said Cristane compeiris
this day and offiris hir self reddie to obey quhat the brethrein of this
assemblie will injone to hir. The brethrein, being advysit with the
said Cristanis confessione, ordanis hir to mak publict repentence in
hir said parroche kirk of S. Niniane ilk Sonday in hir awin clathis
quhill the nixt synnodall assemblie to be hauldin in this brugh on
the first Twysday of October nixt, on the quhilk day the said
Cristane sall compeir in linning clathis and thair to ressave sic
farther injunctionis as than salbe injonit to hir for hir said adultrie
undir the paine of disobedience.

   James Wilsone, fornicatur: The quhilk day Robert Mentayth,
minister at Alvayth, declairit to the brethrein that forsamekill as

thair is ane man dwelland within his said parrochun callit James
Wilsone, son to Andro Wilsone thair, quha hes fallin in the fourt
fault of fornicatioun with thre soverall wemen, and thairfor inquyrit
of the brethir quhat he sould do thairwith. The brethrein ordanis
the said James Wilsone to be summond *litteratorie* to compeir befoir
thame to ressave injunctionis for the said offence undir the paine
of disobedience.

At Sterling the penult day of May, 1587

Presentes: James Andirsone, Mr Arthur Fethie, Andro Forester,
Robert Mentayth, Mr Alexander Wallace, Mr Adame Merschell,
Mr Henrie Layng, Alexander Fargy, Patrik Layng, ministeris;
William Sterling; Mr Alexander Iull, Mr William Moresone and
Mr Richard Wrycht, brethir of exerceis.

The quhilk day Mr Arthur Fethie propheceithe and Mr Henrie
Layng addithe thairto in the secund plaice as thay war ordeinit.

Rober[t] Mentayth, reder: The quhilk day ane summondis beand
producit dewlie execute and indorsit upone Robert Mentayth,
yunger, reder at Alvayth, Symon Patone, reder at Glendoven,
Johnne Hammiltone, reder at Bothkenner, and Alexander Cuthbert,
reder at Falkirk, chairgeing thame to compeir the said day to
produce and delyvir thair penalteis respective, quhilk thai and ilk
ane of thame ar decernit to pay be the last synnodall assemblie for
thair absence thairfra as at mair lynthe is conteinit in the said
summondis, compeirit the said Robert Mentayth and allegit the
caus of his absence fra the said assemblie was first inrespect of
his fathiris presence thairat quha was minister of the said kirk
quhilk he thocht sould have bein sufficient, secundlie, inrespect
of non payment of his stepend and thairthrw wantit to sustein
his expensis quhilk rassonis he remittit to be jugit on be the
brethrein.

Symone Patoun: Compeirit Symone Patoun and allegit that his
wyf was new delyvir of hir birthe the tyme of the last synnodall
assemblie and was in grit dainger of hir lyf and thairfoir could
nocht lave hir, quhilk was the caus of his absence thairfra.

Johnne Hammiltoun: Compeirit Johnne Hammiltoun and allegit
that the tyme of the last synnodall assemblie his mother was dedlie

U

seik and thairfor remanit with hir to confort hir quhilk was the
caus of his absence thairfra.

Alexander Cuthbert: Compeirit Alexander Cuthbert and allegis
that he was seik the tyme of the last synnodall assemblie lyk as he
was befoir and sensyne, quhilk was the caus of his absence thairfra.

Quhilkis excusis allegit be all the saidis personis, the brethrein
tryit and fand thame of varetie and thairfoir admittit thame respective as rassonablle, and farther the brethrein having tryit thair
diligence in thair offecis respective and thair lyf and conversatione
findis nathing in nane of thame reprovablle, and thairfor exhortis
thame to continew in thair officis as becumis.

Thomas Wilsone, fornicatur: The quhilk day ane summondis
beand producit deulie execute and indorsit upone James Wilsone,
sone to Andro Wilsone in Alvayth, chairgeing him to compeir the
said day to ressave injunctionis to be injonit to him for fornicatioun
committit with Chathrein Peresone thair, and that as for the
fourt fault in his persone, as at mair lynthe is conteinit in the said
summondis, compeirit the said James Wilsone and grantis him to
have committit fornicatione with Helleson Clark, secundlie with
Jonet Edmane, relaps, and now the fourt tyme with the said
Cathrein Peresone, for the quhilk he offiris him self in the will of
the kirk. The brethrein ordanis the said James to mak publict
repentence, in his awin parroche kirk four soverall Sondayis in
tyme of sermond, bair fuittit in linning clathis for his said offence.

Waltir Buchannan: The quhilk day compeirit Waltir Buchannan,
brother to Johnne Buchannan of Arnepriour, and grantit him self
summond be William Sterling to compeir this day to the effect
conteinit in the summondis, viz., to heir and sie him self decernit
to be excommunicat as ane papeist, refusar to profes the religione
authoresit be the kingis majestie and his thre esteattis of this realme,
aggreing with the Word of God, and to subscryve the confessione
thairof and for disobedience to the kirk, as at mair lynthe is conteinit thairin, quhairof he confessis him self to have ressavit ane
copie delyverit to him be the said William and als ressavit the
principall summondis for inspectione, quhilk he deteinit in his
awin handis as yit. Eftir the quhilk confessione, the said Waltir
was requyrit be the moderator to declair quhy he frequentit nocht
sermondis and confirrence with sum of the brethrein of the ministrie

sen the xxiiij day of Januar last as he was thane ordeinit, ansorit
that he frequentit his awin parroche kirk of Kippen sensyn to
quhome the moderator declairit that the samin was na obedience
to the said ordinance becaus thair was na minister in that kirk that
hade powar to preiche bot simplie to reid allanirlie. Secundlie, being
requyrit to renunce the papisticall errur and to profes and subscryve
our religione aggreing with the Word of God, the said Walter
ansorit that he was nocht resolvit thairwith as yit concerning the
trewthe and rycht wirschipping of God and thairfor desyrit ane
day as yit to be assignit to him to advys with his answer. The
brethrein being myndfull to remove all occasione that he may
have to allege sudden procedein againis him albeit he hes hade
alreddy sufficient tyme to advys with his said answer, to witt, the
speace of four moneth bypast, nochttheles the brether as yit assignis
to him the xiij day of *Junij* nixt tocum to gif his resoluit answer
quhethir he will imbrais our religione or nocht. And that as for
the last day that was in thair handis to appoint unto him, inrespect
of the neir approching of the conventione of the generall assemblie
in the quhilk the brethrein ar bund to declair and report thair
diligence quhat thai have done concerning the said mater. Als the
said Waltir Buchannan is ordeinit yit as of befoir to frequent and
keip the sermondis preichit be godlie ministeris and quhair he
douttis to confer with sum of the discreit brethrein in thir boundis
quhome he plasis thairby to declair apperancis that he meinis to
have knawlege of the trewthe and to embrais the samin. Attour,
the said Waltir being inquyrit gif his wyf was delyvir of hir birthe
as yit or nocht, the said Waltir answerit and confessit that scho
was delyvir of ane maidin bairn and allegit the samin was nocht as
yit bapteizit. And being desyrit gif he wald promeis to present the
samin bairne to be baptezit according to the Word of God and
ordur reformit in the kirk of Scotland and desyr the samin sacrament to his bairne, he wald mak na direct answer thairto bot
promesit to gif answer thairto on the said xiij day of *Junij* nixtocum,
quhilk continewatioun was grantit be the brethrein siclyk.

Hendirsone contra *Forester*: The quhilk day ane summondis beand
producit deulie execute and indorsit upone Hellein Forester and
Hellein Donaldsone, hir mother, chairgeing thame to compeir the
said day to answer at the instance of Johnne Hendirsone, yunger,

making mentione that albeit the said Johnne Hendersone and Hellein Forester, with consent of thair parentis, in presens of the particular sessione of the kirk of Sterling and Mr Henrie Layng, minister at the said Helleinis parroche kirk, grantit mutuall promeis of mariage is made be thame ilk ane to utheris and appointit ane peremptur day for completing of the samin, nochttheles the said Hellein Donaldson, mother to the said Hellein Forester, sensyne hes past fra the said mariage and dischairgit the said Mr Henrie Layng of ony proclamatione of the samin, and thairfor chairgeing thame as said is to underly disceplein for thair said inconstancie and to declair ane rassonablle caus thairfoir, as at mair lynthe is conteinit in the said summondis, compeirit Johnne Hendersone, persewar, and the said Hellein Donaldsone personallie, quhilk Hellein, being desyrit to declair the caus of hir said inconstancie, could declair na rassonablle caus and thairfor inrespect the brethrein undirstude that the saidis Johnne Hendirsone and Hellein Forester was willing to compleit the said mariage lyk as the said Hellein Foresteris brother was siclyk myndit thairto, thairfor the brethrein ordanis the minister of S. Ninianis kirk to proceid in proclamatioun of the said promeis and to thair mariage gif na farther impediment be opponit agains the samin, nochtwithstanding of the said dischairge of hir mother.

At Sterling the vj day of *Junij*, 1587

Presentes: James Andirsone, Alexander Fargy, Andro Forester, Mr Henrie Layng, ministeris; Mr Alexander Iull, Mr Richard Wrycht, Mr William Moresone and Patrik Layng, brethir of exerceis.

Tryell off Patrik Layng: The quhilk day being assignit to Patrik Layng to gif ane tryell of his doctrein be teichein on the ordinar text of the exerceis, compeirit the said Patrik and teichit on the said text in forme of exerceis as he was ordeinit, viz., on the 10 chaptur to the Hebrewis beginning at the 28 vers thairof inclusive to the 32 vers thairof exclusive publictlie. Quhais doctrein being hard and the brethreinis jugementis cravit thairon and on his doctrein in his additione made in the secund plaice of exerceis the xxiij day of May last, the samin doctrein was fund to be aggreabill with the annalagie of fayth, inrespect quhairof the brethir admittis him to teiche in the publict exerceis.

Laird off Pantascan, adulterar: The samin day compeirit Johnne Levingstone of Pantaskan and grantis him to have committit adultrie with Cristane Waen, for the quhilk he confessis him self to be penitent and repentis of the samin in signe and taikin quhairof he hes put away the said woman furth of his societie, for the quhilk offence he remittis him self in the brethreinis will. The brethrein, praisein God for the said confessione and exhortein him to continew in that esteat and to abstein fra the lyk in the said Cristanis persone and all uthir wemen besyd his awin wyf, thocht gude nocht to continew the geving of injunctionis to him for the said offence quhill the nixt synnodall assemblie of this province, for sindrie gude rassonis knawin to the brethrein. Thairfoir thay ordeinit him fra this furth to mak publict repentence in his awin clathis ilk Sonday in his awin parroche kirk that his minister is thair quhill the nixt synnodall assemblie of this province to be hauldin in the kirk of Sterling the first Twysday of October nixt, on the quhilk day he sall compeir thane and ressave sic injunctionis as the said assemblie sall injone to him undir the paine of dis-obedience, and that he nawayis ressave the said Cristiane Waen in societie with him againe frathisfurth.

Decreit betuix Hendirsone and Forester: The quhilk day compeirit Johnne Hendirsone, yunger, baxter in Sterling, and producit ane summondis dewlie execute and indorsit upone Hellein Forester, dochtir to umquhill George Forester in Schiphaucht, and Hellein Donaldsone, hir mother, makand mentione anent the promeis of mariage made betuix the said Johnne Hendirsone and Hellein Forester, with consent of thair parentis, eftir tryell being tane thairintill be the brethrein upone the penult day of May last bypast thay commandit the samin to be lauchfullie proclamit and mariage solemnizit betuix thame, as the said act beris at lynth, nochttheles sensyne bayth the saidis parteis hes with ane consent cancellat and distroyit the matremoniall contract made thairupone, as was allegit, and thairfor chairgit the said Hellein Forester and Hellein Donald-sone to compeir the said day to heir and sie the brethreinis declaratur pronuncit decerning the said Johnne frie to marie in the Lord, nochtwithstanding of the promeis foirsaid and the said Hellein

Donaldsone decernit for hir oft inconstancie to pay the penaltie
conteinit in the said act of the general assemblie and the said Hellein
and hir dochtir foirsaid to undirly disceplein for sclandering of the
kirk thairby, with certificatioun and thai failze the brethrein will
proceid and decern, as said is, according to Godis Word, as at mair
lynthe is conteinit in the said summondis. The saidis Hellein Forester
and Hellein Donaldsone being oft tymis callit compeirit nocht.
Thairfor the brethrein being advysit with the haill proces deducit
in the said mater findis the said Hellein Donaldsone to have bein
varie inconstant concerning the said promeis oft and dyveris tymis
sen the making thairof and ane grit stayer of hir dochtir in performing of the samin and lykwys findis hir said dochtir now at
last inconstant siclyk for nocht abyding thairat, and thairfoir
decernis the said Johnne Hendirsone fre to marie in the Lord
nochtwithstanding of the said contract inrespect thair hes bein na
carnall copulation betuix the said Hellein Forester and him, and
for the said Hellein Donaldsonis oft inconstancie and diswading of
hir said dochtir to compleit the said mariage according to hir said
promeis, ordanis hir to mak publict repentence in the parroche
kirk of Sterling upone ane Sonday quhen scho salbe warnit thairto
be the officier of this presbytery, undir the pane of disobedience,
for away taking of the sclandir of the said inconstancie done to
the said kirk be proclamein of the said promeis thairin being the
said Johnnis parroche kirk at the command of the said Hellein
Forester, Hellein Donaldsone and the said Johne Hendirsone and
nocht compleiting of the mariage according thairto, and als decernis
the said Hellein Donaldsone to pay x libis., mony to be applyit
ad pios usus according to ane act of the generall assemblie made
thairanent, and farther inhibittis and forbiddis thair minister of
Sanct Ninianis kirk and all uthir ministeris and rederis that nane of
thame minister ony benefeit of the kirk to the said Hellein Donaldsone nor hir dochtir ay and quhill thay satisfie our said decreit in
all pointis alsweill the said penaltie as in repentence as thay and
everie ane of thame will answer upone thair obedience to the kirk.

At Sterling the xiij day of *Junij*, 1587

Presentes: James Andirsone, Robert Mentayth, Alexander Fargy,

Mr Henrie Layng, Mr Adame Mairschell, ministeris; Mr Alexander
Iull and Mr Richard Wrycht, brethir of exerceis.

The quhilk day Mr Alexander Iull propheceithe and Mr Richard
Wrycht addithe thairto according as thay was ordeinit.

Waltir Buchannan: In the terme assignit to Waltir Buchannan,
brother to Johnne Buchannan of Arnepriour, to gif his resoluit
answer gif he will renunce the erruris of the papeistis and profes
and subscryve our religione aggreing with the Word of God or
nocht, compeirit the said Waltir personallie, quha being desyrit to
satisfie the desyr of the terme, viz., to gif his resoluit answer to the
premissis, seing he hes hade sufficient tyme to advys with the samin,
the said Waltir ansorit that he could nocht embrais our religione
presentlie, berassone the samin wald be the tinsall of his wyffis
heritage and leving, quhilk scho hade in Flandiris, and thairfor, yit
as of befoir, desyrit continewatione quhill he tuke ordur thairwith.
The moderator ansorit that the brethrein wald nocht continew him
farther in that respect becaus the samin rassone being alreddie
allegit be him was repellit be the brethrein. Attour, he being
requyrit be the moderatour quhy he frequentit nocht sermondis and
confirrence of brethrein sen the penult of May last, as he was
thane ordeinit, ansorit that thais pairttis of Kippen quhair he
dwellis is undir sic feir of brokin heland men that he could nocht
have his awin dwelling for sudden persute be thame in the cuntrie.
Mairattour, the moderator desyrit the said Waltir to remembir the
grit lavitie that hes bein usit towardis him in granting unto him
varie lairge tyme to advys with his answer and as yit can gait na
direct answer nor na kynd of apperance that he meinis to be
instructit in the rycht worschepping of God according to his Word
berassone he hes nevir bein sein at ane preichein sen he last returnit
in the cuntrie nather yit wald he evir desyr ony confirrence of
brethrein to resolve him of douttis gif he ony hade, and thairfor
his suttein of langer continewatioun apperis to the brethrein to be
rather to drift tyme nor uthirwayis, nochttheles as yit gif he will
promeis and thairupone find cautione undir the paine conteinit in
the act of parliament made anent sic materis that within the speace
of fourtie dayis nixt heirefter he sall athir embraice our religione
and subscryve the confessione of fayth or ellis he and his wyf
within the samin speace to depairte af the cuntrie according to the

lawis of the realme quhairby the sclandir in his persone and wyfis may be tane away, and gif he was nocht resolvit presentlie quhethir he wald do the samin or nocht, the moderatour desyrit him to promeis to compeir befoir the nixt generall assemblie to be haldin in Edinburgh the xx day of this instant moneth and thair to promeis the samin or ellis to satisfie thame uthirwayis. The said Waltir ansorit that he culd nocht mak the said promeis presentlie nather yit wald he compeir befoir the said generall assemblie to the effect foirsaid, nathir wald he appoint na peremptur day quhowsone he wald do ane of thame becaus as yit he was nocht resolvit thairwith in conscience, bot promesis to keip his parroche kirk on the Sabboth day in tyme of serveice and quhen he cumis to the toun of Sterling he sall resort to the sermondis and confer with sum of the ministrie, and in the mentyme sall nocht be sclanderus in word nor behaviour, quhilk being provin, he is content and consentis presentlie to be excommunicat without ony farther proces. Attour, the said Waltir being requyrit gif he wald desyr his maidin bairne, quhairof his wyf is lichter, to be baptezit according to the ordur approvit be the reformit kirk of Scotland and to declair the tyme quhen he will desyr the samin according to his promeis made on the penult day of May last bypast, the said Waltir ansorit that he was nocht yit resolvit quhowsone he wald desyr his said bairne to be baptezit, nather yit wald he promeis directlie to desyr the said sacrament to his said bairne according to the said ordur. And swa (as appeirit) the said Waltir schew litill or na apperance that he is myndit to embraice our religione aggreing with the Word of God, nochttheles the brethrein continewis the pronuncein of thair jugementis on the said answeris quhill thay be advysit with the nixt generall assemblie of the kirk.

Commissionaris to the nixt generall assemblie: The samin day the brethrein hes electit and nominat Mr Arthur Fethie and Andro Forester, ministeris, to pas with James Andirsone, minister, commissionar within the boundis of this province, as commissionaris for this presbytery to the nixt generall assemblie of the kirk to be hauldin in Edinbrugh the xx day of this instant moneth of *Junij* to concur with the said assemblie for traittein of thais thingis concerning the weill and gude ordur to be observit within the kirkis of the said presbytery and haill kirk within this realme that may tend to the glorie of God and promotione of his Word within the samin.

Presentatioun of littis furth of the quhilk ane minister to be admittit to S. Ninianis kirk: The quhilk day compeirit Alexander Saittone of Gargunnok and Duncan Narne of Lokishill, twa of the commissionaris conteinit in the supplicatione undir specefeit, and in the name of the parrochinnaris of S. Ninianis kirk producit ane supplicatione berand in effect that be the deathe of umquhill Patrik Gillaspie, thair minister, thair kirk was presentlie destitut of ane pastur. Thairfoir thai thocht gude to nominat and present to the brethrein the personis follwing, viz., Maister Henrie Layng, Mr Robert Cornwell, Mr Henrie Levingstone, quhome thay desyr the brethrein to try and examin alsweill in literatur as in thair lyvis and conversatione and thaireftir thay that is fundin maist apt to be minister in the said kirk to be presentit to the particular assemblie of the said parroche kirk, thair to be voittit be thame quhome thai sould think maist meit to the said offeice, and thaireftir that persone to be admittit pastour to the said kirk according to the ordur, as the samin supplicatione subscryvit be sindrie of the saidis parrochinnaris in the self at mair lynthe beris. With the quhilk, the brethrein being advysit thocht gude and ordeinit the saidis Maisteris Henrie Levingstone and Henrie Layng to be tryit according to the desyr of the said supplicatione becaus thai war bayth personallie present lyk as also offirit to try the said Mr Robert Cornwall siclyk, quhowsone he wald compeir and offir him self thairto, and thairfor appointis Mr Henrie Layng to mak the exerceis the nixt day on the ordinar text thairof, viz., on the 10 chaptur of the epistill wrettin to the Hebrewis beginning at the [*blank*] vers thairof, and Mr Henrie Livingstone to ad thairto in the secund plaice.

Atour, the brethrein undirstandein that the nixt day of exerceis is nocht to be for the speace of fyftein or xx dayis to cum, inrespect of the generall assemblie that conveinis the xx day of this instant moneth, viz., on the ordinar day of exerceis in this brugh, and becaus nane of the brethrein of this presbytery hes hard the said Mr Henrie Levingstone teiche in publict exerceis at ony tyme heirtofoir, thairfor thinkis gude at his awin desyr that he teiche first privallie on the xviij day of *Junij* instant eftir none in presens of swa mony of the brethrein as may be present the samin tyme on the beginning of the fyft chaptur of the epistill wrettin to the Romanis and that in forme of exerceis.

Tryell of Mr Adame Mairschell: The quhilk day being appointit to Mr Adame Mairschell to gif ane tryell privallie in forme of exerceis on the text gevin to him on the first day of November last bypast, the said Mr Adame compeirit and in presens of the brethrein foirsaid teichit on the said text privallie, viz., on the xj chaptur of S. Mathowis evangell beginning at the 27 vers thairof inclusive unto the end of the chaptur. Quhais doctrein being hard, and the brethreinis jugementis thairon cravit, thay find that he hes nocht satisfeit thame thairin in sic sort that he hes atteinit to the mening of the Spirit of God on this text as becumis, and thairfoir thinkis him nocht meit to be admittit to the secund point of tryell, viz., to exerceis publictlie. Nochttheles, inrespect of absence of sum discreit brethrein and that thair voittis be nocht prejugit, it is thocht gude as yit and the brethrein hes appointit him to teiche privallie on the 3 chaptur of Johnnis evangell beginning at the 16 vers thairof at thir wordis: for God so lovithe the warld, etc., to be teichit in forme of exerceis, and to prepair him self to teiche the samin on sic day as he salbe warnit thairto eftir the desolving of the generall assemblie of the kirk.

At Sterling the xviij day of *Junij*, 1587

[*Presentes*]: James Andirsone, Mr Duncane Andirsone, and Mr Henrie Layng, ministeris; Mr Alexander Iull and Maister Richard Wrycht, brethir of exerceis.

Tryell of Mr Henrie Levingstone: The quhilk day, being appointit to Mr Henrie Levingstone to gif ane tryell prevallie in forme of exerceis on the text appointit to him, compeirit the said Mr Henrie, quha in presens of the brethrein foirsaid teichit on the said text, viz., on the beginning of the fyft chaptur of the epistill wrettin to the Romanis to the 2 vers thairof exclusive, quhais doctrein being hard and the brethreinis jugementis thairon cravit, the samin was jugit to be sound doctrein aggreing weill with the purpos and mynd of the apostill in the said plaice and thairfor the brethrein admittis him to teiche in the publict exerceis according as he was appointit in the last sessione.

Upone the xx and xxvij dayis of *Junij* the brethrein was absent fra the exerceis inrespect of the generall assemblie.

At Sterling the iiij day of July, 1587

Presentes: James Andirsone, Johnne Duncansone, Mr Arthur Fethie, Alexander Fargy, Robert Mentayth, Mr Alexander Wallace, Mr [Henrie] Layng, ministeris; and Mr Alexander Iull, ane brother of exerceis.

Tryell of Maisteris Henrie Layng and Henrie Levinstone: The quhilk day being appointit to Mr Henrie Layng to mak the exerceis and Mr Henrie Levingstone to ad in the secund plaice upone the ordinar text, viz., on the 10 chaptur of the epistill wrettin to the Hebrewis, beginning at the [*blank*] vers thairof, and that for tryell of thair habilitie quha is maist ablle to be admittit minister at S. Ninianis kirk, compeirit bayth the saidis personis and teichit as thay war ordeinit on the said text, quhais doctrein being hard and the brethreinis jugement thairon cravit, the samin was fund sound and proffitablle, and thairfor the brethrein praisis God. Yit for farther tryell of the said Mr Henrie Levingstone, the brethrein ordanis him to teiche publictlie in forme of exerceis on the nixt text follwing the said text teichit this day, and Mr Alexander Wallace to ad to him in the secund plaice on the nixt Twysday eftir the returning of the commissionaris frome the parliament.

At Sterling the viij day of August, 1587

Presentes: James Andirsone, Johnne Duncansone, Mr Henrie Layng, Mr William Cwper and Mr Alexander Wallace, ministeris; and Mr Alexander Iull, ane brother of exerceis.

Tryell of Mr Henrie Levingstone: The quhilk day being appointit to Mr Henrie Levingstone to mak the exerceis on the ordinar text thairof as for ane part of his tryell to knaw gif he be qualefeit to be admittit ane minister of the evangell to S. Ninianis kirk or nocht and appointit siclyk to Mr Alexander Wallace to ad in the secund plaice conforme to the ordur, bayth the saidis personis compeirit and teichit as thay war ordeinit on the said text, viz., on the beginning of the 11 chaptur to the Hebrewis to the 4 vers thairof exclusive, quhais doctrein being hard and the brethreinis jugementis thairon cravit, the samin was fund sound and proffitablle, bot thair jugementis being cravit on the said Maister Henreis doctrein onlie in speciall, seing the samin is ane point of his tryell and gif thay ar satisfeit with him concerning this point, viz., his teichein in forme of exerceis, inrespect this is the thrid tyme he hes teichit in that forme, first privallie, secundlie in adding in the secund plaice in the exerceis and, thridlie, this tyme, the brethrein jugis the said Mr Henreis doctrein this day to be sound and proffitablle according to the purpois of the apostill and mening of the said text. Inrespect quhairof and of his doctrein hard of befoir, thay content thair selffis presentlie with the tryell tane concerning his teichein in form of exerceis and thinkis gude to proceid in the secund point of tryell with him, viz., to knaw his forme of publict doctrein with applicationis, and thairfor ordanis him to teiche publictlie in the kirk of Sterling in presens of the congregatione thairof on the xvij day of August instant on the iij chaptur of S. Johnis evangell at the beginning thairof in the forme foirsaid.

Mr Henry Layng: The samin day the moderator declairit to the brethrein that forsamekill as the parrochinnaris of S. Ninianis kirk in ane supplicatione gevin in be thame hes desyrit the brethrein to try the qualificatioun of Mr Henrie Layng gevin up in lit be thame with utheris conteinit in the said supplicatioun quhairof thay may have ane minister admittit to thame, and seing that the said Mr Henrie Layng gaif ane tryell to the brethrein befoir he was admittit coadjutor with umquhill Patrik Gillaspie, last minister at the said kirk lyk as he hes bein hard sindrie tymis sensyne, thairfor it is askit of the brethrein gif thay will content thame selffis with the tryell alreddie tane of the said Mr Henrie or gif thai will tak tryell of him of new. The brethrein with ane consent contenttis thame selffis presentlie with the tryell alreddie tane of the said Mr Henrie Layng quhill thay have tryit the remanent presentit or to be presentit be the saidis parrochinnaris and continewis thair juge-mentis concerning his habilitie to be onlie minister in the said kirk till have thay have [*sic*] tane full tryell, as said is.

William Sterling: The brethrein undirstandein that albeit thay have ordeinit William Sterling to be tryit of new according to the ordinance of the last synnodall assemblie quhairbe thay may undirstand gif he be worthie to continew a minister in the kirk or nocht, nochttheless as yit thair is na particular text appointit to him, thairfor the brethrein ordanis the said William to be summond to the xv day of this instant moneth to heir and sie farther tryell tane concerning his habilitie to continew and beir offeice in the ministrie undir the paine of disobedience.

At Sterling the xv day of August, 1587

Presentes: James Andirsone, Mr Arthur Fethie, Andro Forester, Alexander Fargy, Mr William Cwper, Mr Henrie Layng, Robert Mentayth, Mr Alexander Wallace, ministeris; Mr Alexander Iull and Mr Richard Wrycht, brethir of exerceis.

The quhilk day James Andirsone propheceithe and Mr William Cwper addithe in the secund plaice as thay war ordeinit.

Fargy, fornicatur: The quhilk day ane summondis beand producit dewlie execute and indorsit upone William Fargy chairgeing him to compeir the said day to heir and se him self decernit to have committit fornicatione with [*blank*] in S. Ninianis parrochun and to undirly disceplein thairfoir, as effeiris, and to answer farther thairanent as he salbe requyrit undir the paine of disobedience, quhilk William being oft tymis callit compeirit nocht, thairfor the brethrein ordanis the said William to be summond of new to the effect foirsaid undir the paine of excommunicatione.

William Sterling: The quhilk day ane summondis beand producit, dewlie execute and indorsit upone William Sterling chairgeing him to compeir the said day to heir and sie farther tryell tane of him concerning his habilitie to continew and beir offeice in the ministrie, compeirit the said William, quha being requyrit to declair the trewthe gif he ministrat the sacrament of the Lordis Supper to the parrochinnaris of Kippen at peace last or thairby or nocht, the said William confessit the samin, and thairfor the moderatour in name of the brethrein declairit to him that he hade gritlie offendit in melling with sa weghtie ane actione, he being nocht onlie suspendit fra ministratioun of the sacramentis bot also fra all offeice in the kirk excep onlie redein contenuallie sen the moneth of September last bypast, as ane act made thairupone beris. Lykas also he confessit of befoir that sen his said suspentione he nocht onlie ministrat the sacrament of baptism to bairnis lauchfullie gottin, bot also to William Fargeis bairne gottin in fornicatione, the kirk nocht beand satisfeit thairfoir, and that besyd mony uthir his offencis conteinit in the actis of this presbytery, for the quhilk it is declairit unto him that he deservis *simpliciter* deprivatione fra all offeice in the kirk. Nochttheles, the brethrein continewis thair jugementis pronuncein quhill thay be farther advysit concerning the saidis offencis and presentlie for farther tryell of his habilitie ordanis him to teiche privallie in forme of exerceis on the xviij chaptur of S. Mathowis evangell beginning at the 7 vers thairof and to tak swa meikill thairof as he plasis and that on the xxij day of August instant, and presentlie of new suspendis him that as of befoir fra all offeice in the kirk excep onlie simpill reidein, proclaming of bandis of mariagis and solemnizatione of mariagis, according to the ordur allanirlie, withe certificatione and he mell with ony farther ather in teichein, exhortein, ministratione of the sacramentis or ather of thame, he salbe deprivit *ipso facto* without ony farther proces, and this suspensione to continew ay and quhill the brethrein be tryell find him meit and ablle to continew a minister in the kirk and thairfor admit thairto *de novo*.

At Striviling the xvij day of August, 1587, beand ane ordinar preichein day in the kirk of Sterlin

Presentes: James Andirsone, Johnne Duncansone, Alexander Fargy, Mr William Cwper, Mr Andro Yung and Mr Andro Yung [*sic*], assessur, ministeris; Mr Alexander Iull, Mr Richard Wrycht and Mr Johnne Millar, brethir of exerceis.

Tryell off Mr Henrie Levingstone: The quhilk day being appointit to Mr Henrie Levingstone to teiche publictlie in the pulpet of Sterling on the iij chaptur of S. Johnis evangell in forme of publict doctrein with applicationis and that for tryell of him in the secund point appointit for examinatioun of personis presentit to the ministrie, the said Mr Henrie having teichit thairon to the 6 vers of the samin exclusive and the brethreinis jugementis thairon cravit, the samin was fund sound doctrein and proffitabill, aggreing weill with the text and the forme prescryvit to him. Nochttheles for farther tryell of him in the samin point, the brethrein ordanis him

to teiche publictlie in the kirk of Sterling on the xxiiij day of this
instant moneth on the iij chaptur of S. Johnis evangell foirsaid
beginning at the 14 vers of the samin in the forme foirsaid with
applicationis.

At Sterling the xxij day of August, 1587

Presentes: James Andirsone, Johnne Duncansone, Mr William
Cwper, Mr Alexander Wallace and Robert Mentayth, ministeris;
Mr Alexander Iull and Mr Richard Wrycht, brethir of exerceis.

The quhilk day Mr William Cwper propheceithe, as he was
ordeinit, and Johnne Duncansone at the desyr of Alexander Fargy
and in his plaice addithe thairto. Quhilk Alexander send excuse for
his absence this day, quhilk was admittit.

William Sterling: The quhilk day being assignit to William
Sterling to teiche privallie on the xviij chaptur of S. Mathowis
evangell beginning at the 7 vers thairof in forme of exerceis, thair
was producit ane misseive wretein send be the said William berand
ane excuse of his noncomperance to teiche as he was ordeinit.
Quhilk excuse was admittit be the brethrein for this day and
ordanis him to prepair him self to teiche on the said text in manir
foirsaid on ony Twysday he plasis betuix and the fyft day of
September nixt. Off the quhilk ordinance, the clark is ordeinit to
mak him advertesit.

Mr William Cowper ordeinit to be placit: The quhilk day compeirit
William Mure in Bathkenner and declairit that the brethrein of
the last generall assemblie hade admittit Mr William Cowper ane
minister of the Word of God and sacramentis, quhome thay hade
appointit to be thair ordinar pastour, and thairfor the said William
for him self and in name of the remanent parrochinnaris desyrit the
brethrein to appoint ane brother to plaice the said Mr William
Cowper pastour to thair said kirk, according to the ordur. Quhilk
desyr was thocht rassonablle, and thairfoir ordeinit James Andirsone,
minister at Sterling, commissionar, to pas to the said kirk ony
Sonday he thocht meit, thair to notifie to the parrochinnaris thairof
his said admissione and to desyr thame to signifie thair consent, as
effeiris, to the said Mr William. Lyk as the said Mr William sall
declair him self willing to accept the samin burdein on him. Quhilk

being declairit affirmative that the samin plaice him ordinar pastor thairat, acceptand promeis of the parrochinnaris that thai sall obey thair said pastour according to Godis Word swalang as he continewis faythfull in his offeice and that the said Mr William promeis solemlie that he salbe ane trew and faythfull pastour to that flock, according to his calling swafar as it sall plais God to assist him with his Holie Spirit.

Potraill, Stein, adulteraris: The samin day compeirit Thomas Potraill in Ester Greinyairdis within the parrochun of S. Niniane and confessis that Marione Stein is lichter of ane bairne gottin be him in incest and adultrie, as his confessione thairof made of befoir at lynthe beris, and desyrit ane command to the minister of his parroche kirk to bapteis the said bairne and he sould obey the kirk as he salbe commandit. The brethrein ordanis the said Thomas to caus cautione be actit in the commissaris buikis of Sterling that the said Thomas and Marione Stein sall compeir befoir the nixt synnodall assemblie of this province to be hauldin in the kirk of Sterling the first Twysday of October nixt, thair to ressave injunctionis to be injonit to thame for adultrie and incest committit be thame and to obey the samin injunctionis, ilk person undir the paine of fourtie pundis mony, quhilk being done, the brethrein ordanis the said bairne to be baptesit.

William Kay and Elizabeth Galbrayth, adulteraris: The quhilk day ane summondis beand producit dewlie execute and indorsit upone William Kay in Arncumrie, within the parrochun of Kippen, and Elizabeth Galbrayth, spous to Donald Neilsone in Campsie, chairgeing thame to compeir the said day to heir and sie tham selffis decernit to have committit adultrie togethir and to underly disceplein thairfoir undir the paine of disobedience, quhilkis personis being oft tymis callit compeirit nocht, thairfor the brethrein ordanis the saidis personis to be summond *de novo* to the effect foirsaid undir the paine of excommunicatione.

Anent chusein of ane minister to S. Ninians kirk: The quhilk day the brethrein undirstanding that forsamekill as according to the desyr of ane supplicatione presentit to thame in name of the parrochinnaris of S. Ninians kirk thay ar enterit in tryell of certan personis gevin up thairin in lit as also will try ony uthir personis that the saidis parrochinnaris sall nominat and present and thaireftir sall

juge as apperteinis, nochttheles befoir the brethreinis declaratur thairin (as thai ar informit) thair is ane particular assemblie of sum of
the elderis and deacunis and utheris of the said parrochun to be
hauldin at the said kirk on the xxv day of this instant moneth of
August to elect and admit ane minister to the said kirk, quhilk is
plaine repugnant to Godis Word and gude ordur, gif swa be, seing
the admissione of all ministeris is onlie in the handis of the presbyteriis and utheris assembleis of ministeris. Thairfor the brethrein
ordanis thair clark to direct inhibitione inhibitand and dischairgeand
Mr Henrie Layng and utheris to be convenit in the said assemblie
that thai unnawayis proceid to the electione nor admissione of ony
man to be minister in the said kirk the said day nor at na tyme
frathynefurth quhill the brethrein pronunce thair jugementis
concerning the habilitie and qualificatioun of the personis alreddie
presentit or to be presentit to us to the effect foirsaid, with certificatioun gif thay do in the contrar the brethrein will decern thair
procedeinis null and of na availl, certefeand thame also that thay sall
admit na minister to the said kirk quhill the parrochinnaris be first
hard in geving thair consentis, according to the ordur.

At Sterling the xxiiij day of August, 1587

Presentes: James Andirsone, Johnne Duncansone, Robert Mentayth, Mr Andro Yung, Mr Alexander Wallace, Mr Andro Murdo,
ministeris; Mr Alexander Iull and Mr Richard Wrycht, brethir of
exerceis.

Mr Henrie Levingstone: The quhilk day being appointit to Mr
Henrie Levingstone to teiche publictlie in the pulpet of Sterling
on the iij chaptur of S. Johnis evangell in forme of publict doctrein
with applicationis, on the quhilk chaptur the said Mr Henrie having
teichit beginning at the 14 vers thairof to the 16 vers of the samin
exclusive and the brethreinis jugement thairon cravit, the samin
was fund sound doctrein and proffitabill aggreing weill with the
mynd of the Spirit of God in that plaice and to the forme of teichein
prescryvit to him. Inrespect quhairof and of the doctrein teichit be
him of befoir in the samin forme on the xvij day of this instant
moneth, the brethrein contentis thame self with this point of tryell
and ar satisfeit with the said Mr Henrie concerning the samin, and

x

seing he is ane in lit cravit be the parrochinnaris of S. Ninianis kirk to be minister to thame, the brethrein thinkis gude and hes ordeinit the said Mr Henrie to teiche in the said kirk on Sonday the iij day off September nixt to the effect thay may heir him teiche, lyk as thay have hard Mr Henrie Layng ane uthir in lit cravit to the effect foirsaid sindrie tymis of befoir, and that the elderis and deacunis and utheris discreit personis of the said parrochun be requyrit to convein thame selffis in ane assemblie immediatlie eftir the sermond to advys quhow thai find thame selffis edefeit with the said Mr Henreis [sic] Levingstonis doctrein, and to caus report thair juge-ment thairof to our assemblie to be hauldin in the kirk of Sterling the fyft day of September nixt that we may be resolvit thairof befoir the pronuncein of our declaratur, and als ordanis Mr Henrie Layng on Sonday nixt to mak intimatioun to the saidis parrochin-naris that the said Mr Henrie Levingstone is ordeinit to teiche to thame on Sonday nixt thaireftir the iij day of September nixt to the effect foirsaid.

At Sterling the xxix day of August, 1587

Presentes: James Andirsone, Alexander Fargy, Robert Mentayth, Mr Alexander Wallace, Mr William Cowper, Mr Henrie Layng, ministeris; Mr Alexander Iull, Mr Richard Wrycht, brethir of exerceis.

The quhilk day Alexander Fargy propheceithe and Robert Mentayth addithe thairto as thay war ordeinit.

Adulteraris, William Kay, Elezabeth Galbrayth: The quhilk day ane summondis beand producit dewlie execute and indorsit upone William Kay in Arncumrie and Elezabeth Galbrayth, spous to Donald Neilsone in Campsie, chairgeing thame to compeir the said day to heir and sie thame selffis decernit to have committit adultrie and to undirly disceplein thairfoir undir the paine of excommuni-catioun, compeirit the said William and grantis carnal deill with the said Elezabeth, quhais husband he grantis to be alyve, and as concerning the said Elezabeth it was testefeit that presentlie scho was seik and thairfor the brethrein continewis thair answer to the said William quhill he and the said Elizabeth be summond *de novo*.

William Fargy, fornicatur: The quhilk day ane summondis beand

producit dewlie execute and indorsit upone William Fargy chairgeing him to compeir the said day to heir and sie him self decernit
to have committit fornicatioun with Agnes Stein in S. Ninianis
parrochun and to underly disceplein thairfoir as effeiris and to
answer farther thairanent, as he salbe requyrit undir the paine of
excommunicatioun, quhilk William being oft tymis callit compeirit
nocht, thairfor the brethrein ordanis him to be summond to heir
and sie him self decernit to be excommunicat for his contemp and
disobedience to the voice of the kirk conjonit with the said offenc
of fornicatioun with certificatioun and he compeir nocht the
brethrein will decern, as said is, according to the Word of God and
disceplein of the kirk havand the warrand thairof thairin.

At Sterling the fyft day of September, 1587

Presentes: James Andirsone, Andro Forester, Alexander Fargy,
Robert Mentayth, Mr Henrie Layng, Mr Duncane Andirsone,
ministeris; and Mr Richard Wrycht, brother of exerceis.

Robert Mentayth propheceithe, as he was ordeinit, and Mr
Henrie Layng addithe in plaice of Mr Alexander Wallace quha
excusit his absence in the last sessione, quhilk was admittit.

William Fargy, fornicatur: The quhilk day compeirit William
Fargy and grantis that he committit fornicatione with twa sindrie
wemen, first, with Elezabeth Wys in Sterling, secundlie, with
Agnes Stein in Carsie, and being requyrit quha baptezit the bairne
gottin on the said Elezabeth Wys, he ansorit that the samin was
ded borne. As concerning the secund bairne, he confessis that
William Sterling baptezit the samin, beand presentit to him be
Andro Ure in name of the said William Fargy, quhilk was done
be his solistein and fand cautione that he sould satisfie the kirk for
the samin. The brethrein ordanis the said William to satisfie the
act of parliament made anent fornicatioun and to mak publict
repentence in the parroche kirk of Sterling the nixt Sonday for his
said first fault of fornicatioun committit in Sterling and to mak
publict repentence in S. Ninianis kirk the nixt twa Sondayis
thaireftir for his secund offence of fornicatione committit in the
parroschun thairof.

Mr Henrie Levingstone: The samin day compeirit Duncane Narne of Lokishill, as commissionar for the particular sessione of the parroche kirk of S. Niniane, and producit thair answer concerning the doctrein teichit be Mr Henrie Levingstone in thair kirk on Sonday last, berand in effect that the haill elderis and deacunis thane present, being requyrit quhat frute and edificatione thay hade ressavit be his doctrein, answerit all in ane voice that thay war gretumlie edefeit thairby and praisit God for the gude apperance thay fand in that mane, as at mair lynthe is conteinit in the samin. With the quhilk the brethrein being advysit efter tryell tane of the parrochinnaris present the said day, it was fund that thair was bot ane few numbir of thais that dwellis bewast the said kirk present and thairfor the brethrein hes ordeinit the said Mr Henrie Levingstone to teiche in the said kirk, yit as of befoir, on Sonday the xvij day of September instant and that the elderis, deacunis and utheris discreit personis of the said parrochun be requyrit to convein in ane assemblie immediatlie eftir the sermond to advys quhow thay find thame selffis edefeit with his doctrein and to caus report thair jugementis thairof to our assemblie to be hauldin in the kirk of Sterling the xix day of September instant that the brethrein may be resolvit thairof befoir the pronuncein of thair declaratur, and als ordanis Mr Henrie Layng to teiche in the said kirk on Sonday nixt and to mak intimatione to the saidis parrochinnaris that the said Mr Henrie Levingstone is ordeinit to teiche to thame on Sonday nixt thaireftir to the effect foirsaid.

Mr Hew Myllis: The quhilk day compeirit Mr Hew Myllis, servand presentlie to the Lady Burlie, quha declairis that [he] is varie willein to entir in the ministrie and thairfor ernistlie desyris the brethir to tak ane tryell of him concerning his habilitie thairto. The brethrein, praisein God for his godlie and lauchfull desyr, appointis him to teiche on the 4 chaptur of the 1 epistill to Timothie beginning at the 12 vers thairof to the end of the chaptur privallie in forme of exerceis upone the xix day of this instant moneth of September.

Sessio 2a

Tryell of William Sterling: The samin day William Sterling teichit privallie on the xviij chaptur of S. Mathowis evangell, beginning at the 7 vers thairof to the 12 vers of the samin exclusive, quhais doctrein being hard and the brethreinis jugement thairon cravit, the said William was fund nawayis to have opnit up the said text according to the mening of the Spirit of God thairin. Inrespect quhairof, he is jugit to be ignorant of the scripturis, nocht instructit thairin him self meikilles abill to instruct utheris. Nochtheles, the brethrein continewis the pronuncein of thair jugementis concerning his habilitie to continew in the ministrie to the xxvj day of September instant, on the quhilk day it is thocht gude that ane uther text be appointit to him to teiche in presens of the nixt synnodall assemblie privallie in forme of publict doctrein with applicatiounis, and that for his farther tryell, to the quhilk day he is warnit *apud acta*.

At Sterling the xij day of September, 1587

Presentes: James Andirsone, Johnne Duncansone, Mr Arthur Fethie, Andro Forester, Mr William Cowper, Mr Adame Merschall, Alexander Fargy, Mr Henrie Layng, ministeris; and Mr Alexander Iull, ane brother of exerceis.

Mr Henrie Layng propheceithe in the placie and at the desyr of Mr Alexander Wallace and Andro Forester addithe in the secund plaice as he was ordeinit.

Adulteraris, Harvie and Yung in Bothkenner: The quhilk day ane summondis beand producit dewlie execute and indorsit upone William Harvie and Marione Yung in the parroschun of Bothkenner, allegit adulteraris, chairgeing thame to compeir the said day to heir and sie thame selffis decernit to have committit adultrie togethir, to undirly disceplein thairfoir, and to separat thame selffis undir the paine of disobedience, quhilkis personis being oft tymis callit compeirit nocht, thairfor the brethrein ordanis thame to be summond *de novo* to the effect foirsaid undir the paine of excommunicatione.

Sessio 2a

Mr Adame Mairschell: The quhilk day Mr Adame Mairschell having teichit privallie on the 3 chaptur of S. Johnis evangell beginning at the 16 vers thairof to the 18 vers of the samin exclusive, quhais doctrein being hard and the brethreinis jugement thairon cravit, thay juget the said text to be nawayis opnit up according to the mening of the Spirit of God thairin and the said

Mr Adame thocht to be ignorant of the scripturis and nocht abill to instruct utheris thairin. Nochttheles the brethrein continewis the pronuncein of thair jugement concerning his habilitie to continew in the ministrie to the xxvj day of September instant on the quhilk day, it is thocht gude that ane uthir text be appointit unto him to teiche in presens of the nixt synnodall assemblie privallie in forme of publict doctrein with applicatiounis and that for his farther tryell to the quhilk day he is warnit *apud acta.*

At Sterling the xix day of September, 1587

Presentes: James Andirsone, Mr Arthur Fethie, Robert Mentayth, Alexander Fargy, Mr Henrie Layng, Mr William Cowper, Mr Duncane Andirsone, ministeris; Mr Richard Wrycht, ane brother of exerceis.

The quhilk day Andro Forester, minister at Falkirk, sould have propheceithe and Mr Alexander Wallace sould have occupyit the secund plaice, as thay war ordeinit of befoir, quha bayth neglectit the samin. Nochttheles laist the making of the exerceis sould have fallit this day, Mr Henrie Layng propheceithe and James Andirsone occupyithe the secund plaice.

Andro Forester, Mr Alexander Wallace: The samin day ane misseive beand producit concerning the excuse of Andro Forester for his absence this day, quhilk being red and considderit, the samin was fund na wayis rassonablle and thairfor he was decernit to pay x s. in penaltie according to the generall act made anent thais that neglectis the making of the exerceis. As concerning Mr Alexander Wallace becaus he hes send na excuse for his absence thairfor, the brethrein continewis pronuncein of declaratur againis him quhill he be first hard to answer for him self.

Mr Henrie Levingstone: The samin day compeirit Duncane Narne of Lokishill as commissionar for the particular sessione of the parroche kirk of S. Niniane and producit thair answer concerning the doctrein teichit be Mr Henrie Levingstone in thair kirk on Sonday last, berand in effect that ane lairge numbir of the elderis and deacunis of the said kirk with sindrie gentill men being conveinit and requyrit quhat frute and edificatione thay had ressavit be his doctrein answerit all in ane voice that thay fand thame selffis meikill profetit thairby and was varie weill satisfeit thairwith, for the quhilk thay praisit the Eternall, and thairfor desyrit the brethrein to proceid in geving and pronuncein thair declaratur, quhilk of the personis conteinit in the parrochinnaris supplicatione thay find maist meit and qualefeit to accept the waightie burdein of that ministrie within the said parrochun and to admit him thairto, quhilk thay crave the brethrein maist ernistlie to do with diligence that thair kirk be nocht destitut of ane pastour, as at mair lenthe is conteinit, in the samin. With the quhilk, the brethrein being advysit, the brethrein yit as of befoir hes ordeinit the said Mr Henrie Levingston to teiche in the said parroche kirk of S. Niniane upone Sonday nixt the xxiiij day of September instant, to the effect that all present the said day may heir his doctrein quhairof it may be that sum of thame have nocht hard him of befoir and that the elderis and deacunis and utheris discreit personis of the said parrochun be requyrit to convein in ane assemblie immediatlie eftir the sermond, and thair eftir gude advysment declair to the commissionaris undirwrittin quhow thay ar edefeit with the said Mr Henrie Levingstonis doctrein, and be quhilk of the doctreinis teichit be the said Mr Henrie Levingstone or Mr Henrie Layng thay ar maist edefeit, and farther to answer to sic thingis as thay salbe requyrit of be our commissionaris, to wit, our brother Mr Richard Wrycht and James Duncansone, our clark, or ony of thame, and to caus report thair oppinionis faythfullie to us in our nixt assemblie to be hauldin in the kirk of Sterling the xxvj day of September instant be our said commissionaris with sum of thair awin numbir to be conjoint with thame. Upone the quhilk ordinance, the brethrein ordanis [thair scrib, *deleted*; the moderator in thair name becaus thair scrib is ane of the commissionaris abone writtin (*signed*) J. Duncansone, *substituted in margin*] to direct testificatione in wret, quhilk thay ordan the said Mr Henrie Levingstone to notifie to the said parrochinnaris to be conveinit the said day.

Mr Arthur Fethie: Compeirit Mr Arthur Fethie, minister at Airthe, and producit ane ordinance of the generall assemblie, of the dait at Edinburgh the xx day of May the yeir of God im vc lxxxvj yeiris, subscryvit be Mr James Richie, clark thairof (as appeiris), upone the bak of ane bill producit be him befoir the said assemblie, berand the wordis follwing: The generall assemblie ordanis the commissionaris to travell with the modefearis and to sie the complenar weill providit or ellis with advys of the presbytery to tak ordur for his transportatione quhair he may be provydit. According to the quhilk and inrespect James Andirsone, minister of Sterling, commissionar within thair boundis, hes according to the said ordinance travellit with the modefearis to have gottin sum augmentatione to the said Mr Arthur for his serveice bot gat na thing, and als becaus it hes plasit the kingis majestie to gif him the personage of Kinnell and thairfor detbund to sairve thair desyris lycence of the brethrein to transport him self fra Airthe to Kynnell. Quhilk commissionar being requyrit be the brethrein to testefie the trewthe quhat he hes done in said mater, quha testefeis that he hes done for his part according to the said Mr Arthuris declaratioun in all pointis and obteinit na thing. Inrespect quhairof and berassone the said Mr Arthur is detbund to serve at the kirk of Kinnell for the caus foirsaid, thairfor according to the said ordinance of the generall assemblie, the commissionar with the advys of the brethrein grantis him libertie to transport him self fra the kirk of Airthe quhair he presentlie servis to the said kirk of Kinnell, provyding alwayis that he se the kirk of Airthe provydit of ane sufficient pastor befoir his passing thairfra.

Adulteraris in Bathkenner, Harvy, Yung: The quhilk day ane summondis beand producit dewlie execute and indorsit upone William Harvy and Marione Yung, parrochinnaris in Bothkenner, chairgeing thame to compeir the said day to heir and sie thame self decernit to have committit adultrie and to undirly disceplein thairfoir and to seperat thame selffis undir the paine of excommunicatione, compeirit the said William and grantis that he was mareit with Cathrein Car, quhome he allegis departit fra him the speace of xx yeiris syne or thairby, and confessis that sen his said mariage he hes hade carnall copulatione with the said Marion Yung, quha is presentlie with him in hous, quhilk William is ordeinit to seperat him self fra the said Marione with all diligence and nocht to repair to hir ony way under the paine of excommunicatione, and that he compeir befoir the nixt synnodall assemblie of this province haldin in the kirk of Sterling the iij day of October nixt to ressave injunctionis to be adjonit to him for his said offence of adultrie undir the paine of excommunicatione, and the said Marione being oft tymis callit compeirit nocht. Thairfore the brethrein ordanis hir to be summond *litteratorie* to heir and sie hir self decernit to be excommunicat for hir contemp and malicius disobedience to the voice of the kirk conjonit with hir said offence of adultrie, with certificatioun and scho failzie the brethrein will proceid and decern hir to be excommunicat, as said is, according to the Word of God and disceplein of the kirk havand the warrand thairof thairin.

Sessio 2a 19 Septembris

Triall of Mr Hew Myllis: The quhilk day being assignit to Mr Hew Myllis to teiche privallie in forme of exerceis on the 4 chaptur of the 1 epistill to Timothie beginning at the 12 vers of the samin, compeirit the said Mr Hew and teichit on the said text to the 15 vers of the samin exclusive in manir foirsaid in the Latein langage, quhilk being hard and jugit upone, the brethrein is nocht satisfeit with his opnein up of the mening of the text and thairfor thinkis him nocht meit to be admittit to the secund point of tryell bot ordanis him to teiche privallie in the samin forme in Ingillis langage on the xxvj day of September instant upone the viij chaptur of S. Markis evangell beginning at the 34 vers thairof.

At Sterling the xxvj day of September, 1587

Presentes: James Andirsone, Mr Duncane Andirsone, John Duncansone, Andro Forester, Mr Henrie Layng, ministeris; Mr Alexander Iull, Mr Richard Wrycht, brethir of exerceis.

Andro Forester, minister at Falkirk, propheceithe as he was ordeinit and the secund plaice, vacand in absence of Mr Alexander Wallace quha sould have occupyit the samin, Johnne Duncansone addithe. The samin day the said Andro Forester was requyrit to pay x s. of penaltie, as he was ordeinit in the last sessione, for nocht making of the exerceis on the samin day as he was ordeinit and becaus the excuse of his absence than send was repellit. The said Andro answerit that he sould pay the samin sasone as he gaittis in his stepend.

Mr Henrie Levingstone: The quhilk day compeirit Mr Richard Wrycht, James Duncansone, commissionaris for the brethrein

appointit to the effect undirwrittin, and Duncane Narne of Lokishill, in name of the particular sessione of the kirk of S. Niniane, and
producit thair jugement concerning the doctrein teichit be Mr
Henrie Levingstone in thair kirk on Sonday last, berand in effect
that ane grit assemblie of the elderis, deacunis, barronis and gentill
men of the said kirk being conveinit, and being requyrit [*recte*,
inquyrit] quhow thay war edefeit with the said Mr Henreis doctrein
answerit all in ane voice that thai war meikill profitit thairby and
lykit varie weill of the samin, and farther being inquyrit quhethir
thay fand thame selffis maist edefeit be the said Mr Henreis doctrein
or Mr Henrie Layngis and quhilk of the saidis twa personis thay
wald rathest that the presbytery sould appoint to be thair minister,
to the quhilk the saidis parrochinnaris answerit that thay wald
continew thair declaratur on that hed to Twysday the iij day of
October nixt, and that at the request of my lord of Cambuskynneth
quha promesit to report to the synnodall assemblie of this province
to be hauldin in the kirk of Sterling the said day ane answer fra
David Home quhethir gif he wald accept on him the ministrie of
the said kirk as was appointit be the generall assemblie or nocht,
as at mair lynth is conteinit in the samin. With the quhilk, the
brethrein being advysit hes thocht gude to continew farther
procedein in the said mater to the said iij day of October nixt, and
the said Mr Henrie Levingston offiris to studie the commone
placis and grundis of religione quhairby he may be prepairit to
answer thairon the said day gif the brethrein of the said assemblie
sall than think gude to examin him thairof, to the quhilk the
brethrein consentis.

Waltir Buchannan: The quhilk day compeirit Waltir Buchannan,
brother to Johnne Buchannan of Arnepriour, and desyrit of the
brethrein that thai sould continue farther procedein againis him
anent the craving ane confessione of his fayth and religione, berassone he was to depart schortlie furth of this cuntrie and promesis
faythfullie to depart furth of the same betuix and the ellevin day
of November and the faist of Mertimes nixttocum without farther
delay. With the quhilk desyr the brethrein being advysit, James
Andirsone, commissionar and moderator in this assemblie, in the
name of God and his kirk present, admonesit the said Walter
Buchannan to profes and subscryve the reformit religione professit

publictlie within this realme and to renunce all contrar religione thairunto, speciallie the heresie of the papeistis, betuix and the feast of Mertimes nixt (gif he be than present in the realme) undir the paine of excommunicatioun and this for the first admonitione.

Tryell off William Sterling, Mr Adame Mairschell: In the terme assignit be the brethrein to pronunce thair jugementis concerning the habilitie of Mr Adame Mairschell and William Sterling to continew in the ministrie, compeirit the said William Sterling, quha is appointit to teiche on the xviij chaptur of S. Mathowis evangell, beginning at the 12 vers thairof privallie in forme of publict doctrein on the iij day of October nixt in presens of the synnodall assemblie of this province to be convenit in this plaice for the tym, to the quhilk day the brethrein continewis the pronuncein of thair jugement concerning his habilitie to continew in the ministrie. As tuichein Mr Adame Mairschell, he being oft tymis callit compeirit nocht. Thairfor the brethrein ordanis him to teiche the said day in presens of the samin assemblie on the iij chaptur of S. Johnis evangell, beginning at the 18 vers thairof privallie in forme of publict doctrein, to the quhilk day the brethrein continewis the pronuncein of thair jugement concerning his habilitie to continew in the ministrie. Off the quhilk ordinance and continewatione, the brethrein ordanis James Duncansone, thair clark, to mak dew intimatione to him in wret that he may be prepairit thairfoir as apperteinis.

Patrik Layng: The brethrein ordanis Patrik Layng to teiche on the xj chaptur of S. Mathowis evangell, beginning at the 18 vers thairof, on the iij day of October nixt in presens of the nixt synnodall assemblie of this province to be hauldin in this plaice the said day and that privallie in forme of publict doctrein. Off the quhilk ordinance, the brethrein ordanis James Duncansone, thair scrib, to mak dew intimatione in wret and also thairby to warne him to compeir the said day to heir and sie the brethreinis jugement pronuncit concerning his habilitie to continew in the ministrie.

Sessio 2a

Tryell of Mr Hew Myllis: The quhilk day being assignit to Mr Hew Myllis to teiche privallie in forme of exerceis on the 8 chaptur of S. Markis evangell beginning at the 34 vers thairof, compeirit the said Mr Hew and teichit on the said text beginning at the vers foirsaid to the 35 vers of the samin exclusive quhais doctrein being hard and jugit on, the brethrein findis the said text to be nawyis opnit up as is requisit and thairfor ar nocht satisfeit with him as yit concerning this point of tryell. Nochttheles, at his awin desyr, he is appointit to teiche on the samin chaptur foirsaid, beginning at the 35 vers thairof, quhair he left privallie in forme off exerceis, and that in presens of the brethrein, on the x day of October nixttocum for his farther tryell. And als the said Mr Hew is inhibit that he nawayis mell with the exerceis of ony part of the ministrie of the kirk at the kirk of Muckert nor na uthir kirk quhill he be lauchfullie admittit thairto undir the paine off disobedience to the voice of the kirk.

The synnodall assemblie of this province was hauldin in Sterling on the iij day of October 1587 and thairfor thair was na exerceis this day bot the doctrein usit at sic assembleis, quhilk synnodall assemblie and materis done thairintill ar conteinit in the buik of disceplein thairof.

At Sterling the x day of October, 1587

Presentes: James Andirsone, Alexander Fargy, Mr Alexander Wallace, Mr Henrie Layng, ministeris; Mr Alexander Iull and Mr Richard Wrycht, brethir of exerceis.

The samin day, Mr Alexander Wallace propheceithe as he was ordeinit and Mr Henrie Layng addithe thairto in the secund plaice at the desyr of Mr Arthur Fethie, quha sould have occupyit the samin, quha proponit in the last sessione ane excuse for his absence this day quhilk was admittit.

Admissione of Mr Henrie Levingstone: The quhilk day compeirit Alexander Fargy, minister at Logy, and declairit to the brethrein that on Sonday last the viij day of October instant he teichit in S. Ninianis kirk and eftir the end of his sermond, accordein to ane commissione gevin him of the last synnodall assemblie of this province, he made dew and lauchfull intimatione to the haill parrochinnaris conveinit for the tyme that the brethrein of the said assemblie, being ryplie advysit with the literatur and qualificatione of Mr Henrie Levingstone, had fund him qualefeit and meit to be admittit ordinar pastur to thame. And thairfor in the name of God

and his kirk desyrit all personis quhatsumevir that hade to oppone
againis him ony way in lyf and conversatione that may unablle
him to be admittit to the said waightie chairge that thay compeir
befoir the brethrein of the presbytery of Sterling in the parroche
kirk thairof the ten day of October instant in the hour of caus,
thair to declair the samin, with certificatioun gif na lauchfull
impediment be opponit the said day that he wilbe fullie admittit
ordinar pastur to thame, according to the ordur, conforme to his
said commissione in all pointis, of the quhilk he producit the extract
befoir the brethrein, quhilk being red and his report jugit on, he
is fund to have execute his said commissione dewlie according
thairto. Eftir the quhilkis, all personis quhatsumevir in generall that
hade to say againis the said Mr Henrie Levingstone in lyf and
conversatione (gif ony was) being oft tymis callit, nane compeirit,
lauchfull tyme of day biddin. The brethrein accordein to the jugement of the said synodall assemblie and the certificatione abone
specefeit hes admittit and admittis the said Mr Henrie Levingstone
ordinar pastour to the said parroche kirk callit of auld S. Ninianis
kirk besyd Sterling with full powar to him to teiche Godis Word,
ministrat the sacramentis and execute disceplein with all uthir
exerceis appertening to his offeice accordein to the Word of God
in all pointis. And also the brethrein ordanis James Andirsone,
minister at Sterling, commissionar, to pas to the said parroche kirk
on Sonday the xv day of October instant and thair eftir sermond
to notifie the said Mr Henreis admissione to the parrochinnaris
thairof, and to plaice him ordinar pastur thairat according to the
ordur, acceptand promeis of the said Mr Henrie solemlie that he
salbe ane trew and faythfull pastur to that flock as Godis Word
prescryvis swafar as it sall plais God to assist him with his Spirit,
and that he crave the said parrochinnaris consent to his admissione
and plaissein, with ane promeis that thai salbe obedient to the said
Mr Henrie, thair minister, according to Godis Word, swalang as
he remains faithfull in his offeice. And ordanis the commissionar to
report his diligence heirin to the brethrein on the xvij day of
October instant.

Mr Andro Kirk: The samin day compeirit Andro Kirk, reder at
the kirk of Muckert, and declairit that he hade ane yung mane to
his sone callit Mr Andro Kirk, quha is reder presentlie at the kirk

of Dysert, and is myndit to exerceis his talent in the ministrie gif he salbe fund qualefeit and meit thairto, and thairfor is willein to offir him self to ane tryell of the brethrein of this presbytery. Quhairfor the said Andro Kirk desyrit that the brethrein wald appoint ane text to be teichit on be the said Mr Andro on quhat day thay sould think meit and he sould report the samin to him. Quhilk desyr, the brethrein findis rassonablle and thairfor thay have thocht gude that the said Mr Andro sall prepair him self to teiche on the xj chaptur of S. Mathowis evangell, beginning at the 28 vers thairof to the end of the chaptur, privallie in forme of exerceis, and that on the xxiiij day of this instant moneth of October quhairof the said Andro is ordeinit to mak him dewlie advertesit.

Sessio 2a

Tryell of Patrik Layng: The quhilk day being assignit be the brethrein of the last synodall assemblie of this province to Patrik Layng to teiche on the xviij chaptur of S. Mathowis evangell, beginning at the 7 vers thairof, privallie in forme of publict doctrein, compeirit the said Patrik and teichit on the text foirsaid to the 10 vers of the samin exclusive, quhais doctrein being jugit upone, the brethrein ar nawayis satisfeit with him concerning this point of tryell, and thairfor he is ordeinit to sustein farther tryell on this point, and to that effect he is ordeinit to teiche on the text nixt follwein the said text now teichit be him, in forme of publict doctrein privallie on the xxiiij day of October instant.

Tryell of Mr Hew Myllis: The samin day being assignit to Mr Hew Myllis to teiche on the viij chaptur of S. Markis evangell beginning quhair he laist laft at the 35 vers of the samin, compeirit the said Mr Hew and teichit on the said text to the end of the chaptur privallie in forme of exerceis, quhais doctrein being jugit on the brethrein findis the samin nocht swa soundlie teichit aggreing with the text as becumis and thairfoir thai ar nocht satisfeit with him concerning this point of tryell. Inrespect quhairof, he is exhortit to continew in studie of the scripturis and pray to God to blis him thairin quhill he be mair abill to profeit in the kirk.

At Sterling the xvij day of October, 1587

Presentes: James Andirsone, Johnne Duncansone, Mr Henrie

Levingstone, Mr William Cwper, Andro Forester, Mr Alexander Wallace, Mr Henrie Layng, Robert Mentayth, Alexander Fargy, ministeris; Mr Alexander Iull, Mr Richard Wrycht, brethir of exerceis.

Mr Henrie Layng propheceithe in the plaice and at desyr of Mr Arthur Fethie, quha sould have occupyit the samin, and Mr Alexander Iull addithe thairto as thay war ordeinit.

Mr Henrie Levingstone placit minister at S. Ninians kirk: The quhilk day being assignit to James Andirsone, minister at Sterling, commissionar, to report his diligence anent the plaissein of Mr Henrie Levingstone ordinar pastour at S. Ninianis kirk according to his commissione, compeirit the said James and declairit that he for obedience of the brethreinis ordinance made thairanent past to the said parroche kirk on Sonday the xv of this instant quhair he aftir sermond made dew intimatioun to the parrochinnaris thairof of the said Mr Henreis admissione as lykwys of the brethreinis ordinance commanding him to plaice the said Mr Henrie ordinar pastour thairat, quhilk he than red publictlie as the samin of the deat at Sterling the x day of October at lynthe beris. Eftir the quhilk, he desyrit the said Mr Henrie Levingstone to declair on his conscience gif he was content to entir minister to the said flock and to accept the chairge thairof, quha answerit that glaidlie he wald according to the commandement of the kirk, inrespect he was assurit in conscience that he was lauchfullie callit thairto be God. And siclyk the said James Andirsone requirit of the said congregatione gif thay war content to accept him to be thair ordinar pastour and wald promeis solemnlie to acknawlaige him for the samin, and to obey, reverence and assist him in his offeice in all thingis according to the Word of God, swa lang as he remainit faythfull in his offeice, quhilk gif thay wald do he desyrit thame and everie ane of thame to notifie the samin to him be uphaldein of thair handis, quhilk thay did, and further Alexander Forester of Garden, ane honerablle mane, zalus in religione, and ane of the principall of the said congregatione, for him self and in name of the remanent parrochinnaris, tuke the said Mr Henrie be the hand and acceptit him as thair ordinar pastour. And als the said Mr Henrie being desyrit to promeis to the saidis parrochinnaris to be faythfull in his offeice, quha promesit solemnitlie to be ane trew and faythfull pastur to thame as Godis Word cravis, swafar as it sall plais God to assist him with his Spirit. And swa the said Mr Henrie was plaissit and admittit ordinar pastur to the said kirk callit of auld S. Ninianis kirk. For blissein of the quhilk wark in his handis, the said James Andirsone, commissionar, made solem prayer. And this was done in presens of the godlie personis follwein besyd the ordinar parrochinnaris of the said kirk, viz., Robert Forester of Boquhen, last provest off Sterling, Mr James Pont, commissar of Dunblane, Mr Alexander Iull, Mr Richard Wrycht, brethir of the exerceis of Sterling, Johnne Auchtmutty and Patrik Kinros, burgessis of the samin brugh, and this for the report of the said James Andirsone, done in the mater abone wrettin according to the commissione gevin to him thairanent, quhilk the brethrein jugit to be formallie done.

At Sterling the xxiiij day of October, 1587

Presentes: James Andirsone, Johnne Duncansone, Mr Henrie Levingstone, Mr Henrie Layng, Robert Mentayth, Alexander Fargy, Mr William Cwpper, Mr Andro Murdo, ministeris; Mr Alexander Iull and Mr Richard Wrycht, brethir of exerceis.

The quhilk day Mr Alexander Iull propheceithe and Mr Richard Wrycht addithe in the secund plaice as thay war ordeinit.

Harvie and Yung, adulteraris in Bathkenner: The quhilk day ane summondis beand producit dewlie execute and indorsit upone Marione Yung in Bothkenner chairgeing hir to compeir the said day to heir and sie hir self decernit to be excommunicat for hir contemp and malicius disobedience to the voice of the kirk conjonit with adultrie, compeirit the said Marione Yung and William Harvie in Bothkainner, quha confessis that thai have had carnall daill togethir sindrie yeiris bygane and hes gottin sindrie bairnis togethir sen he was mareit on Elezabeth Car, quhilk Elezabeth, he allegis, past fra him mony yeiris syne and he hes nocht sein hir and thairfor he knawis nocht gif scho be dade or nocht, and confessis that he hes nevir ressavit ony assurance nor testimony of hir daythe. Inrespect of the quhilk confessione made be bayth the saidis personis, thay ar decernit to have committit adultrie, and thairfor ar commandit to separat thame selffis and remane sindrie at all tymis fra

thisfurth undir the paine of excommunicatioun, quhilk thay promeis to obey. And the said Marione submittis hir self obedient to
the commandement of the kirk, and the said William siclyk offiris
him self obedient to the kirk according to the publict admonitione
gevin be Mr William Cwper, his ordinar pastour, on Sonday last.
Inrespect quhairof, he desyris that the pronuncein of the sentence
of excommunicatioun be stayit againis him. According to the
quhilk desyr inrespect of his said obedience, the brethrein commandis the said Mr William to stay farther proceidein againis him
swa lang as he continewis obedient to the voice of the kirk and
decernis and ordanis the said William Harvie and Marione Yung
to mak publict repentence in thair awin parroche kirk of Bothkenner
ilk Sonday in thair awin clathis as thai salbe commandit be thair
minister quhill the nixt synnodall assemblie of this province to be
hauldin in the parroche kirk of Dunblane the secund day of Aprill
nixt, and thair to compeir the said day and ressave sic farther
injunctionis as salbe injonit to thame and obey the samin undir the
paine of excommunicatioun.

Mr Adam Mairschell, Mr Andro Kirk: The quhilk day being
assignit to Mr Adam Merschell to present ane mane indewit with
gude giftis abill to proffeit in the kirk and namelie worthie to be
admittit ordinar pastour to the kirk of [*blank*], quhair he presentlie
servis, as ane act made in the last synodall assemblie at mair lynthe
beris, compeirit Andro Kirk, reder at Muckert, and producit ane
misseive wretein subscryvit be him (as appeiris) berand in effect
that he hes done his diligence to obey the said ordinance of the
last synnodall assemblie, and hes spokin Mr Andro Kirk thairanent
and hes causit him compeir this day to be tryit be the brethrein
quhairby thay may undirstand gif he be abill and qualefeit
to be admittit to the plaice foirsaid. Quhilk Mr Andro Kirk
being callit on and desyrit gif he wald present him self to tryell of
the brethrein to the effect foirsaid, he ansorit that glaidlie he
wald and declairit that he was prepairit reddie to teiche on the
text appointit to him be the brethrein, viz., on the xj chaptur of
S. Mathowis evangell, beginning at the 28 vers thairof, in forme
appointit to him. The brethrein appointis him to teiche on the
samin this day at twa houris aftir none quhilk he promesit to
obey.

Y

Sessio 2a

Tryell off Mr Andro Kirk: The said Mr Andro Kirk havein teichit on the said text privallie in forme of exerceis, quhilk being hard and the brethreinis jugement thairon cravit, the samin was teichit in the Latein langage and fund sound doctrein, aggreing with the annalagie of fayth, quhairby the brethrein hoipis weill of him. Nochttheles for farther tryell of him in this samin point, the brethrein ordanis him to teiche on the beginning of the xij chaptur of S. Mathowis evangell in Ingillis langage privallie in forme of exerceis on the last day of this instant moneth of October.

Tryell off Patrik Layng: The quhilk day being assignit to Patrik Layng to teiche on the xviij chaptur of S. Mathowis evangell, beginning at the x vers thairof, privallie in forme of publict doctrein, compeirit the said Patrik and teichit on the said text to the 15 vers of the samin exclusive in forme foirsaid, quhais doctrein being jugit the samin is fund aggreing with the annalagie of fayth bot nocht swa sufficient as is requisit to be teichit be ane pastur in the kirk, and thairfor the brethrein as yit continewis him undir farther tryell quhill the brethrein be farther advysit concerning his habilitie to continew in the ministrie, and presentlie admonesis him to frequent the exerceis oftir nor he hes done for his bettir instructione, and that he be reddy to teiche thairin as he salbe commandit.

At Sterling the last day of October, 1587

Presentes: James Andirsone, Mr Arthur Fethie, Mr Henrie Levingstone, Mr Henrie Layng, Robert Mentayth, Mr Patrik Walkinschaw, Mr Andro Murdo, ministeris; Mr Alexander Iull and Maister Richard Wrycht, brothir of exerceis.

The quhilk day Mr Richard Wrycht propheceithe and Mr Henrie Levingstone addithe in the secund plaice as thay war ordeinit.

Admissione of Mr Andro Murdo, minister to Kippen: The quhilk day compeirit Johnne Forester in Daischur within the parrochun of Kippen, for him self and in name of the parrochinnaris of Kippen, and declairit that forsamekill as the brethrein of the last synnodall assemblie of this province hes deprivit William Sterling, thair last nammit minister, from all functione in the kirk except simpill reidein allanirlie, quhairby thay ar destitute of ane pastour to teiche

Godis Word, ministrat the sacramentis and celebrat mariage to thame, and thairfor he presentit ane supplicatione, in name of the saidis parrochinnaris subscryvit be sindrie of the maist discreit men thairof, contenand commissione to him to that effect and to crave answer thairof, berand in effect that thay have thocht gude to mak sute to the brethrein to desyr thame to try and exame Williame Sterling, Mr Henrie Layng and Maistir Andro Murdo or ony ane of thame to the effect that he of thir, quha be tryell of the brethrein salbe fund best qualefeit or maist meit to be thair pastur, may be be us nominat and admittit thair ordinar according to the ordur, as the samin supplicatione in the self at mair lynthe beris. With the quhilk the brethrein being advysit and first concerning William Sterling, the first in lyt desyrit to be tryit in the said supplicatione, it is answerit that becaus the said William is deposit from all functione in the kirk (excep reidein allanirlie) be the last synodall assemblie of this province in this instant moneth of October, cheiflie for ignorance of the scripturis, thairfor the brethrein jugis him nocht qualefeit sufficient to be admittit minister to the said kirk and thairfor refusis to admit him thairto. Secundlie, concerning Mr Henrie Layng, the secund persone in lit desyrit to be tryit in the said supplicatione, he is inquyrit be the moderator gif he will accept the burdein of the ministrie to the saidis parrochinnaris (the brethrein fundein him meit thairfoir). He ansorit negative, and thairfor the brethrein thinkis nocht gude to burdein him thairwith. Thridlie, concerning Mr Andro Murdo, the last persone in lit, desyrit to be tryit in the said supplicatione, quhome the brethrein knawis is alreddie lauchfullie admittit ane minister of the evangell of Jesus Christ in the kirk, and findein him willein to accept the chairge of ane ordinar pastour to the parrochinnaris of the said kirk of Kippen, and of sufficient qualeteis for that plaice thairfoir to have admittit and appointit and be thir presentis admittis and appointis and the said Mr Andro Murdo ordinar pastour to the parrochinnaris of the said kirk of Kippen with full powar to him to teiche Godis Word, ministrat the sacramentis and exerceis disceplein with all uthir exerceis appertening to his offeice, and ordanis him to be placit ordinar pastor thairat according to the ordur.

Sessio 2a

Tryell of Mr Andro Kirk: The quhilk day being assignit to Mr

Andro Kirk to teiche on the xij chaptur of S. Mathowis evangell at the beginning privallie in forme of exerceis, compeirit the said Mr Andro and teichit on the said text to the 5 vers thairof exclusive, quhais doctrein being jugit on, the samin is fund sound aggreing with the annalegie of fayth. Nochttheles, the brethrein as yit is nocht satisfeit with him concerning this point of tryell and thairfor ordanis him to teiche in the samin forme on the text nixt follwein the foirsaid text now teichit be him, and that he prepair him self thairfoir upone adverteisment eftir the plat.

At Sterling the vij day of November, 1587

Presentes: James Andirsone, Mr Andro Yung, Mr Henrie Levingstone, Mr Henrie Layng, Mr Andro Murdo, ministeris; Mr Alexander Iule, Mr Richard Wrycht, brethir of exerceis.

The quhilk day Mr Henrie Levingstone propheceithe and Mr Henrie Layng addithe in the secund plaice as thay war ordeinit.

At Sterling the xiiij day of November, 1587

Presentes: James Andirsone, Mr Henrie Levingstone, Alexander Fargy, Mr William Cwper, Mr Henrie Layng, Mr Andro Murdo, ministeris; Mr Alexander Iull and Mr Richard Wrycht, brether of exerceis.

The quhilk day James Andirsone made the exerceis, as he was ordeinit, and Mr Andro Murdo addithe in the plaice of Alexander Fargy, quhais absence was excusit berassone of disais and seiknes quhilk excuse was admittit.

At Sterling the xvij day of November, 1587

Bischop off Dunblane: The quhilk day the commissionar of this province and certane of the brethrein of the presbyteriis of Sterling and Dunblane being conveinit and undirstandein perfytlie that William Chisholme, bischop of Dunblane, is schortsyne arryvit, within this realme, quha is notourlie knawin to be ane papeist and ennemie to the reformit religione professit publictlie within this realme aggreing with the Word of God, and thairfor the brethrein ordanis him to be summond *litteratorie* to compeir befoir the brethrein of the saidis presbyteriis to gif ane confessione of his fayth and religione and to subscryve the confessione of fayth subscryvit be the kingis majestie and his houshald and the rest of the faithfull within this realme, undir the paine of excommunicatione, with certificatione and he compeir nocht or compeir and refuse to profes and subscryve the said confessione of fayth, as said is, thay will proceid with the censur of excommunicatione againis him for his contemp and disobedience to the voice of the kirk and continuance in that corruptit religione of papistrie repugnant to the Word of God.

Upone the xxj day of November, 1587 beand ane ordinar day of exerceis, thair was na prophecie of the Wo[r]d, berassone the maist part of the brethrein of this presbytery was in Edinburgh the said day all waittein on the lordis modefearis of ministeris stependis this yeir.

At Sterling the xxviij day of November, 1587

Presentes: James Andirsone, Mr Andro Yung, Mr Henrie Levingstone, Mr Alexander Wallace, Robert Mentayth, Mr William Cwpper, Mr Andro Murdo, Mr Henrie Layng, ministeris; Mr Alexander Iull and Mr Richard Wrycht, brethir of exerceis.

The quhilk day Mr Andro Murdo propheceithe in plaice of Alexander Fargy, quha was seik for the present, and Mr William Cwpper addithe in the secund plaice, as he was ordeinit.

Ane publict fast appointit: The quhilk day the brethrein thinkis gude and hes ordeinit for avoidein executione of the plaigis of God, hingand above our heddis for sin, that thair be ane publict humiliatione and fast with ane exerceis of teichein the Word conjonit thairwith, according to the ordur observit and keipit in all the parrochinnis within the boundis of this presbytery on thir twa nixt Sondayis and the oulk betuix for the causis follwein in speciall: 1. for the plaig off pest begun alreddie in Edinburgh and Leyth; secundlie for persecution of the kirk of God in France and uthir parttis be the ennemeis thairof publictlie and privallie in all parttis;

thridlie, the flowein to this realme of grit multitudis of papeistis and Jesueittis without ony respect tane thairto be the civill magistrat, tendein throw thair prive persuasionis to subvert the religione; fourtlie, the grit aboundance of schaddein of blude in this countrie without ony puneisment or remady made thairfoir be the civill magistrat, and thir speciallis besydis mony uthir vycis that aboundis in this cuntrie, quhilk daylie provokis the executione of the just jugementis of God unles we prevent the samin be unfainzit repentence.

At Sterling the fyft day of December, 1587

Presentes: James Andirsone, commissionar; Alexander Fargy, Andro Forester, Robert Mentayth, Mr Andro Murdo, Mr Henrie Levingstone, Mr Henrie Layng, ministeris; Mr Alexander Iull and Mr Richard Wrycht, brethir of exerceis within the boundis of the presbytery of Sterling; Mr Andro Yung, Mr James Burdun, William Drummond, Mr Alexander Chisholme, Johnne Burdun, Mr William Sterling, brethrein of the exerceis of the presbytery of Dunblane.

The quhilk day thair was na prophecie berassone the samin day was ane day quhairon ordinar doctrein was teichit in the tyme of the publict fast.

[*In margin*: The proces concerning the bischop of Dunblane omittit heir, quhilk is to be fund in the 4 paige follwein heirfra. J. Duncansone.]

At Sterling the xij day of December, 1587

Presentes: James Andirsone, Mr Henrie Levingstone, Mr Henrie Layng, Mr William Cwper; Mr Alexander Iull and Mr Richard Wrycht, brethir of exerceis in the presbytery of Sterling; Mr William Sterling, Mr Andro Yung and Mr Alexander Chisholme, brethrein of exerceis and ministeris within the boundis of the presbytery of Dunblane.

The quhilk day Mr William Cowper propheceithe and James Andirsone addithe in the secund plaice as thay war ordeinit.

[*In margin*: The proces concerning the bischop of Dunblane

omittit heir quhilk is to be fund in the 5 paige follwein heirfra. J. Duncanson.]

Mr Henlie [sic] *Layng admittit minister to Airthe*: The quhilk day compeirit Johnne Bruce, brother to Alexander Bruce of Airthe, George Brys in Airthe, elderis of the parroche kirk thairof, and David Thomesone, deacun of the samin kirk, quha exponit and declairit to the brethrein that forsamekill as be the transportein of Mr Arthur Fethie, thair last minister, fra thame to the kirk of Kinnell in Angus thair kirk presentlie was desolat of ane ordinar pastour, and seing that congregatione hade sindrie and dyvers tymis hard Mr Henrie Layng teiche Godis Word unto thame, be quhais doctrein thay fand thame selffis baithe edefeit and confortit, thairfor schew that thair congregatione hade directit thame this day to the brethrein of this assemblie to crave the said Mr Henrie to be appointit and placit ordinar pastour to thame according to the ordur, promesein to him love, reverence and assistance in his callein. With the quhilk desyr, the brethrein being advysit and findein the said Mr Henrie maist willein to accept that chairge and of sufficient qualeteis for that plaice, thairfore to have admittit and appointit and be thir presentis admittis and appointis the said Mr Henrie Layng ordinar pastour to the parrochinnaris of the said kirk of Airthe, with full powar to him to teiche Godis Word, ministrat the sacramentis and execute disceplein with all uthir exerceis appertening to his offeice, and ordanis thair brother Mr William Cowpper, minister at Bathkenner, to pas to the said kirk of Airthe the nixt Sonday the xvij day of this instant, and thair eftir sermond to notifie the said Mr Henreis admissione to the parrochinnaris thairof, and to desyr thame (gif thay consent thairto) that thay declair him the samin be the signe of uphaldein of thair handis, and siclyk to desyr the said Mr Henrie to declair in presens of the parrochinnaris gif he will accept the said burdein on him, quhilk beand declarit affirmative that ye plaice him ordinar pastour thairat, acceptand promeis of the parrochinnaris that thay salbe obedient to thair said pastour according to Godis Word, swalang as he continewis faithfull in his offeice, and that the said Mr Henrie promeis solemlie that he salbe ane trew and faithfull pastour to that flock according to his calling, swafar as it sall plais God to assist him with his Holie Spirit.

At Sterling the xix day of December, 1587

Presentes: James Andirsone, Mr Henrie Levingstone, Mr Henrie Layng, Mr Andro Murdo, ministeris; Mr Alexander Iull and Mr Richard Wrycht, brethir of exerceis.

The quhilk day, James Andirsone, propheceithe as he was ordeinit and becaus Alexander Fargy was absent, quha sould have occupyit the secund plaice, Mr Henrie Levingston addithe in the secund plaice.

The samin day ane excuse of Alexander Fargyis being proponit for his absence and neglecting of the secund plaice, to wit, that he was disaisit be seiknes, the samin was repellit becaus he wald nocht request ane uthir to keip the plaice for him, and thairfor was convict in v s. as for the penaltie appointit to be payit be thais that neglectis the secund plaice in additione, and als ordanis the said Alexander to teiche in the first plaice of the exerceis and Robert Mentayth to ad in the secund plaice on the xxvj day of this instant moneth, and gif the said Alexander may nocht do it him self for seiknes that he caus ane uthir brothir occupy his plaice thairin undir the pain conteinit in the generall act made thairanent.

Sessio 2a

Tryell of Mr Andro Kirk: The quhilk day Mr Andro Kirk compeirit and teichit privallie on the xij chaptur of S. Mathowis evangell, beginning at the 5 vers thairof to the 9 vers of the samin exclusive, in forme of exerceis as he was ordeinit, quhais doctrein being jugit on the samin is fund sound aggreing with the annalagie of fayth, bot yit the brethrein ar nocht satisfeit with him concerning this point of tryell and thairfoir he is appointit, yit as of befoir, to teich privallie in forme of exerceis on the viij chaptur of the [e]pistill wrettin to the Romanis at the beginning thairof on the xxvj day of December instant.

At Sterling the xxvj day of December, 1587

Presentes: James Andirsone, Mr Henrie Levingstone, Mr Andro Murdo, Alexander Fargy, Robert Mentayth, ministeris; and Mr Alexander Iull, ane brother of exerceis.

The quhilk day Alexander Fargy propheceithe and Robert Mentayth addithe in the secund plaice as thay war ordeinit.

Waltir Buchannan: The quhilk day the brethrein undirstandein that upone the xxvj day of September last bypast Waltir Buchannan, brother to Johnne Buchannan of Arnepriour, desyrit of thame continewatione of farther procedein againis him concerning the cravein of the confessione of his fayth becaus he than promesit to pas furth of the cuntrie betuix and the xj day of November nixt, viz., Mertimes, without farther deley, at the quhilk tyme he was admonesit to recant his papisticall errur, profes and subscryve the reformit religione publictlie professit within this realm, betuix and the said day, gif he war than present in the cuntrie, undir the paine of excommunicatioun, as ane act made the said day at mair lynthe beris, and albeit it be of varetie that the said faist of Mertimes be of lang tyme bypast and that the said Walter remanis as yit within this realme undepartit furth of the samin, nochttheles he hes nocht obeyit the said admonitione nather yit hes he repairit to the preichein of the Word of God at ony tym sen he was first challengit be the brethrein knawin to ony of thame quhair he hes chieflie remainit sensyne, to wit, the spaice of ane haill yeir compleit albeit he hes bein oft and dyvers tymis requyrit thairto and thairfor the brethrein ordanis the said Walter to be summond *litteratorie* to compeir befoir thame and the brethrein of the presbytery of Dunblane to heir and sie him self decernit to be excommunicat for his said contemp and disobedience with certificatione and he compeir nocht or compeir and refuse to profes and subscryve the confessione of fayth subscryvit be the kingis majestie and his houshauld thay will decern him to be admonesit publictlie according to the ordur, to renunce all papistrie in generall and in speciall as is set doun in the said confessione of fayth, profes the reformit religione publictlie professit within this realme and to subscryve the said confessione of fayth, quhilk admonitionis being all disobeyit that he salbe pronuncit excommunicat for his contemp and disobedience to the voice of the kirk reformit within this realme and continuance in that corruptit religione of papistrie repugnant to the Word of God, according to the same Word and disceplein of the kirk havand the warrand thairof thairin.

Buchannan of Arnepriour: The samin day the brethrein undirstand-ein that Johnne Buchannan of Arnepriour hes declairit him self in sindrie partis to be ane papeist and hes rassonit for defence of the heresie thairof with sindrie personis, thairfor the brethrein ordanis the said Johnne to be summond *litteratorie* to compeir befoir the brethrein to gif ane confessione of his fayth and religione and to subscryve the confessione of fayth subscryvit be the kingis majestie and his houshald, undir the paine of disobedience.

The quhilk day compeirit William Kay, adulterar, with Elezabeth Galbrayth, as he hes confessit of befoir, and desyris Mr Andro Murdo, his minister, to be commandit to bapteis his bairne gottin on the said Elezabeth and he sall obey the ordinance of the kirk for his said offence. The brethrein ordanis him to caus cautione for him becum actit in the commissaris buikis of Sterling that he sall obey the injunctionis injonit to him in the last synnodall assemblie for his said offence undir the paine of xl lib., quhilk beand done ordanis the said Mr Andro to bapteis his bairne.

Sessio 2a

Tryall of Mr Andro Kirk: The quhilk day appointit to Mr Andro Kirk to teich on the viij chaptur of the epistill to the Romanis at the beginning privallie in forme of exerceis, compeirit the said Mr Andro and teichit on the said text privallie in maner foirsaid to the 4 vers thairof exclusive. Quhilk being jugit upone, the samin is fund sound and proffitablle doctrein inrespect quhairof the brethrein is satisfeit with him concerning this point of tryell, and admittis him to the secund point of tryell, viz., to exerceis publictlie, and thairfor ordanis him to ad in the secund plaice of the privie exerceis on the ordinar text thairof on the nixt Twysday day, the secund day of Januar nixt.

[*In margin*: The proces of the actis tuichein the bischop of Dun-blane, quhilk sould be insert with the actis made respective the fyft and xij dayis of December mentionat on the 4 paige heir precedein and quhilk was omittit thair. J. Duncansone.]

At Sterling the fyft day of December, 1587

Presentes: James Andirsone, commissionar; Alexander Fargy, Andro Forester, Robert Mentayth, Mr Andro Murdo, Mr Henrie

Levingstone, Mr Henrie Layng, ministeris; Mr Alexander Iull and Mr Richard Wrycht, brethir of exerceis within the boundis of the presbytery of Sterling; Mr Andro Yung, Mr James Burdun, Mr William Drummond, Mr Alexander Chisholme, Johnne Burdun, Mr William Sterling, ministeris and brethrein of exerceis within the boundis of the presbytery off Dunblane.

Bischop off Dunblane: The quhilk day ane summondis beand producit dewlie execute and indorsit upone Williame Chisholme, bischop of Dunblane, chairgein him to compeir the said day to gif ane confessione of fayth and religione, to profes and subscryve the confessione of fayth subscryvit be the kingis majestie and his houshald and the rest of the faythfull within this realme undir the paine of excommunicatione, as at mair lynthe is conteinit in the said summondis, quhilk bischop being oft tymis callit compeirit nocht, bot James commendatar of Inchaffray and James Chisholme of Cromlickis compeirand for him and in his name allegit that the said bischop haid ane disais fallin in his leg quhairthrow he mycht nawayis travell to compeir befoir this assemblie and thairfor desyrit the brethrein to superseid farther procedein againis him quhill he war summond *de novo* that in the mantyme he may resolve him self gif he will profes our religione publictlie professit within this realme or ellis to depart aff the cuntrie. The brethrein being advysit with the said desyr findis na testimoniall in wret producit testefeand the said bischopis disais nather yit ony powar of him to the said honorablle men to desyr thair said petitione in his name. Nochttheles, the brethrein for avoydein of all kynd of occasione that may appeir of thair sudden proceidein in the said mater hes thocht gude to proceid in proces againis the said bischop in manir follwein, that is to say, becaus of the said allegit defens thay have ordeinit and ordeinis thair brethrein Maisteris Andro Yung and Henrie Levingstone, ministeris, to pas to the said William, bischop of Dunblane (gif he can be personallie apprehendit), and to confer with him anent his religione, and in the name of God to requyr him to profes and subscryve the confessione of fayth and religione abone mentionat and farther according to the ordur, and gif he refuse that thai admoneis him in the name of God and of his reformit kirk within this realme of Scotland to compeir befoir the breithrein of the presbyteriis of Sterling and Dunblane in the parroche kirk of Sterling the vij day of

December instant in the hour of caus, thair to recant his papisticall erruris, to profes and subscryve the said confessione of faythe undir the paine of excommunicatione, and [*inserted in margin*: ordanis him to be summond *de novo* to the effect abonementionat with certificatioun conteinit in the last summondis and that the brethrein foirsaid, (*signed*) J. Duncansone], or sum uthir brother or officiar execute the summondis direct to that effect, according thairto in all pointis, and quhatsoevir the said brethrein dois heirintill that thay report the samin in our nixt assemblie to be hauldin in the kirk of Sterling the said xij day of December instant. The quhilkis to do, the brethrein of the saidis presbyteriis gevis full commissione and powar to the saidis Maisteris Andro Yung and Henrie Levingstone conjunctlie and severallie.

At Sterling the xij day of December, 1587

Presentes: James Andirsone, commissionar; Mr Henrie Levingstone, Mr Henrie Layng, Mr William Cwper, ministeris; Mr Alexander Iull and Mr Richard Wrycht, brethir of exerceis in the presbytery of Sterling; Mr William Sterling, Mr Andro Yung and Mr Alexander Chisholme, ministeris and brethrein of exerceis in the presbytery of Dunblane.

Bischop off Dunblane: The quhilk day anent the commissione gevin to Maisteris Andro Yung and Henrie Levingstone, ministeris, to pas and confer with William, bischop of Dunblane, anent his religione, as the act thairof at mair lynthe beiris, compeirit the saidis Maisteris Andro Yung and Henrie Levingstone and reportit thair diligence done thairanent, as it bearis in the self, quhairof the tennour follwis.

Bischop off Dunblane decernit to be excommunicat: Upone the vij day of December *anno* etc., lxxxvij yeiris, we, Maisteris Andro Yung and Henrie Levingstone, ministeris withinwrittein, at command of the ordinance withinspecefeit past to the dwellein [hous, *deleted*] plaice of James, commendatar of Inchaffray, callit Innerpaiffrie, quhair William, bischop of Dunblane, was personallie present for the tyme (as the said commendatar confessit), and desyrit to have acces to the said bischop to the effect we mycht have usit our commissione within specefeit. Nochttheles, we could have nane, nather yit wald he gif his presens to us albeit we remainit awaittein thairon fra the said day at twa houris aftirnone to the viij day of this instant at xj houris or thairby befoir none. Inrespect quhairof, we made intimatioun to the said commendatar that the said bischop wald be summond *de novo* agane in the parroche kirk of Dunblane on Sonday nixt, the x day of December instant, to compeir befoir the presbyteriis of Sterling and Dunblane in the parroche kirk of Sterling the xij day of December instant in the hour of caus, to gif ane confessione of his fayth and religione undir the paine of excommunicatione, as at mair lynthe is conteinit in the samin summondis direct to that effect, and siclyk ane summondis beand producit dewlie execute and indorsit upone the said William, bischop, chairgein him *de novo* agane to compeir the said day in the parroche kirk of Sterling in the hour of caus to mak solem declaratione in this assemblie and in sic uthir placis as he salbe ordeinit that he professis the reformit religione preichit and authoresit publictlie within this realm and to subscryve the confessione thairof, subscryvit be the kingis majestie and his houshald and the remanent faithfull within this realme, undir the paine of excommunicatione, with certificatione and he compeir nocht or compeir and refuse to profes and subscryve, as said is, the brethrein will decern him to be admonest publictlie, according to the ordur, to obey thair said desyr, quhilk publict admonitionis being all contemnit that the sentence of excommunicatione salbe pronuncit againis him for his contemp and disobedience to the voice of the kirk reformit within this realme and continuance in that cor-ruptit religione of papistrie repugnant to the Word of God, as at mair lynthe is conteinit in the said summondis. Quhilk bischop being oft tymis callit compeirit nocht, bot James Chisholme of Cromlickis compeirit in his name and declairit that he could nocht persaif be the said bischopis mynd that he was ony wayis willein to profes nor subscryve the said reformit religione bot was purposit to pas aff the cuntrie ane competent day being grantit to him to that effect. The brethrein being ryplie advysit with the proces deducit againis the said William, bischop of Dunblane, and findand him obstinat in papistrie conjonit with malicius disobedience to the voice of the kirk reformit within this realme thairfore decernis and ordanis the ministeris of the evangell within the boundis of thair presbyteriis publictlie in thair parroche kirkis thir nixt thre Sondayis foll~wing~

from thair pulpattis to admoneis him in name of the eternall God and
of his reformit kirk within this realme to compeir befoir the commissionar of this province and his brethrein of the ministrie in the
kirk of Sterling on the Twysday nixt follwein everie ane of thair
saidis admonitionis respective thair to mak solem declaration that
he professis the said reformit religione and to subscryve the confessione thairof abone mentionat undir the paine of excommunicatione, quhilkis admonitiounis, being all contemnit and disobeyit,
decernis and ordanis the sentence of excommunicatione to be pronuncit againis the said William, bischop of Dunblane, and he to be
cuttit aff fra the societie of Christis kirk and delyverit in the handis
of Sathan for destructione of his flesche that his saull may be saif in
the day of the Lord Jesus, incaice of his said comtempt and disobedience, as said is, according to the Word of God, disceplein of the
kirk, and lawis of this realme. And also ordanis the brethrein of the
saidis presbyteriis to report, or at the leist caus be reportit in thair
name to the assemblie to be hauldin in the kirk of Sterling the secund
day of Januar nixttocum, thair diligence in gevein of the saidis
admonitiounis, as said is, togethir with sure declaratione gif the said
William, bischop, or ony in his name offiris to ony of the brethrein
to obey the saidis admonitiounis at ony tyme befoir the said secund
day of Januar [Februar, *deleted*], as thai and everie ane of thame will
answer upone thair obedience to the kirk.

APPENDIX

ABSTRACT of cases unresolved by December, 1587

2 January, 1587-8

Trial of Mr Andrew Kirk: Robert Menteith, minister, prophesied on the 13th chapter of the epistle to the Hebrews, beginning at the 9th verse to the 15th exclusive, and Mr Andrew Kirk added in the second place, as appointed, for trial of his ability to enter the ministry. Menteith's doctrine was found 'sklendir and the text nocht opnit up as is requisit', and so was exhorted to further study and to regular attendance at the exercise. In his first trial in public exercise, Kirk was found to be 'sound and gude' in doctrine, but in some places was 'nocht swa plain and sensabill as is requisit'. He was admitted to prophesy in the first place on Tuesday, 9th January, and urged to mend his former fault.

Bishop of Dunblane: The bishop was admonished from the pulpits within the presbyteries of Stirling and Dunblane on three successive Sundays to profess the reformed religion and subscribe the king's confession of faith. He was required to compear before the presbytery and agree to the same or be excommunicated, but failed to compear in person or by proxy. 'Thairfor the haill brethrein findis that the sentence of excommunicatione maist justlie aucht to be pronuncit agaínis the said William, bischop, instantlie', but for 'grater fulnes of ordur and that na gude occasione of lenitie and gentill admonitione sould be thocht to be omittit', the bishop was to be admonished again to conform before sentence be pronounced by James Anderson, commissioner.

Walter Buchanan, brother of John Buchanan of Arnprior: A summons was produced and executed to the effect that on 26th September last, Buchanan had compeared before the presbytery and had asked for a delay in proceedings against him. He was to depart from the country by Martinmas and admonished to subscribe the reformed faith and renounce papistry. He failed to comply and is decerned worthy to be excommunicated for contempt and disobedience. All ministers of the presbyteries of Stirling and Dunblane were to admonish him publictly from their pulpits on three successive Sundays to compear before the presbytery to make public declaration that he will profess the reformed faith and subscribe the king's confession of faith under pain of excommunication. The ministers were to report their diligence in making the admonitions. Buchanan was found to be 'obstinat and indurit in papistrie'. He had refused to 'renunce the errur of the papeistis and embrais the said reformit religione', and had declined to submit 'his maidin bairn' for baptism 'according to the ordur approvit be the reformit kirk of this realm'.

John Buchanan of Arnprior: Summons executed upon Buchanan of Arnprior charging him to compear to give confession of his faith as subscribed by the king and to profess the reformed faith under pain of excommunication, but he failed to compear.

9 January, 1587/8

Trial of Mr Andrew Kirk: Kirk prophesied on the 13th chapter of the epistle to the Hebrews from the 15th to the 18th verses for trial of his ability to enter the ministry, and Mr Henry Laing added in second place. Kirk's doctrine was found sound and so was ordained to attend the exercise and to preach therein each month, at least, until the brethren were further resolved.

Bishop of Dunblane: James Anderson, commissioner, was appointed to pronounce sentence of excommunication against William, bishop of Dunblane unless the latter compeared and professed the reformed faith. The bishop failed to compear, and the commissioner 'producit ane misseive wretein subscryvit be his majestie direct to him, berand request of his hienes to continew the pruncein of the said sentence on Sonday last and Sonday nixt, the vij and xiiij dayis of this instant moneth of December [*recte*, January], and siclyk ane uthir wretein direct be my lord chancellar at his hienes command to the samin effect, berand alsa that he haid spokin sum of the brethrein in Edinburgh, quha thocht meit that the samin sould be continewit'. The commissioner, therefore, inquired from the brethren whether they agreed that pronouncing the sentence of excommunication should be delayed. It was agreed to defer pronouncing the sentence until 16 January, in obedience to the king's request.

16 January, 1587/8

Bishop of Dunblane: This day was appointed to James Anderson, minister of Stirling, to pronounce excommunication against the bishop of Dunblane, if the bishop failed to render obedience. The bishop failed to compear, but John Drummond, 'servand to the kingis majestie, compeirit, and producit ane misseive wreting', dated Holyroodhouse, 15 January 1587/8, 'direct frome the kingis majestie to the said James Andirsone, subscryvit be his hienes, berand in effect that his grace hade tane cautione of the bischop of Dunblane that he sall, within fourtie dayis, depart out of this realme, and that gif he sa do his majestie thinkis it a sufficient obedience, desyring that all farther extremitie of censuris sould be superseidit againis him'. Anderson desired the brethren to declare their judgment on suspending the pronouncing of excommunication. They agreed to the king's request and delayed pronouncing the sentence till they were advised by 'the brethrein of the kirk and speciallie the nixt generall assemblie of the kirk gif it hauld on the sex day of Februar nixt, as is appointit'.

23 January, 1587/8

Walter Buchanan: Buchanan failed to compear, though admonished to do so by the ministers of the presbyteries of Stirling and Dunblane on three successive Sundays. The brethren therefore found that they might justly proceed to excommunication but they agreed to admonish him once more to compear before the synod to be held at Stirling on 30 January. The ministers of the presbyteries were 'to mak solem prayeris for the said Waltiris conversione, and to exhort thair congregatiounis respective to pray for him'.

27 February, 1587/8

Bishop of Dunblane: The general assembly, it was intimated, had delivered an ordinance on 14 February 1587/8 requiring the whole

z

ministry of the presbyteries of Stirling and Dunblane, after the
expiry of ten days, to proceed, without further admonitions,
to the sentence of excommunication against William, bishop
of Dunblane, in case of disobedience. It was reported by Mr
William Cowper, minister at Bothkennar, Mr Henry Laing,
minister at Airth, Mr Andrew Murdo, minister at Kippen,
Robert Menteith, minister at Alva, Mr Alexander Wallace,
minister at Clackmannan, and Patrick Laing, minister at Tulliallan,
all being personally present, that they had fulfilled and executed
the assembly's ordinance and had pronounced the sentence of
excommunication against the bishop of Dunblane on Sunday,
25 February, cutting him off from the body of Christ and society
of the kirk and giving him over to the hands and power of the
devil to the destruction of his flesh. The remaining ministers were
ordered to make intimation of the sentence in their kirks on
Sunday, 3 March.

William Harvie, adulterer: Mr William Cowper, minister at Bothkennar, reported that he had ordered William Harvie and Marion
Young to satisfy the kirk of Bothkennar for their adultery and
to separate themselves on pain of excommunication, as required by an act made at Stirling on 24 October 1587, but Harvie
had still not separated himself from Marion Young. Harvie
compeared and alleged that he had obeyed the ordinance and
that he had removed Marion Young from his house a long time
ago. He claimed that he had been prepared to make repentance
but that his minister had refused to accept it. Cowper replied
that he would not receive his repentance since Harvie had not
separated himself from the woman. The presbytery ordered Harvie
to satisfy the particular session of his own parish church by
separating himself from Marion Young so that the slander may be
removed.

12 March, 1587/8

Mr Andrew Kirk licensed to preach: Kirk declared to the presbytery
that 'thruche the seindill exercesein to him self in teichein, he
is nocht in use of langage and memorie to uttir his doctrein to
the proffeit of the auditur in sic forme as is requisit and thairfor

desyrit lycence to teiche in the kirkis of Muckert and Dolur or uther of thame ane certane speace quhairby he may have the bettir occasione to exerceis him self in teichein'. The presbytery granted him licence to preach for five or six weeks in the foresaid kirks.

Placing Mr Andrew Murdo minister at Kippen: John Shaw of Broicht, 'ane honorabill mane' and one of the elders of the parish of Kippen, compeared before the presbytery and, on behalf of himself and the remaining elders and deacons of the parish, declared that after the synod of the presbyteries of Stirling and Dunblane had deposed their last minister, William Stirling, from all function in the ministry, 'simpill reidein only exceptit', the presbytery had appointed, at the parishioners' request, Mr Andrew Murdo as their ordinary pastor, as was recorded in an act at Stirling of 31 October 1587, but Murdo had still to be placed pastor at the kirk, and therefore desired the presbytery to appoint James Anderson, commissioner, to place him pastor at Kippen. The presbytery agreed that Anderson should pass to Kippen next Sunday to make public intimation that William Stirling was deposed from all function except simple reading by the synod, and that Stirling who was entered in the books of assignation as reader at the kirk of Port only was not acknowledged to have any office at Kippen. The commissioner was instructed to notify the parishioners of Kippen of Murdo's admission as ordinary pastor, and to desire their consent, to be signified by 'uphaulding of thair handis'. Murdo was to declare in the parishioners' presence his willing obedience to accept office; the parishioners were to promise obedience to their pastor according to God's Word so long as he remained faithful in office; and Murdo was to promise solemnly to be a true and faithful pastor of that flock. The commissioner was then to place him pastor. [*In margin*: At Stirling, 19 March 1587/8 in presence of the brethren of the presbytery, James Anderson, commissioner, reported that he had placed Murdo ordinary pastor at Kippen on Sunday, 17 March immediately after sermon, and testified that the parishioners had given their consent, and that he had received solemn promises from both minister and congregation. The admission had taken place in presence of the whole congregation and of Alexander Saittone, Walter Leckie of that Ilk and James Ramsay, notary.

26 March, 1588

Walter Buchanan: Buchanan compeared before the presbytery and desired the brethren to continue pronouncing the sentence of excommunication against him for the space of 40 days. He promised either 'to pas af the cuntrie or ellis to imbrais and subscryve the reformit religione'. The presbytery postponed its answer till the next synod of the presbyteries of Stirling and Dunblane to be convened in the cathedral kirk of the city of Dunblane on 2 April next, before which Buchanan was ordered to compear. He promised to obey the summons.

9 April, 1588

Buchanan's excommunication: The presbytery inquired whether James Duncanson, reader at Stirling, had intimated to James Anderson, minister of Stirling, that the latter had been ordained by the synod to pronounce sentence of excommunication against Walter Buchanan on the first Sunday after Anderson's homecoming. Duncanson answered that he had made intimation to Anderson on 6 April. The presbytery then asked Anderson if he had fulfilled the synod's ordinance. Anderson replied that he had postponed pronouncing the sentence until he had conferred with the brethren, seeing he had been absent from the synod. 'Aftir lang rassoning and confirrence in the said mater', the presbytery ordained Anderson to pronounce the sentence next Sunday.

16 April, 1588

Walter Buchanan: The ordinance of the synodal assembly of the presbyteries of Stirling and Dunblane on 2 April had required James Anderson, minister of Stirling, commissioner and moderator for the time of the presbytery of Stirling, to pronounce sentence of excommunication against Walter Buchanan. Asked by the presbytery if he had executed the ordinance, Anderson replied that he had fulfilled and executed the same on Sunday, 14 April and had excommunicated Buchanan as an 'ennemie to the trew religione, a proud contemnar and ane membir altogidder pernicius' to the body of

Christ. Ministers in both presbyteries were to make intimation of the excommunication to their congregations. [On 23 April and 30 April, certain ministers reported to the presbytery that they had duly intimated the sentence from their pulpits.]

ERRATUM:

The following passage should be inserted on p. 98 at *

within the boundis of this presbytery caus execute and indorse faythfully all summondis direct on all and quhatsumevir personis that dwellis within thair parrochun, ilk ane . . .

INDEX

Sandilands, Janet, 30
Sands (Sandis), John, presbytery
   elder from Fossoway, 4
Sauchie, laird of, younger, *see*
   Shaw, James
Sawer, Martin, in Alva parish, 117,
   119-20
schoolmasters, xx, xxvii, 15, 18, 22,
   57, 118, 122, 129, 138, 141, 203;
   see also Dunblane, Muthill,
   Stirling *and* Strageith; *and*
   Brown, John; Nevin, Duncan;
   Wood, John; *and* Yule,
   Alexander
Scott, Helen, in Cambus, 132, 135-6
Scott, John, in Dunblane, 57
Scott, William, reader, exhorter and
   alleged minister of Callander,
   xix, 23, 37, 39-40, 66, 68, 85,
   87, 90, 95, 97, 100, 113, 212-13
Seath, John, in Clackmannan
   parish, 34, 38, 42, 115
separation, matrimonial
   (non-adherence), xxix, 32, 55,
   117; 158; *see also* adherence,
   divorce, marriage
Session, Court of, xxxii, 215
Seton (Saittone), Alexander, of
   Gargunnock, xxix, 235-6, 238,
   240-1, 243-4, 246, 267, 309
Shaw (Schaw), James, of Sauchie,
   younger, 182
Shaw, John, of Broich, 17-18, 29,
   31, 35, 228, 309
Shiphauch, 248-9, 252, 254, 263
Shorts (Schorttis), Alexander, in
   Blackgrange, 51
Sinclair, Alexander, in Denny, 227-8
Sinclair, Ewmond, in Denny, 227
Sinclair, Henry, in Denny, 227
slander, xxx-xxxi, xxxiii-xxxiv, xlii,
   31, 38, 43, 79, 82, 94, 114, 144,
   148, 153, 165, 172, 175, 190,
   192, 204, 212, 220-1, 226-7,
   244, 247, 249-50, 264, 266, 308

Smart, Andrew, in Kippen, 201
Smith (Smyth), Archibald, younger,
   in Stirling, 181-2
Smith, James, 112, 210
Smith, James, in Elphinstoun, 162
Smith, Margaret, in Keir, 182, 194
Spain, xxxv, 235
Spanish Armada, xxxvi
Spittal, Adam, of Blairlogie,
   presbytery elder from Logie,
   xxviii, 1, 8, 14, 17, 25, 29,
   39-40
Squire (Squyer), Andrew, in
   Stirling, 48-52, 54, 58
Stalker, Margaret, 169
Stalker, Marion, 32-33, 35, 41
Stalker, William, bailie in Stirling,
   183
Stein, Agnes, in St Ninians parish,
   277
Stein, Janet, 257
Stein, Marion, in St Ninians parish,
   257, 274
Stevinson, John, reader at
   Kincardine, 90-91, 96-97
Stevinson, William, presbytery
   officer, 18, 41-42, 158
Stewart, James, Earl of Arran,
   xxviii, xl
Stewart, James, lord Doune, steward
   of Menteith, xxxix, 115-16
Stewart, Jane, 30, 45, 52-53, 55,
   62-63, 77-78, 81, 86-87, 129,
   138, 146, 155-7, 207
Stewart, John, provost of Stirling,
   8, 40, 56, 64, 88-90, 102
Stewart, John, servant to the king, 81
Stewart, Margaret, in Airth, 112, 210
stipends, xx, xliii-xliv, 16, 61, 91,
   245, 282, 295; act anent, 206
Stirling, xxxv, 3, 7, 42, 46, 55, 59,
   114, 127, 129, 147, 154, 177-8,
   201, 232, 234, 244, 246, 248,
   254, 256, 263, 277, 282, 287,
   308-9; castle of, xxxiii, 87;

MEMBERSHIP

Membership of the Scottish History Society
is open to all who are interested in the history of Scotland.
For an annual subscription of £8.00
members normally receive one volume each year.
Enquiries should be addressed to
the Honorary Secretary or the Honorary Treasurer
whose addresses are given overleaf.

REPORT

of the 93rd Annual Meeting

The 93rd Annual Meeting of the Scottish History Society was held in the Rooms of the Royal Society, George Street, Edinburgh, on Saturday, 8 December 1979, at 11.15 a.m. Professor A. A. M. Duncan, President of the Society, was in the chair.

The Report of Council was as follows:

The volume to be issued to members during the current year, the *Papers of Peter May, Land Surveyor*, edited by Dr Ian Adams, has been slightly delayed by difficulties with the index. Production is, however, well advanced, and it is expected that this volume, the fifteenth of the Fourth Series, will be in the hands of members within a few weeks.

The next volume to be published by the Society will be *Stirling Presbytery Records* of the late sixteenth century, edited by Dr James Kirk. These are the earliest surviving presbytery records, dating from the presbytery's formal erection on 8 August 1581, and they are an invaluable source for both ecclesiastical and social history. In addition to ecclesiastical administration, the records illustrate cases concerning marriage and matrimonial offences, murder and witchcraft, and Roman Catholic recusancy, along with many other aspects of ecclesiastical discipline.

During the past year the Council has accepted one work for future publication by the Society. Dr B. Levack and Mr B. R. Galloway will edit a volume to be entitled *The Jacobean Union*. It will consist of a number of tracts, both English and Scottish, written in 1604 in the hope of influencing the project of James VI and I for a union between England and Scotland. Only one of the tracts has been published previously, and they will illuminate both sides of the question.

Continuous inflation in recent years, reflected in steadily rising printing costs and postal charges, is making it difficult for the Society to carry out its publication programme on the present basis. Members' subscriptions have been maintained at their present level since 1976, and income from them no longer covers the cost of publication of the volume received annually by members, let alone the administrative costs of running the Society. The Council has therefore decided that, in order to maintain the Society's programme and put its finances on a sounder basis, the annual subscription be raised to £8 with effect from the beginning of the financial year which starts in November 1980.

On a happier note financially, the Council acknowledges with gratitude a generous donation of £600 from the Mary Robson Lilburn Memorial Fund. This money has been granted to support the publication of the volume on *Government under the Covenanters* which is being edited for the Society by Dr David Stevenson.

The three members of the Council due to retire by rotation at this time are Professor A. E. Anton, Mrs Enid Gauldie, and Mr E. J. Cowan. The following will be proposed to the Annual Meeting for election to Council: Mr John di Folco, Rev. Mark Dilworth, and Dr Alasdair Durie.

During the year four members have died, five have resigned and one has been removed from membership for non-payment of subscription. Thirty-five new members have joined. The total membership, including 223 libraries, is now 766, compared with 741 in 1978.

In presenting the Annual Report, Professor T. C. Smout, Chairman of Council, apologised for the delay in issuing the current volume to members, and referred to forthcoming publications. The Hon. Treasurer reviewed the financial situation, explaining the unusual nature of the current credit balance.

The Report and the Accounts were approved, and Mr John di Folco, Rev. Mark Dilworth, and Dr Alasdair Durie declared elected to membership of Council. The President delivered an address entitled 'The Burgesses in the Medieval Parliament'.

ABSTRACT ACCOUNT OF CHARGE AND DISCHARGE OF THE
INTROMISSIONS OF THE HONORARY TREASURER for
1 November 1978 to 31 October 1979

GENERAL ACCOUNT

CHARGE

I. Cash in Bank at 1 November 1978:

    1. Sum at credit of Savings Account with Bank of
       Scotland   £2,500·00

    2. Sum at credit of Current Account with Bank of
       Scotland   362·12

    3. Sum at credit of Savings Account with Edinburgh
       Savings Bank   75·41

    4. Sum at credit of Special Investment Account with
       Edinburgh Savings Bank   487·19

                     £3,424·72

II. Subscriptions received   3,946·13

III. Past publications sold   1,238·16

IV. Reprints sold   163·37

V. Interest on Savings Accounts with Bank of Scotland and
    Edinburgh Savings Bank   243·21

VI. Income Tax Refund (1978–79)   248·81

VII. Donations   700·00

VIII. Carnegie Trust Grant   300·00

IX. Sums drawn from Bank Current Account   £5,513·24

X. Sums drawn from Bank Savings Account   £ —

                     £10,300·40

I. Cost of printing Annual Reports, Notices and
    Printers' Postages, etc.   £307·95

II. Insurance Premiums   28·13

III. Miscellaneous Payments   288·15

IV. Sums lodged in Bank Current Account   £6,994·59

V. Sums lodged in Bank Savings Account   £8,194·82

VI. Funds at close of this account:

    1. Balance at credit of Savings Account with
        Bank of Scotland   .   £7,600·00

    2. Balance at credit of Current Account with
        Bank of Scotland   1,481·35

    3. Balance at credit of Savings Account with
        Edinburgh Savings Bank   78·41

    4. Balance at credit of Special Investment
        Account with Edinburgh Savings Bank   516·41
                                          ———— 9,676·17

                                        £10,300·40*

GLASGOW, *7 November 1979.* I have examined the General Account of the Honorary Treasurer of the Scottish History Society for the year from 1 November 1978 to 31 October 1979, and I find the same to be correctly stated and sufficiently vouched.

                                       I. M. M. MACPHAIL
                                              Auditor

    * The large credit balance reflects the fact that no volume has been paid for in the year covered by the accounts.